FOUNDATIONS

*Critical Thinking,
Reading, and Writing*

FOUNDATIONS

Critical Thinking, Reading, and Writing

Victor Shea
York University

William Whitla
York University

Toronto

Canadian Cataloguing in Publication Data

Shea, Victor Norman, 1960–
    Foundations : critical thinking, reading and writing

Includes index.
ISBN 0-13-086366-1

1. Study skills. 2. Report writing. 3. Critical thinking. I. Whitla, William, 1934–   .
II. Title

LB2369.S45 2001   378.1'7028'1   C00-930111-9

ISBN 0-13-086366-1

Vice President, Editorial Director: Michael Young
Acquisitions Editor: David Stover
Marketing Manager: Sophia Fortier
Signing Representative: Christy den Haan-Veltman
Developmental Editor: Madhu Ranadive
Associate Editor: Susan Ratkaj
Production Editor: Susan Adlam
Copy Editors: Marcia Miron, Amber Wallace
Production Coordinator: Peggy Brown
Page Layout: Janette Thompson (Jansom)
Art Director: Mary Opper
Cover Design: Lisa La Pointe
Cover Image: PhotoDisc

2 3 4 5   05 04 03 02 01

Printed and bound in Canada.

Contents

Chapter 13 Preparing the Final Copy 267

PART FIVE: AFTER YOU GET YOUR PAPER BACK

Chapter 14: The Marked Assignment and What to Do About It   274

PART SIX: EXAMINATIONS

Chapter 15 Preparing for and Writing Exams   283

Preface

TO THE STUDENT

The American philosopher Richard Paul defines critical thinking as "thinking about your thinking while you are thinking in order to make your thinking better: more clear, more accurate, or more defensible." At the same Web site, he gives a more extended definition: "Critical thinking is the intellectually disciplined process of actively and skillfully conceptualizing, applying, analyzing, synthesizing, and/or evaluating information gathered from, or generated by, observation, experience, reflection, reasoning, or communication, as a guide to belief and action." In the simplest terms, critical thinking involves being able to move from asserting opinions to formulating a position, from passively receiving ideas, arguments, and readings to actively engaging with them (**www.criticalthinking.org**).

Critical reading and writing applies these same thinking skills. This book teaches you these skills systematically: you will acquire the critical skills to allow you to formulate a reasoned position on a topic, including summarizing readings and arguments, determining their chief components and structure, analyzing them for their validity, bias, omissions, and conclusions, shaping a critique of them, assessing their implications, developing reasoned alternatives, and writing about them in essays and examinations.

Critical thinking is a foundational skill for all other kinds of learning, whether in the traditional disciplines or in interdisciplinary study. At first glance it may appear that the stress on a reasoned position in relation to your course materials is a paradox because many ideas in your course stress the established theories within the particular discipline, such as theories of government in political science, changes in education and social policy in history, or matters of analysis in literature. This book will foster your ability to assess the lectures and readings in your courses from a reasoned position, to analyze and even challenge specific arguments in the texts you read. Moreover, a great deal of critical thinking examines the reasoning behind the positions taken in a course and in your own reading and writing.

Such skills are now being taught in many courses and at many levels of schooling, from grade school to graduate school. They are useful and may be applied with good results to all courses in your university career, as well as to other contexts such as your future employment. Clear thinking, reasoned argument, and good analytical and communication skills are highly valued by both university teachers and employers. Hence, your involvement with this book or a course involving critical thinking is part of a widespread demand in North American society for just those skills that you will be learning in *Foundations*.

Critical Thinking

To inform you more clearly about the goals and expectations of *Foundations*, and to let you know which skills we want to get across by the end of the book, we can spell out these applications a little more fully.

Critical thinking is involved in all aspects of this book, including the sections describing how to develop survival skills, how to use computers for research and academic writing,

how to read course materials, how to argue effectively in the classroom and in written assignments, how to evaluate and document your sources, and how to prepare for and write your
tests and examinations. Critical thinking can be applied to all aspects of your course, but it
has two particular components:

- *Critical reading* involves receiving texts actively (including lectures, seminars, presentations, films, and required readings).

- *Critical writing* involves formulating your own position and arguing it in a variety
  of written and oral methods of presentation.

Critical Reading

Experts on rhetoric and critical thinking would all agree that writing skills are improved
by working on reading skills to become an active reader, one who is engaged in organizing
and analyzing texts. To be an active reader means that you have acquired the critical thinking skills to understand, explain, and either defend or qualify what you have read. That is,
you are not thinking or reading merely to acquire information or to exercise a set of skills that
you have learned routinely. Rather, you are thinking to develop a habit of mind that will
enable you to form your own position on what you hear in lectures and read in the course materials. Critical thinking, therefore, helps you become aware of your options and strategies
for formulating your own position.

Critical reading also involves different kinds of materials and texts in your courses,
whether those are textbooks in a discipline, course kits, packages of readings, documents, critical or scholarly articles, results of lab experiments, or, in some courses, fiction, films,
music, and nonfiction texts (from psychology, history, the social sciences, and criticism). Your
instructors will indicate how you are to read these materials and what particular emphases
they wish to place on them. In some courses, you will read these texts in their social and political contexts from different disciplinary perspectives; in others, you will read them for
their content, and you will have to use your critical thinking skills to master the material, to
understand how it is structured and presented, and to see how it is defended. Critical reading also involves your research in the library, on the Internet, and in lectures and presentations as a process of critical listening.

Throughout this book, you will develop a critical reading vocabulary, one related both
to the materials and concepts of a course, and also to critical thinking as a process of active
engagement. By developing your skills in critical reading, this book will enable you to engage with texts in three increasingly complex ways:

1. Critical reading involves reading texts literally, to understand what is meant by the
   words on a page. That is, you will learn to read for the denotation and connotation of
   words and to assess the strategies of argument used by scholars, researchers, writers,
   and filmmakers.

2. Critical reading involves learning how to position your literal reading in relation to the
   text as a whole structure. Critical reading, in this sense, means understanding the ways
   that a text is put together, how its structure is organized formally into its component
   parts, and how its ideas, themes, and larger concepts are related.

3. Critical reading then helps you to put the literal and structural reading into a context in
   terms of the situation in which the text is produced, the materials that are represented in

the text, and the condition in which the text is read or performed in the present. For instance, the English writer Charles Dickens published his novel *A Tale of Two Cities* in 1848, when revolutions were sweeping Europe. In the novel he represents the events of the French Revolution (1789–91), though we read it in the early twenty-first century with very different assumptions. Another example might be the economist Adam Smith, who published his study *The Wealth of Nations* in 1776, arguing for the first time that competition based on individual self-interest drives an economic system. The context of its publication, at the height of the Scottish enlightenment and in the same year as the American Revolution, can be read very differently in the light of today's global markets. That is, critical reading at this level places the text in a historical context and also addresses the difficulties that a particular text presents, helping us to perceive the gaps and omissions, and especially the assumptions involved when we read older texts through the lens of present-day history and experience.

Critical Writing

Critical writing involves a parallel set of methods and skills that you can expect to become familiar with by the end of this book:

1. Critical writing skills, involving oral and written participation and assignments, will help you to write literate and comprehensible English. The basic structures of standard English will be explained to help you communicate your ideas clearly and persuasively. You will learn methods of valid argument and will learn to recognize basic faults in argument and expression. You will also learn how to prepare a first draft of an essay and how to edit, revise, and proofread your essays. A variety of sources will be provided that you can turn to for help.

2. Critical writing involves placing your arguments in a structure, in an oral argument or essay, in which you can formulate your own reasoned position. You will be able to relate your position to that of the texts you are discussing, and you will be able to move efficiently from primary to secondary materials in your research.

3. Critical writing involves shaping your writing toward a specific audience, such as your fellow students or your seminar leader. To address this larger context in which your writing is produced and received, you need to become aware of your own assumptions and biases, of your gaps and limitations, and of the methods you can use to persuade your particular audience. To do that, you need to become familiar with and use several kinds of rhetorical and logical skills, such as thinking and writing in parallel structures, moving from premises to valid conclusions, or organizing your argument with major and minor points, examples, illustrations, and quotations.

Computers in Critical Thinking

The use of computers is altering the ways in which we think, read, and write. You have probably come to university with at least some computer skills. Computers make important demands concerning critical judgment, but they can greatly aid the writing of essays and assignments and can save you a lot of time in correcting and improving your work. They can also be major distractions from doing your research (especially if you waste time by searching the Internet clumsily). You probably at least use a computer as a glorified typewriter to type out and print the final draft of your essays, and you likely also use the computer for much more sophisticated work. Throughout these chapters on critical thinking, reading, and writing, we draw attention to some implications for students' use of computers and the Web, and we supply many useful Web sites, discuss ways of conducting research on the Web, and provide advice on evaluating your results.

Highlights of This Handbook

In Part One, we introduce strategies for your university studies in the following areas:

- dealing with changes in academic expectations from high school to university
- knowing what is expected of you in a university classroom
- managing your time by organizing priorities
- studying effectively
- taking useful notes in lectures and seminars
- reading and annotating for retention

Then we turn to basic computer literacy and to the kinds of critical reading practices that will help you work effectively with a computer on the Internet and the World Wide Web. We deal extensively in separate chapters with reading and vocabulary skills in an effort to make your assimilation of course materials as effective as possible. The last section of Part One provides an overview of grammar and punctuation.

Part Two helps you become conscious of your position as a student in a university course. Much of the book is devoted to critical writing, including using both traditional and recent electronic methods to write an academic essay, still the predominant form of evaluation for most students in university courses. Chapters 6 and 7 set out ways to develop a critical attitude, to present forms of argument, and to describe formal and informal fallacies in logic.

Part Three goes through the process of undertaking research for an essay. Extensive treatment is given to research methods using both print and electronic sources. Part Four deals in detail with writing assignments, especially formal essays, from the planning stage through to the final copy, drawing on both traditional methods of research and newer methods of electronic information retrieval. This section concludes with information about documenting sources according to the most recent MLA and APA guidelines, including up-to-date treatment of electronic sources such as the Internet, e-mail, and CD-ROMs. Part Five deals with the marked assignment or the returned essay, and Part Six describes how to prepare for and write examinations. Detailed contemporary examples and current resources illustrate each chapter. Bibliographical information is provided throughout, including many references to current Web sites.

A special feature of this book is the attention given to using critical skills with the computer in studying, taking notes, undertaking research, and writing assignments. Useful guidance is provided in the following areas:

- using Corel WordPerfect and Microsoft Word for university writing
- using Microsoft Explorer and Netscape Navigator critically in accessing and assessing Web research sites

- sharing learning and research through e-mail and listservs
- accessing resources through library computers and through your home computer
- organizing your research on the computer
- writing and revising your essay effectively with your computer

At the end of each chapter, further readings and Web sites on all aspects of critical thinking, reading, and writing are provided. A concurrent Web site associated with this book will keep those sites and references up-to-date and will provide additional information and glossaries.

Foundations attempts to chart a way through the complicated process of mastering critical thinking, reading, and writing in a systematic way. By the end of this book, you should have a solid basis in critical thinking, reading, and writing as applied to the readings in whatever course you are studying. You should feel comfortable in formulating a reasoned position on any of the texts in your course, you should be skilled in presenting that position to your classmates and seminar leader in both oral and written form, and you should be well prepared for all of the course assignments. Above all, if you are ever in any doubt about any of the procedures or materials in the course, you should ask your instructor for help or advice: asking such appropriate questions is a fundamental first step in critical thinking.

TO THE INSTRUCTOR

Foundations: Critical Thinking, Reading, and Writing has been written for university students in critical thinking, composition, and introductory or more advanced courses in the humanities and social sciences at various year levels. This book can be used as a text within an introductory or general course in most fields, to teach critical thinking, to introduce research methods, and to explain the conventions of academic reading and writing. It can also be used in more advanced courses to consolidate critical thinking skills among students who have some experience with the general concepts. For those students, a judicious selection of chapters to be used will be important. Increasingly, students have little idea of what is expected of them, and for professors to assume that students have been taught these skills or can meet their unstated expectations is unrealistic. The book addresses these expectations, and students may use it as an assigned text or on their own as a guide to the complex expectations and conventions of university study.

We assume that students, whether making the transition from high school to university or coming to university after a break in their studies for work or family, have a wide variety of skills. Parts of *Foundations*, therefore, might be unnecessary to individual readers—some students might have been taught grammar basics, and some may be well advanced in computer skills. However, based on many years of teaching introductory and advanced courses in English and the humanities, we have tried to provide instruction in what we consider the basic needs of incoming students. If a part of this book is unnecessary for some students because of previous training, then we are certain that other parts will be useful in helping them cope with the demands of university. For professors wishing to use *Foundations* in specific courses, we assume that different parts of the book can be usefully assigned throughout the year to help teach specific critical skills in relation to the course content. Parts of the text, such as Chapters 1 and 2, which deal with survival skills, might be assigned for students to read on their own; other parts, such as Chapters 6 and 7, which explain how to adopt, defend, and assess a position in argument, might be profitable for a detailed treatment in class time. On the whole, *Foundations* is a response to a pressing need for students to develop critical thinking skills in their first years at university.

Clear thinking, reasoned argument, and good analytical and communication skills are highly valued by both university teachers and employers. Many recent comments in the press have pointed out the urgent need for people with these skills in all areas of public life. Recently in Canada, the United States, and Great Britain, public policy makers have made the teaching of these skills a clearly stated goal of educational systems. In a short statement on the Web site of Longview Community College in Missouri, which has a special mandate to encourage critical thinking, Bonnie Duldt gives an overview of how critical thinking as a national standard in the United States has become an essential part of educational policy in the last decade:

> The National Assessment of Educational Progress, which continually surveys the quality of American education..., reported in 1980 only 5 percent of the seventeen-year old high school graduates could synthesize and learn from specialized reading materials.... The U.S. Department of Education established goals mandating critical thinking for all college graduates by the end of the century.... Centers of critical thinking have been established to meet the new educational focus. The most distinguished of these is the Center for Critical Thinking, Sonoma State University. Associated with this Center is the Foundation for Critical Thinking. The National Council for Critical Thinking has developed statements of policy and principles of critical thinking. ("Coaching Winners")

Many other colleges and universities in the United States have set up critical thinking institutes and centres as courses have proliferated. In Canada, a renewed emphasis on literacy in public and secondary schools has replaced the tendency in the 1970s and 1980s to avoid teaching grammar as a rote-learning subject. Emphasis is now placed on grammar as a part of communication skills, often combined with some emphasis on critical thinking. At universities in Canada, critical thinking, often taught across the curriculum, is largely replacing courses in introductory rhetoric and English composition.

A major problem for the present generation of students is that many have missed out on these educational reforms. Furthermore, many analysts of public life have pointed out that as a consumer society, we tend to accept what we are told by the media, advertisers, and government uncritically and without question. Educational reforms that stress critical thinking seek to break this passive acceptance of others' positions by teaching ways of asking reasoned questions and formulating alternatives.

Key Features of This Text

Unlike other texts that deal with critical thinking, *Foundations* integrates critical and computer skills, traditional research and the new electronic media resources, writing in conventional modes in the classroom and using the computer for critical writing skills, and using the computer for sophisticated searches, evaluation, and consolidation of research materials. This handbook assumes that most students use the computer to write essays, but it takes those students further in helping them use their computers to undertake useful research on the Internet. As well, this handbook takes a student systematically from university entrance skills to enhanced research and writing skills at a more professional level, developing those abilities in an analytical way from the first lecture in a course to the final examination, from the first assignment to the final essay in a course, from first efforts at library research to finished essays, and from receiving a marked essay to revising and resubmitting it. Throughout, useful boxes of tips are provided on how to use the computer and critical skills more effectively, along with charts on developing language and research skills, and references to extensive print and Internet resources to expand the dimensions of this text.

This handbook provides an interdisciplinary approach to teaching foundational skills across the curriculum. The authors have taught in interdisciplinary and departmental courses where emphasis has been placed on coherent argument in oral and written presentations, on research, and essay writing. But more recently our own university, like many others, has undertaken a rethinking of curriculum to stress these skills in the broader context of critical thinking, reading, and writing. Our courses became part of this new critical skills curriculum. We prepared and tested earlier drafts of parts of this book in our classes over several years and made chapters available to colleagues. They responded enthusiastically, telling us how they adapted our examples and models to their own teaching materials, as we had hoped they would. In subsequent revisions we emphasized students' concerns by providing reasons for strategic choices in critical reading and writing, by amplifying our examples and suggestions, and by setting out the practical advantages for improvement in academic skills. Throughout, we have stressed conventional writing and research methods, together with an integrated approach to new information technology. Our experience is that *Foundations* can be used in a variety of teaching situations and can be addressed to specific student needs, easily prompting discussion about our proposed methods and suggestions. It will be comprehensible to a student working alone or in a small group.

Our aim is to provide students and instructors with a practical and helpful guide to critical thinking that will promote the worthy goals of the American Philosophical Association in their consensus statement on the topic: "We understand critical thinking to be purposeful, self-regulatory judgment which results in interpretation, analysis, evaluation and inference, as well as explanations of the evidential, conceptual, methodological, or contextual considerations upon which such a judgment is based" (2).

Acknowledgments

We are grateful to our students in Humanities 2640: Modes of Fantasy, who over many years have helped us to hone these skills and direct them as clearly as possible to students' needs and classroom practice. We are particularly grateful to those students who took our courses from 1996 to 2000, for whom much of this material was written in preliminary forms. Various people have helped us by making suggestions and by reading parts of the manuscript, among whom we would like to thank our colleagues in the Division of Humanities at York University and Gabriele Helms of the University of British Columbia, Emmy Misser of Wilfrid Laurier University, and John Reiff of Tusculum College. At Pearson we have been greatly helped by Matthew Christian, Madhu Ranadive, and David Stover. Marcia Miron has been a highly proficient copy editor. Particular guidance and help have come from Kym Bird, Sue Collins, Rob Finlayson, Doug Freake, Lisa Haberman, Jennifer Hosein, Peggy Keall, Rob Lawrence, Steve Mason, Mary Lou McKenna, Kirsten McKnight, Peter Mitchell, Gwen Norman, Ron Sheese, Marlene Shore, Patricia Stamp, Peter Turner, Susan Warwick, and Lisa Wood. Various institutions have also helped us, including Founders College, the Centre for Academic Writing, the Centre for Computer Assisted Writing, and the Teaching with Technology lab at Calumet College, York University.

Victor Shea
William Whitla
Division of Humanities, York University

SHIFTING GEARS: ADAPTING TO UNIVERSITY DEMANDS

Chapter **1**

CHANGING SCHOOLS AND EXPECTATIONS

Most students go on to university or college directly after high school. However, changing economic factors are increasingly requiring students to work for a few years before continuing their studies or to take a part-time job while at university. Other students withdraw to raise children, to care for ailing parents or siblings, or to increase their grades through makeup classes in competition for the scarce spaces at the school of their choice. The old pattern of moving directly after high school to the university that Mom or Dad went to, of getting into residence, of taking a full load of study, of doing lots of partying—this kind of romanticized, ivy-league student existence seems to have vanished as single-parent families have become more common and the need to earn lots of money for the big tuition costs has grown.

Students now come to university with different skills from those of ten or twenty years ago. You probably have a much greater ability to work with computers, but you may have a decreased ability to write well in standard English. You may be an expert in all kinds of music and current movies, but you may have not yet developed many resources for describing, evaluating, or analyzing what you know and learn. You are suddenly faced with many new challenges, not least of which is being on your own in a new environment where you have to take responsibility for your own education in important ways. And just when you are faced with this changing environment and expectations, you are also confronted with new worries about your ability to succeed. This book directly addresses those concerns by providing skills and strategies for academic success.

You might be troubled by other problems that interfere with your academic study. You may have withdrawn from study for several months or years to work and now wonder if your old skills are rusty. You might be worried about how to finance the costs of spiralling tuition and so have taken a part-time job that cuts into your study time, or you might be anxious about your job prospects upon graduation. You might be forced into living at home for financial reasons but would rather live in residence, or you might have moved into a new and ethnically diverse academic community where your former sense of identity is threatened. Almost all students are faced with new challenges in the classroom, not only in their first year but every year, when they have new teachers to understand, new class-mates to relate to, and new course materials to master.

Every university has many facilities to help students cope with problems in their life situations. There are financial aid officers, organizations for mature students, clubs and associations for particular language and cultural groups, and many people with specialized training and resources to help you with accommodation and family or personal difficulties. The helpful and discreet resources of the student association and the counselling offices are available, usually along with handouts and access to their specialized libraries, and you can be sure that staff will treat your problems with sympathy and care. The same professionals, as well as your school's job placement or employment office, can help you cope with worries about your future job prospects or about your present balance of academics and work. They will also help you write your résumé and make plans for finding a good match between your courses and your career plans. All of these student resources have particular roles in smoothing out your university life, and you are encouraged to use them as you need them. Clearing away such worries and personal difficulties will help you focus on your academic life and will make the kinds of academic skills that are addressed in this book far more useful to you.

Your university professors expect you to work independently and to have a number of skills in thinking, reading, writing, taking lecture notes, and making class presentations. Some of these expectations undoubtedly will cause much anxiety—and not only to beginning students.

In what follows we set out some of the skills that will help you survive. Better than that, they will enable you to cope from the start with your lectures and seminars, with your assignments and readings. Even better, they will train you in study methods and instill study habits that will continue to benefit you in the rest of your years at university, and even in life-long learning.

CODES OF CIVILITY

We are all familiar with differing codes of behaviour that are expected in various circumstances: we talk differently in front of our grandparents than we do among our closest friends, and conduct that passes in the college pub would not go down well in the local bank. Some people lament the collapse of etiquette; others welcome such changes, as they lessen differences between the sexes and classes. At university, too, there are codes of civility that are accepted and almost invisible—they are explained only when they are infringed. A brief introduction to these codes follows to help you avoid making mistakes in this area.

We generally comply with such codes to allow others their freedom of thought and action and to maintain the decorum that lets the university get on with its primary business of education and research. Universities are special communities of learning and hence have special rules of conduct different from those of other institutions. As early as 1921, after seven years of student pressure, Stanford University adopted an honour system that required all students to sign a statement concerning academic honesty, and as a result professors agreed not to proctor examinations. In recent decades, however, universities and colleges have been forced by changing social expectations and experiences to develop and state standards, rules, and penalties. These changes sprang, in part, from the years of student unrest in the 1960s and 1970s. In particular, the riots at the University of Mississippi in 1962, when the first black student, James Meredith, was admitted; at Kent State in 1970, when the U.S. military reserves shot protesting students; and in California and later across the United States when students protested the Vietnam War—all these pushed the agenda about civility in two directions: on one side, for greater controls exercised by the institutions over safety, security, and compliance with the law, and on the other, for increasing demands for free speech and action. More recently, especially after the massacre of fourteen female students at the École Polytechnique in Montreal on 6 December 1989, worries about personal safety on campus and about racial and sexual harassment have led to increasing regulations.

Conduct in the Classroom

University publications are often full of high-sounding rhetoric about their aims and accomplishments in the impartial pursuit of knowledge, the qualities of their libraries and laboratories, and the unparalleled teaching abilities of their faculty. We do not dispute these claims, but we do believe that students should have access to these resources without fear of threat, intimidation, or reprisal. The atmosphere in the lecture hall, seminar room, and library should allow for the free expression and exchange of ideas. Within the appropriate limitations (such as proper payment of fees, admission to a course, and the like), all should have equal access to the opportunities for learning and study in any given course. To that end, the rights of others and their access to the same opportunities depend on practices of tolerance, respect for others, and civility. You may not agree with all that your fellow students think or say, but you have a responsibility to hear them out and to disagree as vigorously as you can or as is appropriate. More importantly, your objections and disagreements must fall within the limitations set out in the speech codes of your university, codes that do not allow for the belittling of another student in terms of race, religion, gender, sexual orientation, or physical disability.

Universities and their members must abide by federal, provincial, and municipal laws, but as special communities they also formulate their own laws, regulations, customs, and expectations that govern how the social and learning aspects of the university work. These procedures are usually written down in the student calendar or catalogue, and it is your responsibility to read and follow them. They ensure that classroom work and other academic activities can continue with courtesy and mutual respect between teachers and students, and among students themselves. They outline the kinds of behaviour that are unprofessional or disruptive, and they state those that warrant intervention by university authorities, such as cases of violence or threat of violence, harassment or discrimination in contravention of human rights or conduct codes, and theft or the destruction of property. Penalties for infringements can be severe. But these regulations are not in place to punish the offender so much as to protect those who want to conduct their studies without disruption.

Sometimes conduct in the classroom can be troubling but not a matter for formal intervention or censure. For instance, when a student continually interrupts a lecturer with silly or inappropriate questions, other students, and possibly the teacher, do not always know how to respond appropriately. It might be that the student is just having a difficult time and is using the occasion to make some kind of statement. But there may be a more serious cause, such as mental illness, family stress, or a wish to get back at other students or the teacher. Usually, a teacher will respond by saying that he or she would like to discuss the question with the student after class; if this response fails, the teacher might ask the rest of the class whether they would like to pursue this line of questioning or continue with the lecture. Such a move tends to align the teacher with the rest of the class, though the appeal could backfire. The other students could also intervene and ask that the lecture continue without interruption or ask the student to save the questions until later.

What about students who regard the lecture hall as a kind of movie theatre—who come and go to the washrooms, leave from the middle of a row to get a soft drink and some food, talk noisily with their friends, and generally behave as though nothing important were going on? These students seem to be at the lecture for the social life and are often amazed when the teacher or other students point out their bad manners. But the rest of the class has paid hard-earned money for this lecture hour and should not have it stolen by the bad manners or the discourteous or disruptive antics of one or two students. If you are one of these people, you need to consider how you might be offending not only the students around you, but also the teacher, who, after all, assigns your grade. It might be in your best interest to change your ways, perhaps sitting nearer the front of the room or away from your friends or others who might distract you. If you are one of the students continually annoyed by disruptive students, you can speak to your lecturer or move away from those students, perhaps sitting near the front of the classroom. Again, some comment made by students nearby will help to discourage such antisocial and anti-academic behaviour. It may seem to you that such advice is unnecessary, but increasingly students are coming to university without any idea that such disruptive behaviour is unacceptable. The reasons for the increase in bad manners are undoubtedly complex, having to do with changing social conventions, and more specifically with the conduct tolerated in high school classrooms; nevertheless, you should be aware from the outset that university professors have little tolerance for such behaviour. Students who engage in inconsiderate or offensive behaviour are noticed and penalized. In some courses and institutions, repeated misconduct can lead to expulsion.

You will find that you have teachers with differing teaching methods and abilities. Some are challenging and even charismatic; others, well-informed but shy. Some present their ideas with vigour and force; others, timidly and tentatively. All are in front of a class because the university has hired them for their ability in their field of specialization, and each of them has particular knowledge that will be of use to you. Sometimes you will find it difficult to follow your teacher's train of thought, or the material will appear to be unfocused and off topic, and, indeed, it may well be so. It is at this point that the conventions of civility and decorum are most important. Some students will be tempted to talk and even become disruptive. It is more to your academic advantage to find some way of focusing on an aspect of the lecture or seminar that appears relevant to you. Ways of doing this are discussed in this chapter in the section on taking notes in lectures (see page 17). Some courses are taught by the formal lecture method; some seminars are run on the Socratic method of question and response, controlled by the teacher; and others are conducted through group work, various kinds of interactive or problem-solving techniques, or different kinds of teaching media. Some make use of a variety of techniques. In each case, you have the right to expect that you can ask questions, air your concerns, and meet your academic expectations without impediment.

Student conduct in the classroom and seminar should involve mutual respect and shared responsibility for maintaining the academic goals of the course. That means listening to others, avoiding using offensive language, especially language that is racially or gender biased, and refraining from baiting, belittling, or demeaning others. Students may expect that their seminars and lectures follow the course syllabuses and handouts and the schedules that the university publishes, and any activity that interferes with this objective should be evaluated and dealt with appropriately, either by you or by your teacher after you have brought it to his or her attention.

Gender, Sexual, Racial, and Religious Stereotyping

Universities and colleges and most businesses and professional practices now avoid stereotypical language for gender and race. It is unacceptable for speakers and writers today to refer to *man* as though the collective noun included the whole of humanity, as in the phrase "man has struggled for two hundred years with the problems of poverty." The silliness of this patriarchal usage is demonstrated if the sentence is changed to "man has struggled for two hundred years with the problems of gender bias and equality." Formal academic prose should reflect current standards of treating all people with respect and hence should avoid such expressions as *chairman,* or other words with -*man* as a suffix, in favour of alternative forms, such as *chair*; it should avoid conveying the assumption that all authors, critics, politicians, historians, or theologians are men or are white and Anglo-Saxon; and it should avoid adopting a tone that assumes all readers are male and white. Some writers redress the historic gender imbalance in language by self-consciously using feminine pronouns in their prose, by alternating them with male pronouns, or by using the form *s/he*. This field is one in which language is undergoing rapid modification, and it will likely be some time before usage becomes more settled.

Such is the state of what is generally called *inclusive language*. A more troubling and difficult aspect of stereotyping involves the use of derogatory terms for gender, sexual orientation, and racial and religious groups. Much has been said recently about *political correctness,* a term now used as a buzzword by opponents of the increased sensitivity toward language usage that labels people in a demeaning way. People claiming their right to use abusive language as a principle of free speech often assert that sensitivity to language has been overly emphasized in the interests of political correctness. They do not recognize that such language silences and threatens many people, and as such, is antithetical to principles of critical thinking that support the free exchange of different viewpoints and opinions.

The university community encourages diversity and open thought; therefore, the use of derogatory terms that are threatening to many people is unacceptable. Using derogatory terms such as *bitches* to refer to women, *fags* to refer to gays, or *ginos* to refer to Italians (to take but a few instances) is not only impolite at university, but often is an infringement on the speech codes set down in your university's policy. Whatever the political and ideological implications of these speech codes, they are in place and usually will be enforced. Probably, many infringements are made from ignorance rather than with the intention of direct confrontation, and if you make such an error, you should not be afraid to apologize and amend your practice. When in doubt, it is wise to err on the side of caution. You should not hesitate to ask for advice regarding this controversial and changing area of language usage.

To take one example, ethnic groups should be referred to in the terms that they themselves use. Terms that in the past have been used to denigrate particular groups are unacceptable unless you are directly quoting these terms from a particular source, perhaps in an essay on racial prejudice. For instance, terms like *nigger* or *Jap* are, of course, absolutely unacceptable, as they reflect racist usage in the United States before desegregation and anti-Japanese sentiment during and after World War II. Terms like *negro* and *Indian* are also not accepted usage; the preferred terms now are *African-Canadian* (or *-American*) and *First Nation*. Other terms like *Black* and *Native Canadian* (or *American*) are still in transition, and, while controversial, are generally acceptable.

In your own comments in class and in writing your assignments you should try to follow your university's practices and the codes that are set out in your department or course. Some instructors are only now learning to change their ways; others can be fierce about infringements, so you are far better off to avoid gender and racial stereotyping of any kind in your classroom comments and written assignments.

Humour and Jokes

Humour and jokes often violate acceptable codes and norms by turning a particular physical trait, a stereotypical action, or a characteristic into the butt of someone's remarks. Hence, the dangers of infringing on the university's regulations about appropriate conduct are considerable. Humour in the classroom is often a welcome diversion both to your fellow students and to your instructor. But you need to assess the level and tone of the humour or joke and respect the criteria for general civility and tolerance.

You also need to exercise caution in using jokes in your essays and assignments. You decide early on about the tone and pitch of your paper. If you are serious, engaged, and challenged by it, your reader will take you on the same terms. If you are flippant, dismissive, or superficial, that will also be the reaction of your reader to your position. In this context, the use of humour and irony is a particular problem. On the whole, such attempts should probably be avoided. Humour in an academic essay is very difficult to control, because it involves a destabilizing of the rhetoric and the audience. Attempts to be humorous often backfire, resulting in a collapse of the reader's sympathy with your argument, because such attempts assume a common ideological position, even a chumminess, within which the joke will be shared. Beginning writers often miscalculate the quality of their humour in academic writing.

The same thing applies to parenthetical asides inserted into a paper, often with the addition of slang, or as moments of direct and confiding address to the reader: *Sez you. As though you didn't know! You thought I'd forget this, didn't you? Ha! ha!* Such interjections break the flow of your thought, the rhetorical seriousness of your style, and the reader's attention. They assert an informal conversational tone and friendliness in the place of persuasive argument. Students often use such interjections in examinations, but more often than not such phrases put off a reader. At best they will be ignored; at worst, they might be seen as offensive and will be held against you as an attempt to curry favour or to avoid taking the exercise seriously.

Serious Instances of Harassment or Threats of Violence

In cases of serious or prolonged disruptions, harassment, discrimination, or threats of violence or intimidation by either faculty or other students, there are important avenues to be followed. First, you need to maintain your own safety in the situation, and, second, you need to preserve your academic integrity. Having done that, you should follow the procedures that your university sets out for dealing with each problem. Appropriate people to contact are the course director, the head of a department, the student or faculty ombudsperson, the academic dean or dean of students, the sexual harassment office (anonymity can be preserved in most instances), the women's support office, the campus police, the medical offices, chaplains, and so on. If you live in residence, your residence don or dean can be of help. Whatever happened is very likely not the first occasion of such an event, and your question or complaint should be taken seriously; otherwise, you can move to the next higher official in the hierarchy.

CONCENTRATION

Study Habits

Whether your most common place of study is the library, your residence room, your home, or any number of places in between (the bus, the pub, the lunch room, the park between classes), you are, or should be, in control of your study space and what you bring to it. As noted on the Dartmouth College home page, large numbers of students—from 8 percent to as high as 50 percent—have difficulty concentrating on their studies on a regular basis, and virtually all students have this difficulty from time to time (See Works Cited list, "Concentration"). In general, students blame outside influences, but many studies have been conducted to show that a combination of external reasons (environment, distractions, noise and light levels) and internal reasons (motivational problems, diet, exercise, sleep patterns, and a failure to understand the purpose, goals, and appropriate methods for the particular study task) create problems in concentration or in developing successful study habits. No one can expect that after a summer of vigorous physical activity or mind-numbing repetition in your job, or after a year spent raising children, you can show up for the first week of lectures and plug in immediately to the old study routines that you had learned, or perhaps only partly learned, in your high school days or earlier in your university career. Study skills, including concentration, are learned habits, and they have to be acquired and nurtured carefully to bring appropriate results. You should not be discouraged as you revert to old habits, but rather should try to isolate the cause of losing your concentration and should follow the controls that you set for yourself until you can successfully focus on studying for about an hour. When you are successful, you can give yourself a reward.

It is a good idea to assess the reasons for your distraction. If you can learn what it is that causes poor attention generally, and then determine if that cause applies to you, then you are well on your way to bringing more focus to your studying. The key is to make control over your environment and yourself habitual, so that you can use your time to best advantage.

External Conditions for Good Concentration

Your Environment

Whether you live at home, in residence, or with friends, you will want to spend time with your friends and in various forms of sports and recreation. Sometimes you will just want to talk, watch TV, go to the movies, or have a coffee with your classmates between classes. While it is always useful to take whatever time you can for study—say in that hour or two you may have between classes when you have a chapter to read—that time can best be spent where you can direct your attention toward your reading. Spending the time in the pub, where there is constant coming and going and the big TV screen dominates all conversation, might not be the best choice. The library, where most of the study space seems to be taken over by groups working loudly on joint projects, might also be a poor choice. But one of the study halls or a carrel in the library stacks might give you just the location you need.

Your Equipment

Aside from the occasional time you have for reading, such as on the bus or between classes, you will need a place for study on a regular basis. This place should be equipped with whatever you need: a good reading light, a comfortable chair, a desk, your computer, writing materials, your notes, a bookstand to keep your book propped open, so your hands are free to use the computer or to write in your notebook, and a dictionary.

Music and TV

What about noise, especially music? If you find yourself reading the same paragraph several times because your neighbours in residence are laughing their way through *The Simpsons*, you might be better off either to join them or go to the library. Again, a lot of study has gone into the kind of music that students listen to and how they react to it. Recently, studies have found that the music of Mozart is the best music to listen to because it trains the ear with its mathematical organization and coherence. Similar arguments could be made about Bach, no doubt, or the Beatles, or the Barenaked Ladies, but such arguments have little point here. Probably most students already have developed the habit of listening to music when studying in high school, a habit that is hard to break. Many successful students have reported that when they moved from high school to university, they decided that they would turn the music down or off altogether, to draw a conscious distinction between the habits of high school and those of university, where the stakes are much higher. In any case, you certainly need to be able to control the noise or music level. What applies to music applies to TV even more stringently. You need to set aside your time for watching TV and listening to music, and to follow that timetable carefully. You will get more enjoyment out of your relaxation and out of your studying, too.

Internal Conditions for Good Concentration

Your Physical State

It is important to plan to study your most difficult material when you are most alert. Some people work best in the early morning, and others late at night. You need to choose your time for demanding work carefully and try to prevent other things from encroaching on this special time. Physical hunger is a sure source of distraction, just as a lot of soft drinks (or beer) or snacks will tempt you to turn away from the books to indulge yourself. It is best to have a deliberate snack before you start studying and to do a little physical exercise as a tune-up. Studying when you are drowsy will not produce good results.

Your Mental State

There are any number of inhibitors to good study habits, including boredom, anxiety, personal worries, or poor methods, but the greatest deterrent is the notion that studying is a chore that *must* be performed, when you have to summon every ounce of willpower to open the book and get through that first paragraph. Here, the problem is primarily one of attitude. After all, you have registered for this course, and success in it depends on getting the work done efficiently, block by building block. It helps to shift your attitude to find a reason that satisfies you for taking the class, such as that you are interested in the materials covered or that success in this course will make achieving other goals possible. Talking to your professor or to other students will sometimes help. Getting the readings done for the next lecture so that you see for yourself how much more you get out of it will also result in a lot of satisfaction. If you are anxious about the difficulty of the course, you can try to solve the particular problem that you are stuck on or talk to your instructor to sort out the problem. Or, if this course is more demanding than others, you can find ways of putting its demands in perspective, such as the following:

- breaking up large tasks into their component parts
- doing the most difficult task first, when you are most alert
- identifying your problems in a particular project or reading and addressing each of them systematically
- using a notebook to write out your tasks and striking them out when they are accomplished

Daydreaming or Mind-Wandering

When you find that your attention is slipping, you need to note what is distracting you. If it is part of your environment, you can take steps to correct it. If it is daydreaming that is pulling you away, you might write down the interrupting thought and turn back to the books. The idea is that if you objectify the thought, you will be able to set it aside and more easily regain your direction. Another trick is simply to make a check mark on a piece of paper whenever you catch yourself daydreaming, and try to reduce the number of checks in an hour. On the other hand, you can turn deliberately away from your books and daydream freely for as long as you wish. The idea is to try to avoid studying and daydreaming at the same time.

TIPS: Increasing Your Concentration

1. Set aside a regular amount of time for study.
2. Gradually increase your attention span.
3. Set out your tasks or goals for a particular session in order (the number of pages to be read, the problems to be solved), and check them off when you complete them.
4. Vary your activities among reading, writing, reviewing, memorizing, solving problems, planning for the next day, and so on.
5. Plan your breaks and do something different so that you enjoy them.

Personal Worries

Personal worries can get in the way of all of your academic activities, so you need to try to identify what the problems are and develop a practical and concrete plan to resolve them. Talking to someone who can help—a friend, a counsellor on campus, or a specialist in the area of your worry—can also alleviate problems. The student services centre at your university will have counselling services available and will be able to refer you to other people who can give professional and discreet help.

The Task versus the Clock: Time for Best Concentration

You often will have only a restricted amount of time at your disposal, in which case you have to take advantage of that time to do what you can. But when you set aside a greater amount of time for study, you need to be governed by the demands of the task you set for yourself, rather than the clock. The clock can be a major distraction.

You should do your most demanding studying when you are at your best, whether that is morning or evening, but you should also plan to set aside that premium time when there are the fewest competing activities demanding your attention, from sports to your favourite TV shows. Besides following your timetable, you need to be aware that some of the most demanding tasks should determine their own length of time (see the section below on scheduling). It is best to stop studying when you get tired and your concentration begins to fade seriously, and when none of the tricks to keep in focus seems to be working.

TIME SCHEDULING

"I'd draw up a timetable, but I haven't had a moment," says the frustrated student. Some people think that scheduling their time limits their freedom unnecessarily and destroys spontaneity. In fact, we are, in so many ways, much less free than we think. We are all surrounded by obligations and duties that we can choose to either ignore or comply with, but we are not free to do whatever we want at every moment of our lives. When it comes to studying or not studying, or planning time for deliberate choices about studying, you are really setting in order a series of priorities. At the top of the list of possibilities is passing the course of study for the degree and graduating, and at the bottom is failure. When you schedule time for study regularly and methodically, you are choosing one set of priorities over another: the course and your long-term goals—including graduation and beyond—over other interests. These other interests probably include obligations such as work, child care, and other family responsibilities. These obligations are not frivolous, but they do affect your university study in ways that can usually be managed. However, it may be that in realistically appraising the demands on your time, you will find that a normal five-course load is impossible, or at least that your grades will suffer, if you must maintain the other demands on your time outside university work.

University professors are under continual pressure from students to reduce the workloads in their courses, but there are limits to how much the workload in university courses can be reduced before it becomes watered down. In any case, the workload for a particular course is set at the beginning of the year, and you must assess the demands of that workload in relation to other demands on your time. A normal minimal expectation for university work is that you spend two hours outside class for every hour in class. Following this minimal demand, your time spent in a full-time five-course load will require at least forty-five hours per week: fifteen hours spent in class, and thirty hours spent outside reading and writing. The time commitment to a full-time course load, therefore, is more than a full-time job, which is now usually thirty-seven to forty hours a week. We point out these time frames not to frighten or discourage you, but to provide a reality check. Without the commitment of time to your studies, your grades will suffer considerably.

To speak of completing a course or of graduation means that there is a perspective governed by time. At the end, with a more-or-less fixed date, is the day of graduation. Your years of study are determined by what courses you take, which determine, in some measure, your pattern of study, courses, and credits. Most students find it practical and very helpful to map out the year, the term, the month, and the week.

The Year

If your courses are on a yearly schedule, you need to note the important dates of assignments, essays, reports or class presentations, projects, quizzes, and examinations (mid-terms and finals), as well as any other highlights. You need to be sure to mark down the key dates by which you must drop the course to receive a partial fee refund or to avoid receiving a failing grade, and the last day to hand in term work. Of course, your yearly schedule will also include special events such as religious holidays, sports events in which you are a participant or spectator, and events for which you have tickets (see Box 1.1).

TIPS: Getting Organized

1. Many student organizations make academic timetable forms available in the first week of classes. Get a couple and hang them prominently near your desk.

2. Buy a watch.

3. Keep and use a date book.

4. Most student centres recommend that you spend at least twice the number of hours a week reading or studying for a course as you spend in the classroom. For more difficult work, and when assignments are due, you will have to spend more time studying.

5. Use odd periods of time—such as time spent on the bus—for reviewing or reading that is not too demanding.

6. Always carry some notes or a book with you that you can work on for that fifteen-minute period. Such use of time adds up profitably.

7. If you have a free day with no classes, do not plan to use it for weekly study marathons, as it will be hard to maintain your concentration. Instead, break it up into two-hour sessions (at most), do different work within those sessions, and relax between sessions.

8. Before you go to bed, put some of your material in order for the next day (you won't have time in the morning), and make a brief list of upcoming tasks.

The Term, Semester, or Quarter

Like the yearly schedule, the semester schedule will also record the key dates for university and course deadlines, as well as other events such as concerts and long weekends. But here your time is more compressed. You might also wish to fit the term schedules into a yearly pattern, especially if some of your courses are year-long courses and some are semester courses.

The Month

Most students who draw up this schedule position the month with a week added into the next month. To organize a month of good work and then find that the next week contains two assignments will come as a shock. The week added at the end is insurance that when you schedule the next month, you will have no surprises.

The Week

For the first weeks in the term, it helps to make detailed timetables of your week, first listing all classes, seminars, labs, and other fixed activities such as work or other responsibilities. Then, you should total all of the time that you customarily spend eating, sleeping, shopping, attending meetings, and commuting, as well as any other time requirements, such as family, work, or regular sports activities. You should allow yourself an hour for lunch on most days, if your classes allow, and more time than that for dinner, so you can use some of that time for relaxation. You can include the time that you intend to take off on the weekends and the time that you will spend reading for pleasure or watching TV. After calculating the time that you have left, you can deduct from that a reasonable amount of recreational time for the week. The amount of time that you have left is what you have for your academic study and reading.

Next, you should estimate the time that you need for studying for each course and plan it in blocks, so that you can split your time working on a number of courses in a block to give variety and minimize loss of concentration. Some students find that thinking of blocks of time as morning, afternoon, and evening is a help. It is a good idea to put your most difficult work into the peak study period when you have the fewest distractions and your concentration is at its best. You also need to include in your schedule time for recreation. Of course, things always go wrong ("the Peter principle"), so you should allow some time for an Unexpected Fateful Occurrence (UFO). If this map allows you sufficient time for the two hours of study to one hour of classes, your management is under control; if not, you need to decide where you can make adjustments and check the schedule again to see whether it is practical and realistic.

You can then post your schedule over your desk and be prepared to amend it as the week goes by. You'll likely need to revise the schedule for the second week to fit your needs and goals. It is your strategy map, and all that you do academically can be charted on it.

For example, you might set out a daily timetable based on your weekly timetable with the specifics added about where you are. You can put in the locations and precise tasks that you have to complete and sketch in the details the night before. It might look like this:

7:00 a.m.	get up, breakfast
7:45	leave for campus
8:30	locker; return books to library; look over Geography notes

9:30–11:00	Geography lecture
11:00–12:00	library; look up 2 different encyc. articles to photocopy on Adam Smith and Ricardo for Economic hist. assignment for next week
12:00–1:30	swim and lunch
1:30–2:30	review vocabulary for Spanish class
2:30–3:20	Spanish class
3:30–4:30	coffee with Jim and Linda
4:30–6:30	shopping and dinner
6:30–7:30	TV show
7:30–10:30	study—desk
7:30–8:30	read textbook on Smith and Ricardo
	read and compare the two encyclopedia articles
	notes on text and on articles
8:30–9:30	Spanish vocab. 1/2 hour
	Spanish grammar from text 1/2 hour
9:30–10:30	read chapters 4–8 of Dickens's *Hard Times* for English
10:30	TV news and bed

You can see that the details are set out carefully, especially in the evening study time, but also in the library, so that the time does not drift by. Of course it will not all work out clearly, and there will be problems, but the scheme sets out a pattern that you can then decide to vary or modify. As well, the daily plan fits into the weekly and monthly schedule.

When You Fall Behind: A Schedule to Catch Up

Everybody falls behind, and for a time the schedule does not seem to function as the unfinished school work piles up. That is when you invoke the "catch-up schedule." It has three simple principles: first, keep from falling behind further; second, prioritize the incomplete work; and third, implement a method to catch up on some of it every day.

1. Keep from falling further behind. Be rigorous in what you have to do to keep up. That may mean skimming a bit, or taking some shortcuts—anything to cut free a bit of time that you can use for getting some of the unfinished work done. But in planning for that, you cannot afford to let other things slip. Make careful lists of your readings, decide what you can do, and complete it at least in the overview method (see page 64); go to lectures and labs, concentrating as well as you can; hit on what is most important; and keep up with any new deadline dates.

2. Prioritize your unfinished work. Sort it into four categories: *urgent* (*U:* this work has to be done as soon as possible; grade loss is threatened by this item); *essential* (*E:* this item has to be done soon and is related to understanding a major component or part of the course; direct grade loss is not imminent, but this item is vital to the final examination); *important* (*I:* it would be good and useful to get this item completed within a specific time for general comprehension, but it is neither urgent nor vital); and *postpone* (*P:* this item can safely be postponed until your schedule allows it to be taken up;

BOX 1.1   Mapping Time for All Course Requirements for a Year

How much time does a student have for a full-year course? In this model, adapted from one by Professor Susan Warwick, we assume that a full-year course involves thirty weeks, with three hours of classes a week. In our sample there are 3500 pages of readings to complete in the year, including all texts and a course kit, but not counting any extra reading for assignments. We also assume that our sample student is taking a full course load of five courses and is also working for twenty-five hours a week.

Time Available

168 hours in a week   = 5040 hours in a 30-week year

Commitments

5 courses @ 15 hours a week   = 450 hours
Sleeping @ 8 hours a night   = 1680 hours
Work @ 25 hours a week   = 750 hours
Travel @ 2 hours a day, 10 hours a week   = 300 hours
Entertaining @ 2 hours a day, 10 hours a week   = 300 hours
Misc. (eating, shopping, etc.) @ 2 hours a day,
   10 hours a week   = 300 hours
Total   = 3780 hours
Hence 1260 hours are left   = 1260 hours
To be fair, take only 2/3 of that amount   = 840 hours
Divided by the five courses   = 168 hours per course per year
Realistic estimate of course time available   = 5.6 hours a week per course

That amount of time comes close to the recommended minimum of two hours of studying or reading outside class for every hour spent in class. You will have to schedule more than your allotted time for assignments in some weeks, but for many weeks you can spend the full time on course readings. Two models calculate the reading load. Column A divides the course readings into weekly and daily numbers of pages to read all of the course materials. Column B assumes an average reader and calculates the time needed on the basis of the number of words to be read and average reading speed.

Column A

Actual page count of sample course
   = 3500 pages
   = 116 pages each week
   = 20 pages a day, excluding
      Saturdays and Sundays
With about five and a half hours available, that also comes out to about twenty pages a day for a five-day week.

Column B

3500 pages = 1 225 000 words
   @ 350 per page
Most U.S. college students read 250–300 words a minute. A good reader will read about 500, a slow reader 150–250. Take the lowest of the average readers, 250 words a minute. Therefore, an average student will take 4900 minutes to read all of the readings.
   = 81.6 hours for the year, or
   = 2.7 hours a week to do all the readings, about
      half of the allotted time, with time left over
      for research and assignments.

realistically, you put items in this category only when you are aware that they may not be completed, and accepting that fact does not put you at risk). Next, list all of the work that you have not done, fitting it into one of the categories. Colour code them, with the *U* items marked in red. Then, estimate the amount of time that you will need for each task. Be as complete and as specific as you can, listing all readings unfinished, lectures missed, notes incomplete, work not handed in, and deadlines missed. The chances are that your estimated times will greatly exceed your available time. So, go back over the list and cut back once more, eliminating what you can safely, reducing the time for lesser tasks, and giving the most time to the high-priority items. The aim here is not to get you more and more discouraged or to render you immobile from the shock of what is incomplete, but to set out what you should do to get out of the swamp.

Deal first with the deadlines you have missed or the work you have not handed in. Check with your professors about whether you can still submit it, even if there is a late penalty. Then, make a plan to get the work done, concentrating on what is most difficult first, or what is latest, or what carries the greatest weight or greatest penalty. Mark on your schedule specific times for beginning this work and for each part of it until it is finished, and stick to the time you allot for it. Try to have the first item completed within three days, according to a realistic schedule.

When you are drawing up your priorities, you will see some materials that have long passed in the course, so, unless they are essential for understanding the present concepts of the course or you are missing a gap that cannot be filled later, skip them for now and return to them later when there is a lull in your workload.

Where you are more modestly behind in your readings, again concentrate on moving through the older material to get up to speed. Reading for comprehension rather than for detail would be a good idea here.

3. Catch up bit by bit. In the time that you have saved from your other work, take some time every day to get your overdue work back into shape. Each week you should be chipping away at the unfinished tasks and removing them from your list, and meanwhile you will not be falling further behind.

When you are struggling to catch up, ask for help from your friends or your teachers. Delegate some of the work to others. Perhaps a friend can take notes once for you (do not make this practice a habit) while you complete your library work. Many students, when falling behind, make a habit of skipping classes to make up for lost time; this practice, when habitual, is ultimately counterproductive, because the classes missed result in the student's falling further behind. Class time is usually an efficient way of keeping in touch with course materials and requirements. Even if you do not have time to complete the readings, attendance at lectures and seminars will at least keep you up-to-date. Professors are not sympathetic to repeating material covered in class that you have missed because of your scheduling problems.

When you have fallen behind, give up some tasks as impossible and just accept that fact. Reorganize some part of your life to get a fresh angle and to stimulate your motivation; sometimes just cleaning up your desk or room or reorganizing your work place a little can help. Do not give in, however, to making this the important task in order to avoid doing what you are behind in. Get something done, and you will move ahead with the rest of your list to get caught up.

Problems with Time Management

"I'm supposed to be doing this survey in Psychology on procrastination, but I just can't seem to get around to doing it." Things get put off and put off until the last possible moment, and then, in a frantic flurry of activity, you struggle to get papers handed in and to study for exams, or to complete whatever task has you in a panic at the moment. Typically, procrastinators fail to learn from this pattern of disaster, but when the chance to defer comes up again, even in the face of horrible results, the same behavioural pattern kicks in. Or, they fall back on the excuse that many of us have invoked, "I'll do that when I feel like it"—except that we almost never feel like it. The key problem is that procrastinators really do believe that they do their best work under the extreme pressure of an absolute deadline, and so they cannot move until that moment is imminent. It is as though all of their inertia has accumulated to render them immobile until the final moment—or beyond the final moment, when in a frenzy they struggle to complete an almost impossible task. They argue with themselves like this: "To get to university you must be smart. Smart people do not have to study hard (a fallacy). So if I do poorly, I can blame it on my late start, rather than on my lack of ability, since, after all, it was not my best effort." Such self-justification and apologetic escapism masks real worries and self-doubts.

Dogging the life of a procrastinator is the loss of self-confidence, as all of the promises you have made to yourself are broken. You have feelings of unworthiness, along with a pronounced fear of failure, a fear almost certain to be realized when the countdown begins. But no matter how deep your doubts or how ingrained your habit, many recent studies have assured sufferers (and most students have been sufferers at one time or another—you are not alone) that their problem can be reduced and cured. In an article in *The New York Times,* Jane Brody writes that "there are a host of techniques, many of which have been tested on some of the nation's most egregious procrastinators, to help you overcome the tendency to postpone or ignore tasks you find forbidding, offensive or just plain disagreeable" (C12). She paraphrases from *It's About Time,* a book by Linda Sapadin and Jack Maguire, who argue that there are at least six styles of procrastinators:

- *Perfectionists* are overly preoccupied with details or with the fear of starting or finishing a project that may not meet their high standards. They want things done their way and so have difficulty delegating tasks.

- *Dreamers* have grandiose ideas about what they would like to do but rarely get going on these projects. They wait for opportunities to present themselves instead of just digging in. Despite previous plans or priorities, they do what they feel like doing at the moment. They expect great things from themselves that never seem to happen.

- *Worriers* paralyze themselves before starting a project with a series of "what if's." They have difficulty making decisions, avoid new or different situations, doubt their judgment or ability to tackle projects, and need or seek advice, approval, assurance, or assistance from others before starting.

- *Defiers* resist authority. They become sulky, irritable, or argumentative when asked to do something they do not want to do. They sabotage tasks they do not like doing by working too slowly or ineffectively. They feel resentful or manipulated when asked to do something unexpected and take offence when others suggest ways of being more productive.

- *Crisis makers* ignore important tasks until the last minute, then work frantically to get them done. Many are proud of living "on the edge." Their lives seem chaotic, their moods highly and dramatically changeable. They are easily frustrated and show it by quitting or getting angry. They tend to get very involved with a project, then quit abruptly.

- *Overdoers* run around doing lots of things without really accomplishing very much. They have difficulty saying no when asked for help and often wonder how they got themselves into what they are doing. They are always complaining they have too much to do, too little time. They tend to get overinvolved in other people's problems at the expense of their own.

Professionals in the field of time management agree that some form of stress management is important, and you can seek help with this aspect of your life from your university health centre or from your doctor. One of the essential ingredients in stress management is regular physical exercise, even if it is simply walking for half an hour once or twice a day. Other suggestions are breaking large tasks down into smaller ones to make them easier to start and complete, devoting a regular bit of time each week to working on the larger task so that you chip away at it, and making a list of the tasks that you have completed, rather than a list of those that you need to do. The latter list is often too overwhelming. Another recommendation is to get a study partner with whom you can work well. The aim throughout is to get working up to speed. The story is told of the early French martyr St. Denys, who, after being beheaded outside Paris, bent over, put his head back on his shoulders, and walked back to Paris. Voltaire's comment on this legend was that the first step was the hard one, a remark that applies to the recovering procrastinator.

Above all, you need to be realistic in setting out your academic goals and fixing your timetable to achieve your objectives. Your schedule is not a wish list, but rather a map to help you chart your way to your goals. Your schedule will also change from week to week and month to month as the demands of your coursework change. So, you should be prepared to be flexible about what you can accomplish.

CRITICAL LISTENING: TAKING NOTES IN LECTURES AND SEMINARS

When students first come to university, one of the most intimidating experiences is to be in a large lecture hall with a professor far away at the front lecturing on a subject that you are obliged to take but that you have had little or no preparation for. Above all, the whole format of the formal lecture is strange and frustrating to you. As well as the large lecture, you likely will have a smaller seminar, perhaps attached to the lecture course, in which you are with a smaller group of students and are expected to make a formal class presentation yourself; in fact, you become the lecturer for that time.

In many ways, the lecture to a large class is outmoded and difficult, both for the student and the lecturer. It involves an expert delivering information and argument to a class of learners who have little chance to interrupt or ask questions. Many professors regard the large lecture as a performance and are either good or terrible at such theatrics. Some prepare well and deliver with wit and style, making their arguments pointedly and using the blackboard effectively to write out an outline, to explain difficult terms or concepts, or to supply a list of additional readings. Others are ill prepared, explain little, digress, and plough through their lecture as a chore, making it also a chore for you. Some lecturers talk quickly, or seem to, especially when you are not used to how they lecture or stress their main points. Others lecture so slowly and with so many "ums," "ahs," or other verbal habits that you have difficulty getting from one point to the next. Such differences apply to their treatment of content, use of humour or examples, and ability to attract and hold your attention. Being aware of such differences will make you alert to how they use different methods of indicating what is important.

Universities favour this method of teaching not only because it has been traditional for more than a thousand years, but also because in the days of financially troubled institutions, it is usually economical. In some institutions, this mode of teaching is assigned to the most junior faculty, while the senior faculty with international recognition teach the advanced seminars and graduate courses. Other schools make it a point to share among all faculty the lecturing in large classes, so that in your first year you might have as a lecturer a well-known authority in the field.

Whoever your lecturer is, and whatever method of lecturing he or she uses, your responsibility is to get what you can from the lecture by being an active listener and note taker. Both listening and taking notes are learned skills. These skills are vital to your success in the course, since you will need these notes later to complete the course readings, write your essays, and study for the tests and final examinations.

Six Principles for Being a Good Listener and Note Taker

1. Come to the lecture prepared with your readings completed and with the necessary books and notebooks.
2. Be an active listener.
3. Write down the structure of the lecture.
4. Note the key terms, concepts, and definitions.
5. Note the illustrations, examples, or page references.
6. Learn to question or comment by marking what you disagree with, want to expand later, or do not understand.

Each of these points is worth further discussion.

Come Prepared

To get the most out of a lecture you need to be up and running before the lecture begins. That means that you should have completed the readings or lab work before the lecture. The course syllabus will set out the lecture topics or themes for the year, and often the assignments will be specified, along with readings, page numbers, and so on. Even if you do not have time to complete all of the reading in detail, you should learn to skim and read for general comprehension before the lecture. You should also bring the appropriate text to the lecture, especially if the lecturer customarily refers to passages for more detailed discussion and comment. You also will want to have your notebook ready, beginning each lecture on a new page. We discuss several formats for note taking during lectures in the next section.

Be an Active Listener

Years of TV watching have made many students and others into passive listeners. You watch the program, switch the channel after a moment or two if it does not please, tune out during the ads, or fast-forward the tape on the VCR to the good bits. But you are more limited with the lecturer and have little control over what happens at the front of the room. Or so it seems. In fact, you still have the ability to switch channels mentally, tune out, fast-forward to the next class, sleep, daydream, or just waste your time. On the other hand, the practice of TV watching and doing other tasks simultaneously, such as reading a newspaper or listening to music, has developed skills that you can adapt to become a better listener and note taker during lectures. Just as watching TV while reading a newspaper requires that you divide your attention between two tasks, so, too, a lecture requires that you learn to both listen and record at the same time. When studying, you cannot give divided attention to other tasks, such as watching TV, and concentrate effectively. However, for some academic activities, such as note taking in lectures, dividing your attention is not only desirable, but necessary.

More practically, this hour-long lecture has cost you a good deal of money (perhaps $15, calculated at $1000 per course, for 75 hours per year; in many universities the cost will be four or five times that amount). More importantly, this lecture is giving you the information that you need to pass the course. Therefore, being an active learner makes good sense economically and academically.

Being an active learner means that you approach the lecture as a reading exercise. You are, in fact, "reading" the lecture and making notes about your reading. Being an active listener means using all of your critical thinking abilities, including resisting accepted ideas; listening (or reading) for the structure, the ideas, and the concepts; and resisting the distractions of the lecturer's mannerisms, the classroom rustle, or anything in the content that offends you (at least for the moment).

TIPS: Active Listening

1. Keep the lecture notes for each course in a separate notebook.
2. Date and identify the lecture clearly, and number the pages of the lecture.
3. Write down the lecture outline and any background readings. Use the same numbering scheme in your notes so when you review you know what point you have reached.
4. Maintain your concentration by making notes according to one of the suggested methods.
5. Write on one side of the sheet only; use loose-leaf paper, which may be rearranged later, with inserts; and indent details and skip lines to separate topics.
6. Omit articles and unnecessary adjectives, and use abbreviations and other signs that help you.
7. Note in the margin or underline any words you don't understand, and mark the concepts you need more information about.
8. Use an indent method, and number points.

To become an active listener, you need to choose where you sit in the classroom. Sitting in the middle and near the front positions you to see and hear best, with fewer distractions from your classmates. It also helps to be aware of the many activities that take place when you become an active listener: understanding what is being said, summarizing it for your notes, shifting attention between the lecturer and the notes, analyzing what has been said and evaluating it, and anticipating what will come next. Of course, you cannot undertake all of these activities all of the time with equal balance, but trying to stress two or three in any given lecture will help you hone your skills.

Go for the Structure

Some lecturers write out the structure of the lecture on the blackboard week by week, and then try to follow it in the course of their remarks. Recording this outline at the beginning of the lecture, before the lecture actually starts, is a good way of preparing for the content of the next hour. It enables you to see the transitions and to anticipate where the lecture is going and to some extent how it will get there. Sometimes there are key concepts or ideas in the outline. Finally, the outline will greatly help you in your short review of the lecture after it is over and in the more extensive review of your notes that you will have to undertake in preparing for your final examinations.

Other lecturers do not write an outline on the board, and so you have to listen actively for the shape of the lecture as it proceeds. Many lecturers list or enumerate the items they are covering: "First ... second ..."; "There are three reasons for such a reaction ..."; "Finally...." If you do not get the structure clearly when you are listening to it, you can try to note any of the transitions in the argument and any ways in which points are enumerated, and then, after the lecture, take a few minutes to look over your notes and try to identify the structural elements and mark them in your notes (1, 2, 3; A, B, C; and so on).

Most lectures have several traditional features:

Introduction
There is an introduction in which there might be a summary of last week's lecture, a statement of the thesis for this week, an outline of a theme, or some comments that might in themselves be considered an outline. It helps to be on time for the lecture and ready for this kind of comment when it occurs, and to try to get down as much of it as possible in your notes. In particular, you should pay close attention to stress laid on continuities between this week's lecture and previous lectures. Such stress indicates the patterns being developed over the course, indicating to you what students often ask: "What is important?"

Body
The body of a lecture can take several forms:
- setting out a body of material under headings
- explaining or defining the terms or concepts that will be used in the lecture and commenting on a reading systematically or randomly
- making a point and illustrating it with a reference to the text or with an example
- elaborating or expanding points or illustrations
- rephrasing the argument to explain a difficult concept

Conclusion

The concluding remarks can be a flourish (some clever remark to end the lecture on a high point); a wrap-up or summary ("This week I have outlined ... and have shown that.... Next week I shall...."); a highlighting of the main points made; or an assignment of the readings for the next week.

Being an active listener enables you to read the lecturer's mannerisms and body language for points of emphasis in the structure of the lecture. But you should also be aware of the kinds of signals that a lecturer gives you to indicate where he or she is in presenting the material, such as the following rhetorical devices.

Repetition

The most common complaint students make about lecturers is that they speak too quickly for them to take notes. While some lecturers are insensitive to students' needs and do speak too quickly, usually that complaint means that students have not learned to listen actively and to use paraphrase or synthesis in making notes. But lecturers also know that students cannot keep up with them in their note taking and so repeat central ideas, rephrase them, or elaborate on them to give students a chance to catch up. The following expressions signal repetition:

Let me put that another way....

Once again....

In other words....

That is....

For example.... Another example....

As well.... Also.... In addition....

Emphasis

Lecturers tend to stress main points at the beginning or end of sections and to mark them off in their comments by some phrase or bodily signal, such as tapping the lectern, slowing down, changing the voice, or making a note on the blackboard. These points are those that the lecturer wishes to get across as central to the theme that is being developed, so you should try to get them down as clearly as you can. Signals of emphasis include the following:

This is the first important point....

Most importantly....

The significant fact is....

Specifically....

Definitions

Definitions of key terms or explanations of central concepts in the course are important for comprehending both what the lecturer means and how these terms are being used in the course. Such definitions are usually not available or easily accessible in dictionaries, but rather are specialist explanations given from the particular viewpoint of the course content. For instance, the term *hysteria* can have all sorts of popular meanings, but in a course on Freud's thought it has a clinical and technical meaning that Freud (and probably your lecturer) was at some pains to define. Similarly, many literary terms, such as those defining various genres like classicism or romanticism, *bildungsroman*, fantasy, and so on, may be defined in the handbooks, but the usage in your course may be far more precise and focused. Some teachers explain definitions by means of etymology (word derivations from source languages, often demonstrating shades of meaning that are important though hidden from later usage), popular versus scholarly usage, technical terminology, or example and illustration.

Transitions, turns, or bridges

In shifting from one topic to another, or from one part of the argument to the next, lecturers signal their transitions clearly, but often without enumerating them ("second," "third"). Such transitions indicate a change in direction, a turn in the argument, or a movement from one point to the next. Listening for and noting these transitions by some consistent mark in your note taking will help you to identify the parts of the structure later on (many people use various kinds of arrows). Transitional signals include the following:

- words that draw contrasts: *but, however, on the other hand, conversely, despite*
- words that point to a new direction: *now, next, to continue*
- words that draw cause-and-effect relationships: *hence, accordingly, consequently, therefore, because*

Elaboration

Fuller and fuller explanations in a lecture are often one of the hardest parts for a student to comprehend. One example seems to be significant or even too much for the note taker: Why go on and on? A student later may complain that the example was all a digression or that the instructor did not get to the point. Of course, the student may well be right. Or, it may be that the student failed to catch the point of the elaboration.

Usually, when a matter is explained at some length it is important, and perhaps difficult, and so demands considerable attention from the lecturer. The point might be controversial and thus need justification, support, or documentation; it might be poorly explained in the textbook and so require fuller explanation; or it might be best explained through an analogy to make it clearer. For instance, when we introduce the concept of popular notions of fantasy in a course that we jointly teach, the lecturer demonstrates popular usage by citing a number of recent occurrences of the term *fantasy* in the newspaper, reading the passage and commenting on it in some detail. Students often find this method perplexing, even though its point is explained, because they cannot see the direct connection between the topic of the lecture and their readings or their preconceptions. To them, the lecturer is being self-indulgent and is confusing because the examples are different from each other and their relationship is not immediately clear. In fact, the lecturer is giving a reading of the materials and methods of the course in such an explanation. It is a mini-model of how the course works. And the elaboration is given to you, if you are an active listener, so that you can supply your own elaboration later to further support the point being made. Students often expect a concept or point to be clarified immediately; however, academic study usually requires that concepts are laid out in such a way that they will not be fully understood until later in the course. Such a practice goes against the modes of instantaneous gratification dominant in our consumer society: critical thinking not only uses different methods, but in doing so also challenges preconceived ideas about how knowledge is produced and transmitted.

The key is to hear the introduction to the examples. Why are they being introduced, and to illustrate what? Why is this elaboration important? A lecturer will usually signal that clearly: "I shall illustrate this point with four examples...." So, if you get down the reason for the elaboration, or the point of the elaboration, you also need to note three things: the example, the reference, and the point made about it. Without the examples, the elaboration evaporates, and your notes have a big blank where the lecturer was at pains to give an explanation.

Note the Key Terms, Concepts, and Definitions

We have already commented on how noting the key terms and definitions will reveal the structure of a lecture. Here, we comment on that a bit more. Central terms and concepts are important not only to understanding a particular lecture, but also to comprehending the general structure and goals of the entire course.

Many students underline key terms that a lecturer stresses and then mark them later in the margins for review, often with the definition given in class. These notes can then be expanded by adding definitions from the textbook or from a specialist dictionary, or from some other source on the course. Raising questions about these key terms is an important way of ensuring that you understand them. You may then ask such questions during the lecture if there is an opportunity for questioning, after the lecture by speaking to the teacher, or during a seminar.

Note the Illustrations, Examples, or Page References

Many students turn off mentally when the lecturer says "for example." That phrase, however, indicates that what is coming is intended to illustrate the theoretical or conceptual point just made. You might still be struggling to get down the point and are thrown off by the example with its concrete language or precise reference. To help you understand the theory or concept, you should make a note of the reference in a word or two. You may abbreviate the title of the book to which the lecturer refers, and note the page reference, especially if it is a book on the course. Later, you can use that illustration to understand the theory or concept. In concluding an example, a lecturer often says something like, "By this example I have shown that...." Here, the lecturer is both repeating the point and summarizing the conclusion that the example or illustration alludes to. So if you missed the point at the opening, you can get it again here. Examples are intended to offer fuller explanations, not to while away the time pointlessly, so you should strive in your active listening to understand exactly why they are there and what they are illustrating.

Use Analytical Questioning in Your Note Taking

If your active listening has progressed appropriately, you will be able to question ideas as they are being advanced. This strategy is rather hard to master, since it depends both on having confidence in your own position and on understanding what is being argued in the lecture. You then can adopt some strategies in your notes to mark the places where you do not understand (writing a *?* in the margin), where you disagree (using the symbol *d/a* in the margin), or where you have to expand or explain later (marking *exp* in the margin). These points are also useful to take up with your tutor or seminar leader or with the professor if you have scheduled interviews or want to gather a number of questions before scheduling an appointment to discuss them.

BOX 1.2	The 5Rs of Note Taking

During the lecture write down as much of the argument and concepts as you can. Write legibly and leave spaces for what you cannot get down. Then, take fifteen minutes a night for each lecture to use the 5Rs.

■ *Record.* Soon after the lecture or in the 5R session that evening, fill in the blanks with what you missed, including missing concepts or phrases.

■ *Reduce.* Read through notes, and pick out key words and put them in the left margin as a clue to what was covered.

■ *Recite.* Cover the "record" section, and by going over the key words recall the substance of the lecture and recite it in your own words.

■ *Reflect.* Think about the content of the lecture and your notes; jot down at the end of the lecture notes any questions, problems of interpretation, and other illustrations or examples.

■ *Review.* Take ten minutes each week for a quick review of that week's notes, looking particularly at the key words.

Different Note-Taking Formats for Different Lectures

Many students drift through their lectures week after week not knowing what to write down and end the term with few useful notes, many wasted hours, and the prospect of little material to study for examinations. Others struggle to write down all of the information that they hear and leave each lecture frustrated because they missed some essential points. Others tape lectures and then either transcribe them (which means going through the lecture at least twice—once in hearing it, and once in transcribing it).

Still others take no notes and rely on their friends (which amounts to handing your destiny and intellect over to others). The best-prepared students know which method works well for them, having thought about and tried several. The same method might not work well for each course or in both lectures and tutorials. Most students eventually find that a combination of several methods works best. One of the aims is to avoid recopying without synthesis. If you do choose a method that involves rewriting the lecture, you should do so to add to it, to modify and expand, not simply to copy out again what you could have got the first time. We give several highly respected methods below. All of them involve dividing your page into sections where you add specific items in your review. All of them provide an opportunity to use the 5Rs of note taking (see Box 1.2).

The Cornell Method

Developed at Cornell University, this method involves review, organization and condensation of notes, and highlighting of key words for later study and reference using the 5Rs.

The *cue column* is sometimes called a *key-word column*. Some users also underline or asterisk key terms in their note taking or use another method to flag words or concepts that the lecturer stresses, as well as others that they do not understand or follow (see Figure 1.1).

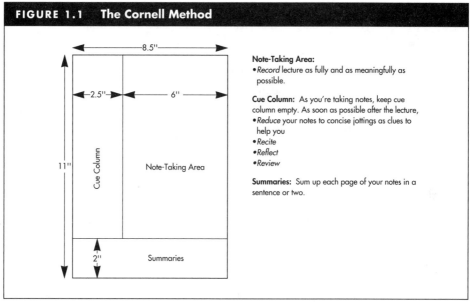

FIGURE 1.1   The Cornell Method

Source: *Cornell Method.* www.dartmouth.edu/~acskills/lsg/cornell.html

Advantages

- It requires no recopying of notes.
- It fills in gaps in the lecture quickly.
- It involves immediate review and consolidation.
- It links lectures and studying for exams.

Disadvantage

- It requires follow-up of fifteen minutes a night for completion using the 5Rs. (Is this not really an advantage?)

The Indent-Outline Method

This method stresses the outline and structure of a lecture, with the most general points beginning at the left margin and the more specific subcategories indented. You do not need to add numbers or letters, but you might find that useful, especially in the 5R stage when you go over the notes in the evening. For instance, in a lecture on the rise of the Third Reich and the causes of World War II, the general outline on the blackboard might be as follows:

1. The aftermath of WWI: the Treaty of Versailles and the Weimar Republic
2. The rise of Hitler to the writing of *Mein Kampf*
3. The development of National Socialism in Germany
4. The stock market crash and world economy
5. Political pluralism in Germany and the emergence of Hitler as Chancellor and President
6. Military and economic policy of the Third Reich

7. Territorial expansionism: Anschluss
8. Austria, Czechoslovakia, and the reaction of England and Russia
9. Poland

You would then start with an outline that might begin as follows:

1. The aftermath of WWI: general conditions
    – The treaty of Versailles, 1919
        Decisions of the Allies re
        Germany: 3 Issues:
            Debt and repayment obligations:
                resentment and inflation
            Military limitation to 100 000
            Land—loss of Alsace-Lorraine to France and disputed territories
            Political situation

    – Italy
        Rise of Fascism:
        Mussolini

    – Russia
        Rise of Communism:
        Lenin and Stalin

    – Weimar Republic
        Political turmoil in Germany
        Relations with allies
            Method of trying to repay debt
            Land constraints and problems
                Political failures: result is development of new political parties
                Rise of Hitler in summary form
                Served in German army in WWI
                President of German Workers Party 1921
                Led Munich Beer Hall putsch, 1923—failure
                Imprisoned, and began writing *Mein Kampf,* 1924
                Nazis increase in power, influence, paramilitary strength
                In political crisis runs for chancellorship, defeated by von
                        Hindenburg, but he cannot form government
                Appointed Chancellor, 1933, President 1934, Führer
                Rise of anti-Semitism and persecution of the Jews
                Policy of remilitarization, land expansion, blood & soil

The last section is in summary form and will be expanded later in the lecture in points 2–9. Each of these points could be filled in with more argument in a paragraph or other notes. Dates and data can be added during the lecture or later from textbooks and readings.

Advantages

- If the lecturer is logical and systematic, this method works well.
- Clear headings are easy to read, and space allows filling in details.
- Reading headings in order of indentation allows connections to be drawn.
- Indenting and analysis increase comprehension.

Disadvantages

- If the lecturer is unclear or lectures by association or explication, this method is harder to use.
- It requires the ability to think ahead and anticipate where the next argument fits in, and so depends on being well prepared with assigned readings.
- It requires analytical skills and concentration; thus, it is useful only when you are alert.

The Concept-Mapping Method

Both the Cornell and the indent-outline methods are linear and depend on your ability to perceive the linear arrangement of the lecture. The concept-mapping method maps out the lecture in terms of a graphic or diagram and allows you to draw connections that you did not see before or that the lecturer may return to later in the lecture. Maps also can capture a lot of information on a single page and are excellent for showing relationships among concepts. For instance, a map of the first part of the lecture on World War II might look like the one in Figure 1.2.

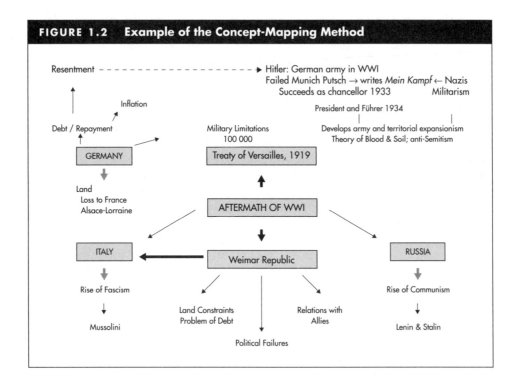

FIGURE 1.2   Example of the Concept-Mapping Method

The central topic is in the middle of the page, with the two major subheads above and below, and the other ideas radiating out from that as appropriate. It is always a good idea to start in the middle of a page with the main topic, and then to branch out in any direction, drawing connections and lines as the lecture proceeds. A new page might be started for the second section of the topic in the outline, and so on. Some students find they can add to only one map for much of a lecture; others find that one map per section of the argument works better. Others find that concept mapping is useful as part of the "reduce" phase of the 5R summary. The map can work to reorganize and synthesize the lecture once you have taken it down in the Cornell or outline-indent format. This reorganization is particularly useful in your review of the course materials when studying for a term or final examination. It allows you to see relationships and patterns that would otherwise have been hard to perceive.

Advantages

- This method stresses critical thinking, since you are forced to find relationships and locate them graphically.
- All of the lecture, or a major part of it, is visible structurally on one page.
- You can later elaborate the map with better arrows, colour coding, further data, and links.
- Review is easy, since the key words are already there, and some students find the graphic format easier to remember, especially in relating ideas.

Disadvantages

- In drawing the map you focus on the grand plan and tend to neglect the details.
- It is more difficult to add the references and illustrations.

The Charting Method

The charting method also depends on graphic or visual representation, and it is particularly useful when your lecturer follows a chronological order that lets you set out a vertical or horizontal timeline. You then fill in the appropriate intervals on the timeline. If you can anticipate the kind of chart that will be used, it is helpful to come to the lecture with one partly prepared.

The charting method can also be used for all kinds of other charts. For instance, a lecturer might set out the distinctions between mental and physical sensations when discussing some phenomenon. The two halves of the chart might then be extended on either side, and might also move vertically. Sometimes, students have no idea when this kind of chart will end and find themselves squeezing information into little space at the top or sides of a page.

It is essential to select specific categories, and then to arrange your note taking by putting the concepts and information under the specific categories. We could set out the same materials listed above as a chart as in Table 1.1.

You can add dates, data, and other information later from your textbook or other readings.

This method is also very useful in drawing together your summaries of large sections of a course in preparation for tests and examinations. You can choose appropriate categories and fill in the information as you undertake your review.

Advantages

- This method forces you to be analytical when you are listening to the lecture, because you have to choose a category for each piece of information.
- The categories help you to make comparisons and draw connections.

TABLE 1.1 Example of the Charting Method

Period of History	Act	Countries Involved	Major Events	Issues or Problems	Major Figure	Effects	Significance
1917–19	Treaty of Versailles	Allies → Germany	settlement of blame, debts, land (same)			unworkable solution	
		Russia	Revolution of 1917	overthrow of Czar	Lenin	feudal → modern	rise of Communism
1920–29		Weimar Republic	war reparations	debt → inflation	von Hindenburg	resentment	helps Hitler
		Germany	Munich Putsch fails Hitler jailed	Germ. Workers Party	Hitler	anti-Versailles writes *Mein Kampf*	rise of Nazis
1930–39		Italy	overthrow of monarchy	remilitarization	Mussolini		rise of Fascists
		Germany	Hitler loses election to von Hindenburg	political instability	Hitler	appointed Chancellor 1933 President 1934 Führer 1935	
				remilitarization	Hitler	territorial expansion anti-Semitism	

- The chart helps with efficient review.

Disadvantages

- You might categorize information incorrectly because your categories were not well chosen and it is difficult to change them once you are started; you should leave space at either end of your chart for new categories if needed.

- You might also have to force some materials into categories where they do not fit well, losing some subtlety.

The Line/Sentence Method

This method involves using a new line for every new idea, topic, or fact as the lecture proceeds, and numbering each line or sentence (the sentence does not have to be grammatically complete—you can abbreviate and omit unnecessary words). For this method it is important to leave a two-inch margin on the left side of the page so you can go back in the 5R stage to mark out the structure and divisions of the lecture and to add the key words.

Advantages

- This method gets down a lot of information efficiently.

- It is particularly useful when you are uncertain about what is important in a lecture or how the parts fit together, or when you are not as prepared as you should be.

- Less emphasis is put on critical thinking (this could be a disadvantage).

Disadvantages

- You cannot determine what the structure of the lecture is as you hear it, but only upon reviewing it.

- It is also difficult to distinguish between major and minor points.

- It involves less critical thinking and analysis.

- It may involve some rewriting to link related ideas.

Notes in Small Classes, Seminars, or Tutorials

All that we have said about lectures applies also to tutorials or to small classes where there is a good deal of discussion. The methods can be modified usefully, especially because tutorials or seminars often do different sorts of work in the class time. Some tutorials or seminars are stand-alone classes, while others are satellite seminars attached to large lecture courses. The stand-alone seminar may well function as an independent course, with some classes given to lectures, some to discussion, some to presentations or other projects. The satellite seminar often has to deal with problems and issues arising from the main lecture in the course, taking up difficult points, explaining terms or concepts, and examining issues or problems raised there. Because the atmosphere might be more informal and the instructor might not deliver a structured lecture, it is probable that the shape of the classroom discussion will be harder to grasp. There might be as many as three or four different kinds of material or modes of teaching used: review of the lecture, close textual work, explanation and question/answer sessions about course concepts, discussion of a series of topics, review of assignments, critical thinking and writing exercises, or class presentations by students. Each of these modes requires a somewhat different approach to taking notes. At the very least, a student has to be aware of the differing shifts in teaching modes and materials. It is most useful to try to indicate such shifts in your seminar notes and to record the important points that are being communicated.

Many students feel that they have to take notes in a large lecture because that is where the information is being set out, but in tutorials, it is a different matter. How do you record the seminar discussion? In general, it is wise to take notes in tutorials as you would in lectures to try to see the structure of the seminar and how it is being shaped by questions and the discussion. You might find that the concept-mapping model works well here.

If students give presentations, they might provide handouts with an outline of what they are presenting, and you can add notes to those sheets. If there are no handouts, you should take notes during the presentation, paying attention to what is particularly strong in it (you can mark it as *G* for good or + in the margin), what you disagree with or want to question in the following discussion (?), and what seems weak or unjustified (*W* or -). Sitting back with your arms folded may give the impression that you are devoting all of your attention to the paper, but it may also suggest that you are not interested and that there is nothing worth writing down. After all, the student making the presentation has done extra work on this topic, and you should be able to benefit from that by going away with some useful notes.

In discussion classes, you can record the general topic and then, if you know the students' names, identify the key points they have made by their initials. It is as though you are recording the process of the discussion. Here, it is important to get the shifts or turns in the line of discussion and to note the conclusions reached, as well as the summary the teacher makes about the conclusion. Some students find that recording a discussion as though they were taking notes of a meeting to later circulate helps them focus on what is important. Some classes designate one or two students each week to do just that—to record the discussion and circulate the record to all the students the next week.

Taking good lecture notes is a minor art form. Becoming proficient in note taking and appreciating its merits will, in the long run, help turn your year into a success story.

Some Final Words of Advice

It is never a good idea to hand over your notes to another student. If you want to lend them, it is better to photocopy your originals and give away the copy. As well, you should take enough paper to class for the lecture, but leave your lecture notes at home unless they are being

TIPS: Using Abbreviations in Note Taking

1. Use conventional symbols: + / $ (money) & # (number) @ = w/ (with) ∴ (therefore)
2. Abbreviate common words in the field: total (totalitarian), ind (individual), cons (conservative). Omit final letters: intro (introduction).
3. Omit vowels: prblm (problem); gvt (government), bckgrd (background).
4. Abbreviate titles of books studied in a course: AW (*Alice in Wonderland*), HT (*Hard Times*), CP (*The Color Purple*).
5. Use *g* to represent *ing:* mrkg (marking).
6. Omit unimportant words: *a, the,* verb forms.

discussed in class or you have points to raise from them. Then if you lose them, you will not have lost an entire set of notes.

If you have a lecturer who talks too quickly, it helps to use a two-page system, in which you write the main part of the lecture on the right-hand side and leave the left blank. During lulls in the lecture, you can fill in the gaps on the left-hand page at the appropriate place, and immediately after the lecture, go back over the lecture to fill in what you can recall.

What about retyping your lecture notes on the computer? Some authorities think this task is a waste of time, but others think it is useful, especially if your handwriting is bad. You might find that you can expand your notes well when you retype, and then can add other information to the computer file when undertaking a review. You also can paraphrase and organize the lecture more efficiently. If you combine this strategy with the 5R method, you might find it useful during the "revise" stage.

There are many useful abbreviations and shortcuts that experienced note takers use that you could adapt for your own purposes. It is important to use abbreviations that you will remember, so that your notes will not be gibberish to you when you return to them to study for examinations.

Finally, it sometimes helps to get together with other students to compare and discuss your lecture notes or to study with a good friend who also takes good notes and see what you can learn from each other, both about the methods of taking notes and about the course.

READING AND COMPREHENDING ASSIGNED TEXTS

From the first class, your professors start assigning readings, but often they do not explain what to look for or what the point of the reading is. You are expected to understand what you read and to fit it into the course in some way. Perhaps the reading will also be discussed in the following class. Learning to read and master assigned texts becomes a survival skill in the first week if you are not to fall far behind, perhaps never to recover. We deal in Chapter 3 with reading and critical skills. Our concern here is to get you started with some methods that will help you to survive.

In a large psychology class at Harvard, students were told to take ten minutes to read twenty pages of the textbook. Then they had to shut the books and take a test in which they had to write out the main argument, describe the supporting arguments and evidence, and finally state the author's conclusions. Only about 10 percent were able to complete the last requirement. Most students began at the beginning and read as far as they could in the allotted time, but they failed to come close to completing the reading. Those who completed the last requirement had learned to read for an overview, to skim, and then to fill in the gaps. Those are essential survival skills in the first weeks of classes, and they can be broken down into a number of steps.

1. Look over the whole of a book before you begin to read it. See how it is set out and what its divisions are (parts, chapters, sections). Often, the table of contents is much abbreviated, so look over the parts or sections to see what each really contains.

2. Look over the subheadings in the parts of the book that you are going to read. If you will be reading it all, look at the other kinds of information that are in the book: illustrations, graphs and diagrams, charts and summaries.

3. Read at least part of the preface. In the preface, the author usually sets out his or her goals and a summary of the literature in the field, how this book relates to it, and how the

argument is organized. That is, you get a neat summary of the whole book in the preface (scholarly articles often contain an abstract at the beginning that serves the same function). As well, the acknowledgments will point you to other people in the field whose works you might wish to consult.

4. Look at the back of the title page. This page records the details of the book's publication, but it also includes information about how it is catalogued, often including the subject headings that classify it in the Library of Congress system used in most university libraries. With this information you can search the subject headings in your university library for books on the same subject.

5. Look to see whether the book has a bibliography. Skimming the bibliography will help you learn which kinds of authors and authorities are referred to in the book, and it may help you determine some of the viewpoints of the author you are reading.

Armed with this preliminary survey, you are ready for a more sustained and detailed approach to the assigned reading. We give a lot of further advice in Chapter 3.

READING PROBLEMS, DISABILITIES, AND REMEDIES

Almost all students find some of the readings they are assigned difficult. So do professors. Some technical works in philosophy, political and literary theory, and branches of science and technology demand considerable concentration. But many students who have difficulty just keeping up with the routine reading and week-to-week assignments for most of their classes, discover that they have badly misunderstood assigned readings, or have frequent and serious difficulty concentrating.

Some of these problems may not be rooted in the normal difficulties that most students experience, but rather may result from an undiagnosed medical condition or a learning disability. The first step you should take if you suspect that this might be the case is to ensure that you are not experiencing vision difficulties that could be treated by a routine checkup.

Reading disabilities are one aspect of more general learning disabilities, which might have physiological causes (eye–brain coordination or eye–hand coordination) or psychological causes (brought on by financial difficulties, home or work environment, family problems, and so on). Many of these difficulties are evident from the first stages of learning to read and write and are now diagnosed much earlier than in former years. Often, reading and writing problems are diagnosed as dyslexia. Originally, the term meant a dysfunction of reading ability, but it now is applied to a wide range of difficulties in short-term memory retention and eye–hand coordination. It is often marked by reversing letters (R as Я or Milton as Mitlon), syllables, numbers, ideas, sequences, and so on. U.S. government data indicate that about 15 percent of the school population (one child in seven) is dyslexic (see the Web page of the Davis Dyslexia Association at **www.dyslexia.com/quest.htm**).

If you know that you have a more serious reading disability, you should follow the procedures that address your particular difficulty. If you suspect that you have a reading disability (or some other kind of learning disability that impedes your reading and comprehension), you can likely have that checked at your university health service or student services centre. Many universities have a special office for students with disabilities that routinely tests for such problems and offers assistance to cope with the problem, including computer assistance, reading recovery programs, individual tutoring, writing assistance, and special arrangements for taking examinations. Much information, including preliminary self-help checklists, is also available on the Web. A number of such sites are linked on a Web site maintained by SNOW (Special Needs Opportunity Windows) at the University of Toronto (**snow.utoronto.ca/Learn2/readisab.htm**).

IMPROVING YOUR MEMORY AND LEARNING ABILITIES

Memory loss is not limited to the elderly or to the proverbial absent-minded professor. All of us are continually learning new materials and integrating new experiences into our memory at almost the same time that we are forgetting other materials and experiences. Forgetting is a fact of life. Wordsworth was at least partly right in saying that "birth is but a sleep and a forgetting." Huge numbers of psychological studies have been undertaken on the subject of memory and forgetfulness. What is clear from many of these studies is that people forget material that they have recently learned very quickly at first, and then the rate of forgetting slows down over time. Hence, the problem is knowing how to learn material the first time so that it will be better remembered, and then ensuring that the rate of forgetting is slowed down.

Memory works by making links between information. Facts are fitted into mental frameworks and then are related to other facts. Stocking those frameworks with information and useful relationships among kinds of information helps to strengthen your memory. In fact, most people can do a great deal to improve their memories. Some material needs to be retained for a short time (and short-term memory is sufficient for that), but other kinds need to be retained by long-term memory. The act of remembering is characterized by three other *r* words: *recognizing, recalling,* and *retaining.* When you recognize something, you can identify or associate it with something that you already know: you can pick it out from among similar items. The emphasis on this part of remembering is on the actual object or idea that you recognize, not on your reaction to it. On the other hand, to recall something is to pull it back into your mind, to reproduce it in some measure. Here, the stress is on what you can do as part of your response to a prompting. Retention is the capability of holding that recognition and recollection in your mind. If you retain a memory, you are defeating the forces of forgetfulness. These functions of the human brain require practice to work well, and more practice to work better.

Two main methods are often used to help train and exercise the memory:

- *Association* relates new information to what you already know in order to create a new meaning, thereby helping both recognition and recollection.
- *Organization* as a mental activity groups the information into categories, smaller portions, or major and minor emphases and so helps you to classify information and perform more apt associations.

Such comments may be useful as explanations of how memory can be said to work; however, the question that most students ask is, "How can I remember it better?" One advantage of using critical thinking practices is that the materials and concepts of the course, the intellectual structures and frameworks in which the course can be placed, are already known to you. Hence, it is a lot easier to fit into the course frameworks the smaller details, such as the data, the individual readings, and the concepts. You already have done some of the work required to aid your remembering—you have organized the components of your course.

It is within this context that a major part of learning and memory comes into play for most students. You are expected to understand the concepts and materials of the course and to be able to discuss them in essays and examinations. To do that you have to recall them, not

TIPS: Improving Your Memory

1. Be clear about what you have to remember.

2. Make sure that what you are setting out to remember is in the form in which you want to remember it. That is, learn it right the first time. It is far easier to do so than to unlearn what was wrong and relearn it.

3. Memorize passages as a whole, rather than line by line. Memorizing passages from texts, especially poetry, in which the rhythms and rhymes aid recall, is comparatively easy. This skill provides a permanent acquisition: what is well memorized will stay with you to be of use later for recollection and pleasure.

4. Try using a tape recorder when memorizing, so you can repeat the passage.

5. Alternatively, write out the passage, and then learn it from the written draft.

6. Practise memorizing. With practice, more and more can be memorized; most of us have our minds filled with details that we do not need urgently, such as many phone numbers, but even that can help you extend the range of your memory.

7. If you have to remember words or definitions or rules verbatim, mark them that way in your lecture notes or texts. Some people find it helpful to write words or definitions on sticky-notes to attach to their mirrors, where they can see them several times over the next few days or weeks. This method often works well for learning new concepts or specialized vocabulary.

necessarily in detail, but in the general ways in which they fit into the intellectual frameworks of the course, and you have to discuss them in that context, demonstrating your competence. You are not expected here to recall the exact words of the lectures or the texts you studied, but you are expected to understand the concepts and to be able to reproduce and analyze them in your own words.

In some coursework, you will need to recall specific details precisely. Medical students have to recall thousands of names of parts of the body, and law students have to memorize details of specific legal cases; students in theatre, mathematics, and foreign languages also have to memorize many details. Indeed, most students have to learn some passages from texts in detail, some dates, some historical figures, some vocabulary and concepts, and so on. This more specialized and particular use of memory can often be frightening. But you will feel less overwhelmed if you reflect on what you have already memorized: you probably know the names of dozens of singers and their songs and many lyrics in detail or the phone numbers of many of your friends, and all of that without effort, because you want to learn it, or it just appears to implant itself in your brain. Hence, you know that you have the ability for precise memory, as well as the more general ability to relate concepts and ideas to your own understanding processes. Still, that nagging question remains, "How can I remember it all better?"

Walter Pauk (168–69) lists eight principles for improving your ability to remember:

1. Creating motivated interest. You will remember things better if you are interested in them. So find some area, even if it is self-interest in passing this course, to focus your interest on.

2. Using selectivity. To learn every detail about the course with the same thoroughness is impossible. Therefore, you have to select what is most important and concentrate first on that. Of course, judgment is involved in making such a selection, but you will have the help of your texts and teachers in this field.

3. Creating intention. It is not enough to hope that the material will pass from the book or the lecture into your head by osmosis. You have to make a conscious effort or intention to remember.

4. Building on your basic background. New knowledge or information, to be useful, has to be related to old knowledge that is part of your background. In this way, you can make proper associations to remember it, and you can organize it better to facilitate recall. Some work that you do for any course is background work for later and better understanding, just as some courses are foundations upon which more advanced courses later build. Hence, that background is being used for training your memory.

5. Organizing materials in ways that are meaningful and useful to you. Your teachers will provide suggestions for organizing the course materials, and they might even demand that you follow their lead in adopting the same plan. Nevertheless, you will still have to arrange some of the materials in categories and patterns that make sense to you. Some researchers think that organizing information into blocks of seven items works best for most students. You might find that establishing patterns based on three, five, or some other number works better for you—the point is that memory works by organizing materials into patterns of association. You need to find a way of patterning the materials you wish to commit to memory, and if it works, follow it.

6. Reciting. Verbalizing what it is that you are remembering consolidates it in your mind. Some psychologists explain this process by saying that when you first read a text or hear a lecture you are incorporating the material in your primary or short-term memory, which seems to have a smaller or more limited capacity. To have it active and available for a longer period of time, it has to be transferred by a reinforcement process, such as recitation, to the secondary or long-term memory. If you know that you will be forcing yourself to recite what you have read or learned, you will be more motivated to learn it. You also will have a direct check on how you are doing, a better one than if you simply re-read the passage or review it. Finally, your critical thinking and speaking activities reinforce learning and memory retention because you think the thoughts again, verbalize them, and hear them, drawing on a number of senses to consolidate memory retention. You can use your own words and recite it as though you were explaining it to your roommate. If you can explain something to someone else, you have learned it for yourself.

7. Consolidating. This principle means that you hold the ideas in your mind long enough to consolidate them and join them to other associations and frameworks of knowledge that you already have in your mind.

8. Distributing practice. There is an advantage to using relatively short periods of time for intensive learning activity involving memory. Distributing your study periods is preferable to amassing them for an onslaught, except when that is to your advantage, such as when you are caught up in reading a novel or need longer periods of time to write a term paper.

All of that said, the most valuable suggestion for improving your memory is to exercise your mind by consciously trying to recall what you have heard in lectures and have read in the books and other materials on the course. As you do that more frequently, building on what you have learned, you will find that you become more successful in remembering.

TIPS: Using Mnemonics

Mnemonics is the name given to memory helpers, to ways of recalling specific data, often through some set of associations. Many of us had to learn them in our piano lessons—for example, the names for the staff lines in the treble clef are "each good boy does fine always," each first letter referring to the line EGBDF. Or in biology, to remember the orders of classification for living organisms, we learned the phrase "kings play cards on fairly good soft velvet" for the classification of kingdom, phylum, class, family, genus, species, and variety. Use mnemonics to recall lists or data.

A DOZEN INFALLIBLE RULES FOR FLUNKING

Most students find that it is possible to flunk with little or no effort. In fact, little or no effort is the key. So here are a dozen of the surest ways to set out on a course of academic suicide. They are, of course, suggestions of what to avoid, but as rules for failure, they are supported by the observations of both of the authors of this book. You can find more of these suggestions at the imaginative Web sites of Dr. Whiz, who also gives "40 Ways to P.O. the Prof" (**monster.educ.kent.edu/docwhiz/poprof.html**).

Use these infallible rules at your own risk. They will guarantee that you will waste your and your parents' (and everyone else's) time, money, and patience, and earn for you everything you wanted to know about misery, anguish, and frustration.

1. Assessing who you are and why you are at university. The cardinal rule is to avoid answering this question. Do not think seriously about your future and why you are at university. Instead, regard your learning as merely serving time or the university as your playground, built for your pleasure.

2. Providing information. When you are forced to comply with university regulations, regard yourself as the number that you were assigned on your application forms, or use the name John Smith or Captain Kirk on your parking application form just to get a laugh from the staff. The same, of course, applies to your interactions with professors, who will laugh heartily when you sabotage their class records.

3. Your personal attitudes. Worry a lot about what others think about you, and do all that you can to win their approval by flattering them, buying them coffee, and otherwise ingratiating yourself into their good books so that they will lend you the notes you need for lectures you missed. But above all, be aware that circumstances not of your own making have made you what you are. You cannot change yourself, and so give in and accept your limitations as your destiny.

4. Your program of study. If you regard the university as a shopping mall, you are on the right track. Load up your shopping basket or timetable with junk food first. Go for the Mickey Mouses of life, whether courses, books, ideas, or friends. Do as little as possible to integrate your courses into a coherent whole.

5. Your courses. Treat your courses with the contempt that you think they deserve. After all, you didn't get the first choices that you wanted, so why put any wasted effort into this dog.

6. Attending lectures and seminars. Although you have paid a great deal of money for your education, consider it all misspent, and skip classes (especially seminars, where your absence will be more noticeable), don't take notes (if by any chance you wander into a class by mistake), hand in no assignments, and complain that you were not warned of the consequences for any of these actions.

7. Justifying your absence. When you run into your profs in the supermarket, remind them of your absence by asking smart questions that they love to hear, such as "Did we do anything important in class today?" or "Are you serious that we have to make a class presentation?" or "Is that assignment really due when you said it was?" or "How much work do I have to do to get a passing grade?"

8. Seeking advice. Do not seek advice of any kind from college advisors, from peer help groups, or, above all, from your teachers. If by some unforeseen chance one of these persons happens to give you advice, ignore it or reject it.

9. Study habits. Resist the temptation to study habitually in any form. You will be helped by losing or, better, throwing away your course syllabus at the beginning of the year. Then, adopt the casual study-as-you-go approach that fits studying into whatever time is left over in the week, preferably after a party on Sunday night.

10. Course assignments. Hand in your papers with the wrong course number and your teacher's name spelled incorrectly. You can imagine how much this flatters your instructor and shows how much you were paying attention. The paper you hand in should be only partly on the topic assigned, and it should have the fringes still on from going through your dot matrix printer. And, by the way, use a worn-out ribbon so your essay will be difficult to read.

11. Reverse all of the expected axioms of life: leap before you look, act before you think, and above all, do others before they do you.

12. Burn this book.

FURTHER READINGS

Albrecht, Karl. *Brain Power*. New York: Prentice-Hall, 1980.

Burka, Jane, and Lenora Yuen. *Procrastination: Why You Do It, What to Do About It*. Reading, MA: Addison Wesley, 1983.

Fiore, Neil. *The Now Habit: Overcoming Procrastination with Guilt-Free Play*. Los Angeles: Jeremy Tarcher, 1989.

Fleet, Joan, Fiona Goodchild, and Richard Zajchowski. *Learning for Success: Skills and Strategies for Canadian Students*. Toronto: Harcourt Brace, 1994.

Pauk, Walter. *How to Study in College*. 5th ed. Boston: Houghton Mifflin, 1993.

Roberts, Susan M. *Living without Procrastination: How to Stop Postponing Your Life*. Oakland, CA: New Harbinger, 1995.

Yates, Frances A. *The Art of Memory*. Chicago: U of Chicago P, 1966.

WEBLINKS

- Critical Thinking Resources at Yukon College
  www.yukoncollege.yk.ca/~agraham/nost202/critical.htm

- Davis Dyslexia Association
  www.dyslexia.com/quest.htm

- The Learning Skills Programme at York University
  www.yorku.ca/cdc/lsp/lsphome.html

- Making a Schedule, the Augustine Club at Columbia University
  www.columbia.edu/cu/augustine/study/schedule.html

- Overcoming Procrastination, Student Academic Services at California Polytechnic State
  University (San Luis Obispo)
  sas.calpoly.edu/asc/ssl/procrastination.html

- Remembering
  www.ucc.vt.edu/stdysk/remember.html

- SNOW (Special Needs Opportunity Windows) at the University of Toronto
  snow.utoronto.ca/Learn2/readisab.htm

- Special Education Legal Primer
  mirconnect.com/journal/legal

- Time Management for University Students, Counselling and Development Centre at
  York University
  www.yorku.ca/cdc/lsp/tm/time.htm

COMPUTERS AND CRITICAL THINKING

Chapter 2

The rapid changes in computer technology, both in hardware and in the amount of electronic information available, have often left students and professors bewildered, lost, or overwhelmed. The amazing speed of the new super Pentium microchips, the amount of information available in print and on the Internet, the elaborate methods of classifying it, the complex search engines used to find the data on the information highway, and the fact that at any moment of the day tens of millions of people are accessing the Internet raise the most serious questions about what kinds of knowledge can be used to function effectively with the new technologies. The way in which computer technology affects modes of critical thinking is a complex and controversial area of debate. It is now more than forty years since Marshall McLuhan redefined the world as the "global village"; it will now have to be redefined again as the "global chip," as all parts of the world can be linked for communication and the sharing of information both simultaneously and polymorphously through multimedia. When you use a computer and gain access to the Internet, you are becoming a part of this vast electronic network of communicators, with greatly varying skills, assumptions, and purposes. In the new millennium, some computer expertise is both useful and necessary to any student who wishes to think, read, and write critically. However, using your computer effectively requires specialized knowledge and newly directed methods of critical thinking to find and evaluate computer-available data.

All students will continue for at least some decades to use a mixture of print and electronic media for their reading, research, and writing of class assignments and research essays. Because of this combined use of print and electronic media, in our discussion of critical thinking we do not separate traditional methods of critical thinking, reading, and writing from new ways of thinking about communicating ideas. Although we draw distinctions between research in print and electronic media, we believe that both require the use of critical thinking. Critical thinking uses methods of induction and deduction, cause and effect, and a sequencing of ideas, matters that we discuss in detail later; all are vital tools in effectively using your computer. The principles of critical reading that we discuss will help you to assess the usefulness of the data that you discover. We also outline methods to find, select, and quote the research material that you find on the Web and explain how to cite it in your bibliographical records.

SOME ASSUMPTIONS ABOUT COMPUTERS AND UNIVERSITY WORK

Advertisements all over North America in the newspapers, on television, and in specialized computer papers urge students to get a computer to improve their work. The popular assumption is that the wired classroom from kindergarten to the end of high school and beyond is a better learning environment than the pre-chip classroom. Only recently has this assumption been challenged by the back-to-books lobby. While these debates will no doubt continue, it is now clear that governments across North America have made the commitment to computer literacy as part of public and high school education, undoubtedly because future employment will require these new technological skills. You and your fellow classmates may have come out of high schools that are in transition in implementing computer technology: some schools are well advanced, and others are far behind. Some students in your classes will be expert in programming, working with HTML language, and maintaining and repairing computer systems. Others will be confused by this language and are at a developing stage of their computer abilities. Almost no students will have learned advanced skills for computers that are helpful to university work or will have related what skills they have to critical thinking.

We assume that users of this book know the fundamentals of using a computer, a word processor, and a mouse, as well as such procedures as how to save your work and the importance of backing up your work frequently. We also assume that you have little experience in the systematic use of a computer in library or Internet research, or in the use of critical skills to evaluate what you find. We expect that you will want to fine-tune your computer skills to make them more effective in your university work, and that you will avoid falling back on tired old excuses about drive crashes or printer failures. Most instructors are not sympathetic to the excuse that "last night, just as I was printing the final copy of my essay, my computer crashed, and I hadn't saved it"; you are expected to save it before you print it and keep a copy on a floppy. We also assume that you regularly use an anti-virus program (McAfee VirusScan, Norton AntiVirus, Dr. Solomon's Anti-Virus, or some other) or have one installed to operate automatically. If these assumptions are incorrect in your case, you should seek assistance from your university's help desk, consult your manuals, or seek advice from your computer retailer to ensure that your computer and your work are protected.

All of our instructions are applicable to users of Macintosh and PC computers. We also assume that most students with PCs now use either Windows 3.1 or later versions or Windows 95/98 or later versions as their operating systems. Working on the Internet with DOS is now virtually impossible, and older word processors (such as WordPerfect for DOS, version 5.1) seem cumbersome, though still perfectly usable. A few other operating systems, like OS/2 or UNIX, can also be used for accessing the Internet, but these tend to be specialties, and chances are that you will be using either a Mac or a PC with some versions of Windows for your home computer. Recent word processors such as Corel's WordPerfect 8/9 and Microsoft's Word 97, or their Office 2000 versions, come with a suite of interrelated programs that connect easily with the Internet and with each other, and that include a desktop manager, a spread-sheet program, a database program, an Internet browser, and other utilities. Inexpensive academic versions (less than fifty dollars and without a manual or telephone help access, but with online access to the manufacturer's site and to user groups) are usually available from your university bookstore or computer shop. Students who buy such a suite of programs can purchase one of the excellent manuals produced for the word processor by independent publishers such as Cue or Sybex.

Increasingly, many courses require that students undertake work on the Internet, either in conducting research on the Web or by conferencing, e-mail, or other inter-classroom communication. To prepare you for the later sections on using the Internet and the World Wide Web for your research and for access through online resources to your library's facilities, we give rudimentary advice on how to connect to the Internet.

A word of caution—if you lend any of your disks to another student, you run two major risks: when your disk is returned to you it could be infected with a virus, so you should run a virus check on it before using it, and you have no control over how anyone else might use your work.

WHAT IS THE INTERNET?

The Internet is a network, a vast set of public and private computers linked together to transfer data to one another. It is tempting to think of the Internet as a machine located in one place, like the giant mainframe computers of the 1970s, but nothing could be further from reality. The forerunner of the Internet was ARPANet, developed in 1969 as a project of the U.S. Department of Defense and NASA for the exchange of scientific and military information among linked research centres in the United States, which were spread out at the time of the Cold War so that if one centre were destroyed the rest could continue to function. This distributed access is one of the keys to the decentralization of the Internet today. Gradually, other countries joined, first those associated through NATO (England and Norway in 1973), and then others. By the mid-1980s, universities and other institutions had joined the Internet; by 1989, there were well over 100 000 hosts. The Internet (or Net) is now a vast interlinked and international network of millions of subsystems, institutional networks, and individual computers. This network transfers data through telephone lines, directly connected computers, fibre optic lines, communications cables, and other means. While relying on a single standard "language" for the exchange of data, TCP/IP (Transmission Control Protocol/Internet Protocol), the Net also included by 1990 such search tools as Gopher (University of Minnesota) and Archie and file transmission tools such as FTP (File Transfer Protocol). It now also includes e-mail, Telnet, newsgroups, and a range of other communications functions, including the World Wide Web (for links to Internet histories see **www.isoc.org/internet/history/**).

WHAT IS THE WORLD WIDE WEB?

In 1991, a particular development in Internet communication changed how browsers search for information. The European Particle Physics Lab at the Centre for Nuclear Research (CERN) began to develop the World Wide Web, access to which was greatly improved by the development of search engines (Mosaic was the first, developed at the University of Illinois) that relied on point-and-click technology with a mouse. As the Web has grown, more and more sophisticated tools for making Web pages, finding and classifying information, and moving it from place to place have been developed. In the Web's early days, a user had to have a variety of software programs, each with their different configurations, languages, procedures, and searching tools. For instance, the Web at first was entirely a text-based environment without graphics or sound. Users relied on a program called Lynx, operated without a mouse, to search and navigate from document to document. Gopher was the name of one of the early compilers of digital information housed at universities and government research centres. Gopher sites are now incorporated into the Web and are accessible through the major Web browsers. Veronica (an acronym for Very Easy Rodent-Oriented Network Indexed Computerized Archives), developed at the University of Nevada, is a search engine that can scan the Gopher sites for information. To move large documents, blocks of text, or software programs from one computer to another, a special file transfer program called FTP is most commonly used. This mode of file transfer, like virtually all of these earlier procedures, is incorporated into Web browsers so that you can access a particular site on the Web to download a specific program, and after indicating your choices, transfer the software to the location on your computer's hard drive that you designate.

To enable faster communication between sites on the Web, pages are not only filled with graphics and multimedia features, but also employ the single most important characteristic of the Web, hypertext. This is a language for writing Web pages, which is embedded in the graphic or text that provides a link or computer access point to another Web page. By clicking on a highlighted hypertext link, the computer is almost immediately logged on to the new site, making fast access to an enormous range of sites possible. Hence, the Web is a hypertext system used to access the information on the Internet. The Web is now the major part of the Internet that is accessed by millions of clients every day. There now are over 320 million hypertext Web pages put up by governments, businesses, public and private institutions (such as universities and professional associations), interest groups, the media, and thousands of individuals who can talk and view in real time through RealAudio, with interactive applet images via Java.

Much Web information is trivial or of narrow appeal, but a great deal is also useful and important. Two questions immediately arise: How can you find what you want? How can you evaluate what you find? To find information, you can use different Web browsers to access the Web and a large variety of search engines that perform different tasks. To evaluate what you find, you need to use the methods of critical thinking. These methods are discussed in the sections and chapters that follow.

CONNECTING TO THE INTERNET

Your first move in connecting your computer to the Internet should be to consult the academic computing help desk or office in your university. Their staff will supply you with information about which hardware you need to get started (the minimal requirements for your computer operating system, such as Windows 3.1 or 95, the speed of modem that you can use, and other details). They will also supply, usually for a small cost, the software needed to connect you to the university's modem pool or Internet access and e-mail, as well as your user identification name and a password to provide secure access.

TIPS: Preparing for Disasters

1. Plug your system into a surge protector.

2. Back up your files regularly, especially your data files; at some point your hard drive will crash.

3. Create a start-up disk to use in emergencies. In Windows 95/98 open Control Panel, double click on Add/Remove Programs, select the Startup Disk tab, and click on Create Disk. Major virus programs also enable you to make a start-up disk to recover from a virus attack.

Your computer should be as powerful and have as much RAM (random access memory) as you can afford, at least 16 MB (megabytes), though 64 MB is common and memory chips are inexpensive. You also should have a hard drive of sufficient size, usually 2 or 3 gigabytes (Gbytes), to run the current large operating systems (such as Windows 95) and a word processor and other software to store your large data and graphics files. Your modem should match or exceed the minimum requirement of a high-speed modem connection through your server (at least 28.8 kilobytes per second, or Kbps, though even modems at that speed are hard to get on new machines that routinely use 56Kbps speeds). You will also need communications software to enable your modem to make connections between your computer and the Internet. Usually, this software is included with your modem package. A CD-ROM drive is not essential if you only download software, but they are inexpensive to install in your computer and most larger programs, including word processors, ship with a CD. For economical reasons you will want to connect to the Internet by a local access phone number, not a long-distance one. The speed of computers and their capabilities and specifications, as well as those of other hardware components (hard drives, modems, back-up/archive units, video and sound cards, monitors, CD-ROM players, and so on), are

BOX 2.1   Minimum System Requirements

To run Netscape 4 or Navigator 4 or later versions you need

Mac:

■ 16 MB of RAM; 68030 or Power PC Mac or better; System 7.5 or higher; hard drive with at least 40 MB of free space; modem (28.8K or better)

PC running Windows 3.1 as operating system:

■ 16 MB of RAM; 486 or faster CPU (almost all are Pentiums or better now, but you might be using an older machine); hard drive with at least 40 MB of free space; modem (28K or better)

PC running Windows 95/98 as operating system:

■ 16 MB of RAM; 486 or faster CPU (a Pentium II or Pentium III is standard now); hard drive with at least 60 MB of free space; modem (28K or better)

continually changing. This month's state of the art quickly becomes next week's bargain. You should consult with your friends, the university computer shop, local publications, and your instructors for up-to-date information on available systems and a good match between your budget and what is available.

There are four ways of connecting your computer to the Internet through an Internet Service Provider (ISP):

1. You can connect through your university, which will already supply this service to staff, faculty, and students. For most students, this method is easiest and cheapest, though there is sometimes a modest charge for online services for a semester or year of study. This service is usually the best choice, since when you dial in with a password through the university's ISP you are recognized as a legitimate university user and can access all of the services that the university supplies free to its members. Some of those services, such as access to some library reference materials and search indexes, might have restricted access for only university members.

2. If you do not have your own computer but want to access the Internet, the Web, and other services such as e-mail, you can use the computer pools at your university. Most universities have terminals that are available for student use. For access you need your own user name and password, available through the computer facilities help desk or some similar service. Then you can log on whenever you wish at the university. Some people who have accounts for their home computers also wish to access a computer at the university from time to time. Having a university password for access is handy for these occasions.

3. If you already have access to an ISP at home through another member of the family or a friend, you can either use that capability or have an additional user added to the same service supplied by the ISP. You will not be able automatically to use this ISP for access to materials that the university has restricted to its members. However, such resources are still available to you in the library or through the computer labs in your university.

4. The fourth alternative is for you to sign up with one of the community or commercial ISPs. Some communities have established Internet link-up facilities that are either inexpensive or free, but space on these servers is in great demand and access might be slow. Commercial ISPs include America Online (more than 7 million clients), CompuServe (more than 3.5 million), and Prodigy (over 1 million), each of which provides its own connecting software. You pay a monthly or annual fee for access to one of these ISPs. Each ISP offers free time to get acquainted (often a month of limited access) so you can decide whether to continue and what level of service to subscribe to. If you wish to browse the Web (called *surfing*) for long periods each day, you will find that you quickly use up your allotted time. Commercial ISPs' software is often distributed free to attract customers.

In the first and last cases, you install the software provided by your university or commercial ISP by following the printed information with the software and online instructions. Some software is more complex than others to install and configure; in each case, the entering of various codes in the on-screen dialogue boxes must be done with great care to ensure a valid connection. Both your university and commercial ISPs have advice available on phone hotlines. University terminals in the computer pools are already programmed with the necessary software, and an opening welcome dialogue enables you to log on and choose the kind of software or service you want.

TIPS: Connecting to the Internet

When you contact your ISP (either your university computer service or a commercial provider) for a user account, be certain to make an accurate record of the following pieces of information:

1. your user name (the name you will use)

2. your e-mail address (used by people who wish to contact you)

3. your password (used to access your account and your e-mail; you might have two different passwords, or a temporary one before you decide on a permanent one)

4. the phone number of your ISP to set your computer and modem to dial when making a connection

5. the server name of your Internet provider, which you will need to configure your connection software

Most Internet access is through a connection called a Point-to-Point Protocol (PPP) or perhaps through an older Serial Line Internet Protocol (SLIP). Your Internet provider will inform you which kind of account you will be using with them, or the connection will work in the background without your knowledge if your software allows it. That connection software will also include the capability of storing your password, phone numbers, e-mail addresses, and the dial-up number you are calling from and that you need to access the Internet. Your university or commercial package will include all of this material, which you should install following the instructions provided. Mac computers need the MacTCP/ConfigPPP software, and Windows 3.1 needs Winsock or Trumpet Winsock, again available as part of the set-up package from your provider and installed directly through their software. Windows 95/98 uses the Dial-Up Networking folder in "My Computer." Using the supplied software, you run "setup" and follow the instructions, both printed with your software and in the on-line dialogue boxes. You will be informed where to include your user name, password, and other information, and then you will need to reboot your computer to have the changes take effect and to run the text connection. If you are connected properly, you can begin to download the Web browser that you will be using. If you run into problems, you should review all of the procedures, make certain that you added all of the information correctly (a single mistake in the password can cause a failure), and if you still have problems, you can consult your computer help desk or provider (or a knowledgeable friend) for assistance. You will need to have all of the information about your user name, password, and so on, available, as well a description of what seemed to go wrong and when.

Once you are connected, let's say from home, you need to install a Web browser, either by downloading one from your ISP or by copying one from a CD onto your hard drive. A Web browser is the interface software program that runs on your computer and connects it to the Web. It provides both a window into the resources of the Web and also a set of controls and tools to allow you to navigate from Web site to Web site and to do specific tasks when you get there. Most users now rely on either Netscape Navigator or Microsoft Explorer. Your university or other ISP will give you advice about which Web browser is recommended for the connecting software you have and the provider system that you are accessing. However, either browser will work with virtually any computer that has sufficient hard-drive space and enough memory and is either a Mac or a PC running Windows 3.1 or Windows 95/98.

If you have connected through your university, it is probable that the system will also supply you with download facilities by FTP to acquire a Web browser. Instructions and help are provided. These are very large files and take some time to download, perhaps an hour or more, depending on the time of day when you try to access the Internet and the speed of your modem and computer. The files are sent in compressed or "zipped" format and automatically unpack themselves and begin the installation process when you run the .exe or setup file.

When the Web browser is installed and configured, it will recognize your connecting software, and all you need to do is make the connection to your service provider and then click on the icon or other active button for your browser (Navigator or Explorer). The program is then activated, and you are ready to begin to use the Internet and the Web.

It is at this point that you can surf the Net or use the Web for research purposes. It is also at this point that your critical judgment about the quality of the sites you visit will help you determine their utility in your study and research projects.

WEB BROWSERS: NETSCAPE NAVIGATOR®
AND MICROSOFT INTERNET EXPLORER®

Navigator and Explorer are the two programs that share the market as basic and comprehensive browser software packages. They enable you to read hypertext Web pages on the Internet. Both have added-on programs to help in setting up Web pages, sending and receiving e-mail, participating in newsgroups and conferencing, and so on. Both are available free—you should check with your university provider to find out which one is maintained through their site licence. Either can be used for access to your university's home page for its calendar, libraries, computing services, and research and writing lab aids and for access to other libraries, research tools, the wider academic communities, and the full resources of the Web. Either can also be used for browsing casually or for more directed research. Most universities have adopted a simple access routine to gain access to these browsers, using software or downloading facilities that are available to students and faculty. Each browser is easy to install and configure and comes with instructions.

BOX 2.2   **Changing Your Browser's Home Page**

To change your browser's home page, the page that is arrived at by default when the browser starts:

1. Choose Edit in the menu bar, and from the drop-down menu choose Preferences.
2. In the Home Page dialogue box, enter the address that you wish to use for your home page.
3. If you wish to use your university's home page, go to that site and repeat these procedures, clicking the Use Current Page button. The current address will be added.
4. Press OK to record your choice.

Using a Browser

Netscape Navigator 4.0 is a typical Web browser and is used here as a basic introduction to browsers, though Microsoft Explorer works in almost the same fashion with similar procedures, screens, and buttons. If you wish to have more information, you can consult one of the many manuals available for Netscape or Netscape's own online handbook (**help.netscape.com/docs/client/communicator/IntroComm/Introcom.html**).

After you establish a connection, you double click on the Netscape icon in Windows to activate the program. By default, the home page is that of Netscape, but you can change it to any page you like; many students and faculty use the home page of their university to have ready access to the library, calendar, and other resources.

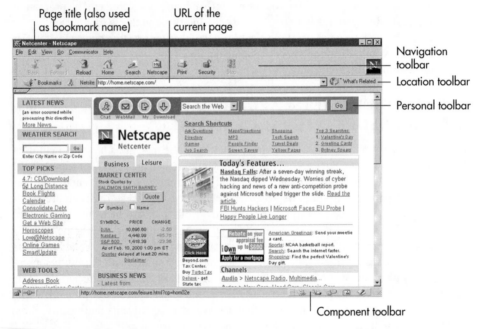

The Browser Screen

The Netscape screen shows a title bar, a menu bar (with several conventional names and functions used in the Windows environment), a Navigation toolbar with icon buttons, a location toolbar, and a personal toolbar.

The Netscape logo is animated when the browser is searching on the Web. The document occupies the large space in the centre of the screen, and scroll bars for moving through the document appear at the right and at the bottom when the document is too large for the screen. At the bottom is a graph bar that indicates the progress of loading a document, as well as the URL (Uniform Resource Locator) or address of the loading document. The other components of the Netscape suite (for e-mail, conferencing, making Web pages, and the like) are indicated by icons in the Component bar at the bottom right.

The title bar at the top of the screen displays the page that is currently loaded and active, with the normal Windows boxes on the right to minimize, reduce/maximize, and exit or close the program. The Netscape icon on the left gives a drop-down menu for the same options.

The menu bar, the next line down from the title bar, offers the features of the Navigation toolbar, along with more advanced features. You can click on any of these six words to display a drop-down menu.

1. *File* gives a series of options about what to do with the present document.
   - *Save As* saves the document to disk, allowing choices about where to save it, what name to give it, and what format to save it in.
   - *Print* prints the current page.
   - *Close* closes the current Netscape window.
   - *Exit* exits Netscape, to be used when you are finished with your Web session. You may also exit by clicking on the Netscape icon at the left of the Title bar.

2. *Edit* allows you perform various functions with the current page.
   - *Copy* allows you to copy selected text (highlighted with your mouse) to be retrieved (or pasted) into your word processor or elsewhere.
   - *Find in Page* gives a dialogue box where you can enter text that you wish to find in the current document. The identified text is highlighted.
   - *Preferences* allows you to specify preferences for how Netscape works on your system.

3. *View* shows commands that allow you to change the appearance of your Netscape page (by choosing which toolbars to show or hide) and your document, or to get information about the document. If the document is slow to load you can sometimes speed up the process by clicking on Reload to have the same page reinstalled.

4. *Go* provides a series of commands to navigate through Netscape.

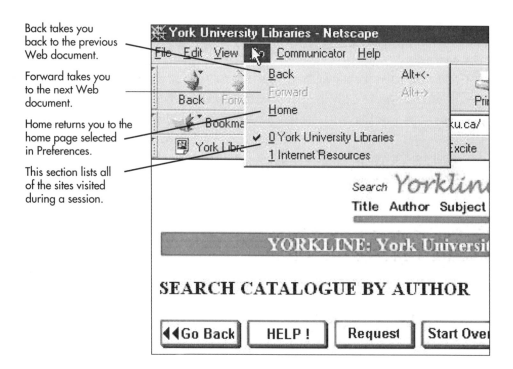

Back takes you back to the previous Web document.

Forward takes you to the next Web document.

Home returns you to the home page selected in Preferences.

This section lists all of the sites visited during a session.

5. *Communicator* provides access to the other programs in the Netscape Suite, including Collabra (for conferencing) and Netcaster (for making your own Web pages). It also provides access to the past history of your searches and to your bookmarks.

6. *Help* provides access to a wealth of information about how to make Netscape work efficiently for you. There is an index of help topics, a handbook, instructions and tips, and access by hyperlinks to other sources of information and assistance, including plug-ins or ancillary programs and updates. This drop-down menu also gives quick access to the Netscape home page for information on current versions and upgrades.

The Toolbars

Clicking on one of the nine icons in the Navigation toolbar performs an immediate function or initiates a dialogue box. The Netscape logo shows passing constellations when the browser is actively searching or downloading data.

Using the Navigation toolbar enables you to move back (to the previous page in the current log-on), to move forward (to the next active window), to return to home (to return to Netscape's default page or to your own home page in the Edit → Preferences menu), or to reload (to reload or refresh the current page).

- *Back* retraces your steps, taking you back to the previous page that linked you to the current page.
- *Forward* takes you to the next page. It works only if you have already used the Back button.
- *Reload* re-enters the current Web page to display a fresh copy.
- *Home* takes you to the home page that came up automatically on starting Netscape.
- *Search* lists hyperlinks to a number of popular Internet search engines to conduct a search.
- *Guide* gives access to a number of Internet directory items to assist in a search.
- *Print* prints the current page or document. A dialogue box lets you select options and begin printing.
- *Stop* interrupts any ongoing transfer of data or loading of a page.

Microsoft's Internet Explorer has a similar-looking toolbar and address bar.

The location toolbar allows you to specify an address or an URL: you type in the address and click Enter or Return. Each URL begins with http://, the protocol used in sending a message. The next item in the address is the Web server that will answer the message.

This part is followed by the complete path to the Web site that is requested. The scroll arrow on the right of the bar displays the other sites that you have recently entered. If you do not know an address, you will have to use a search engine.

The same bar includes a Bookmark icon (in Explorer it is called Favorites) that allows you to bookmark pages by saving page or site names and addresses as hyperlinks in a quickly accessed bookmark file. The bookmark list contains addresses that you want to return to (you click on Bookmark and then Save, Add, or Edit). You can subsequently add headings to your bookmarks, move them to other locations in your list, or remove them when they are no longer useful (Help provides further information).

The personal toolbar can be customized to include buttons for bookmarks, Web sites that you often visit, indexes, search engines, or other features (see Personal Toolbar in Help/Index).

You can download either Netscape or Microsoft's Explorer from their home Web sites. For introductions to Explorer see:

- Introduction to Microsoft Explorer: **www.ie4.aust.com/learnie3**
- Guide to Internet Explorer 3.0: **www.eiu.edu/~mediasrv/ie/tutor1.htm**

For further information on using Netscape, see the Netscape home page at home.netscape.com/ or one of the following:

- Netscape World: **www.netscapeworld.com**
- Netscape Basics: **www.lib.berkeley.edu/TeachingLib/Guides/Internet/**
- Introduction to Netscape: **www.scar.utoronto.ca/cc/newsletter/nsguide**
- Yahoo's list of Netscape Resources: **search.yahoo.com/bin/search?p=netscape**

The component toolbar located at the lower right hand of the screen provides access to procedures for connecting to other features of the Internet. If you have installed a standalone Web browser rather than Navigator or Explorer as part of their suites of interconnected programs, you can either add the rest of the suite or access the other features of the Internet by the procedures described below.

INTERNET TOOLS

There are a number of ways to link your computer to other individuals, to discussion groups, or to special interest information and news.

E-mail

E-mail, or electronic mail, enables you to use your Internet connection to communicate with another person or institution. The transmission is almost immediate, but it is not necessarily secure, since you have no way of knowing who is reading the letter you send.

Your university account is likely set up with the necessary connection protocols; if not, you can purchase software that will make the connections simple for you. The e-mail address normally follows the form of someone@somewhere: a user name, followed by the @ sign and the domain or location name. An e-mail address is assigned through your university, through your Internet service provider, or through one of the Web browsers like Netscape or Explorer. Then the process is straightforward:

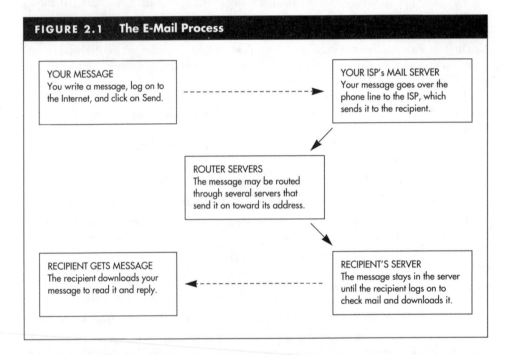

FIGURE 2.1 The E-Mail Process

You will also need an e-mail communications software program such as Pine or Eudora. Pine, though widely used and able to run on most computers, is awkward and difficult to use, especially in handling attachments—files that you enclose with your e-mail letter. Another popular e-mail program is Eudora, available in the Eudora Pro version (with a spell checker) commercially, and the Eudora Lite version at no cost (**www.qualcomm.com**) in versions for both Macs and PCs. This program allows you to work off-line in writing your letters; you can then log on to your server to send or receive mail. Both Pine and Eudora download your mail to your hard drive. You can send and receive plain text and save it in folders or "mailboxes" that you can name. You can remove mail into a trash folder. You can also write messages in your word processor, block them, paste them into an e-mail message, and send them (an advantage is that you can check your message for spelling and other features using the facilities of your word processor, rather than the often more limited resources of your e-mail program). Finally, you can attach whole files to your e-mail message using the program's "attach" function, including graphics and retaining the entire formatting of your original document. To read it correctly, your recipient must have the capability to access the attachment (most word processing programs do) and read it on the receiving computer. All of these possibilities are available, along with mailing to multiple receivers, forwarding mail, and so on.

The e-mail functions of Netscape and Explorer, on the other hand, can be set to use the same method (known as a POP, or Post Office Protocol), or they can be set to keep the mail on the main server (called IMAP, Internet Message Access Protocol) so that it can be accessed from any computer. If you are using a computer at school, on the road, and at home, you can still have access to all of your e-mail through this protocol. Otherwise, you would have bits of your e-mail scattered from computer to computer. You should consult your university help desk or ISP for assistance in enabling your Web browser to receive your e-mail. For instance, there are services available on the Net called Hotmail (**www.hotmail.com**) or "NetAddress" (**www.netaddress.com**) that will give you a free user account. Both operate on the Web browsers, but there is sometimes a wait for access because of the many thousands of users.

Some university classes circulate e-mail addresses for the purposes of keeping in touch or for joint classroom projects. Some set up the whole class as a distribution list (in which some or all messages can be posted to the class), following the procedures for a particular e-mail program as used by the distribution list manager. Not all members of the class, however, need to use the same e-mail software. This function is discussed in the section on listservs, on page 54.

Some helpful sites for e-mail information are the following:

- A Beginner's Guide to Effective E-Mail: **www.webfoot.com/advice/email.top.html**
- E-Mail Etiquette: **www.iwillfollow.com/email.htm**

TIPS: Sending E-mail

1. E-mail is convenient, fast, and easy. But it is not necessarily private. You should be aware that you have no control over who is accessing the mail at the receiver's end of the line.

2. Good manners on the Net (netiquette):

   - Don't type everything in capital letters: it is considered to represent shouting and so is aggressive and rude.
   - Don't type everything in lower case letters either: that is considered mumbling.
   - Follow standard English conventions of spelling and punctuation.
   - Except for personal correspondence keep e-mail messages brief.
   - It is also a convention to acknowledge receipt of an e-mail message, even with a simple "Thanks" or "Got it. Bye," indicating to the sender that the message got through and that you are logging off for now in this exchange.
   - The worst negative action on e-mail is flaming, or sending e-mail that is overly argumentative, hostile, or even abusive.

3. If your file is too large for e-mail, you can compress it (or decompress a message you have received) with file compression software installed on your computer, such as PKZIP from **www.pkwar.com** or WinZip from **www.winzip.com**.

HyperNews

HyperNews uses your Web browser to access public special interest discussion groups. Its particular virtue is that it uses the hypertext format of the Web page that you access in the normal way on your browser, and it is complete with URLs that you can access within documents. In addition, it includes the discussion format of a newsgroup (see page 55). That is, you search for a topic with one of your Web search engines, and if you locate a HyperNews discussion group, it will be indicated as a newsgroup with the use of that or a similar term, such as *user's discussion group*. When you call up the article, you get an onscreen picture of many articles or e-mail entries concerning a particular topic, each linked together, with the responses to messages chained to it in what are called *threads*, which tie together a series of articles on the same topic or responses to the same message. For instance, there are HyperNews groups for the major word processors (such as that for WordPerfect **www.corel.com/support/newsgroup.htm** with the particular URL of **www.corel.com/support/options/online_newsgroups.htm#wp8**), printers, and scanners. There are discussion groups not only on computers, but on almost any topic. You can then view any part of that discussion; search within it for topics that interest you; arrange the topics alphabetically by subject, author, or date; and contribute a response to that thread. If you contribute directly to the HyperNews site, it will immediately be posted for all users to read. If you wish your reply to be private, you can respond to any message in the thread by sending an e-mail to the person who sent it. You will need no additional software or other plug-ins to access this facility.

Listservs

Listservs are mailing lists or associations based on e-mail that allow you to create or to join one of the many thousands of interest groups whose members remain in contact through mass distribution over e-mail. For instance, you could set up a group of people in your class who could work on a particular project, or the whole class could be part of a discussion list maintained and controlled by the instructor. The listserv could be used to send out course information, deadlines, notices, and readings, and it could allow interactive discussion among the class members on various topics in the course. Or you could join an existing discussion group concerned with an author, topic, health problem, or anything else that you are interested in.

A listserv consists of a list of subscribers that is maintained and controlled by the list owner or manager. You apply to this subscriber list to join, rather than through the address of the topic or name of the interest group. You can join or leave at any time by following the procedures for that listserv.

There are three kinds of listservs. An open list allows anyone to subscribe and post messages. A message that is sent to an open list is sent to all subscribers, who receive it in their private e-mail folders. Moderated lists are reviewed by the listserv's manager before they go to subscribers. Finally, closed lists require special permission to join and may require answering questions; only members of the closed group receive and post messages. It is this third kind of listserv that is most often used for class discussion lists.

To search Listserv's list of discussion groups, you can browse through their list at **www.lsoft.com/lists/LIST_Q.html** or **www.lsoft.com/lists/listref.html**. Another listing of discussion groups is in the "E-mail Discussion Groups" category at Inter-Links: **alabanza.com/kabacoff/Inter-Links/**

Another method is to send an e-mail to List Global, an online interactive listserv program that lets you use a keyword to search for listservs that interest you by topic. You simply send a message to **listserv@bitnic.cren.net** and leave the subject line blank. In the body of the message, you then type "list global/[keyword]" (for example, list global/jazz). After you send the message you will get a reply with a list of the discussion groups containing your keyword that you can print or save. Note that List Global cuts off the beginning and ending of words, so that if you ask for war you will get a list that includes warrior, warfare, software, hardware, and warts, as well as war. You should make your keyword specific.

Once you find a listserv that you wish to join, you must find the address to which you send an e-mail requesting a subscription. Some very active listservs require you to confirm your subscription within forty-eight hours by a specified procedure that they send to your e-mail. Once you have subscribed to a listserv you will receive two messages, one telling you that you have been subscribed, and one giving you the detailed protocols for the listserv, including information on how to post messages, view the archived messages, unsubscribe, and so on. It is a good idea to print this document for future reference.

The three major discussion-list programs are Lister, Majordomo, and list proc. It is likely that your ISP (such as your university server or a commercial provider like AOL) already has one of these facilities available to you. You can make an inquiry to find out or search your server's Web site.

Online advice about listservs is provided in the guide prepared by the Rutgers University writing centre at **www.rci.rutgers.edu/~au/workshop/groups.htm.**

Newsgroups

Newsgroups are special interest public discussion groups or online forums devoted to particular subjects, enabled by Usenet, which is the Internet's own bulletin board, a worldwide facility to enable discussion groups to function on the Internet. Messages posted to newsgroups are collected on the news server and are accessible to all who have access to Usenet and wish to retrieve them. Newsgroups are divided into various hierarchies: alt (alternative), biz (business), comp (computers), misc (miscellaneous: family, taxes), news, rec (recreational: arts, hobbies, movies, sports), sci (sciences), soc (social issues, including national cultures, politics, and religion), and talk (debate and opinion). Each of these can be subdivided, as, for instance, rec.arts.sf.tv.startrek. To search for a newsgroup that interests you, you can search through your regular browser, and if you find a group, your browser will automatically enter its subprogram specially devoted to newsgroups. Alternatively, you can search through the newsgroups carried on your ISP. Netscape and Microsoft both make access to discussion groups easy through their Web browsers. The Netscape suite program called Communicator (which includes the Web browser Navigator) also includes a newsreader, Collabra. This program is integrated with your other Internet programs and can be set up to read the newsgroups to which your university provides access. To access this program, you follow these steps:

1. Select Edit → Preferences and then select Mail and Groups and then Groups Server.

2. Fill in the name of your university's news server, and click OK.

3. Select Communicator → Collabra Discussion Groups.

4. Click on the Join Groups icon, which will open a new window within which you can search for a newsgroup that interests you.

Another method is to configure your browser without using the special newsreader. To do so you have to follow a series of steps. Here are the steps for Netscape Navigator:

1. Enter the address of the newserver in the window of the browser to connect with your ISP. Enter this address in the Edit, Preferences, Mail & Groups, Group Server window.

2. Click on the Communicator tab in the menu bar and select Message Center.

3. The names of all of the newsgroups accessible on your ISP will then be displayed once they load (this will take a few minutes if the list is long).

4. Click on Search for a group to open a search window where you enter the term you are searching for. Then, subscribe if you wish.

Similar steps are used in Microsoft Explorer (consult the Help index).

From this point you can subscribe to a newsgroup to read the posted messages, contribute to the discussion (to the sender only, to the general discussion, or to the sender and the discussion), start a new discussion topic, or unsubscribe. You can also use one of the specialized newsgroup browsers to search for you. For instance, Liszt maintains a Web site that you can access through your normal browser, and then you use it to search for newsgroups (**www.liszt.com/news/**). Most of these groups are public, allowing you to browse through the entries; others are private and require you to join (usually free of charge, but you may have to supply your e-mail address and other information). You can respond either to an individual or to a topic or have your message posted (as is customary) for everyone else who has access to the site. Your university site may have access to a Usenet search engine, such as DejaNews, or you can access it directly at its Web address (**www.deja.com/home_ps.shtml**).

When you access a newsgroup, you are presented with a list of articles that have been posted to that group. You can then choose which to access and decide whether you wish to respond. If you do respond, your answer is threaded, or linked to that topic. Newsgroups allow you choose what you read and answer; however, listservs send all of the mail to all subscribers to the list.

Good sources of information concerning Newsgroups and Usenet include the following:

- Usenet FAQs [Frequently Asked Questions]: **www.faqs.org**
- Usenet Info Center Launch Pad: **metapod.unc.edu.usenet-i**

Finally, the Internet has many interest groups that are accessible directly on the Internet itself through your Web browser. For instance, there are discussion groups maintained by the major word processors that allow users to correspond about the virtues and defects of their programs or to seek advice about how to overcome difficulties. There are also user groups for all kinds of medical conditions, for specific kinds of pets, for historical events (such as the military history of World War II), for popular culture (such as *The X-Files*), and so on. These user groups are normally located not by searching for the discussion group, but by activating a link to them on a Web page that you have already found. For example, *The X-Files* page (**www.fox.com/thexfiles/index2.htm**) has a link to the discussion group, which you can read, join, contribute to, or ignore. Such discussions contain a lot of trivial information as well as some useful contributions. The trick, here, as with all newsgroups and listservs—not to mention Web pages in general—is to evaluate what you find.

In many ways, the rapid technological developments that allow information to be distributed more quickly and easily have made critical reading and thinking even more important. The Web provides information from diverse sources, many of which have no monitoring procedures or accountability. While it is important to think critically about all aspects of your reading and research in more traditional formats such as the lecture, textbook, and academic monograph or journal article, the Internet, with its instant access to Web pages, discussion groups, and e-mail, makes these demands for critical skills all the more urgent.

OTHER SOURCES OF INFORMATION

Most of the large publishers issue helpful how-to books on setting up your computer and configuring it. Similar books are available for your word processor and for Internet browsers. Your campus bookstore will have a large selection of these books, often at sell-off prices as older versions are taken over by even newer versions of popular software. You need to be certain that you are getting a guide that is near to the release version of your software; otherwise, it will be too outmoded to be of much help. Nothing dates faster than old computer manuals, unless it is the computers and the software themselves. Companies like Cue (**www.cue.com**), Osborne (McGraw-Hill) (**www.osborne.com**), and Sybex (**www.sybex.com**) produce many of these manuals.

Another good source of information is the series of booklets produced by *PC Novice* and *Smart Computing* magazines, including the following:

- *PC Novice Guide to Computing Basics*
- *PC Novice Guide to Going Online*
- *PC Novice Guide to the Internet*
- *PC Novice Guide to the Web*

These booklets are printed in an inexpensive magazine format, are reliable and up-to-date (at the time of issue), are packed full of information, and can often be found still in stock at magazine retail stores. Back orders can be placed by filling in the form in a recent issue of *PC Novice* or *Smart Computing* or at the publisher's Web site (**www.smartcomputing.com/Default.asp**).

Some specialized sites for computer information are the following:

- BABEL: A Glossary of Computer Oriented Abbreviations and Acronyms: **www.cis.columbia.edu/glossary.html**
- ILC Glossary of Internet Terms: **www.matisse.net/files/glossary.html**
- EFF's Guide to the Internet: **www.hep.net/documents/eegtti/eeg_toc.html**
- The Internet Companion: **www.obs-us.com/obs/english/books/editinc**
- Learn the Net Internet classes: **www.learnthenet.com/english/index.html**
- PC Friendly Internet Page: **darkwing.uoregon.edu/~wharmon**

FINAL WORDS OF WISDOM

- If your computer has not crashed yet, it will. So BACK UP, BACK UP, BACK UP— onto tape, floppies, or wherever—so that you have your important files, especially the document files that you have made for your courses, safe and secure.

- Use a virus-checking program. If you share disks or download any programs that can be executed, you are in danger of importing a virus. Even if you use your own disks in a machine in the library, you are imperiling your system. So when you get home, or before you use any disk that comes from another source, run a virus check on it. It is probable that your university already has an on-site licence for one of most popular programs: McAfee, Norton Anti-Virus, Dr. Solomon's, and so on. Install it now, use it, and keep the virus program updated.

- Consult your instructors, your university's computing help desk, the library, and your friends for advice on how to make your use of your computer effective and enjoyable. The many facilities each university provides are there for your use. You have already helped to pay for the facilities in your fees, so take advantage of them.

- If you run into problems, first consult your manual. Then, a knowledgeable friend can help if it is not a hardware or major software problem. The Internet user-group information, the university computer help desk for students, or a computer retailer or service agency are other sources of help and information. If the deadline approaches and your problem is not yet solved, take your backed-up disks to a friend or to the university computer lab and print your essay, writing a note to your instructor explaining your difficulty.

FURTHER READINGS

Barron, Billy, and Jill Ellsworth. *The Internet Unleashed*. Indianapolis, IN: Sams, 1997.

Coffee, Peter. *Peter Coffee Teaches PCs*. Indianapolis, IN: Que, 1998.

Computing for Parents: Help Your Student Excel in School. PCNovice Learning Series 10 (1997). An excellent introduction for university students.

Kent, Peter. *The Complete Idiot's Guide to the Internet*. 4th ed. Indianapolis, IN: Que, 1997.

Norton, Peter. *Peter Norton's Introduction to Computers*. New York: Glencoe-Macmillan; McGraw-Hill, 1998.

WEBLINKS

- BABEL: A Glossary of Computer Oriented Abbreviations and Acronyms
  www.cis.columbia.edu/glossary.html

- EFF's Guide to the Internet
  www.hep.net/documents/eegtti/eeg_toc.html

- ILC Glossary of Internet Terms
  www.matisse.net/files/glossary.html

- The Internet Companion
  www.obs-us.com/obs/english/books/editinc

- Learn the Net Internet Classes
  www.learnthenet.com/english/index.html

- Library of Congress Brief Guides to the Internet
  artemis.simmons.edu/~christen/assignmt/resource/overview/biblio.htm

- PC Friendly Internet Page
  darkwing.uoregon.edu/~wharmon

CRITICAL READING STRATEGIES

C h a p t e r

3

WHAT IS CRITICAL READING?

Many recent studies on the preparedness of students for university work indicate that the most serious problem students have is an inability to read critically. The skill of critical reading is not widely taught, and many students lack an interest in improving their reading on their own. A wide range of recent scholarship (see the references at **www.kcmetro.cc.mo.us/ longview/ctac/reading.htm**) suggests that old methods that postponed critical reading until basic and intermediate reading skills were learned are being questioned. More recent views suggest that reading is always an integrated and interactive process. Learning critical reading skills should not be postponed, but rather should be undertaken at least in high school, and probably much earlier, and should certainly be consolidated at university. Nevertheless, most students have not had the advantage of learning critical reading practices. So if you feel that you are stumbling in the dark when you sit down with a reading assignment, you are not alone. Most of your classmates share your situation.

Critical reading makes you a more effective reader by helping you adapt different methods of reading for different kinds of material. Critical reading and retaining what you read are strengthened by learning to annotate in different ways and for different purposes, by drawing connections between your reading and your studying and writing of assignments, and by systematically improving your vocabulary and reading skills.

Critical reading at its simplest involves reading any text with interest, comprehension, and a questioning frame of mind. You will be looking not only for what an author is saying, but also for the links in argument, the bridges from one point to another, the patterns of words and thoughts, and the stated and unstated assumptions. You will be reading to question the validity of the argument, and so you will be engaged in ongoing analysis. And when you are done, you will be able to summarize the main points of the argument and to offer a critique of it, stating its strong points and its weak ones. Best of all, this process will happen with greater and greater efficiency and ease as you become more accustomed to practising it. Then you will find that, far from being intimidated by the reading assignments, you will be well prepared to begin them and to carry them out effectively.

Any argument can be questioned and tested: critical reading involves a constant process of challenging and testing the validity of a text's claims based on its logic and the relationships between its premises and the supporting evidence. Valid arguments depend on proper use of logic (see the more detailed discussion in Chapter 7). In reading fiction, the testing of arguments is not quite so straightforward; nevertheless, critical reading can question all kinds of assumptions that are made in texts about human nature and character motivation, about what constitutes a good or a bad action, about what is a legitimate or an illegitimate challenge to represented social orders, and so on.

Above all, critical reading is an integral part of critical thinking. When you have learned how to exercise these skills, your reading and thinking will become part of the same learning process and your work will improve. The rewards include better grades and much greater satisfaction and pleasure in your studies.

LEARNING TO READ: PHONICS VERSUS WHOLE LANGUAGE DEBATES

What Are the Debates and Why Discuss Them Here?

Reading is a process of acquiring more and more meaning from a text, whether it is printed, electronic, visual (artwork, film, or video), or musical. "Reading" such texts involves you in the acquisition of vocabulary, factual knowledge, and relational meaning. As a skill, reading is acquired in elementary school, though many children learn to read before entering school. Two methods have generally been used to teach reading as a process in North America, the phonetic method and the whole language method. The merits of these two methods have in recent years been heatedly debated in academic circles, as well as in boards of education. Students have been subjected to one method, now to another, and, less frequently, to a blend of both. This section is included to give readers some sense of the debates in educational theory and policy making that have shaped their reading experience and that have been, at least in part, the major reason why so many students at university urgently need to improve their critical reading skills.

The Phonic Method

Teaching the alphabetic code, or phonic methodology (how letters are pronounced in combinations), has changed in its details, but overall it has been remarkably consistent from about 1910 on and has roots that stretch back to Noah Webster's *American Spelling Book* (1783), John Newberry's *Spelling Dictionary* (1745), and Solomon Lowe's *Critical Spelling-book* (1755).

Phonetics, phonics, or phonology is the study of speech sounds, including their production by the speech and hearing organs. Phonics is one method used in elementary schools to teach beginning reading; it is the systematic teaching of the correspondence of letters to sounds, and it results in progressive skills in word recognition, spelling accuracy, and the comprehension of meaning. In English, there are about thirty-six basic sounds (or *phonemes,* the smallest units of language that distinguished one sound class from another). For example, the *p* sounds in *pit, spin,* and *hip* are all slightly different, but the *p* sounds all belong to the same phoneme. The *p* and *b* sounds in *pit* and *bit,* however, have two different phonemes. It is in this distinguishing feature of phonemes that differences in meaning are allowed. Furthermore, the sounds of letters differ from the names of the letters in the ABC. The letter *c,* for instance, has the ABC name that sounds like *see,* but in a combination of letters it is pronounced as *k* (as in *car*). Hence, the words *cat* and *dog* have very different sounds phonically from the names of the letters in the ABC. The sounds of phonemes are described and identified in dictionaries in the pronunciation guide for each word.

When phonemes are combined, they make up a string of sounds that give meaning. This shape of a sound that imparts meaning is called a *morpheme* (the smallest combination of sounds that gives meaning). Such short morphemes as *un-, non-,* and *-ly* indicate meaning differences, but so do particular case endings, verbal forms, and so on. Hence, morphology combines phonemes into words of clear and distinct meanings. Morphemes are the smallest units of speech that are recurrent and meaningful: they are the minimal grammatical unit, whether part of a word or a whole word. They cannot be further subdivided without loss of meaning.

In learning to read by the phonic method, a student learns to sound out the words according to already learned patterns of sound recognition based on the combinations of letters and their pronunciation. The meaning of the words is arrived at by recognizing the morphemes that are then combined to make meaningful words, and those words are then combined into sentences. So the word *teacher* is made up of two morphemes, *teach* and *er*. The phonic reader can sound out the morpheme *teach* and can combine it with *er* to arrive at the meaning of the completed word. Such a method appears simple and straightforward, but in fact it gives rise to many problems for many students who have failed to learn any part of the phonics method. When faced with complex terms in technical subjects (in psychology, classics, biology, and literature), they cannot easily pronounce the words, apart from understanding them. Most teachers of English and foreign languages will be acutely aware of

Solomon Lowe. *The Critical Spelling-book.* London, 1755. Permission of the Osborne Collection, Toronto Public Library.

this problem when students have difficulty in pronouncing (or deriving meaning from) unfamiliar words or characters in Shakespearean plays or proper names in the novels of
Dostoevsky. But the same problems occur with various descriptions of clinical conditions
in psychology, names in Greek, Roman, or contemporary history, the names of chemical com-
pounds or parts of an organism, and so on.

The Whole Language Method

The whole language method of teaching reading stresses the fact that language is learned in
a variety of social situations (through interaction with parents, friends, students, and teachers) and oral and visual contexts (through TV, video, computers, the radio, and books).
Whole language teaching, then, in the words of a pamphlet produced by the (U.S.) National
Council of Teachers of English (a strong proponent of whole language teaching of reading
and writing), is "a lot like learning to talk," sharing "language naturally as a part of everyday experiences." As in the home, where oral language acquisition is "celebrated and accepted
without criticism," so in school, "through using reading and writing and observing others reading and writing in everyday situations ... children can learn to read and write." Hence, the
classrooms where this learning takes place are those that foster a holistic approach to language,
encouraging conversation and projects, considerable reading (especially of "whole," "real,"
or complete books, rather than extracts or kits), listening to others read, and writing. Little
attention is paid to correction, standardized testing, spelling, and many of the conventions
of standard English grammar or punctuation, as noted at the National Council of Teachers
of English (NCTE) home page ("Elementary School Practices"). Similarly, the Board of
Education for the City of London (Ontario) issued in 1990 "A Parent's Guide to Whole
Language" in accordance with the policy of the Ontario Ministry of Education: "Children learn
in a holistic manner, integrating what they are learning into that which they already know.
Learning is difficult when it is focused on isolated parts."

Whole language teaching was first adopted officially in the United States in 1987, after it
had been used in New Zealand. But it had already been widely deployed in schools before
1987, partly in reaction to the rigid teaching of phonics in the 1960s. By the mid-1980s it was
widely used throughout the United States, becoming the accepted policy of the National
Council for the Teachers of English from about 1990 to the present. In Canada it has dominated
the curricula during the same period, so that in Ontario, Circular 14 (the list of government-ap-
proved school texts) approved only whole language materials for teaching reading, and whole
language was the program taught by the faculties of education throughout the 1990s.

Recent Discussions and Their Implications
for University Students

During this entire period, the debate between the phonics and whole language advocates
rose in intensity and rhetorical levels. Phonics teachers maintained that they did not teach
by the drill or memorization method, while whole language advocates asserted that phonics
should be taught only as needed. Phonics advocates countered with an attack on the whole language position (promulgated by one of the chief supporters of whole language, Ken Goodman,
of the University of Arizona) that learning to read is as natural as learning to talk. Learning
to talk, according to the phonics advocates, proceeds in a situation of family and peer socialization, and to that extent it is natural; however, in learning to read, a nonreader has to be

taught by a reader. Effort is required to follow instructions to learn to read; you will not learn to read unless someone teaches you how to do it. Hence, the opponents of "natural" reading acquisition want to develop the best possible means of making the teaching of reading effective.

The collapse of phonics capabilities among postsecondary students in Canada has been one of the hidden causes of what many have called the current crisis of literacy in universities. Many students cannot read unfamiliar words, cannot sound them out, cannot link them to known words in their vocabulary, and, in a related set of skills, have almost no ability to write accurately or spell the simplest of definitions. Such students have been the products of a too-limited approach to language acquisition, and their almost complete lack of phonics has greatly disadvantaged them. Hence, the reaction against the whole language teaching of reading without simultaneous teaching of phonics, and without some standards of spelling, correction, and testing, is long overdue. But faculties of education, as well as local boards of education and individual schools, will take some time to shift curricula and teachers' abilities to modify their almost total emphasis on whole language. So, despite efforts to curb the literacy decline, the process of recovery will be long and difficult.

Opposition to the exclusive use of the whole language method to teach beginning reading has been loud and prolonged, but until recently it has made little headway with the ministries and boards of education in Canada and the United States. This opposition was anticipated by the indictment of reading skills by Rudolf Flesch in his 1955 book *Why Johnny Can't Read and What You Can Do About It*, followed by his second scathing attack, *Why Johnny Still Can't Read: A New Look at the Scandal of Our Schools*. Of the major studies conducted in the United States sponsored by the major national educational policy organizations and foundations, none supported whole language or its precursors as the sole preferred method (see Chall; Anderson et al.; Adams; and Snow et al.).

Preventing Reading Difficulties in Young Children, by Snow et al., is a major report written by seventeen of the leading scholars in their fields and sponsored by the major funding agencies and policy-making bodies of the U.S. government and by the most prestigious scientific organizations. The report recommends teaching reading to all children, not only to those with reading problems, through instruction in the alphabetic codes, phonetics, letter–sound correspondences, and word families; through wider experience in reading and writing independently and with other children; and through discussions to develop conceptual knowledge and comprehension strategies.

In many provinces and states there has in the past several years been a revision of whole language teaching as the only approved method, in favour of whole language with systematic teaching in phonetics and other language skills. For instance, in 1995 California passed a law requiring the teaching of fundamental spelling and phonics skills for grades one to eight. Michigan followed suit, and the Center for the Improvement of Early Reading Achievement at the University of Michigan School of Education has been at the forefront of advocating an integrated approach to reading using both the systematic teaching of phonics and some whole language methodologies (see their ten research-based principles to improve reading at **www.ciera.org/ciera/information/principles/index.html**). Similarly, in Ontario in 1997 and 1998 new curricular guidelines were approved to teach basic skills. For many teachers and boards of education, this change of policy has meant increased time in teacher training, the learning of new skills, and the writing of new textbooks; for many students it will mean radical changes in the ways that they are taught to read. However, for those students who have been reared on the whole language methodology and who are entering university in the next ten or twelve years, the problems of reading at a university level are considerable.

he age of two, most children can combine words into meaningful sentences.
re able to use those skills almost from the first stages of learning to read, which
ar some children well before kindergarten, for others kindergarten or grade one.
nately, many parents (and children) complain that by grade four they are still read-
a grade one level and have not made the transition to pleasurable reading and to the
ability to cope with the syntax of a sentence and its meaning. Students already know the
rules for oral English and have internalized some of them through their knowledge of the spoken language, but the written language presents additional problems.

Current research in word recognition (cited above) suggests that effective early readers
have learned to move from letters to sounds (phonics) and then to meaning (morphology)
through observation, being read to, learning to read, and reading to others. Young readers learn
that words have separate and identifiable shapes that can be recognized, sometimes with
and sometimes without phonemic processing. Whole language is particularly useful for
readers who have some skills with phoneme processing. At the same time, the majority of
university students with reading problems or disabilities have difficulty with these first
steps in early reading: proceding from phonics to meaning levels.

Critics of the whole language method have repeatedly pointed out the problems high
school and university students have with the conventions of standard written English, but a
less obvious problem is students' general lack of ability to read unfamiliar words, to pronounce
words correctly according to conventional practice, to link unfamiliar words to other words
in families, to recognize prefixes and suffixes as carriers of meaning, to move to the se-
mantic level (the level of meaning) for unfamiliar words in sentences, and to rapidly and efficiently comprehend what they are reading.

It is partly to overcome these difficulties that this chapter has been introduced. It is intended to explain the situation in which many students find themselves. In the rest of the chapter, we address ways of improving your reading skills.

READING STRATEGIES

Increasing Comprehension and Concentration

Whether you are reading a book for a course or for pleasure, in an area of knowledge that you
are studying in detail or about which you know little but are interested, at an introductory or
advanced level, there are some basic approaches to reading that will greatly increase your comprehension and your pleasure. We summarize them for you here.

Skimming for an Overview or Preview

Experienced academic readers skim books all the time, and they have learned to skim with efficiency and purpose. Even glancing over a book because you have no time for more systematic
reading can be useful. If you are glancing over it because you have budgeted your time poorly
and just need to have some acquaintance with the text before class, knowing how to use
skimming skills will help you. Skimming, however, is not a substitute for careful and systematic
reading. But for many books it is all you will have time to do. Skimming a book, if done
purposefully, can give a vital overview, or it can be a preview to a more systematic and analytical reading. Skimming means that you look over a whole book or article to determine the

BOX 3.1   **Readings on the Phonetics–Whole Language Debate**

Adams, Marilyn. *Beginning to Read: Thinking and Learning about Print*. Washington: Sponsored by the Office of Educational Research and Improvement of the U.S. Department of Education, 1990.

Ainsworth, Lynne. "Teaching Reading: Are Our Schools Failing the Test?" *Toronto Star* 18 Apr. 1992: D1, D5.

Carbo, M. "Reading Styles Research: 'What Works' Isn't Always Phonics." *Phi Delta Kappan* 68.6 (Feb. 1987): 431–35.

Chall, Jeanne S. *Learning to Read: The Great Debate*. 3rd ed. Fort Worth, TX: Harcourt Brace, 1996.

Evers, Williamson M. Ed. *What's Gone Wrong in America's Classrooms*. Stanford, CA: Hoover Institute Press, Stanford U, 1998.

Flesch, Rudolf. *Why Johnny Can't Read and What You Can Do About It*. New York: Harper and Row, 1955.

———. *Why Johnny Still Can't Read: A New Look at the Scandal of Our Schools*. New York: Harper and Row, 1981.

Fletcher, J.M., and G.R. Lyon. "Reading: A Research-Based Approach." In Evers 49–90.

Goswami, Usha, and Peter Bryant. *Phonological Skills and Learning to Read*. Hillsdale, NJ: Erlbaum, 1990.

Hall, E.M., and L.A Dennis. *Living and Learning: The Report of the Provincial Committee on Aims and Objectives of Education in the Schools of Ontario*. Toronto: H. Newton, 1968.

Hanson, R.A., and D. Farrell. "The Long-Term Effect on High School Seniors of Learning to Read in Kindergarten." *Reading Research Quarterly* 30 (1995): 908–33.

Hiebert, Elfrieda H., David Pearson, Barbara Taylor, Virginia Richardson, and Scott G. Paris. *Every Child a Reader*. Ann Arbour, MI: CIERA (Center for the Improvement of Early Reading Achievement), U of Michigan School of Education, 1998.

Hiebert, Elfrieda H., and Barbara M. Taylor. Eds. *Getting Reading Right from the Start: Effective Early Literacy Interventions*. Boston: Allyn and Bacon, 1994.

Karlin, Robert, and A.R. Karlin. *Teaching Elementary Reading: Principles and Strategies*. New York/Toronto: Harcourt Brace, 1981.

"Let Battle Commence." *Times Educational Supplement* 10 Nov. 1995, sec. 2: 5.

Rieben, Laurence, and Charles A. Perfetti. Eds. *Learning to Read: Basic Research and Its Implications*. Hillsdale, NJ: Erlbaum, 1991.

Symons, Sonya, Vera Woloshyn, and Michael Pressley. Eds. "The Scientific Evaluation of the Whole Language Approach to Literacy Development." Spec. issue of *Educational Psychologist* 29.4 (1994).

Vanderwolf, Case. "Teaching Methods in Elementary Schools [in Ontario]: A Brief Review of the Evidence." *Orbit* 22 (1991): 20–22.

Williams, J. "Reading Instruction Today." *American Psychologist* 34 (1979): 917–22.

general organization and contents. Reviewing the table of contents in a book, or the sub-headings in a chapter or an article, is the quickest way to determine what the text covers. Perhaps you are used to skipping rather than skimming the boldfaced or italicized passages that highlight the organization of a section of a book. In skimming it is important not only to notice these signals, but also to see how they fit together. Often, there is a point being made in the arrangement of chapter headings or subheadings: perhaps they are set out chronolog-ically, conceptually, or cumulatively. Authors want you to be able to recognize the way that their ideas are put together, so skimming such headings for clues gives you an important preview of the argument. Sometimes, the book's purpose and argument are outlined in the pref-ace or introduction in a little more detail. Sometimes there are comments there too about a book's intended audience or about the situation for which the author is writing.

Skimming can also mean that you move from chapter titles and headings to some of the con-tent of the chapters. Many experienced readers look at the opening of chapters or the first paragraphs of an article, where many authors summarize their goals and positions. The final chapter and the last paragraphs often summarize the argument again or place it in a wider perspective. Reading over these sections quickly will enable you to comprehend the book's or article's range and methods. Then you can narrow your focus in skimming the chapters or sections that are particularly interesting or relevant to you. When you look them over, you can read the opening and closing sentences of paragraphs to get the gist of the argument, not-ing any lists of points set off by numbers or paragraphs that enumerate them: "First ... second ... and third," or "The four most important causes of the...." Key words are also important to this overview—*reasons*, *causes*, *results*, *effects*, and so on. The argument may also be organized to balance both sides of a question, so you should be alert to signals of pro and con arguments (such as the use of "On the one hand ... on the other hand...."). Italicized type is sometimes used in definitions, which can be a great help to you in understanding how important concepts are being used. Finally, the repetition of arguments in slightly different terms or as summaries (sometimes with such a phrase as "In other words ...") will help you to comprehend the main concepts. After you have completed your skimming of a text, you will know how the argument is organized and where it is proceeding and can then to go back for more concentrated read-ing, from which you will reap much greater understanding and pleasure (see Box 3.2).

Reading Actively

To read actively means that you set a goal for yourself in your reading, usually focusing on where you are in the course and the questions raised about the text in lectures and seminars. Without such goals, you have little idea of what to concentrate on, and everything you read tends to have the same value. You are unable to focus on major themes or ideas and often miss important connections. The organization of a textbook, novel, or journal article with its head-ings and divisions is a help in focusing your goals. Reading actively also involves critically thinking as you read, assessing your attention span and focus, noting difficulties and problems, questioning the argument, and determining what is crucial and what is less important.

Reading for the Literal

The only way to understand a text and to build your vocabulary, critical concepts, and cul-tural knowledge is to use a good dictionary, the course's reading aids, and other reference books. We deal with developing your vocabulary and with dictionaries in Chapter 4. To get to the literal level of any reading, you need to develop specific reading skills. But you should also draw on other materials that will aid your comprehension of what a text means at this most basic level, the accumulative meaning of the words on the page as they lay out an argument or develop a narrative. This point may seem obvious and even trite; however, many students do not bother to use this reading practice, and so they bypass the first stage of understanding the words on the page.

Reading for Context

Critical reading involves locating the text in its own time of writing and production and in the context of your own reading. That is, you need to establish, at least in a preliminary way, an understanding of the text's position in history (including its cultural role and the author's biography) and of the text's position in the present. You bring all kinds of assumptions from your present context into the reading of any text. This critical reading strategy helps you to become aware of and question those assumptions.

Preparing Outlines and Summaries

To make a useful outline of an argument or a narrative, you need to be aware of its general

---

BOX 3.2   Skimming

- Note the author and what angle the title takes on the field of study.
- Study the table of contents or headings to discover the range and coherence of the materials covered. Note boldfaced subheadings.
- Survey the preface or introduction to find a summary of the book's argument and audience.
- Scan the opening chapter and/or paragraphs for a summary of the argument.
- Scan the last chapter and/or paragraphs for a summary of the argument and a discussion of its implications.
- Zero in on the main topic or section that concerns you and read the opening and closing sentences in each paragraph. Do not get distracted and read what is in between. You are looking for the general shape of the discussion.
- Go back and note any itemized or numbered lists or places where key stages are stressed.
- Note key phrases, such as the *main point, the chief reason, three issues,* or *the key idea.*
- Note points of transition in the argument by key words: *in contrast, on the other hand, however,* and so on.
- Note words and definitions that are set in italics or bold type.
- Scan the index for terms or concepts relevant to your topic, and check the references for other pertinent books.

shape or structure. You should distinguish between the main line and supporting ideas, illustrations, and examples, or, in narrative, between the main plot and the subplots or digressions. An outline is a map of the text. A summary begins with an outline but moves from a list of words or points to a whole new text in your own words. This step requires creating an overview or synthesis of the text. If you use the text's actual words, you should be certain to put them in quotation marks and indicate the page references to avoid mistakenly using them later as your own ideas, and thus laying yourself open to charges of plagiarism.

Drawing Connections with Other Readings

As you are reading week by week in a course, you should draw relationships with previous readings by situating them within the course's overall argument. This process will give you a map of the entire course, into which you can fit individual readings. As well, you might want to draw relationships with other readings in other courses, in which similar issues or historical contexts are addressed.

These strategies are intended to get you started in becoming a more engaged reader. You can adapt them or add to them as you become more self-reflexive about the reading process. The general thrust of these strategies is to have you begin to consider a reading as a dialogue in which you participate with the text in constructing meaning.

Using the SQ3R Method

One widely used reading strategy is the SQ3R method, which stands for "Survey, Question, and then apply the three Rs to answer your questions: Read, Recite, and Review." This method has three stages. In the first you survey the whole contents of the book or article you are examining, and in the second you question it. The third stage involves the three R responses to your question: read, recite, and review. In detail, the system looks like this:

1. First, survey the whole contents of an assigned book or article when you begin it. Include the preface, introduction, table of contents, bibliography, and index. Try to get a feel for the ideas and argument of the whole text. When reading an article or a particular chapter, read the introduction to it, the summary at the end, and the headings used throughout—take only a minute or two on this process.

2. Next, frame a question about the introduction or first main point to increase your concentration and to develop a critical attitude. Your question can be on the level of content. For instance, What does the author argue were the main factors in Hitler's rise to power? Or, your question may position the book's argument in relation to other works in the field. For instance, How does this particular author modify or disagree with other explanations for Hitler's rise to power? The second question is more difficult to formulate; however, the purpose of this stage of reading is to create a device to make you an active reader, to focus your attention as you read, and to alert you to the ways that your question is answered or modified. See if this question is responded to in the paragraphs or pages that immediately follow.

3. Finally, apply the 3 Rs

   • Read to the end of the first section, trying to find the answer to your question in the introduction to the book, chapter, or article. If you are unsuccessful, consider again the question you asked and reformulate it.

   • Recite the answer. When you finish the section, look away and try to recite the answer to your question. Now is the time to take brief notes or underline key passages. Complete the entire chapter like this, adding to your notes.

- Review the argument. Test your memory by trying to recall the main points in each section.

This method is particularly useful in reading books that have a sustained argument. It is less successful when used for works of fiction. When reading fiction, you can follow the survey stage and then approach each chapter as a unit in the development of the entire text. When you are reading, you can keep in mind some of the following traditional aspects of prose fiction:

- What can be said about the setting? What is its time period? Its location? Its atmosphere?
- Who is speaking and to whom?
- What are the main events?

Some students find it helpful to write two- or three-sentence synopses, or just points, at the end of each chapter to summarize the characters and their interaction, to note the main events, and to pose any questions. You might also like to keep your own index to the book, especially of the terms that strike you or that are particularly important for the course in which you read it. Then, when you finish the book you already have it summarized, making it far more accessible for class discussions and examinations.

You can extend your questioning of a text to a deeper level by asking how it is constructed: What are its parts? What is its genre? What are its stylistic features? What does it mean, and how does it construct that meaning? The assumptions of the text can also be questioned in such a reading: What are the theoretical assumptions of this text? What theory of human nature or of art does this text assume? What is its audience? How does it deal with controversial issues of race, gender, and class? What are its political and social assumptions? On what does it rely for proof and evidence? Are its truth claims appeals to religious belief, morality, scientific or statistical evidence, or common sense? How can the text be opened up to contrary readings?

Critical reading involves planning a strategy before you begin reading any text; that is, you need to have a purpose to address the different kinds of readings that are required in university courses. Not all assigned reading is of the same level of difficulty. For instance, some readings pass on information in a succinct form, others are in textbook format with headings, explanations, and summaries, and others are critical articles. Some readings are fictional narratives, in popular or sometimes difficult language, which require you to pay attention to the different structural patterns, rhetorical devices, or shifts in argument that are being made. At other times you are reading for specific information and can skim quickly through material until you find what you are looking for. The strategies that follow present different critical skills for different levels of material. Not every strategy is appropriate for each kind of reading.

Reading an Article or a Chapter Effectively

Most courses have weekly reading assignments, consisting of chapters from a textbook, a selection from a course kit, or an article located in the university's periodical or reserve collection, where your instructor has deposited it for short-term loan. If you own the textbook or the course kit, you are free to mark it up as you choose for best comprehension (see the section on annotation on page 72). If it is a library holding or on deposit there, you cannot mark it and must use other reading strategies. One possibility is to photocopy the article, if allowed

TIPS: Being an Active Reader

1. To get a clear overview of an argument, read the first and last sentences of each paragraph. See the detailed tips on skimming above.

2. Look for the indications in the text of important information, such as when a paragraph begins with a phrase that highlights it (e.g., *most important*).

3. Note any unfamiliar words and look them up in a dictionary. Keep a record of them as you build your vocabulary.

4. Learn the basic Latin prefixes of words so that you can begin to understand even unfamiliar words, such as *ante-* (before), *contra-* (against), *extra-* (outside), and *post-* (after). (See suggestions about this process in Chapter 4.)

by copyright law and library rules. In any of these instances, there are specific strategies that make your critical reading of such an assignment more productive. Some instructors encourage cooperative learning among two or more students. If that is the case for your assignment, you should work through these steps together and after skimming discuss your responses concerning the main point of the article, what is being argued, and how it is being argued.

First, you should note the name of the author and the title of the article. You will likely not have time to return to this reading, so you need to make adequate notes that you can look over before your class, assignment, and any final examinations; the author's name and the title of the article may help you to locate other works by the same author, and the title will indicate the general topic. A quick read through or skimming of an article acquaints you with the author's thesis, general argument, and main points and prepares you for a more systematic reading. From this overview, you should try to summarize the author's thesis by answering such questions as, What is the main point that the author is making? What question or issue is the author examining, and what does he or she conclude about it? What principle is being examined in this article, and what is the evidence and method used to support it? You might find this information set out clearly in the first or concluding paragraph.

You want to come away from a detailed and systematic reading with a clear sense of the author's argument, including evidence, data, and conclusions, and with a sense of how the argument is organized into major and minor arguments. Above all, you need to understand the relationship between the author's ideas or concepts and the facts or data that are used to support them. It is important to note key transitions in the argument, along with outlines, summaries, and conclusions. You should circle any words you do not understand and look them up in your dictionary.

Most readers find that it is important for their understanding to make notes, either in the text by means of annotation if the document is your own copy or in a notebook if you are using a library copy. Underlining or copying out the thesis statement, numbering the stages in an argument, writing key definitions in the margins, and writing in questions or queries all help with understanding. You might also want to outline the main argument in your own words and perhaps summarize the conclusions of the article. Above all, you should clearly mark out or make a note about the divisions of the article: the introduction, the main points of the body of the essay, numbered if possible, and the conclusion. Within this skeleton outline, you can go back and refine the analysis of the major points by noting the concepts, ideas, or principles and the evidence to support them, the minor parts of the argument, and so on.

Finally, you can move to some evaluation. Are you convinced by the argument? Do the data and evidence support the argument and conclusions? For whom is the author writing this article? What are the author's assumptions about the audience and the subject of the article? Do you see implications beyond the article's conclusions?

Reading a Difficult Book

Many books that you will read at university are written by specialists in a field, who are writing with the assumption that their readers are other specialists. A relatively small number of the books and articles that are assigned or that you will come across in your research are written as introductions to a field or for the general public. That kind of book is often found in a good public library and sometimes in your university library. Books that are devoted to a specific topic of research are often called *monographs* (Greek *monos,* alone; *graphein,* to write; written on one particular subject).

To use a book in your study and research you need to approach it as though you were an intelligent reader, though not necessarily a specialist in the field. It might be that you are working in that field or one related to it, and so you bring some prior knowledge to your reading. You also have a goal in reading this book. You should try to define explicitly your prior knowledge of the field and your reasons for reading this book—not just that it is a part of an assignment, but how it fits with the materials in your course of study.

The skimming approach outlined above is most useful to you in reading a difficult book. You have probably already begun the process of skimming just by looking over the book in the library, checking the title, contents, and general range of the work. Now you can skim more systematically. Part of your skimming might involve checking the chapter headings for particular materials relevant to your research project or assignment. You might also check the index for key terms and look up the list of works cited to see whether the references are pertinent to your topic. Then, you should get down to the reading of the book, refusing to get bogged down in passages that you do not understand, but also refusing to just let them drift by you. If you do not understand something that seems crucial, it is a good idea to note the location and return to it later after you have read further. Chances are, you will later understand it far more readily. Looking up all of the footnotes and references will slow you down. The purpose of this initial reading is to acquaint you with the argument in general and with some detail.

After the first quick overview, you can return to the same passage and read it more carefully. In all probability, you will already have fallen into this habit in your skimming stage as you were attracted or challenged by part of the argument and stopped there to get it in detail before moving on. In this second-to-last stage you will likely want to make some notes for future reference. In any case, you will likely not have time to go back to the book again, and so will have to rely on the notes that you make now. You should be certain to copy any direct quotations accurately (including the punctuation) and to make a careful note of the reference (author, title, place of publication, publisher, date, and page reference). Finally, you can skim over the book again to make certain that you have all of the information from it that you need and that you have the arguments and data copied down accurately.

TIPS: Annotating Your Own Copy of a Book

1. Mark up your text appropriately if it is your own copy. *Do not mark up library copies*—other readers' purposes might be quite different from yours. Underlining in your personal copy is useful for the *most significant* passages, but underlining or highlighting whole pages simply means that you know how to run your hand, not your mind, over the page.

2. Draw connections and relationships between ideas in the text.

3. Number the stages of the argument in the margins to keep track of them.

4. Take some notes on what you read, choosing a method appropriate to the book and the assignment.

5. If you record quotations, record them accurately and note the source. Save time by doing it now, rather than later, when another reader may have the book out from the library.

Annotating

In general, annotation is fundamental to each of these strategies. Mechanical highlighting of page after page, either continuously or in a random fashion without any thought-out strategic principles, makes little sense. If a particular passage is focused on in a lecture or seminar to illustrate specific points of argument or rhetoric, you should mark and annotate it. Many critical readers annotate their own books (*not* library books) by underlining key words, phrases, or sentences; by writing brief comments or questions about difficult passages in the margins; by marking important sections of the text; by drawing connections between ideas through numbering ideas in sequence; by drawing arrows; or by using question marks or other shorthand annotations to indicate concepts you do not understand or points that are particularly important for your reading. Many readers make indexes of important words or concepts inside the back cover. Others annotate fiction by writing a brief summary of the action, setting, and characters at the end of each chapter. Such practices give you important ways of reviewing your entire reading list at the end of the course.

Annotation Styles in Different Subject Areas

It may seem obvious, but it needs to be pointed out that different subject areas use different kinds of writing patterns, and so demand different kinds of reading practices. Science subjects depend on classification and process, stress problem-solving methods, may introduce instructions on experiments, and summarize evidence and statistics. In the social sciences, definitions of concepts shape the argument, which proceeds with details and illustrations as evidence. Kinds of argument include comparison and contrast, cause and effect, and complicated arguments that move through the addition of layer after layer. In humanities subjects, some texts are constructed analytically, like those in the social sciences. Others are read for the narrative, as in fiction. But here, too, a reader can use critical thinking and analytical tools to question the narrative.

Making reading notes is like making lecture notes, and some of the same methods can be followed. Concept-mapping and the indent-outline methods are particularly helpful (see Chapter 1). For a discussion of various ways to organize your reading notes into files on your computer, see Chapter 9.

For some self-testing reading programs on the Internet, see the Regents' Testing page at

---

BOX 3.3	How to Calculate Your Reading Speed

To determine your reading speed in words per minute (WPM), read something that you enjoy for exactly ten minutes. Then make the calculations as in the following sample:

Complete these calculations for your sample reading:

Calculate the number of lines per page	27
(count the lines on several pages and average them)	
Calculate the number of words per page	237
(count the words on several pages and average them)	
Total number of pages in the book you are reading	339
Total (approximate) number of words	80 343
$(237 \times 339 = 80\ 343)$	
Total (approximate) number of lines	9153
$(27 \times 339 = 9153)$	
Total (approximate) number of words per line:	8.8

Complete these calculations to determine your WPM rate:

Number of pages you read in 10 minutes	11
Any additional lines beyond those 11 pages	12
1. Multiply the number of pages by the number of words per page	2607
$(11 \times 237 = 2607 \text{ words})$	
2. Multiply the number of additional lines by the number of words per line	106
$(12 \times 8.8 = 106 \text{ words})$	
3. Add the products of steps 1 and 2	2713
$(2607 + 106 = 2713 \text{ words})$	
4. Divide the total number of words by the reading time	271
$(2,713 \div 10 = 271 \text{ WPM})$	
5. Your reading speed = 271 WPM	

The overall WPM value is affected by round-off error. Average university students read between 250 and 350 WPM of fiction and nontechnical writing. A good score is about double that, and some people can read four times that speed. Checking your speed over several weeks should show steady improvement in your WPM rate.

Source: Adapted from Student Academic Services, California Polytechnic State University: **sas.calpoly.edu/asc/ssl/ personal.reading.imprvmnt.html**

the Georgia State University, which uses U.S. national magazines to test and assess reading speed and comprehension, along with a self-analysis of the results you achieve (**www.gsu.edu/~wwwrtp**).

POWER READING

Speed reading is a tremendous asset in courses with a heavy load of assigned texts. Most universities provide advice on speed reading, and some give classes in it or can recommend books. A number of self-help books on this topic will be available in your university bookstore. Different kinds of books and articles make different kinds of demands on your time and energy. A philosophy textbook, or one in computer science or mathematics, requires that you understand each step of the argument, and very likely requires rereading as you are progressing. On the other hand, some books can be read very quickly. You would not attempt to read a magazine article at the dentist's with the same kind of attention that you give to your psychology course. Many students read much too slowly. If you are a word-by-word reader, chances are that you are not taking in nearly as much as you could if you increased your rate and read by phrases or even lines. Most speed-reading books have exercises to test yourself. For instance, David Yarington includes one in his book *Surviving in College* and comments that by exercising conscious will you can improve the rate of your reading; he shows how using the simple device of saying "Read faster!" to yourself can help you double your reading speed and comprehension.

One of the first steps in learning to read faster is to follow quickly over the line with your finger (the finger method) or with a pointer (such as a pen or pencil) without relaxing the pace. The act of following with the finger provides some motor concentration and increases your speed and comprehension. Others find it useful to use the whole hand for this method. The point is to keep going in order to reduce the temptation to skip back to the previous sentence or

TIPS: Improving Power Reading

1. Twice a day read something you enjoy for ten minutes without stopping. Time yourself to within thirty seconds.
2. Record your reading rate (WPM) and chart your progress for a week. Recording and charting are essential if you wish to make real progress.
3. Push yourself gently as you read. If your mind wanders, get it back on track.
4. Wait until you've finished reading to look up unfamiliar words.
5. To improve comprehension, recite the chapter after closing the book. See how many specific details you can recall. Use the SQ3R method.
6. Sign up to use one of the speed reading computer programs in the academic skills centre of your university for an hour twice a week. It will help you boost your rate.
7. Set reading rate goals for yourself. A 10 percent increase in your reading rate over the previous record is a good rule of thumb.

Source: Adapted from Student Academic Services, California Polytechnic State University: **sas.calpoly.edu/asc/ssl/personal.reading.imprvmnt.html**

to an earlier phrase to reread it. Most teachers of power reading agree that the speed of y
ing depends to a large degree on the speed at which you move your finger or hand down

People who study the psychology of reading have been greatly interested in how
works in relation to the printed page and in terms of comprehension. Beginning read
to focus on a word at a time: their fixation zone is the single word, or, to make things even
slower, vocalization. Vocalization means that words are actually sounded out or pronounced
mentally, on the assumption that if the word is pronounced it will be understood. More experienced readers avoid vocalization because they have increased vocabularies and recognize
most words they come across, and they also extend their fixation zone to take in a block of
words by a single fixation of the eyes. Many university students fear missing something in the
textbooks or assignments that they are reading, and they often revert to the much earlier fixation on a word-by-word zone. That process is invoked especially when the reading is difficult or contains many unfamiliar words or concepts. Reading is thereby greatly slowed down.

Reading analysts are also interested in the duration of each fixation of the eyes. Beginning
readers look longer at each word, and even experienced readers, as we all know, slow down
in reading when they are tired or when their mind wanders. The fixation time greatly increases,
and the fixation zone is reduced. When you are slowed down in your reading by poor attention
or lack of sleep you also tend to skip back to recover some of the words or phrases that you
missed in the first pass of the eyes over that zone. Power reading attempts to address the issue
of reducing the fixation time by spending less and less time to "read" a passage, and by increasing the fixation zone from a word-by-word process to four or five words or a whole line
with experienced readers. When these processes are implemented, usually by some pointer
or finger method of ensuring a steady progress down the page to minimize skipping back,
you will be well on the way to becoming a power reader.

Power reading puts the materials you read into your short-term memory, so that you
can better comprehend the general structure and the details of what you are reading. However,
you still have to consolidate that information into your long-term memory (review the discussion of this process at the end of Chapter 1). Of course, the conditions for concentrated
reading have to be in your favour. Reading in the college pub to the accompaniment of
Jerry Seinfeld is not the best way to get the most out of your reading.

LEVELS OF READING

In this section, we take an apparently trivial example of a text, a well-known fairy tale, to show
how reading the story with an awareness of different levels of comprehension and understanding can yield increasingly valuable results. The illustrations suggest ways in which
those levels can be interpreted visually.

Literal Level: Reading for Content

When you were a small child, you likely read the fairy tale *Little Red Riding Hood* in some
simplified version or in a collection of children's stories. You were caught up in the narrative, with its repetitions and violence, and were probably slightly frightened too, especially
by the three scenes usually illustrated: the mother sending the girl to her grandmother's
cottage, the encounter with the wolf in the woods, and the girl's meeting with the wolf in bed
in the cottage. If you were asked what the story was "about," you could provide a summary
of the content on the literal level.

The Blue Beard Picture Book. London, 1875. Illus. Walter Crane. I. Permission of the Osborne Collection, Toronto Public Library.

It is at this level that most students remain when reading works of fiction; even many students in English and the humanities do not read at a more intensive level. It is comparatively easy to test for literal comprehension at this first level by asking what happened in each of a narrative's sections. Problems arise only over difficult words, complicated relationships, or complex plots. Nevertheless, the reading at the literal level for comprehension of content is vital to further levels of understanding. When the same approach is carried over to critical or scholarly articles, however, this method becomes shakier, and literal comprehension becomes more difficult. What must be followed now is not a plot, but an argument, and the normal supports for a plot (such as characters, setting, di-

alogue, and action) are missing. To make the content accessible at this stage, students often rely on highlighting a text with a marker, thinking that if all is marked, the content will move directly from the page into the brain.

Sometimes, of course, a reading for content at the literal level is followed by another leading question: How did you like the story you read? This question evokes an "appreciative" or "affective" response, since it involves the reader or auditor in a reaction on the basis of likes or dislikes. Responses at this level can be mere knee-jerk reactions and are difficult to evaluate, compare, or discuss. Critical reading practices require that such responses be assessed by asking for the basis or criteria used in a statement of likes or

The Blue Beard Picture Book. London, 1875. Illus. Walter Crane. II. Permission of the Osborne Collection, Toronto Public Library.

dislikes. Until there are some criteria in place that can be discussed and compared, there is no basis for appreciation except individual taste or opinion. To carry an appreciative response to a level of evaluation involves moving from a reactive phase to analytical levels of reading.

Expository Level: Reading for Content and Meaning

You might be asked a different question, such as, What does *Little Red Riding Hood* "mean"? Then you are forced to explain in your own words what you have read about. You have to assess what you understand the story to mean and relate what you read as content to what you think that content means in a larger sense. You are being asked to generalize and abstract from the content its significance, to explain it, and to translate its content into meaning. At this level you are giving what is often called an *expo-*

The Blue Beard Picture Book. London, 1875. Illus. Walter Crane. VII. Permission of the Osborne Collection, Toronto Public Library.

sition or *explication*. At this point you move from what the story has "said" to how it can be read, from "what" to "how." Your interpretation might be quite simple, based, perhaps, on what you have been taught: "Don't talk to strangers," or "Stay out of danger," or "Don't go to visit your grandmother alone." Many versions of the tale exploit such meanings: illustrations of the opening scene often suggest a direct moral meaning as a conventional mother sends a potentially rebellious daughter into a world of temptations with warnings and a cautionary shake of her finger.

It is at this second expository level that reading becomes evaluative. Your responses are moving well beyond the affective or appreciative response, and you can begin to see how a text is making its meaning effective. You are evaluating the means by which its conceptual and rhetorical controls are put into place. You are evaluating the "how" of the story—how the story communicates its content and meaning—and your interpretation makes this level of critical reading possible.

While such responses may seem trivial when applied to fairy tales, the same process can be applied to any work of fiction or to a scholarly or critical article on any topic. The move from content at the literal level to meaning at an interpretive level does not usually happen, however, at a successive reading (though, of course, many works benefit from repeated readings, and some difficult sections have to be read through more than once to get the meaning clear, even at the literal level). Instead, reading for the literal meaning and at the expository level usually take place simultaneously. This simultaneous reading is especially true with fairy tales, since most readers have internalized the ways in which they construct meaning; however, this exposi-

Ludwig Bechstein. *Märchenbuch*. Leipzig, 1857. Illus. Ludwig Richter. 200. Collections of the authors.

tory level is established by structural relations within the text. The meaning or moral of fairy tales is conditioned by an author's comments, which traditionally come at the beginning and after the end of the tale.

The version of *Little Red Riding Hood* you were reading was probably based on *Le Petit Chaperon Rouge* ("Little Red-Cap") by Charles Perrault. It was first published in his *Histoires ou Contes du temps passé avec des Moralitez* ("Stories or Tales of Times Past, with Moralities," 1697). The collection's subtitle gave its name to an entire genre of children's stories: *Contes de Ma Mère l'Oye* ("Tales of My Mother Goose"). Perrault's version begins:

Once upon a time there was a little village girl, the prettiest in the world. Her mother doted on her, and her grandmother even more. This good woman made her a little red hood which suited her so well that wherever she went, she was called Little Red Riding Hood.

One day, after her mother had baked some biscuits, she said to Little Red Riding Hood, "Go see how your grandmother's feeling. I've heard that she's ill. You can take her some biscuits and this small pot of butter." Little Red Riding Hood departed at once to visit her grandmother, who lived in another village. In passing through the forest she met old neighbor wolf, who had a great desire to eat her. But he did not dare because of some woodcutters who were in the forest. Instead he asked her where she was going. The poor child, who did not know that it is dangerous to stop and listen to a wolf, said to him, "I'm going to see my grandmother, and I'm bringing her some biscuits with a small pot of butter that my mother's sending her." (Zipes 58)

Charles Perrault. *The Histories of Passed Times, or The Tales of Mother Goose. With Morals.* Brussels, 1785. Trans. Robert Samber. vol. I, 10–11. Permission of the Osborne Collection, Toronto Public Library.

At the end of the story are the "moralities" that Perrault promised in his title. At the beginning of the story, the meaning or morality is suggested in the phrase "who did not know that it is dangerous to stop and listen to a wolf." At the end of the tale, however, he wrote this meaning out in verse, so that the reader need not stop at the literal level of the story, but could move to the meaning level under his guidance:

MORAL
One sees here that young children,
Especially pretty girls,
Who're bred as pure as pearls,
Should question words addressed by men.
Or they may serve one day as feast
For a wolf or other beast.
I say a wolf since not all are wild
Or are indeed the same in kind.
For some are winning and have sharp minds.
Some are loud, smooth, or mild.
Others appear plain kind or unriled.
They follow young ladies wherever they go,
Right into the halls of their very own homes.
Alas for those girls who've refused the truth:
The sweetest tongue has the sharpest tooth.
(Zipes 58–60)

At this stage of our example, the literal content of the text remains unchanged, but the meaning is conditioned by the structure and details of the tale and its apparatus. The moral is anticipated in the introduction to the story and is explained on its own terms in the morality appended to the tale. In fact, it is this morality verse that is structurally controlling the meaning of the entire text.

Analytical Level: Reading for Content, Meaning, and Context

To move to an analytical level of interpretation, you have to consider a text's content, meaning, and context together. To do that means that you need to have knowledge of the context in which the text was produced, as well as the context in which you are reading it. From general knowledge you might know something about the intellectual context of the seventeenth century, or you might know about the use of moral tags as advice from adults to children about appropriate kinds of behaviour necessary in order to fit into society. When you make an interpretation you necessarily draw on other kinds of information to contextualize the reading within your own resources. Whether or not those are adequate depends on your stock of information and concepts as a developing reader. In your reading of the story you have to be able to recognize where you have to undertake further reading to fill in the gaps in your knowledge.

At the analytical level, part of the context involves drawing on the methodologies and systems of knowledge of other disciplines in order to illuminate your reading. This intellectual context often means that you can apply the methods of one discipline to another, putting your reading of *Little Red Riding Hood,* for instance, into the context of psychology, gender studies, or social analysis. While some influential psychoanalytical interpretations of the story have considered the mother to be the superego and the child's ad-

Charles Perrault. *Histoires ou Contes du temps passé, avec des moralitez.* Amsterdam, 1721. Illus. Charles Perrault. I. Permission of the Osborne Collection, Toronto Public Library.

venture as learning to conform to parental values (Bettelheim 181), many modern interpretations consider the story a rape narrative, moving from domestic order to transgression in the wood and punishment by rape. Most illustrations suggest the power of the wolf by making him larger than the girl and showing him touching her, intimately sizing her up, and casting knowing glances, a convention from at least the time of Doré (1862). A key moment in this reading is the violent double action of the bedroom scene in Perrault's version, in which the wolf first rapes the grandmother before forcing or beguiling the girl to undress and get into bed:

Charles Perrault. *The Histories of Passed Times, or The Tales of Mother Goose. With Morals.* Brussels, 1785. Trans. Robert Samber. vol. I, plate 2. Permission of the Osborne Collection, Toronto Public Library.

Charles Perrault. *Les Contes de Perrault.* Paris, 1862. Illus. Gustave Doré. IV. Collections of the authors.

Grimm, Jakob, and Wilhelm Grimm. *The Fairy Tales of the Brothers Grimm.* London, 1909. Illus. Arthur Rackham. Facing 118. Permission of the Osborne Collection, Toronto Public Library.

Upon seeing her enter, the wolf hid himself under the bedcovers and said to her, "Put the biscuits and the pot of butter on the bin and come and lie down beside me." Little Red Riding Hood undressed and got into the bed, where she was quite astonished to see how her grandmother appeared in her nightgown.

"Grandmother, what big arms you have!" she said to her.

"All the better to hug you with my child."

Susan Brownmiller rereads the story in this context, drawing out the associations and implications at the analytical level and commenting on the details. She concludes:

> *Red Riding Hood* is a parable of rape. There are frightening male figures abroad in the woods— we call them wolves, among other names—and females are helpless before them. Better stick close to the path, better not be adventurous. If you are lucky, a good *friendly* male may be able to save you from certain disaster. (343–44)

A number of modern versions of the story seek to draw out its feminist potential. For instance, Marcia Lieberman writes on all of the volumes of Andrew Lang's collections of fairy tales (*The Blue Fairy Book,* 1889, containing part of the Perrault version of *Little Red Riding Hood*). She argues that the happy-ever-after endings have "been made the repositories of the dreams, hopes, and fantasies of generations of girls," each awaiting their Prince Charming—so she challenges Bruno Bettelheim's theory that the fairy tales are gender-free stories that help children of both sexes solve problems and come to maturation and self-definition (383–95). Whether or not you agree with her analysis, the point is that her reading is based on placing the meaning of the story in the context of the role of fairy tales in the seventeenth century in educating children. This analytical level relates the well-known content of the story (the literal level) to a new meaning. Her exposition (the second level) does not depend only on the morality of the tale or on its structural organization, though these aspects are important. Lieberman rereads the story in the political and social context of seventeenth-century France; her analysis allows her to conclude that the story was used

Charles Perrault. *Les Contes de Perrault.* Paris, 1862. Illus. Gustave Doré. xxiii. Collections of the authors.

Charles Perrault. *Les Contes
de Perrault.* Paris, 1862.
Illus. Gustave Doré. xix.
Collections of the authors.

to socialize children in conventional behaviour. The validity of her argument can be tested on
its own merits and depends on the ways she establishes how this socialization to conventional
behaviour relates to her feminist analysis. We shall discuss how you can analyze critical articles
like Lieberman's in the following sections.

Other analytical readings of the story include Marxist interpretations, which consider how
fairy tales have been used in the process of socialization, especially in legitimizing the
vested interests of capitalist societies by relying on conditions of servitude and standards of
courtly conduct watered down to bourgeois respectability. To resist those bourgeois readings,
Catherine Storr relocates Red Riding Hood in contemporary urban North America in "Polly
and the Wolf" (1955). The wolf cannot get to the grandmother's house easily, and so he
takes the bus when the train fails. The child takes whiskey for her grandmother and is wily
and street-smart, taking along her boyfriend, who is called Hunter. The American poet Anne
Sexton has retold seventeen of the traditional Grimm versions as psychological studies in her
book *Transformations* (1971).

Such modernized versions suggest that there is yet another level of reading, in which older
versions can be compared, and these too can be contrasted with modern rewritings and with
other tales from either similar or different contexts.

Comparative Level: Reading for Associations and Implications

It might be that you were not familiar with Perrault's version and his morality, but rather with
the version told by the Brothers Grimm:

> There was once a sweet little maid, much beloved by everybody, but most of all by her grand-
> mother, who never knew how to make enough of her. Once she sent her a little cap of red vel-
> vet, and as it was very becoming to her, and she never wore anything else, people called her Little
> Red-cap. One day her mother said to her, "Come, Little Red-cap, here are some cakes and a flask
> of wine for you to take to grandmother: she is weak and ill, and they will do her good. Make
> haste and start before it grows hot, and walk properly and nicely, and don't run, or you might
> fall and break the flask of wine, and there would be none left for grandmother. And when you
> go into her room, don't forget to say, Good morning, instead of staring about you." (Grimm 132)

The Brothers Grimm version begins with a conventional, pretty young woman, often depicted in illustrations. It continues with Red-cap's telling the wolf the location of her grandmother's cottage, and his advice that she take longer to get there by gathering flowers on the way (so that he might get there before her and eat her grandmother whole). In the Grimm version, the wolf eats Red-cap too, and it is only the timely arrival of the woodcutter that saves both of the eaten victims, who step forth fully clad and alive when he slices the wolf open.

When you take on a more systematic reading and study of *Little Red Riding Hood* you become aware that the story has many analogues, or parallel versions. Until recently, it was believed that Perrault invented the tale and that the Brothers Grimm had transcribed one of the oral versions; we now know from the research of Marianne Rumpf, Marc Soriano, and others that the tale is medieval and that it was still popular in France in the seventeenth century, partly because Europe was in the last stages of the witch hunt and there was widespread fear of werewolves. Furthermore, research into the manuscript of the Brothers Grimm shows that they "improved" the version considerably.

Further study of the story would, therefore, involve the reading of its analogues (parallel or similar versions from related or even very different literary traditions). Such readings are conducted not only to bring out the parallels, but also to examine the roots of the story—here, in its instruction about the appropriate roles for working-class and bourgeois children, about parental warnings concerning sexual exploits, and about conventional gender roles (some of the implications of which we have already suggested at the analytical level). Hence, with fairy stories, as with many forms of writing, a comparative reading of variants of the tale will involve not only a comparison of near contemporary versions, but

Grimm, Jakob, and Wilhelm Grimm. *Grimm's Fairy Tales*. London, 1900. Illus. Eddie J. Andrews. Facing 26. Permission of the Osborne Collection, Toronto Public Library.

Grimm, Jakob, and Wilhelm Grimm. *The Fairy Tales of the Brothers Grimm*. London, 1909. Illus. Arthur Rackham. Facing 116. Permission of the Osborne Collection, Toronto Public Library.

will also consider how the history of those versions has yielded modern rewritings. The story has associations with rural or village life, and it reflects the values and habits of a peasant community that was closely related to nature. These associations have to be questioned when the story is read in the context of the twenty-first century and in an urban setting. The implications of the story in the warnings against the wolf, the responsibilities of parents and grandparents, and the ability of the child to follow instructions are all part of the comparative reading level that places the narrative in its own time and in other times when it is rewritten or consumed. One way of illuminating such questions is to see whether other versions of the tale stress some of those aspects of current life that were called into question in earlier versions.

For instance, in an effort to modernize the tale, James Finn Garner published this version:

> There once was a young person named Red Riding Hood who lived with her mother on the edge of a large wood. One day her mother asked her to take a basket of fresh fruit and mineral water to her grandmother's house—not because this was womyn's work, mind you, but because the deed was generous and helped engender a feeling of community. Furthermore, her grandmother was not sick, but rather was in full physical and mental health and was fully capable of taking care of herself as a mature adult.
>
> So Red Riding Hood set off with her basket through the woods. Many people believed that the forest was a foreboding and dangerous place and never set foot in it. Red Riding Hood, however, was so confident in her own budding sexuality that such obvious Freudian imagery did not intimidate her.
>
> On the way to Grandma's house, Red Riding Hood was accosted by a Wolf, who asked her what was in her basket. She replied, "Some healthful snacks for my grandmother, who is certainly capable of taking care of herself as a mature adult." (1–2)

The Book of Nursery Tales. London, 1845. Third series. Frontispiece. Permission of the Osborne Collection, Toronto Public Library.

Other versions draw on ecological, sociological, and other implications and associations by carrying the reading even further, such as this version by Stan Greenberg posted on the Web:

> There once was a young person named Little Red Riding Hood who lived on the edge of a large forest full of endangered owls and rare plants that would probably provide a cure for cancer if only someone took the time to study them.
>
> Red Riding Hood lived with a nurture giver whom she sometimes referred to as "mother," although she didn't mean to imply by this term that she would have thought less of the person if a close biological link did not in fact exist. Nor did she intend to denigrate the equal value of non-traditional households, although she was sorry if this was the impression conveyed.
>
> One day her mother asked her to take a basket of organically grown fruit and mineral water to her grandmother's house.

"But mother, won't this be stealing work from the unionized people who have struggled for years to earn the right to carry all packages between various people in the woods?"

Red Riding Hood's mother assured her that she had called the union boss and gotten a special compassionate mission exemption form. (**www.otherside.net.redhood.htm**)

In both of these modern versions, the writers have used a comparative reading. They accept the fact that fairy tales are meant to teach children, which, as we have seen, was established in Perrault's making explicit the morality of the tale after the conclusion of his version. The particular moral of the seventeenth century, however, is updated to the context of the late twentieth century. Hence, both modern writers satirize various contemporary political movements by adapting Perrault's morality to fit their own contemporary context. A comparative reading makes each of these moves apparent.

In a different contemporary context, one reading of the version by the Brothers Grimm has resulted in a case of censorship. As recently as 1989 an illustrated edition of *Little Red Riding Hood* was banned in two California school districts. The fact that the story involved Red Riding Hood's taking "this piece of cake and bottle of wine" to her grandmother raised to the school boards a concern about the approving of alcohol use in the story.

The comparative level of reading can involve many other kinds of writing, and, indeed, other media. For instance, many students are interested in the ways that a piece of writing is transformed from one medium to another, as when films are made of well-known books, such as the novel and film versions of Alice Walker's *The Color Purple*. But there are many other examples, some very controversial, such as the reworkings of children's classics by Walt Disney Studios, or the many film versions of Mary Shelley's *Frankenstein.* Other reworkings include taking a piece of fiction as a model for a text in another medium, as Francis Ford Coppola's *Apocalypse Now* did with Joseph Conrad's *Heart of Darkness.* Reading such texts at the comparative level (as well as at the other levels) would be a productive exercise. But the scope of such a reading can go further, so that a particular reading stressing social analysis or historical background can be read comparatively against another reading drawing on different disciplinary materials or a different historical context. Two studies of the American Revolution, for instance, can be read comparatively, or one can be read with prior knowledge of the other, so that throughout a critical reading at the comparative level there are grounds for questioning assumptions, assertions, and analysis of similar data. These kinds of comparative approaches to historical, social, economic, intellectual, or scientific data lead to the modifications of historical or scientific theories; therefore, this reading method is an important part of critical reading strategies.

Reading for Keeps: Summary

All that has been said in these sections on the four levels of reading concerning *Little Red Riding Hood* can be applied to other kinds of reading. When you have to read a scholarly article or book, the same levels of reading come into play. For instance, if in your sociology or psychology course you were assigned the chapter "Language Development" in *Child Development: An Introduction* by John Santrock and Steven Yussen (Dubuque: Wm C. Brown, 1992), your reading for content at the literal level would be a matter of simple comprehension of what the words mean. A number of technical terms about language are used (*morphology, phonology, syntax, surface* and *deep structure*), as well as some words concerning areas of the brain associated with language learning (*Broca's area* and *Wernicke's area*). While a number of definitions are given in the chapter, other terms (*biological evolution* and *abstract speech*, for example) are not explained, and some other words might be unfamiliar to some readers (*traversed, brain hemisphere, ingenious,* and so on). So the acquisition of the most literal reading of the article might take some time and work for an inexperienced reader.

If, however, you are a more experienced reader, with some knowledge of the field that you are reading in and perhaps even of the particular topic, your reading for content and meaning together moves you to a level of exposition: you are reading to follow the development of the ideas and you are seeking to link the content to the larger meanings that are being presented. In the chapter by Santrock and Yussen, you will perceive that the argument is arranged to examine first the definition and systems of rules of language, and then to consider how language is acquired. It is this latter part of the discussion that takes up the most space in the chapter (eight out of ten subdivisions). At the same time, as an experienced reader, you are also performing at an analytical level: you are attempting to understand the concepts as they are presented (content level), to place those concepts into the argument that the authors are making and to explain that argument (expository level), to relate that argument to the more general argument that the article and the book are making (context), and to analyze the means used to make that argument effective (analytical level). For instance, you would have observed that the chapter is divided into subsections, each with a heading and subcategories. The headings summarize what each subsection contains and help to keep the reader on track. So your comprehension of the major part of the chapter places in sequence the main points that are being made: in the process of biological evolution, humans have developed sophisticated means of acquiring language, and some thinkers, such as Noam Chomsky, argue that human brains are, so to speak, prewired with a language acquisition device (LAD), by which he means a predisposition or innate capability to acquire language. Other positions concerning language, which supplement the biological argument, stress the cultural context of language, and at least two schools of thought dispute the precise ways in which language is acquired: the psychological behaviourists and those who stress cognitive interaction. The final section of the chapter places these arguments into the context of other developmental processes, examining language acquisition in infancy, early childhood, and late childhood.

By reading for associations and implications at the comparative level, you can assess these different views in the light of your other knowledge. In one sense, this linking of language acquisition to other kinds of development (motor, visual recognition, and physical development) raises questions about the extent to which the developmental model is inherent or imposed. At the level of implications, the research into the acquisition of more than one language simultaneously, or at least by late childhood before the onset of puberty, raises questions about the role of bilingualism in education, a major issue in education in Canada and the United States. The article raises some of the socioeconomic dimensions of the problem in the largely unilingual United States, but the highly criticized bilingual education in Spanish in some of the states bordering on Mexico has greatly complicated education, with both supporters and detractors arguing that bilingual education socializes Spanish-speaking people to a servant class. In Canada, bilingualism is an educational and political issue, and multilingual education and heritage language funding crises raise additional implications for language acquisition when the implications of the chapter are applied to practical teaching situations.

Hence, the reading of the chapter with awareness of the various interfunctioning reading levels can help in a more effective comprehension. With increasing practice and familiarity with the critical reading practices, you can actively use a variety of these levels at the same time with comparatively little effort but impressive results.

Almost everything that you read at university can be read on these four different levels. That certainly will be true of the fiction that you might read in a social science course, or the films that you might see in a course on Dickens dealing with concepts of realism. But the same is true of almost everything that you read. One of the problems is that you likely try to read only for the content at the literal level; you are not quite certain what "content" you are supposed to get from the assignment, and even less certain about what points are going to be raised in class, unless there have been reading guides or in-class instructions about how to proceed. As a result, you often remain on the first or literal level, taking what is presented at its face value, whether in fiction, a scholarly article, or a book. Dominated by the urge to gain some command over the material, you resist all temptations to question, analyze, or summarize. No doubt that is a useful and necessary stage to go through: you must at least read the text through with understanding of the content at the literal level. But you should be aware of reading that makes use of other levels, too. As you become a more experienced reader by using the suggestions in this chapter, you will be able to incorporate the apparently separate levels of reading into one or two readings of the text, getting far more out of your reading than you thought possible at first. You will then have prepared yourself well for classroom discussions, writing assignments, and greater enjoyment of your reading and studies. These levels of reading are not restricted to the written word: increasingly, university courses include other media in their curricula.

READING FILMS AND TV CRITICALLY

Reading films and TV critically means that you use similar critical responses in viewing and analyzing films and TV as in reading texts in other media. At the very least, these readings involve drawing a distinction between subjective responses ("I like this or dislike that") and reasoned positions ("This works in the film because of that, and by this method"). Hence, the language and logic of films, their form and content, can be subjected to description and analysis. Similarly, TV has been subjected to much study concerning the use of episodes, soaps, serials, and specific programs. Part of this analysis is also devoted to the use of TV advertising, the use of one-minute clips in news broadcasts, music videos, and other forms of mass communication.

Most of the comments below relate to the reading of movies, but the methods can also be applied to the analysis of TV programs, since many of the same techniques are used in video production. To undertake a critical analysis, a first viewing is needed to comprehend the content of the film—such matters as the storyline, the rearrangement of chronology in terms of plotting, the use of characters, setting, dialogue, rising and falling action, and so on. Subsequent viewings for study enable you to analyze the transitions between scenes and shots more carefully, noting shifts in camera work, specific dialogue, details of the setting, symbolic elements, parallels from shot to shot in composition and framing, and various problems in the film, such as unexplained gaps in scene, dialogue, or detail.

Reading Narrative Discourse in Films and TV

Many students take notes while viewing a film for critical reading (possibly not at the first viewing, but often at the second or third). When you are using a film as one of the sources for one of your writing assignments, detailed notes or annotation are a necessity. In assessing these aspects of a film, you can draw parallels with reading fiction, noting particularly the following issues.

Chronology and Film Narrative

The distinction between the chronological "story" and the rearrangement of that story in terms of narrative discourse is widely exploited in films. The events or actions set out in the order in which they "happened" is known as the *histoire* (French for "story," "history"), a term borrowed from narrative theory or narratology. Films rarely represent the events or actions in the sequence in which they would occur in the real world. One exception is the documentary film, of World War II, for example, which attempts to present a narrative that makes breaks in space but not in time, so that a fairly strict sequence, often of cause and effect, is maintained. Films, on the other hand, take particular delight in rearranging the events so that they are full of flashbacks and flashforwards, as in *Catch-22*. But in most films this *histoire* never exists. A supposed chronology might underlie the film's frame-by-frame sequence, but viewers see only portions of the *histoire* rearranged in the film. The narrative discourse of a film, its *narrative,* is the sequence of retold events arranged in the order of scenes in the film.

Narrative Framing

Films usually use the formal frame of the title and cast in the beginning and end credits. But frequently the title and cast are overlaid visually and sonically on scenes from the film or opening background shots. In *Marat/Sade* the opening and closing credits are the title and credits entered a word at a time in silence. What is the effect of this stress on the linear and visual sequence of written text? In *Apocalypse Now* the opening and closing shots and the credits are different in various versions, but they provide important implications, contexts, and conclusions. For instance, the 70 mm version of the film concludes with Willard's leading Lance back to the patrol boat while the tribesmen and soldiers drop their weapons and a cleansing rain falls on all but Willard. Added to the 35 mm video version are the credits, which appear over the shots of an air attack destroying Kurtz's compound with napalm. What is the effect of the framing of the sound overlay of "This is the End" by *The Doors*? A different kind of formal narrative framing is used in the James Whale film of *Frankenstein,* in which one of the actors steps through a curtain (as on a stage) to warn the audience.

Time and Space

Time and space are manipulated in films with significant visual clues. In older films (here, Whale's *Frankenstein* films are particularly useful), the allusions to time and space are verbal as well as visual (the dialogue "Where is Henry?" anticipates a scene shift to where Henry is, in his lab). A cliché drawn from the captions used in silent films points to this shift in scene: "Meanwhile, back at the ranch...." Later films provide important transitions to the modern use of various kinds of cuts to indicate shifts and juxtapositions in time and space. *Anachronies* (or sequences out of time) and sequences without spatial logic (a coined term might be *anatopies*) are familiar to contemporary viewers of films, who have learned to read this new grammar partly from video clips and music videos. In music videos the sound sequence is sustained and continuous, but the visuals shift in time and space, partly according to the lyrics, partly according to the separate (and possibly only tangentially connected) narrative in the visuals. Woody Allen has experimented a good deal with these shifts in time and space, as have many other modern filmmakers.

Focalization

Focalization in films, as in fiction, is the vantage point from which events are "seen" or from which they are narrated visually. From information in the film, in the way that scenes are shot or directed, viewers are informed whose "eye" is seeing or who is narrating the scene. Sometimes that focalization is accomplished by the lens of the camera in a kind of objective scrutiny (external focalizer), and sometimes by a character, as in a dialogue when the focalization shifts from one to the other character (internal focalizers).

Metafiction

Metafiction draws attention to the process of making the film itself (sometimes called *metafilm*), as in *Apocalypse Now,* when an assault on a village includes Coppola himself making a film of the making of another film. The role of the photographer later in the movie is another reference to the notion of the image photographing itself. The self-consciousness of the filmic techniques is foregrounded in Resnais's *Night and Fog,* in which the focalization (then and now) is juxtaposed with documentary footage of Auschwitz. On the other hand, the notion of metafiction in *Marat/Sade* is more narrowly focused on the notion of the drama of making a drama. How far are these notions incorporated in metafilmic implications in the film?

Signification and Film Syntax

In the last three decades, critics of films and film theorists have been much influenced by the work of Ferdinand de Saussure and other structuralists and post-structuralists. To them the notion of the film sign, or signification, and of the grammar and logic of a film, or its syntax and structure, are very important analytical tools. In spoken and written language, a signifier is the word or sound (the word *tree,* for instance), while a signified is the concept that the word evokes (the concept of tree). Together, these elements constitute a linguistic sign, the building block of language and communication. The signifier in film is usually considered the image (or even a single frame). But the signified is more difficult to define and to isolate from the signifier in films. One critic, Christian Metz, thinks that in the cinematic sign the signifier and the signified are almost identical since the image of anything— a tree, a rose, a person—comes very close to expressing its concept. While a film is not a language, it functions *like* a language, with its significance, scenes, sequences, and syntax. Signs function within this order and make sense within the logic of the film, and their signifieds work there, not independently of other connotations that the signifieds have in other language systems (such as English), but in concert with those associations and conventions. The syntax of films has also changed as the technology has changed, so that we can accept all sorts of shifts in perspective and cuts that earlier viewers could not accept. In earlier films, links in the plot had to be explained either through captions in the silents or through sequences that allowed for the shifts (which is one reason that some earlier films seem particularly slow). The syntax, then, usually involves the modifications to time and space and the conventions of filmmaking that allow for those categories of "reality" to be indicated.

The modification of space is referred to as *mise en scène* (French for "put into the scene"): the positioning of the actors in the setting, the angles and lenses of the cameras—all that takes place on the movie sound set or an actual location. Composition, meaning the arrangement of the details of the scene as a visual composition (including planes, perspective, balance of objects, angles, and so on), is an essential part of the mise en scène. In *Marat/Sade,* for instance, the love scene between Corday and Duperret, in which they are sitting on the same bench, with golden light coming through the sheet behind them, gives to the scene all of the traditional romantic connotations of two lovers in a park at sunset. The composition of the scene underlines those associations. However, these associations are undercut by the irony of the attempted seduction that continually overtakes the romantic love song that Corday sings and by the actual words of her song. The various kinds of shots (see page 91) contribute to the effect of the mise en scène.

The modification of time is called *montage* (French for "putting together"), the cutting that takes place in the editing room to juxtapose different shots and to interpose different time conditions. See the different kinds of cuts described at the end of this page.

Metonymy is also often used in films, as in literary or other texts, to indicate the part standing for the whole, so that the spinning of train wheels indicates travel; the flipping of calendar pages, the passing of time; the hand on the forehead, thinking; and the shot of marching feet, an army.

Film Genres and Film History

Genre studies and the historical study of films have also had an impact on film study and criticism. The conventions whereby films are classified according to accepted types are fairly well established. In your local video store, for instance, films are classified according to such genres as war, adventure, horror, musical, drama, classic, children's, adult, and so on, often without much clear information about what makes a film fit into one category or another. To what extent are the literary terms we have been using applicable to film? Do film genres have institutionally sanctioned criteria concerning narrative, plot lines, and expected audience identification and reaction? You might consider, for instance, the wide critical literature available on the horror/slasher films or on the *Frankenstein* industry, with the crossover between romance and horror.

Understanding Technical Terms

The following technical terms are often used in film production, criticism, and analysis to describe the formal structure of scenes, camera work, and editing.

Cuts

- *Straight cut:* A transition from one scene to another with no intermediary footage.
- *Intercut:* An interjection of one cut into a sequence, often for irony.
- *Crosscuts:* Cutting back and forth from one scene to another, often to communicate a sense of urgency or parallel action.
- *Jump cut:* Showing the beginning and end of an action and leaving the viewer to supply the interim action, as when a character enters a room and is immediately at the destination.
- *Dissolve:* Merging one scene into another—related to *form cuts,* where the shape of one image on the screen suggests the shape of the next image; superimposing a fade-

out with a fade-in. Both are used now to shift from black and white to colour, from one colour hue to another, or from one intensity to another.

- *Fade-out:* The screen gets darker as the image disappears.
- *Fade-in:* The screen changes from black as the image gradually emerges into full brightness.
- *Iris:* A new scene appears in the centre of the old scene and expands to take over the screen; uncommon today, but still used in some films to give the feel of the early days of the movies.
- *Wipe:* The scene is wiped off from one side to another; or one shot shoves another off the screen.

Shots

- *Long shot:* A general setting, with full figures of the subjects.
- *Medium shot:* The object is shown in its immediate context.
- *Close-up:* The camera is stable, the lens moves (cf. *zoom, zoom freeze*) to show the subject's face or any object close at hand.
- *Pan shot:* The camera swings from left to right or right to left, and the base is stable.
- *Tilt shot:* The camera aims up or down while fixed on its axis.
- *High- or low-angle shot:* As described.
- *Overlap shots:* Several shots of the same scene from different angles.
- *Two-shot:* A shot of two people (also a three-shot).
- *Tracking:* A single, continuous shot made with a moving camera, where the relationship and distance between the subject and the camera are constant.
- *Zoom:* The focal length of the camera lens is changed as the camera zooms in on the scene or on a detail, greatly shifting the relationship between the camera (the viewer) and the subject.

Montage

This technique includes the impressionistic juxtaposition of brief shots, but it refers especially to the process of controlling the manipulation of time in film by cutting and editing to combine shots of apparently unrelated material, generating new, meaningful relationships. Famous instances of the use of montage include Eisenstein's treatment of the Odessa Steps in *Battleship Potemkin* (1925) or of the battle on the lake in *Alexander Nevsky* (1938), or more recently the shower murder in Hitchcock's *Psycho* (1959) and the park and disappearing body scene in Antonioni's *Blowup* (1966).

Mise en scène

Mise en scène refers to what takes place on the set and so is the opposite of montage. Literally, it is "the putting into the scene"—the use of the set or location, the direction of the actors, placement of cameras, choice of lenses, and so on—to determine the use of space in shots and scenes.

Frame

Frame refers to the single image on the film but also to the compositional unit of design in each image. Frames may be open, bounded, closed, or marked out with lines in the composition parallel to or echoing the shapes in the image.

FURTHER READINGS

Critical Reading Practice

Benner, Patricia Ann. *Breakthroughs in Critical Reading Skills.* Chicago: Contemporary Books, 1996.

Cheek, Earl H., and Martha D. Collins. *Strategies for Reading Success.* Columbus, OH: Merrill, 1985.

Knight, Theodore O. *Mastering College Reading.* Chicago: Irwin, 1995.

Phillips, Anne Dye, and Peter Elias Sotiriou. *Steps to Reading Proficiency.* 2nd ed. Belmont, CA: Wadsworth, 1987.

Speed Reading

Berg, Howard S., and Marcus Conyers. *Speed Reading: The Easy Way.* New York: Barrons, 1998.

Buzan, Tony. *Use Your Head.* London: BBC Books, 1995.

Carver, Ronald P. "Speed Readers Don't Read; They Skim." *Psychology Today* Aug. 1972: 22–30.

Dudley, Geoffrey A. *Speed Reading.* London: Thomson, 1977.

Frank, Steven. *Speed Reading Secrets.* Holbrook, MA: Backpack Books, 1998.

Smith, Nila Banton. *Speed Reading Made Easy.* New York: Time Warner, 1966.

Films and Television

Allen, Robert C., ed. *Channels of Discourse.* Chapel Hill: U of North Carolina P, 1987.

Bluestone, George. *Novels into Film.* Berkeley: U of California P, 1961.

Bordwell, David, and Kristin Thompson. *Film Art: An Introduction.* Reading, MA: Addison Wesley, 1980.

Burnett, Ron, ed. *Explorations in Film Theory.* Bloomington: U of Indiana P, 1991.

Cook, David A. *A History of Narrative Film.* New York: Norton, 1981.

Deleuze, Gilles. *Cinema.* 2 vols. Minneapolis: U of Minnesota P, 1986–89.

Fiske, John, and John Hartley. *Reading Television.* London: Routledge, 1989.

Goodwin, Andrew, and Garry Whannel, eds. *Understanding Television.* London: Routledge, 1990.

Kellner, Douglas. *Media Culture: Cultural Studies, Identity and Politics between the Modern and the Postmodern.* London: Routledge, 1995.

Lipsitz, George. *Time Passages: Collective Memory in American Popular Culture.* Minneapolis: U of Minnesota P, 1990.

Mast, Gerald, Marshall Cohen, and Leo Braudy, eds. *Film Theory and Criticism.* New York: Oxford UP, 1992.

McCabe, Colin. *Theoretical Essays: Film, Linguistics, Literature.* Manchester: Manchester UP, 1985.

Monaco, James. *How to Read a Film: The Art, Technology, Language, History, and Theory of Film and Media.* New York: Oxford UP, 1981.

Spottiswoode, Raymond. *A Grammar of the Film.* Berkeley: U of California P, 1959.

WEBLINKS

Critical Reading Practice

- Columbia University
  www.columbia.edu/cu/augustine/study/focus.html

- Dartmouth College
  www.dartmouth.edu/admin/acskills/lsg/reading.html

- Georgia State University
  www.gsu.edu/~wwwrtp

- York University
  www.yorku.ca/cdc/lsp/read/read1.htm

Speed Reading

Some computer sites offer software to help learn speed-reading techniques. A number that cost between $20 and $500 can be checked out at:

- Self-Growth
  www.selfgrowth.com/reading.html

- RocketReader
  www.rocketreader.com

- Acereader
  www.stepware.com/acereader.html

Films and Television

- Film and TV publications online from University of Alabama
  www.tcf.ua.edu/ScreenSite/res/pub/

- J. Purcell's Cinemaniac
  www.mtsu.edu/~jpurcell/Cinema/maincinema2.htm

BUILDING A CRITICAL VOCABULARY

C h a p t e r

4

EXTENDING YOUR VOCABULARY

From earliest childhood we make sounds, at first babbling to indicate happiness or crying to indicate needs, but by the age of three we are well on our way to learning a basic vocabulary, and by the age of six we have a vocabulary of between 5000 and 8000 words. By the early teen years that number has increased fourfold to 30 or 40 000 words. The average adult has a vocabulary of about 50 000 words (Breland, Jones, and Jenkins 2). These numbers can seem intimidating, since most people have no idea how many words they know or can control. But the problem is much greater, as Breland and his colleagues report in *The College Board Vocabulary Study:*

> A large vocabulary is difficult to acquire and maintain because many important words occur infrequently in a language. [One study] found that only about 3,000 words occurred more than 10 times per million words of running text and only about 10,000 words occurred more than once per million words of running text. If a college student is to maintain a vocabulary of 50,000 words, four-fifths of those words will be encountered relatively infrequently in normal reading and thus must be stored in memory for long periods of time. (2)

The College Board study attempts to indicate the levels of expertise that advanced high school and first-year university students have with a core vocabulary and how well they fare in defining more difficult words. Many teachers are aware that their students have a limited grasp of many of the words that are used in lectures and readings for courses. The incidence of vocabulary failure increases dramatically when the materials are either technical or literary. Students have considerable difficulty with the vocabulary on any page of a novel by Charles Dickens or a play by Shakespeare. In a recent classroom exercise, the authors found that students could not comprehend the meaning of many fairly common words in a short essay by a Victorian novelist. In one sample, out of a class of thirty students, ten or more admitted (more might have been uncertain of the words but did not admit it) they could not understand the meaning of the following words: *adduced, allegory, burlesque, cockney, postulates,* and *sonata.* Five or more could not identify the following: *assail, breadth, consorting, embodiment, engendering, mastery, vitality.* In a lead article on homework in *Time* magazine, the following words occurred on one page, almost all of which would cause difficulty for many university students: *acclimates, almanac, bolster, confound, diorama, gauge, loquacious, ratcheted, requisite, rigor, rote, scant, decade,* and *sonata* (Ratnesar 38).

Some philosophers and psychologists think that our ability to know anything is directly related to the size and functioning of our vocabulary. Without language we might still be able to think (though some studies of "wild children" who are raised with no human contact or language raise important questions about how the critical functions of the brain are limited by language and vocabulary impairment), but without an adequate vocabulary we cannot organize or communicate what we know.

What, then, can you do to build a more effective vocabulary? One easy answer is to read more effectively. The *College Board Vocabulary Study* estimates that children learn between 800 and 1200 words a year from their reading. You should aim to learn at least double that number of words during each year of your university study. As your vocabulary increases, you will read faster and more accurately, and you will be able to communicate your ideas more effectively in oral and written presentations.

TIPS: Improving Your Vocabulary

1. Carry a pocket dictionary with you and use it frequently to check words you are uncertain about.

2. Keep a vocabulary book and enter unfamiliar words as you read.

3. At the end of a week, go through your vocabulary book, write out the ten most important words for the week with brief definitions on sticky notes, and put them on your mirror.

4. Use an association method (*mnemonics,* or memory jogging) to help you learn the words.

5. Go over the words each night as you brush your teeth, and check the meanings in the morning. When you are certain you know them, replace the sticky note with a new one.

6. Learn to recognize the roots of words, especially if you know any languages other than English.

7. Learn some basic prefixes and suffixes to see how the meanings of words are modified (see the section on these last two tips on page 114).

The most effective method for vocabulary building is to be methodical. You should mark unfamiliar words in your reading (many students use a small *x* in their own books, or note words from library books in their own vocabulary books). You can figure out definitions from the context and note that down, or you can look up a number of them in your dictionary at the end of a reading period. If you are power reading, you should not pause to look up words, since that will slow you down, but should remember to look them up at the end of your reading session. You can keep your own reading dictionary as a file in your computer and add words as you come across them. In the evening, you can add to the dictionary words that you jotted down during the day in your reading or at lectures. In this way you maintain a continuous review. Each week you should set aside some time to review the words more systematically, focusing on a page or on several letters. Above all, keeping a good dictionary at your desk or accessing a good dictionary on the Web (sometimes access is difficult or slow because of the number of clients trying to get onto your server, so the desk dictionary is always a safer bet) should be a routine part of your study habits.

In the sections that follow we discuss what you can learn from a dictionary, what kinds of dictionaries you will use regularly and what kinds you will need only from time to time, and ways to build vocabulary through a knowledge of word sources (in other languages, or through root words in English) and word parts (such as prefixes and suffixes). But first, it is important to distinguish between dictionary meanings and definitions (denotation) and contextual associations (connotation).

DENOTATION AND CONNOTATION

The meaning of any word is the result of a long process of social agreements and language usage stretching back through several thousand years of language history. Meaning is not inherent in words but is the result of usage and agreements, so that any word, say *tree,* is used in English to designate specific phenomena, in this case both evergreen and deciduous plants with a large, single trunk and many branches. The ancestry of the word can be traced to the Anglo-Saxon word *treo* and to similar words in other Scandinavian languages (Icelandic *tre;* Danish *træ;* Swedish *trä*). The word also is allied to the Russian *drevo* (the letters *t* and *d* being variants in some languages), all from the Greek *drus* (an oak tree) and the Sanskrit *dru* (a tree). Other languages derive their word for *tree* from different language roots, so that the French *arbre,* the Italian *albero,* and the Spanish *arbol* may be traced back to the Latin *arbor* (a word that is also used in English). The sound and shape of a word is determined by its difference from other words and by its likeness to other words in its family (such as plurals, adjectives, and adverbs).

This long process of the development and changing of words and their meanings results in both fairly precise definitions and also suggestions of implications. Precise definitions are called *denotations,* and associations of words with other words and implications are called *connotations.* That is, denotation is what the word means according to dictionary definitions, while connotation is what a word suggests by usage and context. Many students remember the difference by aligning the first letter of each with its major basis of meaning:

denotation = dictionary definition

connotation = contextual or association meaning

Denotation

Denotation is the explicit meaning as determined by a dictionary. A dictionary summarizes the root of the word and gives the literal and established meanings for a term, often providing information about how usage has modified the definition over time. Such denotations will help you understand the subtle differences in meanings between words that might seem alike or that might even have the same definition in a thesaurus or shorter word guide but that have, in fact, very different shades of meaning. However, dictionaries, especially concise or desktop dictionaries, often define by listing synonyms, which, when examined more closely for *their* definitions in a larger dictionary, can be shown to have quite different shades of meaning. For instance, in a popular dictionary published at the beginning of the twentieth century, *Chambers's Twentieth Century Dictionary,* the word *thin* is said to mean "having little thickness: slim: lean," and so on. So it might be appropriate to speak of a particular book or a person as *thin.* It would also be proper to speak of the same person as slim, but if the book were spoken of as slim, that would mean that its contents were slight or not intellectually challenging. Indeed, to speak of the person as *lean* would suggest that, as with bacon, there is little fat or all muscle, meanings that are not involved in the word *thin.* That is, the synonyms are not always perfect matches in more abbreviated dictionaries. To get the fuller definitions you have to use the larger dictionaries. Other synonyms, such as those given as possible alternatives for *thin* in a thesaurus, such as *slender, bony, gaunt, flimsy, trim, narrow,* or *slim,* raise many more problems of appropriateness and push denotation back to the level of connotation, where the implications of particular words and their use in context come into play.

One of the frustrations of using a dictionary, especially the brief paperback dictionary that many students find useful to carry to class but continue to use when doing more advanced academic work, is precisely the problem of synonyms. When you are uncertain of the denotation of a word, you might look the word up in a dictionary, only to be faced with a series of synonyms that are equally mystifying. Such is especially the case with technical or scientific terms ("*Cumin*: an umbelliferous plant common in Egypt"; "*Pecten:* a genus of molluscs"). The denotation of many words can be confusing. For instance, the word *pedant* is defined in *Chambers's* as "one who makes a vain display of learning," but the word *vain* might present further problems, since the meanings given for it include "unsatisfying: fruitless: unreal: silly: conceited: showy: vacant: worthless"—all of which do not apply equally to the word *pedant.* The denotations *conceited* and *showy* best apply to the kind of "display of learning" that a pedant would exhibit, though a reader seeking enlightenment would have to dig further to find a way through this thicket.

Still, the problem remains. Often an essay topic introduces problems in terminology, perhaps derived from the course, from the text examined, or from the pertinent critical commentaries. To clarify procedures and method, such terms should be defined, since they might be open to confusion or misunderstanding. Most students think that they can solve the central problem of the interpretation by finding a short dictionary definition. However, such a denotative meaning might be too short, wrong, or insufficiently focused on the materials of a course. It is often best to use course materials to arrive at such definitions. For instance, a course might use the concepts of gender, race, and class to discuss important readings. An essay on a topic that requires consideration of ways that gender codes function in some of the readings might require that notions of masculinity, femininity, gender and genderism, and so on, be discussed. Many short dictionaries will not define such terms helpfully for developing a comprehensive argument. It would be better to use a specialized dictionary or encyclopedia, such as Maggie Humm's *Dictionary of Feminist Theory* or Lisa Tuttle's *Encyclopedia of Feminism*. But perhaps the best approach would be to use the definitions used in the course, given in lectures, or provided in the texts being examined. In this way, problems of misunderstanding are avoided, and the discussion is far more likely to be directly related to the topic.

Connotation

Connotation refers to the associations of a word, drawn partly from how a word is used in a sentence, partly from the other associations that a word has in related or even different uses, and partly from the social context in which the word is used. The word *horse,* for instance, signifies a quadruped that eats grain, but that definition can be applied to many other animals— for instance, to a mule, an ox, or a cow—as well as to different types of horses—broncos, ponies, colts, steeds, stallions, studs, thoroughbreds, and so on, each with different connotations. Similarly, the word *car* can mean very different things in different contexts. It can mean the new car in advertising: it can suggest freedom and power as it drives over empty highways in desert sunsets, or over rocky mountain terrain that no sensible driver would ever traverse. Or it can mean family values, as mom, dad, three kids, and a dog get in the car with their stuff and head for the family cottage. Or it can mean the getaway car associated with a bank holdup, the problem for the city planners, the ecological nightmare, and so on. The connotation of *car,* then, depends on the associations that refer to the way of life of the user, the conventional codes associated with the word in a culture in general, and the use of the word in a particular context. Furthermore, other words for *car* that carry the same denotation (or dictionary meaning) might have very different connotations. For instance, many car-rental firms advertise "rent a car," and others, somewhat downscale, advertise "rent a wreck," with roughly the same denotation but with the distinct connotation of a car in less reliable shape and at a more modest rate. The terms *automobile, auto,* and *motorcar* all suggest a more archaic period, probably before the 1950s. The term *vehicle* is a generic category much loved by government licensing bureaus, and the term *wheels* is teen slang from the 1960s.

Such connotations have all kinds of social values, both positive and negative, attached. For instance, in the three categories of odour, human weight, and mistakes, it is possible to draw up words that indicate roughly the same meaning but that have very different positive and negative connotations.

Category	Negative	Positive
odour	smell	scent
weight	skinny	slender
mistake	screw-up	slip

In another example, the term *buck* denotes the male of the deer, goat, hare, and rabbit, especially the male of the fallow deer. In a recent legal judgment in Ontario in the case of Terri-Jean Bedford, a dominatrix known as Madame de Sade, Judge Roy Bogusky acknowledged that there was "overkill" on the part of the fifteen officers who entered her premises to investigate and possibly arrest her. There was, according to the judge, no reason to submit Bedford to a body search, and "she was not well done by." However, he excused the rowdiness of officers who donned wigs and had mock whip fights as the understandable actions of "young bucks" exposed to an unusual environment (Levy A6). Here, the connotation of "young bucks" has aroused the rage of many people because it is a way of excusing police actions in the name of stereotypical gender roles. The comments are widely seen as sexist. The term "bucks" carries with it the connotation of aggressive pranksterism, or of the good-natured, wholesome sport of males having mildly sexual fun—when the context demands something quite different. So the judge's use of the phrase, his connotation, excuses the officers on the basis of their youthful masculinity; to justice watchers, feminists, and people concerned about the implications of legal language, the term has the connotation of excusing conduct on the basis of sexism.

Connotations also carry social codes and values and can be read for their political power and ideological content. For instance, when a newspaper reports on a strike, the two opposing sides refer to the same stage in their proceedings by different terms that emphasize their political positions. Hence, the union leaders stress the "strike demands," while the CEOs stress the "management offer," and these values are set in order based on their relative positions in the dominant power hierarchies of the opposing sides:

To the CEOs:

Negative connotations	Positive connotations
strike demands	management offer
bargaining position	settlement process

To the union leaders:

Negative connotations	Positive connotations
management offer	strike demands
settlement process	bargaining position

DICTIONARIES AND WHAT THEY TELL YOU

Dictionaries come in many shapes, sizes, and range; they can be encyclopedic and make claims of recording all of the words in a language, or they can be brief word lists with simple definitions; they can be devoted to a particular topic (dictionaries of metals, chemical formulae, literary terms) or directed to a particular audience (dictionaries for new learners of a language, for high school students, and so on). Some knowledge of how most dictionaries work is a useful tool in becoming a better reader. The preface in a dictionary explains the conventions used, the ordering of the alphabet and the system used in the word entries, and the special marks and abbreviations that indicate pronunciation, usage, and derivation. Entries in dictionaries usually include abbreviations (either as a part of the main word list or in a special section of abbreviations at the back of the book). Hyphenated words or compound words are also included (for example, *lynx-eyed*). Some dictionaries also include foreign words or phrases that are often used in English, such as *fait accompli, gesundheit,* or *homo sapiens,* though, again, they may be listed at the back of the book. Some desk and student dictionaries (such as *The Canadian Oxford Dictionary*) include encyclopedic entries, such as short biographical and geographical identifications, and illustrations.

You may use a good dictionary regularly for conventional spellings and meanings (such as *The Concise Oxford Dictionary*, *The American Heritage Dictionary*, *The Random House College Dictionary*, or *Webster's Ninth New Collegiate Dictionary*). But it is recommended that you consult the *The Oxford English Dictionary (OED)* in twenty volumes for detailed historical commentary on words (see "Parts of Speech," on page 101) when you need technical or literary definitions.

Usually, a dictionary provides the information in the sections that follow.

Spelling and Syllabification

The usual spelling (or *orthography*) of a word is given first, and variants are usually noted, such as differences between British and American spelling. The entry word also shows capitalization. The word is divided into syllables, an easy way to determine where the word should be hyphenated at the end of a line. Different principles for dividing words into syllables are used in Great Britain and Canada and in the United States. In Britain and Canada words are divided according to derivation, so that the smallest meaning-parts of words (morphemes) make up the basis of syllables (for instance, *know-ledge*). In the United States words are divided into syllables according to pronunciation (for instance, *knowl-edge*). Such differences have important implications for both phonics in learning to read through familiarization with conventional syllables and for learning to spell. In both systems, however, the same general rules for dividing words apply (see Box 4.2). Modern newspapers use computer dictionaries to divide words, but often the divisions are arbitrary and make nonsense words or comical splits, such as *bar-bed, forest-all, mans-laughter, men-swear, ong-oing, real-locations, roman-tic, sung-lasses, superb-owl, wee-knights, line-age* (culled from the *Globe and Mail*, 1998).

Pronunciation

After the word heading, the pronunciation is given, often in parentheses, and variants and annotation may indicate special uses or regional differences. Some dictionaries use re-spellings to indicate the pronunciation of each syllable according to a phonic method. Others use special typographical symbols or diacritical marks, explained either at the bottom of the page in brief form or in a longer form at the beginning of the book. Increasingly, the

---

BOX 4.1   *Dictionary "Dos" and "Don'ts"*

■ Do use your dictionary to learn the meaning and use of unfamiliar words.

■ Do not use general dictionaries to reduce complex terms in your courses or writing to simplistic definitions. An essay on the Holocaust or Totalitarianism might need complex definitions of terms. Simple dictionary definitions are not helpful in beginning an essay.

■ Do define technical terms in a course (such as *fantasy, romance, horror, obsession,* or *monster*) through course readings or lectures, specialized subject dictionaries, or the *OED*.

BOX 4.2 | **Syllabification**

■ Words are divided after a vowel *(a, e, i, o, u)* so that the next syllable begins with a consonant.

■ Where a single vowel is a syllable in the middle of a word, the word is split after the syllabic vowel (e.g., *physi-cal, he-si-tant*; not *phy-si-cal* or *hesit-ant* or *hes-i-tant*).

■ Double consonants are usually separated in syllables *(mil-len-ni-um).*

■ Two consonants are usually separated *(ad-ver-si-ty).*

■ Single-syllable words are not divided.

■ Prefixes and suffixes (such as *con-, pre-, mis-, -tion,* or *-ing*) are a single syllable, and it is preferable to break the word after a prefix or before a suffix rather than elsewhere.

International Phonetic Alphabet is being used, and older dictionaries that are reprinted often convert older systems to this international standard.

Parts of Speech

After the indication of pronunciation, the part of speech is identified by means of an abbreviation. Many of these abbreviations are obvious: *n.* (noun), *adj.* (adjective), *adv.* (adverb), *conj.* (conjunction), *interj.* (interjection), *prep.* (preposition), *pron.* (pronoun), and *v.* (verb). Some dictionaries (chiefly the *Oxford* series) use the abbreviation *sb.* (substantive) for nouns. If you do not recognize any others, you may identify them in the list of abbreviations in the front matter of the dictionary. When a word functions as more than one part of speech, for instance as both a noun and a verb (such as *fly,* which can be used to mean both a winged insect and moving through the air), the meanings for one part of speech are given together before the meanings for the other. Some dictionaries list the nouns first (the *Oxford* series, for instance), while others list verbs first.

From this point, dictionaries differ in the order of information given, though usually they provide similar kinds of information.

BOX 4.3 | **Typographical Conventions of Hyphens**

■ Do not leave one or two letters at the end of a line before a hyphen.

■ Do not put fewer than three letters on the next line.

■ Do not divide the last word in a paragraph or the last word on a page.

Etymology

All dictionaries, except for the smallest pocket dictionaries, provide some explanation of a word's origins, sometimes before the definitions (as in the *Oxford* and *Webster's* dictionaries), sometimes after. For students these explanations of word origins are often puzzling because of unfamiliar abbreviations, typographical symbols, and foreign words. But this information is often very useful in indicating shades of meaning and in pointing to a word's history. Usually a dictionary will use an opening symbol, such as < or — to indicate that the word in English is "from, taken from, or derived from" a word in another language, indicated by an abbreviation such as those in Box 4.4. Some dictionaries (like *The Shorter Oxford*), give Greek roots in Greek, so some knowledge of the Greek alphabet is necessary to read these words; other dictionaries usually transliterate other language scripts (the Cyrillic alphabet for Russian, Arabic, and so on) into the Latin alphabet.

Restrictions of Usage

Dictionaries usually indicate any usage limitations, either in time (old, rare, obsolete, or archaic usage: e.g., *avaunt* or *aroint* to mean "begone"), or by different classes of society, language groups, regional communities, or forms of discourse. Hence, some uses are informal or colloquial (such as abbreviated verb forms, *I'll, can't, couldn't,* which are acceptable

---

BOX 4.4	**Common Abbreviations Used in Etymologies**

AS	Anglo-Saxon
F	French
G	German
Gk	Greek
Hindu	Hindustani
Indo-E	Indo-European
Ital	Italian
L	Latin
ME	Middle English
OE	Old English
Scand	Scandinavian
Skt	Sanskrit
Sp	Spanish

Abbreviations used in etymologies to indicate the ways in which words are derived from their source languages:

a.	adopted without change in form or pronunciation
ad.	derived by adaptation
f.	from, or formed on (that is, a word in English formed on the basis of a foreign word)

in conversation though not in formal writing), others are slang *(butt, rip off, screw)* or vulgar. Vulgar usage may refer to semiliterate usage *(ain't)* or to terms with sexual or scatological references that are not generally acceptable in formal public discourse *(ass, shit)*. Some words that formerly were vulgarisms, especially swear words, have now moved up to slang or informal words in the conventional hierarchy of acceptable usage *(Hell! Damn!)*. Some words belong to a local dialect (*crick* for creek), and some may be poetic usage (*aweary* for "weary," *even* for "evening"). Some dictionaries explain any peculiar uses of a word in detail. Any use of a word in a specialized field of knowledge is also indicated (for instance, *med.* for medical, *chem.* for chemical, or *nav.* for naval terminology).

Definitions

The list of meanings is the reason most people use a dictionary. Users of a dictionary should be aware that the meanings are not set out randomly, but according to one of two organizational principles: some dictionaries give meanings in chronological order *(Oxford* and *Webster's)*, beginning with the meaning that entered the language at the earliest date; others try to give the most common meaning first, followed by more minor meanings and specialized ones, and grouping related meanings close together *(Random House* and *American Heritage)*. This latter method of organization eliminates much of the history of a word, but it gives faster access to the most common meaning. In either method, the meanings of a word are grouped according to the part of speech. That is, all of the uses for a noun are given first (for instance, *fly* as a noun would include the insect, a baseball hit into the air, a flap in clothing to cover buttons or a zipper in trousers, a fish hook used in fishing for trout, the space backstage and above the stage where the scenery can be hoisted and stored on ropes, and a light, double-seated coach drawn by a horse); the meanings for the verb follow (to move through the air on wings, to flee, to cause to fly, as *to fly a kite,* and so on). Meanings are usually given by a brief statement, in a phrase or a single word. More complex meanings have expanded definitions, sometimes with an indication of special idiomatic usage, such as which preposition follows a particular word (for example, *adhere* may be defined as "stick fast [*to*]"; or particular uses of the verb *to read* might need fuller explanation: *to read into something* means to read more meaning into something than the text warrants; *to read out of* means to expel, as to expel from a political party). Most desk and reference dictionaries also include definitions that illustrate a particular sense with a phrase or sentence, adding a level of connotation to the denotative meaning. Dictionaries based on historical principles date these examples and indicate the sources. You should read the prefatory material in the dictionary that you own and be aware of some of the conventions of those that you most often consult in the libraries or on the Web.

TIP: Using the Dictionary

Be wary of brief pocket dictionaries that do not give full enough definitions or etymologies. Pocket dictionaries often provide definitions only by means of synonyms, the meaning of which may be no clearer than the original word. A user then has to look up several words until a meaning that is understood is reached, and by that point, all of the shades of meaning will be lost.

Derived Forms

Dictionaries normally list the words that are derived from the main entry word, either within the same entry but following the definitions of the main entry or in separate entries in alphabetical order (for instance, *read* might be followed by definitions for *readability, readable, reader, readership,* and *reading*).

Compound and Combination Words

Compound words are those that use the main word or its derivative together with another word, with or without a hyphen *(reading-desk, livingroom)*. Combination words are those that combine two words together into one idea *(reading room, income tax),* though the distinction between compound and combination words is not hard and fast. When meanings are not evident or easily inferred from the words that make up a compound word, dictionaries usually give additional definitions, either as subheadings under the main entries or as separate entries.

Related Words

Modern English words that are not easily recognized as being closely related may, in fact, be derived from the same root, though their subsequent history has been different. For instance, the word *fancy* is an abbreviation of *fantasy*, and the words *essay* (trying or testing, an attempt, a short composition on any subject) and *assay* (a testing of the virtues or qualities of a thing or person) are related because both are adopted from the Old French *assai, assay,* and *essai*, from the Latin *exagium* (weighing), and from the verbs *exagere* and *exigere* (to weigh, examine, or test). Most dictionaries draw attention to these relationships by some system of cross-referencing (using *see* or the Latin abbreviation *cf.* [*confere,* compare]) to an entry with additional information.

Synonyms and Antonyms

Synonyms are words with meanings close to the entry word, though shadings of differences and different connotations mean that no two words are exact synonyms. Accordingly, many dictionaries (the *Thorndike-Barnhart High School Dictionary*, for instance), provide more extended discussions of synonyms to explain usage and shadings of meaning. *Antonyms* are words that are opposite in meaning to the entry word. A *thesaurus* is a book or collection of words or information, but the term is usually applied to a work that lists synonyms systematically.

Usage Notes

Particular phrases might have special meanings, might be used in special circumstances, or might be undergoing changing usage. Some dictionaries indicate which word is generally accepted or preferred when there is a confusion between words (such as *accept* and *except* or *disinterested* and *uninterested*), when a word takes a particular preposition *(adherent to),* or in other instances of idioms or conventional practice.

There are many sites on the Web related to dictionaries. Some consist of English and foreign language dictionaries, and others provide introductions to dictionary work and links to other sites. A general site is Doctor Dictionary (**www.dictionary.com/**).

For general information on dictionaries by the major publishers, see the publishers' Web sites, as, for instance, that of Longmans (**www.awl-elt.com/dictionaries/**).

KINDS OF DICTIONARIES

Dictionaries that university students use are generally of five different kinds:

- pocket dictionaries
- desk dictionaries
- reference dictionaries
- foreign language dictionaries
- special subject dictionaries

Pocket Dictionaries

Mass-market paperback dictionaries can be carried to class and are useful on a daily basis for quickly identifying meanings that you are unfamiliar with in your reading. You usually cannot consult them during lectures, since you will be too busy taking notes: in lectures you should write down unfamiliar words as they sound and asterisk or otherwise mark them in the margins to be checked once you get home and revise your notes. Pocket dictionaries usually cost between five and ten dollars. All have about 100 000 word entries and additional user helps such as lists of abbreviations. Suitable choices are the following:

American Heritage Dictionary. 3rd ed. New York: Laureleaf, 1995. 60 000 word entries.

The Merriam-Webster Dictionary. Springfield: Merriam-Webster, 1995. 70 000 word entries.

The New American Webster Handy College Dictionary. Ed. Philip D. Morehead. New York: Signet, 1995. 115 000 word entries.

Oxford American Dictionary. Ed. Eugene Erlich and Stuart Berg Flexner. New York: Avon, 1983. 70 000 word entries.

Pocket Oxford Dictionary and Thesaurus: American Edition. Ed. Frank R. Abate. New York: Oxford UP, 1999. 50 000 word entries.

Pocket Oxford Dictionary of Current English. 8th ed. Ed. Della Thompson. Oxford: Clarendon, 1996. 140 000 word entries.

Desk Dictionaries

Most dictionary publishers produce a substantial dictionary that is not as complete as a reference work, but far more complete than the pocket dictionary. It should at least contain more than single-word definitions and word origins. Your instructors might recommend a desk dictionary, and a variety will be available in your university bookstore. Examples of desk dictionaries that will continue to be useful long after university include the following:

The American Heritage Dictionary of the English Language. 3rd ed. Ed. Anne H. Soukhanov. Boston: Houghton Mifflin, 1992. 350 000 word entries.

The Canadian Oxford Dictionary. Ed. Katherine Barber. Toronto: Oxford UP, 1998. 130 000 word entries.

The Concise Oxford Dictionary of Current English. 9th ed. Ed. Della F. Thompson. Oxford: Clarendon, 1995. 150 000 word entries.

The Merriam-Webster's Collegiate Dictionary. 10th ed. Springfield: Merriam-Webster, 1998. 215 000 word entries.

Webster's New World College Dictionary. 3rd ed. New York: Macmillan, 1997. 150 000 word entries.

Webster's Ninth New Collegiate Dictionary. Springfield: Merriam-Webster, 1987. 160 000 word entries.

Even larger desk dictionaries include the following:

The Random House Dictionary of the English Language. 2nd ed. Ed. Stuart Berg Flexner. New York: Random House, 1987. 315 000 word entries.

The World Book Dictionary. 2 vols. Ed. Clarence L. Barnhart and Robert K. Barnhart. Chicago: World Book, 1998. 225 000 word entries.

A comparison of entries for the word *critical* in several of these dictionaries allows us to set out a number of important distinguishing features and differences in the meanings of the word, which is the most important topic of this book.

An older dictionary widely used in secondary schools is the *Thorndike-Barnhart High School Dictionary.* It uses some special phonetic letters to indicate pronunciation, so that the symbol ə represents the *a* in *about* in the pronunciation of *critical.* In addition, the word is divided into syllables, its part of speech is identified (adjective), and seven definitions follow, their usage exemplified in some instances by a phrase. No etymology is given: for that you have to read the entry for *critic,* where the derivation of the word is "< L. *criticus* < Gk. *kritikos* critical < *krinein* judge, decide." None of these meanings, however, covers the sense of analysis, central to the notion of critical thinking used in this book.

> **crit i cal** (krit′ə kəl), *adj.* **1**. inclined to find fault or disapprove: *a critical disposition.* **2**. skilled as a critic. **3**. coming from one who is skilled as a critic: *a critical judgment.* **4**. belonging to the work of a critic: *critical essays.* **5**. of a crisis; being important at a time of danger and difficulty: *the critical moment.* **6**. full of danger or difficulty: *His delay was critical.* **7**. of supplies, labor, or resources, necessary for some work or project but existing in inadequate supply. —**crit′ i cal ly**, *adv.* —**crit′ i cal ness**, *n.*
>
> *Thorndike-Barnhart High School Dictionary.* 3rd ed. Ed. E.L. Thorndike and Clarence L. Barnhart. Chicago: Scott, Foresman and Co., 1962. 234.

The entry for *critical* in *The Canadian Oxford Dictionary* uses a somewhat different method for indicating pronunciation (with symbols at the bottom of each page), lists the meanings, and points out that the etymology is located under *critic,* the root word. The first four meanings (1a–c and 2) correspond roughly with the first three in the *Thorndike-Barnhart.* The one closest to our sense of the word in this book is meaning 1c. The fourth meaning of the *Thorndike-Barnhart* does not have an equivalent in *The Canadian Oxford.* The *Canadian Oxford's* 4a and b correspond roughly to the *Thorndike-Barnhart's* meanings 5–7. The special subject area meanings in mathematics and physics have no correspondence in the earlier dictionary. The etymology is a little fuller and more accurate typographically: "Latin *criticus* from Greek *kritikos* from *kritēs* judge from *krinō* judge, decide."

> **critical** / ′ kritikəl / *adj.* **1 a** making or involving adverse or censorious comments or judgments. **b** expressing or involving criticism. **c** involving judgment or discernment (*use your critical*

sense). **2** skilful at or engaged in criticism. **3** providing textual criticism (*a critical edition of Milton*). **4 a** of or at a crisis; involving risk or suspense (*in critical condition*; *a critical operation*). **b** decisive, crucial (*of critical importance*; *at the critical moment*). **5 a** *Math. & Physics* marking transition from one state etc. to another (*critical angle*). **b** *Physics* (of a nuclear reactor) maintaining a self-sustaining chain reaction **criticality** / - ' kæliti / *n.* (in sense 5). **critically** *adv.* **criticalness** *n.* [Latin *criticus*: see CRITIC]

The Canadian Oxford Dictionary. Ed. Katherine Barber. Toronto: Oxford UP, 1998. 314.

A more detailed dictionary, *The Random House Dictionary of the English Language,* uses a somewhat different method for indicating pronunciation (supplied in a concise form at the bottom of the page) and lists the meanings. The first four are close to the first four of the *Thorndike-Barnhart Dictionary*, using similar examples. The fifth, however, is different and has no equivalent in the *Thorndike-Barnhart*. The Random House sixth and seventh definitions separate the meanings of the Thorndike fifth and sixth, but eliminate the notions of difficulty and danger. Those meanings were given in the earlier *Random House Dictionary*, but they are omitted now, indicating a shift in usage. The specialized definitions in medicine and physics have no correspondent entries in the *Thorndike-Barnhart*, but they are close to those in *The Canadian Oxford*. The etymological reference to *critic* is given with a date when the term first entered the language, and examples of synonyms are given.

Crit•i•cal (krit′i kəl), *adj.* **1**. inclined to find fault or to judge with severity, often too readily. **2**. occupied with or skilled in criticism. **3**. involving skillful judgment as to truth, merit, etc.; judicial: *a critical analysis*. **4**. of or pertaining to critics or criticism: *critical essays*. **5**. providing textual variants, proposed emendations, etc.: *a critical edition of Chaucer*. **6**. pertaining to or of the nature of a crisis: *a critical shortage of food*. **7**. of decisive importance with respect to the outcome; crucial: *a critical moment*. **8**. of essential importance; indispensable: *a critical ingredient*. **9**. *Med.* (of a patient's condition) having unstable and abnormal vital signs and other unfavorable indicators, as loss of appetite, poor mobility, or unconsciousness. **10**. *Physics.* **a**. pertaining to a state, value, or quantity at which one or more properties of a substance or system undergo a change. **b**. (of fissionable material) having enough mass to sustain a chain reaction. [1580-90; CRITIC + AL[1]] —**crit′i·cal·ly,** *adv.* —**crit′i·cal′i·ty,** —**crit′i·cal·ness,** *n.*

—**Syn. 1**. captious, censorious, carping, faultfinding, caviling. **3**. discriminating, exact, precise.

The Random House Dictionary of the English Language. Ed. Stuart Berg Flexner. New York: Random House, 1987. 477.

Having given roughly equivalent definitions, *The American Heritage Dictionary* adds synonyms and antonyms, with a comment on usage:

SYNONYMS: *critical, captious, censorious, faultfinding, hypercritical*. The central meaning shared by these adjectives is "tending or marked by a tendency to find and call attention to errors and flaws": *a critical attitude; a captious pedant; censorious of petty failings; an excessively demanding and faultfinding tutor; hypercritical of colloquial speech.*

ANTONYM: *uncritical*.

The American Heritage Dictionary of the English Language. Ed. Anne H. Soukhanov. Boston: Houghton Mifflin, 1992. 443.

A more extended range of synonyms and antonyms is given in *Webster's Ninth New Collegiate Dictionary*:

syn CRITICAL, HYPERCRITICAL, FAULTFINDING, CAPTIOUS, CARPING, CENSORIOUS mean inclined to look for and point out faults and defects. CRITICAL may also imply an effort to see a thing clearly and truly in order to judge it fairly; often it implies harshness in judging; FAULTFINDING implies a querulous or exacting temperament; CAPTIOUS suggests a readiness to detect trivial faults or raise objections on trivial grounds; CARPING implies an ill-natured or perverse picking of flaws; CENSORIOUS implies a disposition to be severely critical and condemnatory. *syn* see in addition ACUTE.

Webster's Ninth New Collegiate Dictionary. Springfield: Merriam-Webster, 1987. 307.

Hence, these desk dictionaries supply many meanings and shades of meaning, and some of them give detailed advice about connotations as well. Most give illustrations for the most important meanings, as well as help with word origins and synonyms.

Some desk dictionaries also include "encyclopedic" information that extends beyond word definitions. For instance, they often list countries and major cities and towns (information found more completely in a gazeteer) with some details about location, population, and features. They also often include famous people, with birth and death dates and brief biographical notes (information usually found in biographical dictionaries); time charts; lists of abbreviations; diagrams of such items as the geological ages or the relationship of language groups; tables of weights and measures; special signs and symbols; forms of address; and common phrases from other languages.

Some of the introductions to these dictionaries are available on the Web, as is that for *Merriam-Webster's Collegiate Dictionary*, 10th edition (**www.m-w.com/pronguid.htm**).

Reference Dictionaries

Reference dictionaries are comprehensive in their coverage of a language and attempt to record usage exhaustively (usually including archaic or obsolete usage). Some of them also attempt to record the history of usage, especially by citing quotations rather than examples coined by the authors of the dictionaries.

Among such reference dictionaries are the great dictionaries published by Oxford University Press, originally edited by Sir James A.H. Murray, and *Webster's Third International,* published by Merriam-Webster. The *Oxford English Dictionary,* commonly known as the *OED,* began to be published in 1884 and was completed in 1928 in twelve volumes. It was corrected and reissued in 1933, and then reissued again (1971–87) as *The Compact Edition of the Oxford English Dictionary* in three volumes as a micrographic reprint of the 1933 edition and the four volumes of supplements. The second edition was published in twenty volumes (Ed. J.A. Simpson and E.S.C. Weiner) in 1989. Yet another edition, the *New Oxford English Dictionary* (*NOED*) is in progress. A CD-ROM version is also published and is available in most university libraries; often, it can be accessed online if you have a university modem account as a registered user.

The advantage in using the *OED* is that it lists in chronological order the first recorded uses of every word, so that you can study a word according to its meanings and different uses over time, with precise references to specific texts. However, the *OED* does not cover standard vocabulary completely: it is limited in its treatment of scientific and technological terms, slang, dialect, and English usage outside the British Isles. An abbreviation of the multivolume dictionary, the *Shorter Oxford English Dictionary,* reduces the space given to obsolete and archaic terms and to citations, while retaining the historical approach to the English language found in the larger edition. The pronunciation is marked by a more complex method of notation, explained in detail in the introduction and set out on each page in abbreviated form. The word sources are given in the original languages and orthography: "**Critic** *a.* 1544. [ad. L. *criticus,* a. Gr., f. (ult.) κρίνειν to decide, judge]."

> **Critical** (kri•tikăl), *a.* 1590. [f. L. *criticus* (see CRITIC *a.*)+ –AL.] **1**. Given to judging; *esp.* fault-finding, censorious. †**2**. Involving or exercising careful judgement or observation; nice, exact, punctual 1716. **3**. Occupied with or skilful in criticism 1641; belonging to criticism 1741. **4**. *Med.,* etc. Relating to the crisis of a disease; determining the issue of a disease, etc. 1601. **5**. Of the nature of, or constituting, a crisis; involving suspense as to the issue 1664. **6**. Decisive, crucial 1841. **7**. *Math.* and *Physics.* Constituting or relating to a point at which some action, property or condition passes over into another; constituting an extreme or limiting case 1841. **8**. *Zool.* and *Bot.* Of species: Uncertain or difficult to determine 1854.
>
> **1**. I am nothing, if not criticall *Oth.*II.i.120. **3**. a c. writer 1766. C acumen FREEMAN. **4**. And so the Fever terminates in a c. Abscess. CHEYNE. **5**. Mrs. H–'s throat was badly cut; her condition is deemed c. 1883. **7**. *C. angle* in *Optics*: that angle of incidence beyond which rays of light are no longer refracted but totally reflected. *C. point* or *temperature*: that temperature above which a substance remains in the gaseous state and cannot be liquefied by any amount of pressure. Hence **Critica•lity** (*rare*), c. quality; a criticism; a crisis. **Critical•ness.**
>
> *The Shorter Oxford English Dictionary.* Ed. C.T. Onions. Oxford: Oxford UP, 1933. I:424.

The *New Shorter Oxford English Dictionary on Historical Principles* reduces the *New Oxford Dictionary* to two volumes. It places far greater stress on scientific usage and on contemporary citation. Many of the older historical citations have been reduced or eliminated. It includes specific instances of usage, gives quotations from authors, and identifies and dates the source.

> **critical** / 'kritik(ə)l/ *a.* M16. [f. late L *criticus* (see CRITIC *a.*) + –AL[1].] **I 1** Of or pertaining to the crisis of a disease; determining the issue of a disease. M16. **2** *gen.* Of, pertaining to, or constituting a crisis; of decisive importance, crucial; involving risk or suspense. E17. **3** *Math. & Physics.* Constituting or relating to a point of transition from one state etc. to another. M19. **b** Of a nuclear reactor etc.: maintaining a self-sustaining chain reaction. M2o.
>
> **2** H. MACMILLAN We made a serious error, at a critical moment when France was already nervous and uncertain. H. KISSINGER Their need for American grain was critical. A. HAILEY They were vulnerable, critical installations and could take weeks to repair or replace completely.
>
> **II 4** Given to judging, esp. unfavourably; fault-finding, censorious. L16. **5** Skilful at or engaged in criticism, esp. of literature or art; providing textual criticism. L16. **b** Belonging to criticism. M18. †**6** Involving careful judgement or observation; nice, exact, punctual. M17-M19.
>
> **4** SHAKES. *Oth.* I am nothing if not critical. W. GOLDING She was severe and very critical of my playing. **5** J. M. MURRY These two finely critical minds—in their separate provinces the finest critical minds we have in England to-day. A. WILSON A critical edition of the text of *Lamia*.
>
> *Special collocations & phrases*: **critical angle** the angle of incidence at which a ray of light must strike an interface with a less dense medium so as to be refracted parallel to the interface. *critical apparatus*: see APPARATUS 2c. **critical damping** *Physics* damping just sufficient to prevent oscillations. **critical mass** the mass of a body of fissile material of critical size (see below). **critical path** a sequence of stages determining the minimum time needed

for the execution of an entire project. **critical point** a set of conditions of temperature, pressure, and density at which a liquid and its vapour become indistinguishable. **critical pressure** the pressure required to liquefy a gas at its critical temperature. **critical size** the minimum size of a body of a given fissile material which is capable of sustaining a nuclear chain reaction. **critical temperature** above which a gas cannot be liquefied by pressure. **critical volume** the volume of unit mass of a gas or vapour at its critical temperature and pressure. **go critical** (of a nuclear reactor etc.) begin to sustain a nuclear chain reaction. *New Critical*: see NEW *a*.

criti'cality *n*. the state or quality of being critical; *esp*. the condition of sustaining a nuclear chain reaction: M18. **critically** adv. M17. **criticalness** *n*. M17.

The New Shorter Oxford English Dictionary on Historical Principles. Ed. Lesley Brown. Oxford: Clarendon, 1993. I:551.

The equivalent American dictionary is the *Dictionary of American English on Historical Principles* in four volumes, which deals with words that originated in the United States, with a cut-off date of 1900. Other related dictionaries extend the range to recent times. The comprehensive American dictionary, however, is *Webster's Third New International Dictionary*. It lists definitions in historical order and gives illustrative quotations, chiefly from twentieth-century sources. It is particularly useful for American usage, spelling, pronunciation, and abbreviations. It does not include any proper names and has omitted usage labels (such as *vulgar, slang,* and *colloquial*), although it has been much criticized for abandoning its duty to specify proper usage. Students who want to find out whether a usage is appropriate for formal prose should consult another dictionary, such as one of the desktop dictionaries.

Dictionary of American English on Historical Principles. 4 vols. Ed. William A. Craigie and James R. Hulbert. Chicago: U of Chicago P, 1938–44. Word entries end at 1900.

New Shorter Oxford English Dictionary on Historical Principles. 2 vols. Ed. Lesley Brown. Oxford: Clarendon, 1993. 500 000 words under 98 000 word entries, with 83 000 quotations.

Oxford English Dictionary. 12 vols. Ed. James A.H. Murray. Oxford: Clarendon, [1884–1928] 1933. About 478 000 words based on several million quotations.

Oxford English Dictionary. 2nd ed. 20 vols. Ed. J.A. Simpson and E.S.C. Weiner. Oxford: Clarendon, 1989. 600 000 word entries.

Shorter Oxford English Dictionary on Historical Principles. 3rd ed. Ed. C.T. Onions. Oxford: Clarendon, 1973. 170 000 word entries.

Webster's Third New International Dictionary. Ed. Philip Babcock Gove. Springfield: Merriam-Webster, 1993. 450 000 word entries.

See also the Web sites associated with the *OED:*

- **www.oed.com/**

- **www.chass.utoronto.ca/chass/oed/oedpage.html**

Foreign Language Dictionaries

Often, you will come across words or phrases in another language in your reading or research. Sometimes the context is sufficient to provide an explanation, or there may be a translation given in the text or in a footnote. But at other times it is necessary to consult a foreign language dictionary. These dictionaries are of two kinds. First, foreign language dictionaries are written for native or bilingual speakers of the language, with all of the information, including definitions, given in the foreign language. These are the basic dictionaries of any given language. The second kind consists of bilingual dictionaries, among which the most commonly used are those that translate from the original language into English and from English into the original language. Some examples of both types of foreign language dictionaries are the following:

Grand Larousse de la langue française. 7 vols. Ed. Louis Guilbert, René Lagane, and Georges Niobey. Paris: Larousse, 1971–78. One of the standard French-only dictionaries.

Grand dictionnaire français-anglais, anglais-français. Paris: Larousse, 1993. A bilingual dictionary in French and English.

Collins-Sansoni Italian Dictionary. Ed. Vladimiro Macchi. Firenze: Sansoni Editore, 1981. A bilingual dictionary in English and Italian.

Collins German-English/English-German Dictionary. Ed. Peter Terrell. London: Collins, 1988. A bilingual German and English dictionary.

On the Web a number of dictionary sites have direct or linked access to major English and foreign language dictionaries. Some sites have dictionaries that allow searching through the dictionary page by page, while others offer immediate translation of a word from one language to another. As an instance of the latter, the site at Bucknell University has a large number of languages available at **www.facstaff.bucknell.edu/rbeard/diction.html**.

French–English dictionaries on the Web include the ARTFL Project—the University of Chicago Project for American and French Research on the Treasury of the French Language, at **humanities.uchicago.edu/forms_unrest/FR-ENG.html**; German–English dictionaries can be found at **dictionaries.travlang.com/GermanEnglish/**; and another collection of Web dictionaries is located at **dict.leo.org/dict/dictionaries.html**.

Special Subject Dictionaries

Almost every subject has a special dictionary of the terms that are particular to that topic. There are dictionaries for almost every nation, historical period, major field of study, and interest group. There are dictionaries on law, dogs, Marxist thought, computer terminology, and so on, available in both printed and electronic forms. The following useful dictionaries for university students are a mere sampling of several fields:

A Dictionary of Marxist Thought. 2nd ed. Ed. Tom Bottomore. Oxford: Blackwell, 1991.

Black, Henry Campbell. *Black's Law Dictionary: Definitions of the Terms and Phrases of American and English Jurisprudence, Ancient and Modern.* 6th ed. Ed. Joseph R. Nolan and Jacqueline M. Nolan-Haley. St. Paul: West, 1990.

Blackwell Dictionary of Twentieth-Century Social Thought. Ed. William Outhwaite and Tom Bottomore. Oxford: Blackwell, 1993.

Dictionary of Slang and Unconventional English. 8th ed. Ed. Eric Partridge; rev. Paul Beale. New
    York: Macmillan, 1984.

Dorling Kindersley Ultimate Visual Dictionary. London: Dorling Kindersley, 1994.

New Dictionary of American Slang. Ed. Robert L. Chapman. New York: Harper, 1986.

New Grove Dictionary of Music and Musicians. 20 vols. Ed. Stanley Sadie. London: Macmillan, 1980.

New Palgrave: A Dictionary of Economics. Ed. John Eatwell, Murray Milgate, and Peter Newman. New
    York: Stockton, 1987.

Oxford Dictionary of English Etymology. Ed. C.T. Onions, G.W.S. Friedrichsen, and R.W. Burchfield.
    Oxford: Clarendon, 1969.

Special interest dictionaries of English are available that explain particular difficulties in
meaning, connotation, and pronunciation for ESL students:

Collins Cobuild English Dictionary. 2nd ed. Ed. John Sinclair. New York: HarperCollins, 1995. Provides
    extensive information on usage and idioms, and adds complete sentences as examples to definitions.

Oxford ESL Dictionary for Students of American English. Ed. A.S. Hornby. Oxford: Oxford UP, 1991.

ETYMOLOGY, OR THE ORIGINS OF WORDS

Word Sources

Words contain within their structure—within their parts or syllables, shape, sound, and
use—the whole history of the language from which they come and, in an important sense,
the history of the people who use them. Because words have histories that are, at least in part,
embedded in their shape, sound, and meaning, they contain the records of the languages
with which they interacted, and they record the important contacts between peoples of different languages over many thousands of years. Philologists (from the Greek, *philos*, loving,
and *logos*, word, discourse, account, or study), or historical linguists, are those who study the
history of language and its use. One of the branches of philology is etymology (from the
Greek, *etymos*, true sense), the investigation of the derivation and original meaning of words.
Knowing the etymology of a word means that you will have a clearer sense of its meaning,
and certainly of its history. Many words in English are derived from other languages and reflect periods when English-speaking peoples interacted with the speakers of other languages
to such a degree that there was significant borrowing and sharing of words; gradually, words
from one language were adopted and perhaps adapted by the borrowing language.
    English is one member of the Indo-European family of languages that originally shared, so
it is conjectured, a common source language, usually called Proto-Indo-European. This source
dates to between 5000 and 6000 B.C.E., when its speakers began over the next several thousand years to move in two opposite directions from the grasslands in eastern Europe between
the Carpathian and Ural mountain ranges and north of the Black Sea, which separated these peoples from the Semitic language speakers of the south. The Indo-Europeans moved in one
branch to the east into southern Asia, the Indo-Iranian branch. The other branch moved very
slowly to the west, appearing in Europe between 3000 and 2500 B.C.E. and branching further
into yet other related families. The Anatolian subgroup had already gone into Asia Minor,
the Hellenic (Greek) branch moved to the south, the Italics across the Alps, the Celts furthest

to the west, and the Germanic peoples to the north and west. Within this vast family of languages, many of the commonest words that refer to kinship (such as *mother, father, brother, sister*) are still alike in important characteristics of both sound and shape. For instance, the word *mother* is *madre* in Italian and Spanish, *Mutter* in German, *mater* in Latin, *meter* in Greek, and *matar* in ancient Persian and Sanskrit. Such words that have descended from the same form in a common parent language are called *cognates*. Most of the European languages have numerous cognates, even in the various daughter families that branched off from their ancestors. Among the Germanic languages, that in the north was Old Norse, which was spoken by the Vikings and from which modern Icelandic, Norwegian, Swedish, and Danish have descended. The western Germanic language was the ancestor of German, Dutch, and English.

As a number of groups from the north invaded, the Roman empire began to break up, and some of those western German peoples, the Jutes, Angles, and Saxons, began the conquest of Britain, driving out the Celtic-speaking peoples or absorbing them, and inaugurating a new linguistic period for Britain—the Old English or Anglo-Saxon period of the English language. About 60 000 words in the language were chiefly Anglo-Saxon, with some Norse words that were incorporated during the Viking invasions of the eighth and ninth centuries. From about 1100 to 1500, the Middle English period was characterized by the absorption of thousands of words from the new invaders, the Normans, who from about 1066 brought the French language to England. French was a Romance language (named after the Romans), and one of the daughter languages, along with Spanish and Italian, of Latin, and so many of the thousands of French word imports were of Latin derivation. With Gutenberg's invention of the printing press in about 1455 and its inauguration in England in 1476, the language tended to become stabilized. However, in the last 450 years many thousands of new words have been added to the language: from other languages brought home in the process of colonization, from a new awareness of the classical languages of Greek and Latin during the Renaissance and after, from new science and technology that drew extensively on Greek terms for the new vocabulary, and from new coinages and English dialects from North America, South Africa, Australia, and other parts of the world.

Currently, much of the particular vocabulary of Anglo-Saxon has disappeared from modern English, but many of the most common words in modern English are Anglo-Saxon, including the definite and indefinite articles, many conjunctions and prepositions, and many verbs. Writing in 1966, Mario Pei calculated that "a straight vocabulary count from the dictionary will show that barely 40 per cent of English words are of Anglo-Saxon origin" (160). Nevertheless, many of the Anglo-Saxon words occur in English frequently. The influence both of the Roman occupation of Britain and of the Latin of the medieval church had a tremendous impact on all of the language of learning, especially history, philosophy, and theology. Again during the English Renaissance in the sixteenth century, the impact of Latin (and of Greek) was widespread in scholarly circles and increasingly in scientific and technical discourse. In everyday writing, such as friendly letters, about 15 percent of the words are of Latin and Greek origin, but in a literary or scientific work, that number increases, according to Pei, to over 30 percent (161). Of course, the words from Latin likely have been passed down through French forms, and a few have come from Italian or Spanish forms, the three major Romance languages derived from Latin.

Therefore, some knowledge of another language is very helpful to a reader of English, partly owing to the awareness of how another language works in its grammar and syntax, but especially for its vocabulary. You can begin to trace for yourself some of the etymological roots of English words. A dictionary that includes etymologies, or word origins, is a great asset in building your vocabulary. You should make it a point when consulting a dictionary to note the word origins and to try to fit them together with other words that you know. Even students who have little or no knowledge of another language can pick up clues from the English words themselves about what the parts of words mean. In the next sections we show how a knowledge of the parts of words—their roots, prefixes, and suffixes—can help expand your vocabulary and deepen your reading comprehension.

The Roots of Words

An English word consists of three possible parts, though not all parts will be present in every word. The parts are the root, the prefix, and the suffix.

The root is the part of the word that contains the basic meaning or denotation of the word. It is the base form of a word from which other forms of words are derived. That is, the root of a word is the basic morpheme (the smallest form of a word that conveys meaning). Some linguists call this part of a word the *stem,* though technically the stem is the part of a word to which prefixes and suffixes can be added. This root in English can often be traced to a different kind of root—to its etymological source in another language—and some linguists use the term *root* to refer both to the smallest meaning-part in an English word and also to the word's etymological source in another language.

A prefix is a word element that is placed in front of the root word, and a suffix (there may be more than one) is an element placed after the root. A prefix changes or modifies the meaning of the root element to make a new word. A suffix also changes the meaning, but it changes the grammatical function of a word or its use, as well. Suffixes tell us whether the word is a noun, an adjective, or a verb, and convey the comparative degree of an adjective: *smaller, smallest.* Two suffixes may be added to a root to create a word, as in *uncritically.*

Unscientifically can be broken down into the following parts:

English Root

Science

Prefix

Un- [from the Old English *un-* or *on-*] expresses a negative meaning of the following root.

Suffixes

1. *-ific > -fic* making, causing, or producing [from the Latin suffix *-ficus*, making or doing, from the Latin verb *facere*, to make or do]

2. *-al* of the kind of, pertaining to [modelled on the ending of the Latin adjective in *-alis*]

3. *-ly* befitting, characteristic of [from Old English *-lic*, like]; also grammatical function of the adverb

Etymological Root

Latin: *scientia*

From another root, Lat. *sciens,* knowing, the present participle of the Latin verb, *scire,* to know.

In the *OED* the prefix *un-* has twenty-two columns dealing with the history of the prefix alone, independent of any root words to which it is attached. There follow 373 pages of definitions of words that use the prefix *un-*.

Dictionaries normally give the roots of words, both in the sense of the English stem and the etymological root from other languages. Most dictionaries that are larger than the concise or pocket dictionaries also list prefixes and suffixes among their meanings. In the *OED*, the commentaries on these prefixes and suffixes are extensive. Many common English words are made up of combinations of roots from other languages; thus, one of the best ways to develop your knowledge of English roots is to take a course in another language. Some of these etymological roots are used as English roots (for instance, *amiable* and *amatory* are two words both deriving from the Latin *amo, amare,* I love, to love), or as prefixes (*advent,* from the Latin *ad*, to or toward, and *venire,* to come). The list below gives a number of these words, the language source, the meaning in the original language and in modern English, and an example.

Common Words from Other Languages

English	Language	Meaning	Examples
ad	Lat.	to, toward	admit
amo	Lat.	love	amiable, amatory
anthro	Gk.	man	anthropology
anti	Lat.	against	antimatter
aqua	Lat.	water	aquarium
astro	Lat	star	astronaut
aud	Lat.	hear	audience
auto	Lat.	self	automatic
bi	Lat.	two	bisexual
biblio	Gk.	book	bibliography
bio	Gk.	life	antibiotics
card	Lat. > Gk.	heart	cardiac
carn	Lat.	meat, flesh	carnival, carnivore
chron	Lat. > Gk.	time	chronic, chronicle
cide, ciss	Lat.	cut, kill	genocide, regicide
circu	Lat.	around	circumference
claus, clud, clos	Lat.	closed	exclude, include
cogn	Lat.	know	recognize, cognition
contra	Lat.	against	contradict
corp	Lat.	body	corpse, corporeal
counter	Lat.	against	counter-revolution
cred	Lat.	believe	credit
cyber	Gk.	direct, guide	cyberspace
dent, dont	Lat.	teeth	dental, orthodonty
derm	Gk.	skin	epidermis
dextra	Lat.	right	dexterity
di	Gk.	two	disect
dict	Lat.	speak	dictionary
div	Lat.	God	divine

dyn	Gk.	power	dynamic
ego	Lat.	I	egomaniac
epi	Gk.	on top	epitaph, epigraph
eu	Gk.	happy, good	euthanasia
ex, exo	Lat.	out	exorcist
extra	Lat.	over, above	extrahepatic
fid	Lat.	faith	confident
fin	Lat.	end	infinite
gamy	Lat.	marriage	polygamy
gen	Lat.	begin, race	generation
gig	Lat.	giant	gigabyte
glot, gloss	Gk.	tongue	glossary
gno, gni	Gk.	know	agnostic
graph, gram	Gk	write	paragraph
gyny	Gk.	woman	gynecology
hemi	Gk.	half	hemisphere
hep	Gk.	liver	hepatitis
hetero	Gk.	other, different	heterosexual
hex	Gk.	six	hexadecimal
homo	Gk.	same	homogenized
homo	Lat.	man	homocide
hydr	Gk.	water	hydrogen
hyper	Gk.	over	hyperactive
hypo	Gk.	under	hypotension
inter	Lat.	between	international
intra	Lat.	within	intravenous
kil	Gk.	thousand	kilowatt
lingua	Lat.	tongue	linguistics
logo	Gk.	word, study	logic (see *ology*)
lux, luc	Lat.	light	lucid
mal	Lat.	bad	malpractice
man	Lat.	hand	manufacture
mania	Lat.	crazy	pyromaniac
mar	Lat.	sea	marine
mega	Gk.	great, large	megabyte
meter	Gk.	measure	thermometer
metro	Gk.	mother	metropolitan
micro	Gk.	very small	microbe
mil	Lat.	1000	million, mile
mini	Lat.	small	minimum
mis	OE	bad	misunderstand
mit, miss	Lat.	send	mission
mono	Gk.	one	monogamy
mort	Lat.	death	mortal, mortician
mot, mov	Lat.	move	promote, motion
multi	Lat.	many	multitude
nat	Lat.	birth	natural

naut	Gk.	ship	nautical
nav	Lat.	ship	navy
neo	Gk.	new	neolithic
nov	Lat.	nine	November
nova	Lat.	new	Nova Scotia
nul	Lat.	nothing	annulment
oct	Lat.	eight	octave
-ology, log	Gk.	study of, words	logical
omnia	Lat.	all	omnipotent
pan	Gk.	all	pan-American
pan	Lat.	bread	companion
pax, pac	Lat.	peace	pacify
ped, paed	Gk.	child	pediatrics
ped, pod	Gk.	feet	pedestrian
pend	Lat.	hang	independent
pent	Lat.	five	pentagon
phil	Gk.	love	anglophile, philosophy
phobia	Gk.	fear	claustrophobia
phon	Gk.	sound	phonograph
phos, photo	Gk.	light	phosphorescence, photography
phyte	Gk.	little plant	neophyte
poli	Gk.	city, state	politics
poly	Gk.	many	polygon
port	Lat.	carry	portfolio
poss, pon	Lat.	put, place	impose
post	Lat.	after	postpone
pre	Lat.	before	prenatal
pro	Lat.	for, forward	promote, provide
pyr	Gk.	fire	pyromaniac
rupt	Lat.	break	rupture
scio	Lat.	know	omniscient
scope	Gk.	see	telescope
scrib, script	Lat.	write	inscribe
seme	Lat.	seed	inseminate
semi	Lat.	half	semicircle
sinestra	Lat.	left	sinister
somn	Lat.	sleep	insomnia, somnolent
soph	Gk.	wisdom	philosophy
spect	Lat.	look at	inspection
sta, sti, stu	Lat.	stand	standard
stella	Lat.	star	constellation
sub	Lat.	under	submarine
super	Lat.	over	superior
tab, taph	Lat.	table	tablet
tele	Gk.	far away	telescope
tetra	Gk.	four	tetrarch, tetralogy

thana	Gk.	death	euthanasia
theo	Gk.	God	theology
tort	Lat.	twist, turn	torture, torment
tox	Lat. > Gk.	poison	toxic
trans	Lat.	across	transfusion
tri	Lat.	three	triple
twe, twi	OE	two	twice
vis, vid	Lat.	see	video
vita, viva	Lat.	life	vital, vivacious
volu	Lat.	wish	volunteer
xeno	Gk.	strange	xenophobic
zoa	Gk.	animal	protozoa

Prefixes and Suffixes

Old English had numerous prefixes and suffixes. During the period when the language was first developing, they were combined with root words to form new words by combinations. With the coming of the Normans, English was influenced by more French and Latin forms, and the number of prefixes and suffixes that were used to make new words declined. Indeed, many of the old prefixes and suffixes began to disappear as the language changed. For instance, the Old English prefix *for-* was attached to verbs and verbal forms to change the meaning of the root to which it was attached (like all prefixes). *For-* intensified the meaning of the verb to which it was attached, or it could add the notion of negativity or destructiveness to the verb. Formerly widely used, this prefix began to be used much less frequently after about 1050. In modern English the Old English prefix appears in only a few verbs:

forbear	forbid	fordo (to destroy)
forget	forgive	forsake
forswear	forlorn (participle)	

Similarly, the prefix *with-,* meaning "against," largely disappeared, except for such words as *withdraw* and *withhold.*

A number of Old and Middle English suffixes have survived:

Suffix	Language	Meaning	Example
-ness	OE	the quality, state, or condition of being	blessedness
-ful	OE	full of, characterized by, tending to	cheerful, harmful
-less	OE *leas*	free from, without	homeless
-some	OE *sum*	causing	awesome
-ish	OE *isc*	somewhat, resembling, like	sweetish, childish

Some other suffixes have almost disappeared. For instance, the suffix *-lock* from the OE *lāc,* an intensifier referring to the condition of the word to which it is attached, is extinct except in the word *wedlock* (OE *wedd,* a pledge + *lāc*). Another example is the suffix *-red* from the OE *raedan,* the condition or state of, now surviving in only a few words like *hatred* and *kindred.* In wider use is the OE suffix *-dom,* meaning a position, realm, state, or condition, surviving in such words as *kingdom, freedom, wisdom,* and *martyrdom.* Indeed, this suffix took on new life in the late twentieth century, with new coinages such as *stardom.* Other OE suffixes that survive include *-hood* (the condition or state of: *likelihood, sainthood, girlhood*) and *-ship* (the office or status of: *dictatorship, governorship*).

New prefixes and suffixes from Latin were attached to Latin roots, and the words replacing Middle English forms were anglicized from Norman words:

Middle English	Meaning	Norman French and Latin Roots
withsay	renounce	< Fr. *renoncer* < Lat. *renuntiare* < *re-* [back] + *nuntius* [message]
withspeak	contradict	< Fr. *contredire* < Lat. *contra-* [against] + *dire* [to speak]
withset	resist	< Fr. *résister* < Lat. *re-* [back]+ *sistere* [to make a stand]

Many Latinate prefixes and suffixes were added to the English language during the Middle English period, and most have survived to modern times. Many prefixes give directions, such as toward (*in-, epi-, ad-*), away from (*ab-, ex-*), above, below, and so on. Others indicate time and age or size and number. Others redirect the positive and negative meanings of the root they are attached to or intensify the meaning of the root. The following is a list of common prefixes:

Prefix	Language	Meaning	Examples
a-, ab-	Lat.	from, away	avert, abstain
a-, an-	Gk.	without	atheist
		not	anarchist
ad-, af-	Lat.	to, toward	adhere, affix
at-, ag-	Lat.	to, toward	attain, aggressive

This prefix, like a number of others (see *en-* and *im-/in-,* below), undergoes a process called *assimilation,* adopting the following letter as part of the prefix. In some prefixes, the letter *n* (in *in-* and *en-*) changes to *m* before the letters *b, m,* or *p* of the root. In the prefix *ad-* the letter *d* changes according to the first word of the root to *ac-, af-, ag-, al-, an-, ap-, as-,* and *at-* (*accord, affable, aggressive, alleviate, annotate, appal, arrogant, assume,* and *attract*).

ambi-	Gk.	both	ambidextrous
amphi-	Gk.	around	amphitheater
ant-	Gk.	against	antonym, antagonist
anti-	Gk.	against	antipathy
ante-	Lat.	before	antedate
cata-	Gk.	down	cataract, catacomb
con-	Lat.	with	convene
cor-	Lat.	together	correlate
com-	Lat.	with	compare
contra-	Lat.	against	contradict
de-	Lat.	from	descend
		down	debase
di-	Lat.	apart	divert, divorce

dia-	Lat.	through	diameter, diagonal
dis-	Lat.	not	disagree, disappear, disfunctional
e-, em-	Lat.	out of	evaluate, emanate
ex-	Lat.	over	exponent
el-	Gk.	in	elliptical
em-	Gk.	in	embark, empathy

The last letter of the root prefix *en-* changes to *el-* before *l* and to *em-* before *b, m,* or *p.*

en-	Gk.	in, into	enclose
epi-	Gk.	upon	epigraph, epitaph
hyper-	Gk.	above, over	hypercritical
hypo-	Gk.	under	hypodermic
il-, im-, in-, ir-	Lat.	not	illegal, illegible, illogical import, impossible inactive, inept irresponsible

The last letter of the prefix *in-* changes according to the first letter of the root. *In-* changes to *il-* before the letter *l*. *In-* changes to *im-* before *b, m,* or *p* and to *ir-* before *r*. Before words of French origin, *in-* changes to *en- (encroach, engender)*.

in-	Lat.	in, into	inject
intra-	Lat.	within	intramural
intro-	Lat.	within	introduction, introspection
per-	Lat.	through thorough	permeate perfect
peri-	Gk.	around	perimeter
post-	Lat.	after	postpone, posterity
pre-	Lat.	before	predict, precede
pro-	Lat.	for forth	pronoun procession
re-	Lat.	back again down	recall revive retreat
sub-	Lat.	under	subordinate
sup-	Lat.	under	suppose
super-	Lat.	over above	supervise superscript
trans-	Lat.	across	transport transmit

A suffix tells how a word is being used, with respect to its meaning and to how it is being used in the syntax or grammatical structure. For instance, words ending in the suffix *-ly* are adverbs, while those ending in the suffixes *-tion* and *-ment* are nouns. Hence, suffixes can help in identifying word functions or parts of speech in sentences. In the word *uncritically* the parts can be divided as follows:

un	-	critic	-	al	-	ly
prefix		root		suffix 1		suffix 2
(negativizes				(makes the root		(makes the root +
the root)				into an adjective)		suffix 1 into an adverb)

The same principle operates with other words. For instance, in the word *fatalists* there are three suffixes added to the root, *fate*. The first two work by changing the root's grammatical category: *-al* turns the root into an adjective, and *-ist* turns it back into a noun, indicating the condition of one who is determined by fate. The final suffix, the letter *-s,* does not change the grammatical category, but simply indicates the plural of the noun. It is often spoken of as an *inflection,* a suffix that indicates such grammatical relations as singular/plural (cat > cats), possessive (girl's), tenses (walk > walked) and comparisons (small > smaller > smallest) (Traugott and Pratt 91). Many other languages, such as Greek, Latin, German, and Russian, are heavily inflected and change the suffixes on the basis of grammatical function. For instance, the ending of the Latin word for girl, *puella,* determines the grammatical function of the word, wherever it is placed in the sentence (though some endings are identical, leading to occasional ambiguity). In English the grammatical function of words is indicated in part by the suffixes, but largely by the location of words in sentences. In Latin the suffixes as inflections are added to the root, *puella:*

Nominative	puella (a girl)	puellae (the girls)
Genitive	puellae (of a girl)	puellarum (of girls)
Dative	puellae (to or for a girl)	puellis (to or for girls)
Accusative	puellam (a girl—object)	puellas (girls—as object)
Vocative	puella (O girl)	puellae (O girls)
Ablative	puella (from, with, or by a girl)	puellis (from, with, or by girls)

Linguists have pointed out that most suffixes are *nomenalizers,* whose function is to change adjectives or verbs into nouns. Another large group, *adjectivalizers,* converts nouns into adjectives. The other groups are much smaller.

Nomenalizers (turn verbs or adjectives into nouns):

-acy	accuracy, delicacy, democracy, piracy, privacy
-ance	guidance, deliverance, governance, significance
-ician	beautician, mortician, musician, technician
-ism	alcoholism, egoism, republicanism, sexism
-ist	fatalist, finalist, pianist, vocalist
-ity	calamity, majority, parity, plurality
-ment	banishment, measurement, parliament, preferment
-ness	dreariness, happiness, goodness, kindness
-ship	comradeship, fellowship, kinship
-ster	barrister, gangster, holster
-tion	congregation, discretion, fruition, institution

Adjectivalizers (turn nouns or verbs into adjectives):

-able	considerable, fashionable, pardonable, preferable, valuable
-al	fatal, frugal, marginal, nominal, poetical
-an	Canadian, republican

-atic	aristocratic, bureaucratic, democratic, systematic
-ful	hopeful, grateful, wistful
-ic	bibliographic, bishopric, chivalric, graphic, iambic, rhetoric
-ine	feminine, masculine
-ish	coolish, devilish, waspish, yellowish
-ory	ambulatory, dormitory, refectory, statutory
-otic	antibiotic, erotic, idiotic, psychotic
-ous	delirious, monstrous, meticulous, preposterous
-y	balmy, clammy, mouthy, slimy

Verbalizers (turn nouns into verbs; often, beginning writers coin new words by turning nouns into verbs, a practice that many stylists attack):

-ate	demonstrate, candidate, evaluate, vaccinate
-en	lighten, weaken
-ify	identify, glorify, magnify, simplify
-ize	dramatize, rationalize, systematize, verbalize

Adverbializers (turn adjectives into adverbs):

-ly	blandly, clearly, happily, warmly
-ward	award, reward, toward

The following is a list of common suffixes:

Suffix	Use	Language	Lang. root	Meaning	Examples
-able	adjective	Old French (OF)	< Lat. *-abilis*	capable of inclined to	obtainable peaceable
-ible	adjective	OF < Lat.	*-ible < -ibilis*	that can be	terrible
-ac	adjective	Lat. < Gk.	*-acus < -akus*	pertaining to	maniac, zodiac
-acy	noun	Lat. < Gk.	*-acia < -ateia*	pertaining to	accuracy, lunacy
-age	noun	Fr.	*-age*	result of, process of	sabotage, voyage
-al, -ial	noun	Lat.	*-ale*, neut. of *-alis*	act of —ing	refusal, facial
-an	noun	Lat.	*-anus*	of	Canadian
-ance	noun	Fr. < Lat.	*-ance < -antia*	state of being	importance
-ence	noun	Fr. < Lat.	*-ence < -entia*	state of being	independence
-ant	adjective/ noun	Fr. < Lat.	*-ant < -ans,-antis*	one who does—	compliant
-ent	adjective/ noun	Fr. < Lat.	*-ent < -ens, -entis*	one who does—	competent
-ate	noun/verb/ adjective	Lat.	*-atus*	to make—	confiscate, collegiate
-ation	noun	Lat.	*-atio*	act of —ing	partition, civilization
-en	verb	OE	*-an*	forms verbs	listen, enlighten
-er	noun	OE < Lat.	*-ere < -arius*	one who—s	doer, officer, thinker

Suffix	Use	Language	Lang. root	Meaning	Examples
-or	noun	Lat.	*-or*	one who—s	assessor, professor, terror
-ery	noun	OF < Lat. < Gk.	*-erie < -arius < -ia*	place for —ing place for —s work of state of	hatchery, nunnery, dentistry, slavery
-esce	verb	Lat.	*-escere*	become, begin to	effervesce
-escence	noun/ adjective				effervescence
-escent	noun				effervescent
-hood	noun	OE	*-had*	of condition	childhood, falsehood
-ic	noun/ adjective	Fr < Lat.< Gk.	*-ique <-icus <-ikos*	like	artistic, heroic
-ify	verb	Lat.	*ficere < facere*	to become—	deify, rectify, simplify
-ion	noun	Lat.	*-io, ionis*	act of —ing	attention, fascination
-ian	noun	Lat.	*-ia*	person from	Torontonian
-ish	adjective	OE	*-isc*	the quality of	childish, British, youngish
-ism	noun	Fr. < Lat. < Gk.	*-isme < -ismos*	doctrine, system of	nationalism, sexism
-ite	noun	Fr. < Lat. < Gk.	*-ite < -ites -ite*	person assoc. with	Carmelite, socialite
-ity	noun	Fr. < Lat.	*-ité < -itas*	the quality of	absurdity, sincerity
-ive	noun/ adjective	Fr. < Lat.	*-ive < -ivus*	of, state of being	active, imitative
-less	adjective	OE	*-las*	without	formless, homeless
-ly	adjective or adverb	OE	*-lice*	like	daily, sweetly
-ness	noun	OE	*-nes*	state of	carefulness

Words are the vital instruments of thought. Increasing your vocabulary by any of the methods outlined above will increase your ability in critical thinking, reading, and writing. Knowledge of how words are formed from other languages, how they are related through their roots and prefixes and suffixes in English, and how they function in communicating meaning is a lifetime learning project. You can greatly increase your ability to use words effectively by learning some of the prefixes and suffixes outlined above. But much also depends on how you use those words accurately in building sentences. To that topic we turn in Chapter 5.

FURTHER READINGS

Vocabulary

Black, John W. *The Use of Words in Context: The Vocabulary of College Students.* New York: Plenum Press, 1985.

Espey, William R. *Thou Improper, Thou Uncommon Noun: An Etymology of Words that Once Were Names.* New York: Clarkson N. Potter, 1978.

————. *Another Almanac of Words at Play.* New York: Clarkson N. Potter, 1980.

Funk, Wilfred, and Norman Lewis. *30 Days to a More Powerful Vocabulary.* New York: Pocket Books, 1971.

Silverthorn, J.E., Devern J. Perry, and John W. Oberly. *College Vocabulary Building.* 5th ed. Cincinnati: South Western, 1971.

Safire, William. "On Language." Weekly column in the *New York Times Magazine.*

————.*You Could Look It Up.* New York: Times Books, 1988.

Language

Baugh, Albert C., and Thomas Cable. *A History of the English Language.* 3rd ed. Englewood Cliffs, NJ: Prentice-Hall, 1978.

Byrne, Mary. *Eureka! A Dictionary of Latin and Greek Elements in English Words.* Newton Abbot: David and Charles, 1987.

Crystal, David. *The Cambridge Encyclopedia of Language.* Cambridge: Cambridge UP, 1987.

Danner, Horace G., and Roger Noel. *An Introduction to an Academic Vocabulary: Word Clusters from Latin, Greek, and German: A Vade Mecum for the Serious Student.* 2nd ed. Lanham, MD: University Press of America, 1990.

McCrum, Robert, William Cran, and Robert MacNeil. *The Story of English.* London: Faber and Faber; BBC Books, 1988.

Nurnberg, Maxwell, and Morris Rosenblum. *All About Words: An Adult Approach to Vocabulary Building.* New York: Mentor-New American Library, 1966.

Pei, Mario. *The Story of Language.* Rev. ed. Toronto: Mentor-New American Library, 1966.

Pyles, Thomas, and John Algeo. *The Origins and Development of the English Language.* 4th ed. New York: Harcourt Brace, 1993.

Shipley, Joseph T. *In Praise of English: The Growth and Use of Language.* New York: Times Books, 1977.

Stevenson, Victor, ed. *Words: The Evolution of Western Languages.* London: Methuen, 1983.

Traugott, Elizabeth Closs, and Mary Louise Pratt. *Linguistics for Students of Literature.* New York: Harcourt Brace, 1980.

WEBLINKS

Vocabulary

- The Wordmonger
  www.geocities.com/Athens/Forum/8962/wordmong.html

- The Word Detective
  www.word-detective.com

- The Word Wizard
  wordwizard.com/newuser/default.htm

- Vocabulary University
  www.vocabulary.com/

Language

- For an account on the Web of the various Indo-European languages, their characteristics and chronologies, with graphs and maps, see the Web site of Cyril Babaev:
  members.tripod.com/~babaev/map.html

- Indo-European Documentation Center at the University of Texas at Austin
  www.dla.utexas.edu/depts/lrc/iedocctr/ie-culture/ie-culture.html

- Daniel Mosser at Virginia Tech
  ebbs.english.vt.edu/hel/hel.html

- Historical linguistics from the University of California at Berkeley
  alumni.eecs.berkeley.edu/~lorentz/Ancient_Scripts/hl_links.html

- Rick Branscomb's history of the English language at Salem State College
  www.mv.com/ipusers/heb/HEL/Resources.html

Using the Dictionary

- Doctor Dictionary
  www.dictionary.com/

- Longman Dictionaries Home Page
  www.aw-lelt.com/dictionaries/

- Web sites associated with the *OED*
  www.oed.com/
  www.chass.utoronto.ca/chass/oed/oedpage.html

RECOGNIZING HOW GRAMMAR AND PUNCTUATION WORK

In English the sentence and its parts, along with appropriate punctuation, are the basic units of thought and expression. Understanding how the sentence and its parts work in relation to one another is fundamental to expressing your thoughts with clarity and purpose. In the simplest sense, grammar (Greek, *grammatikos,* knowing one's language) is the study of the ways that the vocabulary or words of a sentence can be arranged to give meaning. Grammar involves what it is possible to express in a language. Rhetoric (Greek, *rhetorikos,* having the skills of an orator or public speaker) enables you to make choices about putting your words together persuasively. Critical writing involves communicating your reasoned ideas in appropriate grammar and rhetoric.

Most students now coming to university have learned to write by the whole language method, using as models what they read or how they speak. Many teachers identify and explain English grammar and rhetoric, word classes, sentence structure, and punctuation, especially to those students who need help with making their writing conform to conventional practices. Other teachers pay little attention to such matters, in the belief that their students will eventually adopt appropriate language skills. Our view is that some knowledge of grammar and rhetoric is an important part of critical writing, and that this knowledge cannot be gained without some application and practice.

Some students coming to university may suddenly find that their writing is an inadequate vehicle for their ideas and that it is severely criticized by their professors. These students have little equipment to rely on to correct their writing, and they cannot identify the word classes (or parts of speech) and punctuation problems that are marked as inadequate in their writing.

This chapter is directed at just those students, to give them the information about the kinds of terminology, concepts, and practices that will help them improve their writing.

Standard written English is expected in universities and colleges, but many students have had little or no formal training in writing skills (rhetoric), grammar, or punctuation, and have rarely had their work corrected in ways that will help them to improve. Hence, they are at a tremendous disadvantage when they have to write assignments that meet university expectations. Furthermore, standard written English is the acceptable language for job applications, letters of introduction and reference, and all sorts of other communications.

First, grammar as a *structure* refers to the system of a language according to its word classes (called *lexis*) and its arrangement of words into phrases, clauses, and sentences (called *syntax*).

Second, grammar is also a *description* of how that structure works according to the conventions and practices people follow when writing or speaking. Descriptive grammars are used by linguists to study changes in usage and shifts in conventions, without saying what is good or bad usage. They are also used to describe the structure of a language, setting out its terms and definitions. Such descriptive grammars can be traditional, and most grammar handbooks, including this one, define and classify terms largely according to the conventions derived from the classical languages of Greek and Latin (which dominated so much earlier education). At the same time, this traditional grammar has been modified by other kinds of grammar, such as the study of large sentence structures that transform the relationships of words to meaning by adding endings or other changes and by generating expectations as a sentence unfolds (as in transformational-generative grammar).

Third, grammar is *prescriptive* in that it often refers to what is deemed to be correct or to the so-called rules of grammar when the customs of acceptable usage become obligatory, pointing to the benefits of clarity in communication. Most students have already assimilated many of these conventions and use them acceptably in their writing. They are able to reformulate sentences and are at least partly aware of the differences in meaning that are open to them. Such choices are both grammatical (that is, students have to meet the conventions of the language) and rhetorical (they are able to assess the persuasive effect of different choices). At times, however, many students get tangled up in their expression of ideas and cannot understand how to improve or even how to follow an instructor's corrections. This chapter addresses such problems by setting out both a description of the structure of standard English grammar and also a guide to usage for those places in student writing where the structure is weak or falls apart. We do indicate unacceptable usage, but rather than asserting that one usage alone is the correct one, we point out that several choices are possible and explain how each meets the requirements of standard English, the acceptable mode of writing in universities, government, business, and the workplace.

We maintain that some knowledge of grammar and rhetoric improves a good writer and is essential for a weaker writer, at least in understanding the corrections and instructions that are marked on returned essays. For some students, practice in correcting faults in grammar will almost immediately improve their writing and grades. For all students, a knowledge of grammar basics will enable them to read and write with greater fluency and precision. You should use this chapter both as a review to cover the points of grammar that you are unsure of and also as a reference to help you understand your instructor's marking of your assignments. You should also use your instructor's help in dealing with any questions of grammar or punctuation in your work that you do not understand or with areas in which you need more work. Finally, you should use the grammar checker on your word processor, along with its advice and explanations, once you have a draft that you want to correct.

WORDS, PHRASES, CLAUSES, AND SENTENCES

Language determines the ways in which we think by influencing how we perceive, understand, remember, and communicate. Without words and the commonly accepted structures that hold them together, human thought and communication would be virtually impossible. Hence, any understanding we gain about language, especially the ability to use it more clearly and forcefully, marks an advance in our ability to think. The fundamental unit of the English language is the word, and words are combined into larger structures, called phrases and clauses, that together compose a sentence. Sentences are the instruments of thought, and the way people use words and sentences dictates the ways in which they think. Sentences, then, contain fully formulated thoughts, and analyzing a sentence requires examining its parts.

Each English sentence has two major parts: the subject and the predicate (see Figure 5.1).

Word Classes

The basic building blocks of standard English are words held together in sentences. Even in a nonsense sentence you know whether it fits a standard English grammatical pattern or not. If I say, "The forbles grobed a dindle," you have no difficulty in recognizing that the pattern is correct, even though the meaning is nonsense. We understand that the words *forbles* and *dindle* are the same types of words and that *grobed* is a different type. To verify our understanding we can substitute real words, "The judges picked a winner." So, in the sentence "My brother plays basketball after school," we sense that *brother, basketball*, and *school* are similar types of words. We also know that *brother* and *plays* are different types of words, and we can say that they belong to different word classes. Categorizing words into their classes enables you to describe their relationships and to understand how they function. Words can have different forms *(brother, brothers)*, different positions in a sentence (we can rearrange it as "After school my brother plays basketball"), and different functions

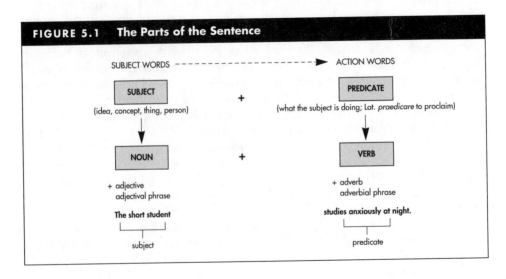

FIGURE 5.1   The Parts of the Sentence

SUBJECT WORDS ---------------------→ ACTION WORDS

SUBJECT
(idea, concept, thing, person)

+

PREDICATE
(what the subject is doing; Lat. *praedicare* to proclaim)

NOUN

+

VERB

+ adjective
adjectival phrase

+ adverb
adverbial phrase

The short student

studies anxiously at night.

subject

predicate

in relation to each other (*brother* says who is playing; *basketball* says what is played; and *play* says what my brother does). Word classes (called *parts of speech* in some grammars) provide a system of categorizing words so you can identify their characteristics and fit them together coherently.

In English there are eight word classes:

- nouns, pronouns, adjectives
- verbs, adverbs
- interjections, prepositions, conjunctions

There are various ways of classifying them. One method is to distinguish among meaning words, asserting words, and function words:

Meaning words (specify objects, persons or things, actions, qualities, ideas, or abstractions):

1. naming words (name things, persons, feelings, ideas, or concepts)
   - nouns
   - noun substitutes: pronouns
2. describing words for nouns and pronouns: adjectives

Asserting words:

1. action words
   - verbs
   - the verb *to be,* the copula, or other linking verbs
2. describing or intensifying words for verbs, adjectives, and other adverbs: adverbs
3. intensifying exclamations inserted suddenly into a sentence: interjections

Function or linking words:

1. linking words for nouns in phrases: prepositions
2. linking words for words, phrases, and clauses: conjunctions

Nouns

Nouns (French, *non, nom* < Latin, *nomen,* name) are naming words that specify objects, persons, things, actions, qualities, ideas, or abstractions. Nouns may differ with respect to number (singular and plural), gender, and case.

Case refers to the relationships between nouns and pronouns and the other parts of the sentence. The *subjective* (or nominative) case refers to nouns or pronouns that are the subjects of a sentence or clause; the *objective* case refers to nouns or pronouns that are the objects of the action of a verb or of a preposition. The third case for nouns and pronouns in English is the *possessive* case, which is used to indicate possession or ownership. Here, the spelling is changed by the use of the apostrophe and the letter *s: the girl's hat* (one girl); *the students' essays* (several students).

Pronouns

Pronouns substitute for, stand for, or replace a noun (Latin, *pro,* for). The *antecedent* of a pronoun is the noun to which it refers. Like nouns, pronouns are distinguished by number (singular and plural), by gender (as with nouns), and by case. However, the case of pronouns is indicated by differences in spelling or by inflections that indicate the case. There also is a wide variety of pronouns:

Personal pronouns refer to the speaker or the person spoken to, or about.

Person	Case	Singular	Plural
first	subjective	I	we
	objective	me	us
	possessive	my, mine	our, ours
second	subj.	you (thou)	you (ye)
	obj.	you (thee)	you
	poss.	your (thy)	your
		yours (thine)	yours
third	subj.	he, she, it	they
	obj.	him, her, it	them
	poss.	his, her, hers, its	their, theirs

Impersonal pronouns refer to no person or thing in particular, but rather to a general reference: *One must be careful. It is getting late.* Other impersonal pronouns include *there* (*There is no end to the trouble*), the editorial *we* (*We cannot praise the people enough*) and *they* (*They say it will get colder*). A common mistake is to confuse the possessive pronoun *its* (*The dog wags* its *tail*) with the contraction of the impersonal pronoun *it's* (*It's a sunny day* = *It is a sunny day*).

Relative pronouns relate an adjectival clause to its antecedent: *who, which, that. That* refers to persons or things, and *which* refers to things. Only *who* has a full declension:

- who (subjective)
- whom (objective)
- whose (possessive)

The difference between the subjective and objective cases gives students the most problems. *Who* is used as the subject of a verb: *The student who is sick missed the exam. Whom* must be the object of a verb or of a preposition: *The student to whom I gave that grade was very pleased.* Another common mistake is to confuse the possessive relative pronoun (*whose*) with the contraction for *who is* (*who's*): *Whose is that? Who's late for class?* (= *Who is late for class?*).

Interrogative pronouns ask a question: *Who? Whom? Whose? Which? What?* and the same words with *-ever* added (*Whoever? Whatever?*): *Who called? You gave it to whom? Whose coat is torn? Which is unclear? What is that?*

Demonstrative pronouns point to the thing referred to: *this, that* (singular), *these, those* (plural): *This is acceptable work, but that is not.*

Indefinite pronouns imply but do not have a specific antecedent: *all, each, either, one, someone, anyone, nobody, everything, nothing,* and so on.

Reflexive and *intensive pronouns* combine some form of personal pronoun with *-self* or *-selves.* Intensive pronouns are used for emphasis: *He himself came. They themselves found her.* Reflexive pronouns signal that the subject receives the action of the verb: *She is working herself to death.*

Adjectives

Adjectives (Latin, *adjicere* < *ad*, to; *jacere*, to throw, to add to) modify nouns or pronouns by describing or limiting them. Adjectives usually precede or immediately follow the noun they modify (*the* red *house, the day* following). Adjectives that follow linking or copula verbs are called *predicate adjectives* (*The bus was* crowded. *This milk smells* sour). *Verbal adjectives* are made from the present and past participles of verbs, like *following* and *crowded* above. A special group of adjectives are called *articles.* The adjectives *a* and *an* are *indefinite articles;* the adjective *the* is a *definite article.* Adjectives may be compared (positive, comparative, and superlative degrees: stem, stem + *er*, stem + *est:* e.g., *smooth, smoother, smoothest*). Some adjectives are irregular (*good, better, best; little, less, least; much more, most*).

When many words discussed in the pronoun section above are used to modify a noun, they function as adjectives. That is, a pronoun is an adjective when it is used with a noun. This category includes *possessive adjectives* (*my, your, their,* and so on: *my coffee*); *relative adjectives* (*which* and *whose,* as well as *what* and *whatever: We know which road to take and whose car; we shall take whatever car runs*); *interrogative adjectives* (*what, which, whose: What book is lost?*); *demonstrative adjectives* (*this, that, these, those: These exercises are easy*); and *indefinite adjectives* (*all, each, either,* and so on: *Each question must be answered*).

Verbs

Verbs (French, *verbe,* verb < Latin, *verbum,* a verb, a word) designate an action, condition, process, or state of being. That is, they assert or predicate something. There are three principal parts to the English verb as shown here with the verb *to be.*

1. infinitive or base form: (*to*) *walk,* (*to*) *play*   (*to*) *be*
2. past tense, or imperfect: (I) *walked*   *was, were*
3. past participle: (I have) *walked*   *been*

Some grammars add two other verb forms:

4. present tense: I *walk,* he/she *walks,*   *am, is, are*
5. present participle: (I am) *walking*   *being*

Types of verbs

Regular (or "weak") *verbs,* the most common category of English verbs, form their principal parts by adding *-ed* to the stem; many verbs have omitted the *-ed* of the past tense and so have all three parts identical (*cut, hit, set, shut*). In a few cases the past participle is formed by adding *t* (*slept*). Fewer than one hundred *irregular* (or "strong") verbs form their past tense and past participles in irregular ways with a change in *spelling* (*run, ran, run; do, did, done; eat, ate, eaten; begin, began, begun*).

There are twenty-six *auxiliary* (or *helping*) *verbs* in English that combine with the root form of the verb (e.g., *can walk*) or a participle (e.g., *were walking, had played*) to convey time and other meanings:

Auxiliaries

have, has, had
do, does, did
be, am, is, are, was, were, being, been

Modal auxiliary verbs

can	could
shall	should
will	would
may	might
must	ought to
used to	had better

Inflection

Verbs in English are inflected, or change their forms, according to the usage demanded by voice, mood, tense, number, and person.

Voice can be active or passive. In the active voice the subject is the actor and there is a direct statement of the action of the subject: *I walked the dog. The cat eats its tuna. Mike played the guitar.* In the passive voice the subject is acted on: *The tuna is eaten by the cat. The guitar was played.*

Mood signifies a writer's position concerning the fact or action being expressed. There are three moods. *Indicative* states a fact or asks a question: *Susan studies in the library every day. Did you walk the dog? Imperative* expresses a command: *Study harder and sleep less. Subjunctive* indicates a wish, desire, regret, or hope: *If I were to win the lottery, I would buy a new car. I wish I were a better student.*

There are six *tenses* in English. For example, here are the six tenses of the active voice of *to take*:

1. present (simple, progressive, emphatic): *I take, I am taking, I do take.*

2. past (imperfect): *I took, I was taking, I did take.*

3. future: *I shall take, I shall be taking* (no emphatic).

4. present perfect (uses *have, has* + past participle): *I have taken. I have been taking.*

5. past perfect (uses *had* + past participle): *I had taken. I had been taking.*

6. future perfect (uses *shall/will have* + past participle*): I shall have taken. I shall have been taking.*

Verbs also change their form according to whether the subject is singular or plural in number and whether it is first, second, or third person: *I take, you take, he or she takes, we take, you take, they take.*

Conjugation

To conjugate a verb, we set out all of the principal parts and the tenses and variants of a verb; a *synopsis* summarizes a conjugation in one person and number only, as in the example of *to take,* above.

Verbals

Verbals continue to be a verb, but they are used as another part of speech as well:

A *participle* is a verbal adjective with *-ing* added to the base form. As a verb it will have tense and voice; as an adjective a participle will modify a noun: *the coming decade*.

A *gerund* is a verbal noun with *-ing* added to the base form. Before a gerund, the possessive case of a noun or pronoun is required: *Her working in San Salvador was dangerous*; *The journalist's departing from San Salvador was dangerous*.

Infinitives

An *infinitive* is a verbal noun, adjective, or adverb: *To lie in court is foolish* (noun). *This question is the exercise to write for next week* (verbal adjective, modifying *exercise*). *Use a computer to check your spelling* (verbal adverb, modifying *use*).

Classification

Verbs can be classified as transitive, intransitive, copulative, or auxiliary.

A *transitive* verb needs a direct object to complete the meaning: *I told a story*.

An *intransitive* verb does not need a direct object to complete meaning: *Birds fly*.

A *copulative verb*, also called a *linking verb*, links the subject to its description. Common copulas include *be, become, appear, seem, feel, grow*, and *prove*. The verb *to be* is irregular throughout.

An *auxiliary verb* helps form tenses of other verbs: *have, be, shall, will, can, may, must, ought, do, should, would* (see above).

Adverbs

Adverbs modify verbs, adjectives, and other adverbs and often use the suffix *-ly* (*coldly, happily*). Adverbs say where, how, why, when, to what extent, and under what circumstances something happens. Like adjectives, they may be compared (*fast, faster, fastest*); some are irregular (*little, less, least*).

Some adverbs function also as conjunctions to connect a complete sentence to a preceding sentence. They are called *conjunctive adverbs* (*especially, hence, however, therefore, nevertheless, then, besides, also, so, further, furthermore, moreover, still, only, consequently, accordingly*, etc.).

Other types of adverbs include adverbs of time (*now, soon, never, yesterday*), of place (*away, here, downstairs, outside*), of manner (*bravely, fondly, sadly, wearily*), and of degree (*very, truly, completely, extremely, rarely*).

Prepositions

Prepositions link a noun or pronoun (called the *object*) to other parts of the sentence (preposition + object = a prepositional phrase). Prepositions give the location or position (hence, pre-position is their name) of the noun or pronoun they are attached to. Many of these usages are *idiomatic* (a conventional phraseology accepted in popular usage, but with a meaning that cannot be determined by its separate words). We use specific prepositions in certain phrases: *accuse a person of a crime*; *different from* (not *to* or *than*); *in respect of* (not *to*); *inferior to* (not *than*); *superior to* (not *than*); *with a view to* (not *of*), and many more. A long list is given in Eric Partridge's *Usage and Abusage*. Other prepositions include *in, over, from, beside*, and *after*.

Conjunctions

Conjunctions link words, phrases, and clauses and indicate whether the relationship between the parts is equal or unequal. *Coordinating conjunctions* connect words, phrases, or clauses of equal grammatical rank:

- additive coordinating conjunction: *and*
- contrasting coordinating conjunction: *but, yet*
- separative coordinating conjunction: *or, either, neither, nor*
- final coordinating conjunction: *for, so*

Subordinating conjunctions connect subordinate clauses with independent ones (minor to major ones). Some of these conjunctions are *after, although, as, as if, as though, because, before, even if, even though, if, in case, in order that, no matter if, once, provided, since, so that, than, that, though, till, unless, until, when, whenever, whereas, wherever, whether,* and *while.*

Correlative conjunctions are used in pairs to join equivalent parts of a sentence: *either ... or, neither ... nor, so ... as, both ... and, whether ... or, not ... but, not only ... but also.*

Interjections

Interjections express sudden and strong emotion and are followed by an exclamation point or a comma. They intensify the emotion of the speaker or the assertion being made. Common interjections include *Golly, Gosh, Wow! Oh, Alas! Help! Hurrah! Ouch!* and *Well!* In analytical writing interjections should be used sparingly, if at all.

Parts of the Sentence

A sentence has two parts, a subject and a predicate. The *subject* names the person or thing that acts, and the *predicate* consists of the verb and all of the words that are associated with it (such as adverbs). The *direct object* of a sentence is the person, place, or thing that receives the action of a transitive verb. A *complement* completes a verb by adding additional information about a subject or object. A *subject complement* is a noun or adjective that describes the subject of a copula verb: *This essay* is excellent. An *object complement* follows a direct object and completes it, with an implied *to be*: *The examiners found the answer* acceptable (*acceptable* is an adjective modifying *answer* and functioning as an object complement to the direct object *answer*). The sentence could read: *The examiners found the answer* to be *acceptable.*

There are five basic sentence patterns in English:

1. subject + verb: *The cat eats.*
2. subject + verb + object: *The cat eats its tuna.*
3. subject + verb + indirect object + direct object: *The student writes her mother letters.*
4. subject + verb + subject complement: *The student is a visitor.*
5. subject + verb + direct object + object complement: *Some teachers call articulate students cheaters.*

To add precise details and variety to your writing, you can expand such basic sentence patterns by using modifiers (adjectives and adverbs), by adding phrases or clauses, or by rearranging the sentence order.

The Phrase

A *phrase* is a group of words that does not contain a subject, a predicate, or both. A phrase is marked by a preposition, an infinitive, or a participle with related words. There are several common kinds of phrase, each of which functions as a single part of speech:

A *prepositional phrase* is introduced by a preposition, followed by an object: *in the summer*. Prepositional phrases function as modifiers in either adjectival or adverbial phrases: *The heat* in the summer...; *we came* after the summer.

An *infinitive phrase* is introduced by an infinitive: *to try harder*. It may function as a noun, adjective, or adverb: *He hopes* to try harder (noun); *It is time* to try harder (adjective); *He is careful* to try harder (adverb).

A *participial phrase* is introduced by a participle: *seeing the end*. It may function as a noun (sometimes called a *gerund phrase*) or as an adjective: *He hated* seeing the end *of a play* (noun—object); seeing the end *of a play was difficult for him* (noun—subject); *the audience,* seeing the end, *understands him* (adjective).

The Clause

A *clause* is a part of a sentence having a subject and a predicate. *Independent* (or *main*) *clauses* can stand by themselves as single sentences. An independent clause is not introduced by a subordinate conjunction, but it may be introduced by a coordinating conjunction. *Dependent* (or *subordinate*) *clauses* are not complete in themselves and cannot stand as simple sentences. They depend on an independent clause and appear to be part of a sentence. In fact, dependent clauses function as parts of speech—as nouns, adjectives, or adverbs.

A *noun clause* functions as a noun, as the subject of a verb, as the object of a verb, as the object of a preposition, in apposition to a noun, or as a predicate nominative. Most noun clauses begin with *that, what, whatever,* or *whoever*:

That he is right is clear. (subject of verb)

They swore *that he told lies.* (object of verb)

Do you agree with *what she said?* (object of preposition)

The goal *that he accepted* is won. (apposition: noun or noun clause in parallel with another noun)

The end is *what I always feared.* (predicate nominative: noun or noun clause in the predicate that renames the subject)

An *adjectival clause* modifies a noun or pronoun. Most adjectival clauses begin with a relative pronoun: *who, whose, whom, which,* or *that.*

The man *who ate the pie* left. (modifies *man*)

The jewellery box, *which I loved,* was stolen. (modifies *box*)

The Dickens character [*that*] *I like best* is Oliver Twist. (modifies *character*)

An *adverbial clause* modifies a verb, an adjective, or an adverb. Adverbial clauses can be recognized easily because they answer the questions, When? Where? Why? How much?

He came *when you called.* (modifies verb: when?)

He cried *because you hit him.* (modifies verb: why?)

He is older *than you think he is.* (modifies adjective)

He works faster *than I do.* (modifies adverb)

In addition, there are two special kinds of adverbial clauses. A *conditional clause* describes the condition necessary for the rest of the sentence to be true; it usually begins with *if: If you shout, I'll leave.* The other kind of adverbial clause is a *concessional clause,* which states a concession opposed to the intent of the main clause; it usually begins with *although: Although she is rich, she buys second-hand clothes.*

Subordinate clauses may also be restrictive or nonrestrictive. A *restrictive clause* restricts or limits the meaning to one particular person, place, or thing: *The shirt that you bought yesterday has shrunk.* A *nonrestrictive clause* merely adds more information to the idea in the main clause: *Economics, which is a hard subject, is popular among first-year students.* A nonrestrictive clause is always separated from the rest of the sentence with commas.

The Sentence and Sentence Types

The sentence is a structural unit of written or spoken composition that contains a subject and a predicate, expressing a complete thought. Every sentence must have a substantive to indicate what the sentence is about (a noun or pronoun, or some other noun equivalent, such as a verbal), and also a verb. *Noun* and *verb* refer to parts of speech; *subject* and *predicate* refer to the functions of those parts in a sentence:

noun	*verb*
Birds	fly.
subject	*predicate*

The predicate may contain much more than the verb, of course, to complement or complete the meaning of the verb: *Birds fly south in the winter. Fly* and all that follows is a predicate.

In conventional or standard English ideas are usually put together in sentences that first name a thing or concept and then say what the thing or concept does. There are four kinds of sentences in English (see Box 5.1).

Simple sentences contain only one main clause (only one subject and one predicate), though either the subject or the predicate may be compound:

noun conj. noun	*verb*
Dogs and cats	howled.
compound subject	*predicate*

noun conj. noun	*verb conj. verb*
Dogs and cats	howled and fought.
compound subject	*compound predicate*

Compound sentences combine two or more simple sentences as two parts of one thought, joined by a coordinating conjunction. Each of the former sentences becomes an independent clause. Normally, a comma separates the clauses joined by a coordinating conjunction:

BOX 5.1	The Four Sentence Types

1. one idea or subject + one action = a **simple sentence**
2. two or more simple sentences combined = a **compound sentence**
   (with a linking word like *and* to link equal parts together)
3. one simple sentence + a subordinate clause = a **complex sentence**
4. two simple sentences joined with a linking word + a subordinate clause =
   a **compound-complex sentence**

You may not pass. (simple sentence)

You should at least try. (simple sentence)

You may not pass, but you should at least try. (compound sentence)

Complex sentences have one main clause and one or more subordinate clauses:
If the weather is fine, we shall go on a picnic.

Compound-complex sentences have two or more main clauses and one or more subordinate clauses:
   If the weather is fine, we shall leave, but they will stay.

PUNCTUATION MARKS AND THEIR USES

Punctuation has a purpose—to mark off the units of thought in your writing so that your reader can understand your meaning fully. In speech, those marks are pauses, intonations, inflections in the voice, and gestures. In writing, these devices are changed into punctuation marks that over time writers and readers have agreed to use in specific ways. That is, punctuation is conventional, and when you break with what a reader expects, such as by putting a comma where a period would be customary, the reader is confused and has to reread your sentence. Your train of thought is interrupted, and your reader is left unsure of your meaning. Where your punctuation should be helpful it becomes misleading. Proper punctuation will greatly facilitate a reader's apprehension of your argument.

Literacy in standard English requires facility in the use of punctuation. An academic essay will not be praised for proper punctuation, but it will be criticized and possibly downgraded if it contains punctuation errors. The discussion of punctuation that follows is intended as an introduction to, rather than as an exhaustive treatment of, the subject. An understanding of the definitions and usage we discuss will enable you to communicate your ideas clearly; you will be able to supply helpful guideposts to lead your reader through your ideas—and through your prose.

Period

A *period* is used at the end of a sentence that is a statement or a command. It indicates a full stop after a completed idea in an indicative or imperative sentence. If a period follows a partial sentence, one lacking a subject or a main verb, the error is a sentence fragment: *The castle, overgrown with moss and cobwebs* (incorrect—needs a main verb). A run-on sentence omits periods, combining independent clauses, fragments, or complete sentences without the necessary internal or final punctuation:

✗   Industrialization began in Canada during the late nineteenth century it greatly expanded however during World War I helped by European immigration.

✔   Industrialization began in Canada during the late nineteenth century. It greatly expanded, however, during World War I, helped by European immigration.

Comma

A *comma* chiefly connects but also separates the parts of a sentence. It indicates to the reader a pause in the thought, a grouping of words for another thought, and a point of emphasis. It has a wide variety of specific uses, of which we mention the most important. It should not be used haphazardly. When you are writing a first draft or taking notes, you should not get into the habit of adding a comma randomly, just when you stop to think. To guide your reader effectively, you need to use commas deliberately according to the following conventions:

1.   Use a comma before coordinating conjunctions (*and, but, yet, or, nor, for,* and *so*) in compound sentences (with two independent clauses, each a complete sentence): *Frankenstein crossed the ice, and the monster moved toward him.*

  • Do not use a comma when the compound elements are not independent clauses: *Frankenstein crossed the ice and lost his way* (the *and* introduces a predicate only, not an independent clause with its own subject; hence, no comma is used).

  • Do not use a comma to join independent clauses without a coordinating conjunction:

  ✗   The monster lept toward him, he could not escape. (comma splice)

  ✔   The monster lept toward him, but he could not escape.

2.   Use a comma to separate items (words, phrases, and clauses) in a series of more than two, including before the last item: *The parrot eats carrots, corn, and peas. It fluffs its feathers, clears its throat, and sings "Yankee Doodle."*

3.   Use a comma after introductory modifiers (words, phrases, or clauses): *After work, I still had to study.*

4.   Use a comma with nonrestrictive (nonessential) modifiers such as dependent clauses, appositives, and participial phrases. Modifiers are nonrestrictive when they are not essential to the basic meaning of the sentence, even though they may add important information: *My sister, the smartest of the family, is older than I.* But with a restrictive modifier, no commas are used: *Coppola's film* Apocalypse Now *stars Marlon Brando.* The appositive *Apocalypse Now* restricts or limits the meaning: without it we would not know which of Coppola's films is referred to. Hence, there are no commas. Another

way of thinking about restrictive and nonrestrictive modifying phrases or clauses is to consider them as essential or nonessential. Commas are used to indicate the fact that this information is not essential. To see whether the information is essential or not, read the sentence without the modifier, and if the meaning is fundamentally unchanged, the modifier is nonessential (or nonrestrictive) and should be set off by commas.

5. Use a comma after and around conjunctive adverbs (such as *hence, however, therefore,* and *thus*) and transitional phrases (such as *for example, in addition, it seems to me, on the contrary,* and *that is*): *That is, she died. It is true, however, that Rover has fleas.*

   - Do not use a comma to join a sentence to an independent clause introduced with a conjunctive adverb. You are misusing the conjunctive adverb as a coordinating conjunction and also are committing a comma splice:

   ✘ Our cat never scratches, however it is true that Rover has fleas. (this example also omits the comma after *however*)

   ✔ Our cat never scratches, but it is true that Rover has fleas. (use a coordinating conjunction with a comma before it)

   ✔ Our cat never scratches; however, it is true that Rover has fleas. (use a semicolon to separate the independent clauses)

   ✔ Our cat never scratches. However, it is true that Rover has fleas. (separate the independent clauses into separate sentences)

6. Use a comma between coordinating adjectives (that is, adjectives equal in value that modify the same noun): *Death of a Salesman is a disturbing, absorbing play.* Or, *Death of a Salesman is a disturbing but absorbing play.*

   - Do not use a comma with cumulative adjectives that build meaning from word to word. The order of coordinating adjectives can be interchanged, but that of cumulative adjectives cannot be changed without writing nonsense.

   ✘ The lecturer stressed several, common, grammatical, mistakes. (the three adjectives cannot be interchanged)

   ✔ The lecturer stressed several common grammatical mistakes.

7. Use a comma with quoted words introduced by a verb of saying or an equivalent word: *She said, "It's a cold winter."* Or, *The poet Blake wrote, "In every cry of every Man ... the mind-forged manacles I hear."* Or, *"In every cry of every Man," claimed Blake, "the mind-forged manacles I hear."*

   - Do not use a comma when the quoted words are introduced with *that* or *as: Blake referred to the misuse of reason as "mind-forged manacles."* Also, do not use a comma when a quoted phrase is part of your own sentence: *Blake claimed that "mind-forged manacles" were heard in "every cry of every Man."*

8. Use a comma with titles and degrees (*Mary Jones, M.D., gave expert testimony*), addresses (*Hamilton, Ontario*), dates (*Friday, June 2, 1998*—but omit the second comma when the date is reversed: *Friday, 2 June 1998*), and letter openings and closings (*Dear Cynthia,*).

   - Do not use the comma in numbers to mark off thousands—use a space instead. Four-digit numbers can be grouped together. This usage represents a change resulting from conversion to the metric system in Canada: 333 000 or 4500.

The most frequent comma error is the *comma blunder* (also called the *comma curse* or the *comma splice*). This fault joins independent sentences and clauses together with commas (often with no conjunction). It is extremely confusing to a reader: *Johnny flipped the egg over, the lady at the counter watched him.* Comma blunders can be corrected by separating the sentences with an end stop punctuation mark such as a period. Another common comma fault is using it to separate the subject and verb: *The man with the red coat, ran away.* Similarly, a comma is often used mistakenly to separate a verb from the rest of the predicate: *The military defeat of Germany in World War I crippled, the country economically.* Correct these mistakes by omitting the commas.

Semicolon

A *semicolon* is made up of both a period and a comma and has some of the functions of each: it separates and connects. The semicolon has only two uses. First, it joins two independent and complete statements that form one logical unit. The major use of the semicolon, then, is between main clauses that you want to link together because they are closely related: *It rained incessantly; the camping trip had to be postponed.* Often, the thought in the second main clause contradicts the first. In such a case the second clause is usually introduced with a conjunctive adverb: *The essay had mistakes in punctuation; nevertheless, it received a good grade for content. It was raining; however, the sun still shone brightly.*

Second, the semicolon separates items in a series that already has internal commas: *The new student had attended high school in Burnaby, British Columbia; Red Deer, Alberta; and Deep River, Ontario. In his cabinet of 1935 Hitler assumed the role of chancellor; Göring, prime minister; and Goebbels, the minister of propaganda.*

Colon

A *colon* means continue: it announces a continuation. It is preceded by an independent clause and announces that a continuation of the idea or examples follows in the second part of the sentence. Its most frequent use is to introduce formal lists, illustrations, explanations, and examples. It is often preceded by an expression introducing the list or explanation, such as *the following* or *as follows.* The colon is also used to introduce a formal quotation, to separate the main title from the subtitle in the title of a book (*Essays and Reviews: The 1860 Text and Its Reading*), and to separate the chapters and verses of the books of the Bible (*Genesis 3:24*).

Apostrophe

An *apostrophe* signifies an omitted letter or letters and is used in the following instances:

1. to form possessives: *the boy's cat* (one boy, one cat); *the boys' cat* (several boys, one cat); *the boys' cats* (several boys and cats). The singular possessive is formed by adding *'s*: *John's hat.* English and Canadian usage adds the *'s* even when the proper noun ends in *s*: *Charles's friend*; *Burns's poems*; or *Dickens's novels.* Exceptions to this custom are ancient proper nouns: *Jesus' disciples*; *Xerxes' army*; *Ulysses' wanderings.* American usage drops the second *s* in all possessives: *Charles' friend.*

   Plural possessives ending in *s* add only an apostrophe: *several nations' rights.* Plural and collective nouns ending in a letter other than *s* add an apostrophe and then *s*: *the children's fate*; *the people's choice.* Compound possessives add *'s* after the last subject: *Bill and Jill's home.*

2. to indicate omitted letters in contractions: *we've = we have; don't = do not.* But in formal essays, such contractions are not used.

   NOTE: The apostrophe in *it's* indicates the omitted letter of *it is*: It's not hard to remember. The personal pronoun in the possessive case (*its*) never uses an apostrophe: *The cat chases its tail.* It is important, then, to distinguish between the possessive (or genitive) case in English and the contraction. A common mistake in journalism and on the Internet is using an apostrophe with a plural noun: *link's, essay's, street's.*

3. to indicate possession by a noun of the action of a gerund (a verbal noun ending in *-ing*): *Alice's falling asleep* or *John's failing his test.*

4. to form plurals of letters, numerals, and symbols by adding *'s: Mind your p's and q's! Build it with 2 x 4's. Try not to use &'s; instead, spell out the word.*

Other Punctuation Marks

Question marks are used to end a sentence that asks a direct question: *Have you enjoyed that novel?*

- Do not use a question mark for an indirect question. An indirect question is contained in a subordinate clause, often beginning with *if* or *whether,* and the subject and verb are in normal order, unlike in the direct question: *Her friend asked whether she had enjoyed the novel.*

- Do not use a question mark to express sarcasm or irony. Instead, explain your point more fully.

✗ The Vietnam War was great (?) for the United States.

✔ The Vietnam War was a useful testing ground for American military technology, but for the United States it was a political and military disaster.

Exclamation marks are used to end a sentence that demands special emphasis or that expresses a strong emotion such as anger or surprise. It is most often found in dialogue, but it is used rarely in academic prose. *Watch out for that driver! I hate arriving late for class!*

The *dash* (marked in typed essays by a double dash —) replaces the comma for added emphasis when words are taken out of their normal order. It also should be used sparingly.

Parentheses ( ) are used to interrupt a sentence in order to add information that would otherwise intrude on the flow of thought:

W.B. Yeats (1865–1939) is probably the most famous Irish poet.

The violence in the two Alice books (unlike that in *The Color Purple*) occurs entirely within a make-believe world.

Brackets [ ] are used to enclose explanatory material within a quotation. They indicate that you have added information to the quotation:

The Doormouse claimed that "they lived on treacle [molasses]" (*The Annotated Alice* 100).

Ellipses (three periods) are used to indicate omitted material in quotations:

"So she [Alice] was considering ... whether the pleasure of making a daisy-chain would be worth the trouble of getting up and picking the daisies" (*The Annotated Alice* 25).

Italics

The term *italic* derives from fifteenth-century Italian handwriting, and italic letters are slanted (*like this*), unlike upright roman letters. Italics are used for titles of books, newspapers, magazines, journals, plays, longer poems, TV and radio programs, movies, musical compositions, art objects, and foreign words. Italics are indicated in typed or handwritten essays by <u>underlining</u> words once. Most computers have italic fonts; if you can, you should use them instead of underlining.

Hyphen

The *hyphen* joins compound words: *a six-year-old*; *twenty-one*; *pre-World-War-One*; *anti-abortion*; *ex-wife*. When a century term is used as a noun it has no hyphen (*the twentieth century*); when it is used as an adjective modifying a following noun, it requires a hyphen (*nineteenth-century literature*). Hyphens also indicate a break in a word at the end of a line. The break comes only after a syllable. A good dictionary will indicate syllabification. Conventionally, each syllable begins with a consonant, double letters are usually split, and prefixes and suffixes (such as *con-, pre-, mis-,* or *-tion, -ing*) are a single syllable.

Quotation Marks

Double quotation marks are used to indicate the following:

- titles of short works or parts of longer works—short poems, short stories, songs, chapter headings, and magazine and journal articles
- a direct quotation, of either speech or written sources. For long quotations (in verse, three or more lines; in prose, over ten lines), the convention is to indent the passage and single space it, omitting the double quotation marks.

Single quotation marks are used to indicate direct speech within the material that you are quoting:

> "'Curiouser and curiouser!' cried Alice (she was so much surprised)." (*The Annotated Alice* 35).

COMMON ERRORS AND WHAT TO DO ABOUT THEM

Errors in standard written English get in the way of easy comprehension of your ideas by your readers. As well as minor or mechanical errors in punctuation, they involve problems in grammar, including faults with subjects and verbs (agreements, for instance) or with treating phrases or clauses that lack main verbs as though they were complete sentences. The eight most common errors are listed below, along with methods of correcting them. These errors account for most of the basic problems in students' writing. If you learn to avoid them you will have solved most of your grammar and punctuation problems. If you do not learn how to correct them, you will continue to be downgraded by your teachers and will be regarded as, in some measure, functionally illiterate.

1. **A comma splice, fault, or blunder** is the separating of two independent clauses with a comma:

   ✗ Alice goes to Wonderland, she meets many strange characters. (comma splice)

✔ Alice goes to Wonderland. She meets many strange characters. (The faulty sentence is split into two separate sentences.)

✔ Alice goes to Wonderland and meets many strange characters. (The two independent clauses are joined with a coordinating conjunction, giving both clauses equal weight.)

✔ Alice goes to Wonderland, meeting many strange characters. (The second clause is subordinated with a participle, thereby putting more weight on the first clause.)

✔ When Alice goes to Wonderland, she meets many strange characters. (The first clause is subordinated with a subordinating conjunction, thereby giving weight to the second clause.)

2. **A fragment** is a group of words that is punctuated as though it were a sentence, but that does not contain a main (or independent) clause: *Such as these fragments. No main verb.* Effective though they may be in creative writing, fragments are hard for a reader to follow in discursive prose. They can be corrected by attaching the fragment properly to a main clause.

✗ Freud who lived in Vienna at the turn of the century. Produced several studies on hysteria.

✔ Freud, who lived in Vienna at the turn of the century, produced several studies on hysteria.

✗ The castle, overgrown with moss and cobwebs. It was transformed from evil to an utopia.

✔ The castle, overgrown with moss and cobwebs, was transformed from evil to an utopia.

Two of the most common forms of the fragment use a *which* clause or a participle instead of a complete verb:

✗ This study of perception involved only adult males. Which is why it was not reliable. The study indicating, of course, the bias against women.

✔ This study of perception involved only adult males, which is why it was not reliable. The study indicated, of course, the bias against women.

✔✔ Because this study of perception involved only adult males, indicating a bias against women, it was not reliable.

3. **Run-on sentences** are a more serious error than either the comma splice or the sentence fragment. Run-on sentences combine two independent clauses as if they were one.

✗ The professor was speaking too quickly the students could not follow him.

✔ The professor was speaking too quickly. The students could not follow him.

✔✔ Because the professor was speaking too quickly, the students could not follow him.

4. **Dangling modifiers** are subordinate phrases that are not clearly related to or dependent on a definite subject.

✗ Going to the store, it was raining. (dangling participle)

✔ Going to the store, I noticed it was raining.

✔ When I went to the store, it was raining.

5. **Incorrectly placed modifiers** are either too far from the words that they modify or divide words that should remain together. Modifiers (such as adjectives or adverbs) should be placed near the words they modify. The parts of an infinitive should not be separated by an adverb: not *to boldly go* but *to go boldly*. The recent editors of the *Oxford English Dictionary*, however, have declared that split infinitives are now acceptable usage.

6. **Agreement problems** usually involve mixing plural and singular subjects and verbs. Verbs agree with the subject in number and person.

✘ Celie and Nettie writes letters to each other.

✔ Celie and Nettie write letters to each other.

The use of a prepositional phrase between the subject and the verb often confuses students:

✘ The aim of Celie's efforts are to gain economic freedom.

✔ The aim of Celie's efforts is to gain economic freedom. (The aim ... is)

✘ Shug, one of the main female characters, are independent of masculine control.

✔ Shug, one of the main female characters, is independent of masculine control. (Shug ... is)

With the conjunctions *or, either ... or,* and *neither ... nor,* the verb agrees with the part of the compound subject next to the verb:

✘ At the end of the novel, neither Celie nor Shug are under masculine control.

✔ At the end of the novel, neither Celie nor Shug is under masculine control.

Also, the subjects of sentences beginning *there is* [*are*] follow the verb: *There is a bird at my window; there are many birds at my window.*

Collective nouns (which refer to a collection of things as one, for example, *nation, army, herd, crowd*) are singular and take a singular verb: *The crowd is unruly.*

7. **Noun–pronoun antecedent problems** usually involve having a plural pronoun refer to a singular noun as its antecedent. A pronoun must agree with its antecedent noun in person, gender, and number.

✘ The student must write their essays carefully.

✔ The students must write their essays carefully.

✔ The student must write his/her essays carefully.

The indefinite pronoun without an antecedent supposes that a reader understands what might be a complicated sequence of ideas, when in fact the pronoun glosses over the precise meaning that is intended. The error usually takes the form of beginning a sentence with *this is.* This error is easily corrected by adding a noun that sums up the argument.

✘ Nettie, Shug, and Sophia are Celie's role models. Albert is not a role model. This shows the text's feminist strategy.

✔ This modelling shows the text's feminist strategy.

8. **Contractions** such as *I'll, we'll,* and *couldn't* should not be used in academic essays; they should be reserved for informal use and e-mail. Contractions are often confused with the possessive case of the personal pronoun. Contractions are verb forms that abbreviate (or contract) the verb and connect it to the subject: *it's* (= it is; often confused with *its*); *they're* (= they are, often confused with *their* and *there*); *who's* (= who is, often confused with *whose*). By far the most common of these mistakes concerns *its* and *it's*.

   ✗ This dog walks on it's hind legs when its doing circus tricks.

   ✔ This dog walks on its hind legs when it's doing circus tricks.

There are many resources that you can turn to for help with these and other common problems with grammar and punctuation. Many handbooks for writers have sections on grammar; all discuss style and argument. One of the best is Lynn Quitman Troyka's *Quick Access: A Reference for Writers*. As well, there are many online sites that give help on all aspects of grammar, common mistakes, and usage. The advice in the online manual from the Writing Center at Purdue University is particularly complete and includes other documents. See their site at **owl.english.purdue.edu/writers/by-topic.htm** to access their publications. Another example is the Grammar Handbook at the University of Illinois at Urbana-Champagne: **www.english.uiuc.edu/cws/wworkshop/grammarmenu.htm/**.

FURTHER READINGS

Handbooks

Buckley, Joanne. *Fit to Print: The Canadian Student's Guide to Essay Writing.* Toronto: Harcourt Brace, 1991.

Connor, William. *Harbrace College Handbook for Canadian Writers.* Toronto: Harcourt Brace, 1994.

Gefvert, Constance. *The Confident Writer.* New York: Norton, 1988.

Messenger, W.E., and Jan de Bruyn. *The Canadian Writer's Handbook.* Scarborough, ON: Prentice Hall, 1995.

Strunk, William, and E.B. White. *The Elements of Style.* 3rd ed. New York: Macmillan, 1979.

Troyka, Lynn. *Quick Access: A Reference for Writers.* 2nd ed. Upper Saddle River, NJ: Prentice-Hall, 1995.

Grammar Reference

Harris, Muriel, and Joan Pilz. *Reference Guide to Grammar and Usage.* Scarborough, ON: Prentice Hall, 1994.

Quirk, Randolph, Sidney Greenbaum, Geoffrey Leech, and Jan Svartik. *A Grammar of Contemporary English.* London: Longman, 1972.

WEBLINKS

- The Online Writery at the University of Missouri
  web.missouri.edu/~writery

- ESL Grammar and other links
  depts.gellaudet.edu/englishworks/tablecontent.html

- The Grammar Doctor
  www.grammardoctor.com

- The Grammar Lady
  grammarlady.com/

- The Internet Grammar
  www.ucl.ac.uk/internet-grammar/

- National Writing Centers Association (NWCA)
  departments.colgate.edu/diw/NWCAOWLS.html

- Online English Grammar
  www.edunet.com/english/grammar/index.cfm

- Study Web
  www.studyweb.com/links/1239.html

- Writing Center at Purdue University
  owl.english.purdue.edu/writers/by-topic.html

DEVELOPING A CRITICAL ATTITUDE

C h a p t e r

6

Your position in the classroom has already been discussed in Chapter 1 concerning where to sit, how to avoid classroom distractions, and what to do about disruptions. But the larger question is, How do you present yourself through your conduct, interest, and performance as a valuable member of the class? At issue here is how you are positioning yourself with respect to your own abilities, the course materials, the other students, and the professor. In all sorts of ways you communicate important messages about your intellectual attitudes and about how you are using the skills in critical thinking that you are learning.

Your physical deportment, your arrival time, how and where you sit, how alert you are—all of these may seem trivial and inconsequential. But professors notice when students continually arrive late for class, sneak into the back corner seat, arrive without books or pens, fall asleep ten minutes after arriving, and wake up early enough to slide out (sometimes noisily) ten minutes before the end of the class. This conduct suggests that such students regard their course, their classmates, and their professor with contempt—or at least they treat them with contempt. On the other hand, arriving with work ready and with a lively and engaged attitude will earn you the respect of other students and the teacher too. It is certain that enhancing those attitudes of mind will make you a better and more successful student and will nourish your own abilities.

Your attitude toward the course materials, your classmates, and the teacher relates to matters of critical thinking. Virtually any course can be open to methods of critical thinking, and in many courses the instructor will encourage a questioning attitude toward the course materials. In some courses, there appears to be a body of material that the professor simply has to cover, perhaps more or less without question. In still other courses, the professor has taken a set position that discourages disagreement, and in such a course a questioning attitude might prompt a negative response.

If we assume that a course encourages critical thinking, an analytical and questioning attitude of mind, and an openness to legitimate student enquiry, then positioning yourself with regard to the course content, lectures, and texts is vital. You will be learning the skills for reading the texts according to the principles of analysis and critical reading that the course advocates, and you will be noting points of disagreement or questioning in the margins of your lecture and seminar notes.

CONSIDERING YOUR AUDIENCE IN CLASS PRESENTATIONS

For many students speaking in class is a frightening experience. You should be aware, however, that other students are also frightened. Your performance in the class is an important basis for the impression you make on your fellow classmates and your instructors. Hence, it is important that you take part in classroom discussion and demonstrate yourself to be an active member of the ongoing intellectual work in the course. Above all, though, you have paid for this course, and you are seeking to get the most benefit from it. You should develop the skills to formulate the questions that will clarify understanding of the course. Your classmates and your instructor are your audience for any questions that you might ask or for any presentations that you have to make. That is not to say that you are seeking an edge over your classmates, or that you are engaging in intellectual bullying or mental aggression. Instead, you, along with your classmates, will be expected to raise questions about what you do not understand, to have a position on the course readings and lectures up to that point, and to be able to articulate the course's goals, methods, and interim conclusions. After all, it is your right to take part in this discussion, to make this presentation, to speak on this book report, or to ask this question.

Many courses require you to make seminar presentations to your classmates. For many students, presenting is an extremely intimidating experience; however, these presentations give you a chance to demonstrate, in an isolated instance, your grasp of the course materials and your ability to work with them. Classroom presentations raise the questions of the appropriate audience and of your position with regard to that audience. You are usually expected to assume that everyone in the class has read the assigned material. Many students have been taught to assume that their audience knows nothing and that the materials have to be explained from the ground up, or that the audience is made up of literate but nonspecialist readers or listeners who are unfamiliar with the course materials. Such a view is often manifested at the beginning of a class presentation or an essay when a nervous student explains what the book is and who the author is—facts already evident to the whole class from the syllabus. You need to ask yourself, "To whom am I speaking?" The answer is usually to your fellow students. However, while you can assume that the rest of the class has some familiarity with the materials (and you, like the seminar leader, must assume that all have done the assigned readings), you cannot expect that they will know the definitions of technical terms or difficult concepts or that they will have the background information that you have acquired in preparing for your presentation. Hence, you should speak with some authority and assurance, but from your reading you will also be aware that you have selected only several aspects of the material to highlight and that your treatment, while comprehensive, is not exhaustive.

Your purpose in class presentations is usually to present information, argument, and interpretation and to provide a basis for discussion. Often, you determine the focus of the topic, within the week's readings and any additional readings you select, and within the guidelines for presentations that have been distributed or discussed in class. You should follow any specific instructions scrupulously. You should undertake your preparation and presentation in close discussion with group members if you are working as a team and in consultation with the professor or seminar leader. After you have thought about the topic well in advance of the presentation and have looked up some of the information about it, you need to discuss your approach with your instructor.

As the presentation continues, or at the end, the students and the instructor might ask you to define your terms, to explain further difficult concepts, or to clarify your method: "Why did you choose to do this?" and "Why did you do it this way?" You must be prepared to field these questions. It is best to relate the presentation to the details of the texts or assignments for the week—for example, by stressing the application of the week's methods to the materials to be read by considering some of the issues that the lecture or the readings raised. You can stress two or three particular questions that you bring to the topic, text, or problem, leaving the class with some directions about how to proceed, open up the topic, and ask some further questions at the end to prompt further discussion.

A handout with some of the data (dates, names, key points, technical information, terms), thesis statement, and a short bibliography that you have developed are useful, but not necessary. As well, you could write an outline of your presentation on the blackboard or on an overhead sheet beforehand. Secondary reading may or may not be required, but it may be helpful; the presentation should be based on your careful reading, thinking, and preparation. In large classes or seminars where the discussion time is limited, your presentation is the only opportunity you have to display your skills in organization, argument, and response to questions on a topic on which you are something of an authority. It is a good chance to make an impact and to consolidate your position in the classroom.

CONSIDERING YOUR AUDIENCE IN WRITTEN ASSIGNMENTS

Your audience for written assignments in university courses is usually limited to one reader, your instructor. You can assume that he or she has read the books and knows the concepts of the course, so you do not have to waste time on plot outlines or explaining concepts as though you were writing the paper for a different audience. You should not "dumb down" your arguments and style to the level of a reader who is ignorant of your topic. Just as important, you should be judicious about not writing in the mode of sensationalist journalism or book blurbs in an analytical essay. Phrases such as "wonderful book," "splendidly written," "excellent economic [or military] strategy" most often indicate empty assertions based on hollow clichés—critical thinking involves reading and writing that challenges or questions such clichés. Most university instructors will be put off by such undemonstrated and extravagant assertions.

Finding the right "voice" is not an easy thing for many students. Generally, it is a good policy to adopt the style of the kinds of books and articles that the instructors recommend in the course. You are demonstrating your academic skills and are being evaluated for your mastery of them, and so you should strive for an appropriate pitch directed to your audience. Consideration of your audience does not mean tailoring your arguments to what you think your instructor might agree with; rather, it means being conscious of the language and strategies of argument appropriate to the level and purpose of your assignment. In writing other than academic essays, a different consideration of audience is necessary: you should take into account the background knowledge of your audience on a particular topic, their expectations, the appropriate degree of difficulty in concepts and diction, and the specific mode of presentation effective for your audience.

Writing an academic essay to defend a thesis, present information, analyze an argument, or criticize a text or document is a skill you learn. If you can do it well, you will get good grades because your arguments will be taken seriously. If you write poorly, with weak punctuation, faults in standard English grammar, spelling mistakes, and feeble use of examples, logic, and quotations, you will receive low grades. The skills learned in writing an essay, in analyzing and presenting your ideas, can be exported to any course and are essential after university in getting a job and keeping it.

The academic or analytical essay is, in a simpler form, the kind of work that many academic faculty undertake in writing scholarly articles. Many do so without questioning accepted knowledge or argument. But as a genre the very nature of the critical essay is to question and to challenge the fundamental attitudes that the university as an institution is supposed to foster.

Usually, the instructor assigns your essay topic. Occasionally, however, you will have to formulate a topic yourself as part of the assignment. In either case, it is essential to become aware of the scope of the topic, of its terms and limitations. In preparing to write an essay on an assigned topic, you will usually undertake some systematic reading, perhaps augmented with library research. Normally, you are free to determine both the direction taken to the destination of the completed essay and the length of time taken to get there. Sometimes, you will begin with an impression, later developed into a hypothesis that has to be proved from some passages in the text under consideration. You might also begin with a problem or contradiction that the text or issue raises, or with an idea that needs to be developed, again with specific citation and documentation. In any case, you will eventually develop several hypotheses about the text or problem, and as you "assay" or test these hypotheses, you will begin to construct the thesis of the essay, the central argument that is to be made in the course of the essay. This developing of the kinds of arguments to be used in defending the thesis is called the discovery stage in traditional rhetoric. At every stage in the preparation of arguments, choices about how to write effectively for the audience and about whether to write as though one were an expert or as an investigator are necessary. In short, all kinds of rhetorical decisions have to be made about writing strategies. In what follows, we set out a number of skills to elaborate on this process.

USING DIFFERENT APPROACHES FOR DIFFERENT ASSIGNMENTS

Different kinds of writing require different approaches or a combination of approaches. A concept essay requires you to write about a specific concept in the course, often applying it to one or more texts or examples from the course to demonstrate your ability to use the concept. A single-book essay usually requires you to use a particular theme or idea in your paper and to "read" the text in light of that notion, citing appropriate evidence. A comparative essay requires you to do the same with one or more ideas or texts, and it involves greater problems in organization. Finally, a research essay requires that you undertake library work on your topic and, after analyzing and arranging your materials into an argument, apply that research to your topic in a coherent and clear way. Most university assignments require a combination of these different kinds of writing.

STRESSING YOUR OWN ANALYSIS

It is important to stress your own analysis rather than hide behind banal assertions like "It is obvious," "It is clear," "The author reveals," or "It is evident from the text." In each of these instances you are asserting something without demonstrating it. You need to change the phrasing to say what you are arguing: "From the evidence of ... I shall demonstrate how...."

You also need to say what you mean or exactly what you want to be heard. When you refer to yourself or to your own ideas, you should be direct and unapologetic, but unobtrusive: "Bradley is wrong, I believe, to exclude *Antony and Cleopatra* from consideration in his *Shakespearean Tragedy*." Here, the direct personal opinion is more acceptable when embedded in the sentence. "I" references may sometimes be generalized to apply to others, and "we" phrases can be used sparingly to involve your readers in your argument. Like "I" references, they are better when included inside the sentence, rather than at the beginning.

SPEAKING AND WRITING TO THE ASSIGNMENT

One of the most powerful misconceptions about a written or an oral presentation is that it is a free expression of an individual's ideas and feelings about a particular subject. In reality, most assignments are done under particular conditions: the due date of the assignment, the scope of the topic, or the time of the meeting when the minutes or brief you were to prepare has to be presented. Failure to comply with or address these requirements often leads to drastic devaluation of your work, leaving you with little recourse to appeal because you simply did not follow the requirements. Almost all academic work is done according to specific instructions about the topic and scope of your paper, the kind of essay you are to write, the number of texts you are to use, and so on. It is impossible to overstate the importance of considering carefully the terms of your assignment. Neglecting this step leads not only to mechanical mistakes in formatting or to dealing with too few texts, but also to the more general criticism, which we have all received at one time or another, that we failed to address the topic of the assignment or to answer the question. In what follows, we outline steps to ensure that you examine closely the terms of an assignment. These steps can be applied to any assigned work in university courses. In chapters that follow we discuss in detail how to research and write academic papers; however, at this point, which we might call the prewriting stage, it is important to assess the terms and requirements of an assignment in order to position yourself effectively in your presentation.

The first step upon receiving an assignment is to look at its terms to figure out what kinds of skills you are being asked to demonstrate. Most undergraduate essays follow a format of stating or assuming an abstract concept, a theme, a mode of character analysis, an historiographical principle, a psychological phenomenon, and so on, and then asking you to apply that concept to a limited number of texts or documents. In some cases, it is clear from the instructions and from the mode of presentation in the course that this concept or analytical principle is not really open to question; in other cases, the terms of the question and the mode of the course encourage questioning, qualification, and perhaps even the rejection of these concepts. In either case, the essential skill that you will be asked to demonstrate usually involves moving between these two levels, the principle and the application.

The second step is to consider carefully the ways in which the abstract principle is framed or expressed in the assignment. Key words or operative terms indicate the scope of your topic. A common strategy instructors use in framing an assignment is to give a quotation that states a definite position about a topic. This quotation or statement accomplishes two things: first, it directs and limits the topic, and second, it establishes a firm position to be qualified or agreed or disagreed with. This quotation is often followed by a statement of qualification or by a series of questions that reflect on the quotation in a "neutral" way. The important tasks here are to find the key concepts and to draw relationships between the position stated in the quotation and the qualifications introduced in the following statement; you then will be able to state your own position regarding the topic. At the prewriting stage, you need not have a specific position already formulated, but you should have a clear sense of the range of possibilities within the assignment.

The third step upon receiving the assignment is to separate this subject matter from the formal requirements. If the assignment says to write on "at least two texts from the course syllabus" or to hand in a paper of "six to eight pages," or whatever, then you need to comply with these instructions. At this stage of assessing the assignment, you need not decide exactly how you will follow some of these specifications—for instance, you may consider four texts from the course as a basis upon which to narrow your final choice of two. Your work at this stage may be recuperated later in at least two ways: first, the broader your range in thinking about the topic, the more you will have to work with in choosing the most effective texts and examples from which to make your argument, and second, specific examples from texts that you do not select can be used as points of illustration, comparison, and contrast throughout your argument, not only clarifying it but also demonstrating a more extensive reading knowledge of the course materials.

ASSIGNMENT EXAMPLES

In considering the following two examples of assignments, you should not get bogged down in the specifics of their content, but rather try to understand the principles we are stressing. At the prewriting stage, you should think about the operative terms of the question, the limitation of the topic, the resources that you have or need to work within these limits, and the research that will be required. Then, you can take preliminary steps in planning the time available to ensure that you do not neglect any phase in the writing process.

Example 1

Quotation

"Themes of anxiety, disillusion, and despair are prevalent in all the works of Thomas Hardy."

Instructor's Qualifications

This critical evaluation was conventional until the 1980s; however, recent commentators have qualified themes of despair in Hardy's works by noting his strategies of maintaining hope and even optimism in the face of cosmic gloom.

Formal Requirements

Write an essay of eight to ten pages in which you discuss at least one poem and a novel in relation to despair and optimism.

This assignment example on Hardy specifies consideration of an author within a range of operative terms that can be summarized as moving between hope and despair. The qualifications indicate that recent commentators have reassessed the earlier conventional position.

Therefore, in establishing your position, you must consider two areas: first, the themes of despair and hope in Hardy's works, and second, the ways in which critics reading Hardy have changed their emphasis. Within these limitations, wide possibilities are open to you in forming and arguing your position. But in order to do so, you will have to address both levels of the question: the themes and the critical readings. Hence, in considering the research necessary you will have to have adequate knowledge of Hardy's work, as well as of the critics' positions. Finally, you are governed by the limitation of length, by the choice of critics, and by the choice of a novel and a poem. You will likely have enough material for a much longer paper, and thus will have to select the best examples to use in the most effective arguments. The choice of critics, novels, and poems again opens possibilities for you. Although your choice will likely be determined by the readings in the course, expanding this range will add depth and persuasiveness to your position. The assignment also leaves open the possibility for at least two fundamental disagreements: first, that themes other than despair and hope are "prevalent," and second, that the critics' positions have not fundamentally changed since the 1980s. While these levels of disagreement are logically possible from the terms of the question, they should be used with caution, as to address them requires considerable expertise.

Example 2

Axiomatic Statement

Canadian society changed radically in the period from 1880 to 1920.

Instructor's Qualifications

Through a consideration of immigration, urbanization, and industrialization,

Formal Requirements

outline the benefits and disadvantages of these changes in an essay of ten to twelve pages.

The second assignment example posits "change" in a specific historical period as a given and then goes on to specify three areas to consider in explaining the change. The topic introduces the possibility of making some judgment about the value of each area in explaining the change, but it does not require you to do so (as in the Hardy assignment, concerning "recent commentators"). Your range of choice in disagreeing with the statement is much more limited than in the first example. To disagree by arguing that there was little or no change, or that there were other more important categories than the three specified, redirects the assignment in ways that you probably should check with your instructor before moving in that direction. You establish your position in argument in this assignment with the qualification that these changes are to be explained as benefits or disadvantages. These qualitative terms force you to ask the question, For whom were they benefits or disadvantages? In answering this question, you are required to establish a reasoned position; therefore, your thinking and research should be directed to examining a range of possibilities within the specific areas indicated. Finally, the formal requirements do not specify the materials you are to consider: statistics, economic or demographic analyses, secondary sources or scholarly positions, and so on. The course materials are an obvious place to start. *After* you have done some preliminary reading and have some specific questions to ask about other kinds of sources you might use, there are two strategies to pursue. First, you might consult your instructor; often, however, an instructor will not specify method or materials, leaving you to your own devices.

A second possibility, then, is to consider how this kind of problem was dealt with in the course readings, lectures, and source materials, and then to use one of those methods.

These two examples and our critical reading of the assignments in the prewriting stage do not exhaust the possible kinds of assignments. Many assignments vary the order of the steps we have outlined, omit a step, or conceal the assumptions of the topic. The important thing here is to establish the limits and possibilities of the writing process in the prewriting stage by reading the assigned topic critically. It is important to observe, also, that the same methods can be used in analyzing questions on examinations.

Another approach to assigning essay topics might require you to formulate your own topic. This kind of exercise also requires considerable thinking at the prewriting stage. An effective way to formulate your strategy is to follow the same principles outlined in our reading of the two assignments above. That is, you pick a topic on the course that interests you, formulate a statement concerning it, introduce some qualifications that indicate a range of possibilities, and select the materials for analysis to conform to the length of the assignment. In much advanced undergraduate work, such as honours theses, or in postgraduate work up to the Ph.D. dissertation, you can follow the same procedures.

Some courses include writing assignments that ask you for reaction, opinion, the expression of feelings, or interaction with other students. For example, you may be asked to keep a reading diary or journal of reactions to texts on the course or to engage with other students by networking through computers and exchanging opinions about course material. Such writing implicitly asks you to suspend judgment and to defer critical evaluation in favour of impressions and reactions. These assignments give weight to your opinions and feelings, but they also conceal a contradiction. On the one hand, you are being invited to offer your own opinions and to state your feelings—on the other, your work will be judged and evaluated. Your opinions and reactions are as good as anybody else's, but they will be evaluated according to criteria that might well be concealed or unstated. The methods of critical argument and analysis we have outlined can still be used in such assignments to provide the basis upon which you establish your opinions and reactions.

FURTHER READINGS

Browne, M. Neil, and Stuart M. Keeley. *Asking the Right Questions: A Guide to Critical Thinking*. Upper Saddle River, NJ: Prentice-Hall, 1998.

Gordon, Jeffrey. *The University in Your Life*. Madison, WI: Brown and Benchmark, 1996.

Fleet, Joan, Fiona Goodchild, and Richard Zajchowski. *Learning for Success: Skills and Strategies for Canadian Students*. 2nd ed. Toronto: Harcourt Brace, 1994.

Inch, Edward S., and Barbara Warnick. *Critical Thinking and Communication: The Use of Reason in Argument*. 3rd ed. Boston: Allyn and Bacon, 1998.

Lieb, Anthony. *Speaking for Success: The Canadian Guide*. Toronto: Harcourt Brace, 1993.

Ruggiero, Vincent Ryan. *The Art of Thinking: A Guide to Critical and Creative Thought*. New York: Longman, 1998.

WEBLINKS

- Critical Thinking Across the Curriculum, a Longview Community College, MI site with links
www.kcmetro.cc.mo-us/longview/CTAC/toc.htm

- Effective Presentations, a University of Kansas Medical Center site
www.kumc.edu/SAH/OTEd/jradel/effective.html

- Resources for Critical Thinking
www.sjsu.edu/depts/itl/graphics/resource.html

- University of Indiana Resources
www.indiana.edu/~eric_rec/bks/ct.html

ARGUING AND ASSESSING A POSITION

An academic argument involving critical thinking is not a contest or a confrontation that you try to win by destroying your opponent. Nor is it a series of assertions in which two opposing sets of opinions are left up in the air with the oversimplified conclusion, "Well, that's just my opinion"—the implication being that all opinions are equal and the reader can take it or leave it. Critical thinking involves breaking down a position into its various components, separating assumptions from hypotheses and premises from evidence. Strategies of argument allow you to critique other positions and help you to formulate your own in a manner that will move or persuade your reader.

ARGUMENTS BASED ON FACT AND OPINION

It is often assumed that there are only two kinds of argument, those based on fact and those based on opinion. Arguments of fact, common in science, have one right answer: for example, the boiling point of water is 100°C. In arguments of fact, then, there is generally agreed-upon knowledge within which specific questions have only one right answer; that is, the right answer is conditioned by the accepted knowledge in the relevant field or discipline. Matters of opinion depend on human preference: for example, I prefer blue jeans to dress pants. In matters of opinion the position asserted is governed by the personal preference asserted at the beginning of the statement—what *you* prefer cannot be disagreed with. However, if we begin to take apart the opinion and look at the conditions of this preference in relation to different circumstances, then we begin to move to a third kind of argument. This move involves questions for which the answers are neither right nor wrong and are not matters of opinion, but are based on positions established as better or worse. If you are going for an interview for employment at a bank, then the matter of appropriate dress moves from your mere opinion ("I prefer ...") to a set of choices governed by other circumstances. If you want the job at the bank you should not wear jeans to the interview.

ARGUMENTS BASED ON JUDGMENT AND CRITICAL THINKING

This third kind of argument, which has no absolute right or wrong answer and which moves from opinion to matters of judgment based on the formulation of a reasoned position, is involved in what we are calling critical thinking. Moving from opinion to reasoned position in the instance of choice of dress involves taking account of the conditions within which the choice is made. These conditions can be argued about in a form outside of personal preference. Your preference or opinion has to be placed in the context of dress codes, social expectations, and appropriate behaviour. Your choice of what to wear, then, should not be a matter of opinion or preference, but a matter of reasoned judgment, whereby you weigh the implications of your choices. The example of appropriate dress at the bank interview may seem unconnected to the kinds of critical judgments you are asked to make in an academic essay. However, just as you need to be aware of the implications of what you wear in applying for a job, so too you need to be aware of how you use your opinions and preferences in adopting a reasoned position in your essay. To substitute for a reasoned judgment, as many students do, the view that your opinion on this text is as good as anyone else's is not critical thinking. On the other hand, to take at face value everything you read, being completely intimidated or overwhelmed by the authority of someone else's assertions, is not critical thinking either. Your critical thinking and writing depend on arranging your ideas in arguments that are clear, logical, and convincing.

The arguments you make are set into a course and discipline where conventions of knowledge and power positions are already established. To argue effectively does not mean that you must agree entirely with these conventions or positions. However, in challenging or opposing them you cannot ignore their existence or dismiss them in an offhand manner. Indeed, the assumptions of a course often establish precisely this movement between the acknowledgment of conventions and positions of power as they exist in the classroom and the critique of them by faculty teaching in the course or by students. Well-established disciplines (like history and English) often use their power and knowledge to produce "truth systems" that make claims for veracity—for instance, these wars or political figures are important, or these authors are great, or these books are classics. And in the media we encounter regularly, in the press, on television, and in the classroom, such truth claims are often asserted as though they cannot be questioned. However, such statements can be challenged and critiqued by adopting an oppositional position from which to open these claims to question. This questioning is based on a critique of the ideological positioning of the argument being advanced, an analysis (or deconstruction) of the terms the argument uses or the positions assumed, and an application of logical analysis to the propositions of an argument. Here, what is called *traditional logic* can serve a useful purpose in indicating the *validity* of arguments (whether the arguments are put together correctly according to the rules of formal logic), and a knowledge of informal fallacies will often expose the gaps where an oppositional reading of a truth claim may be launched. Furthermore, a knowledge of basic principles of formal logic will help you in formulating your own arguments.

While some kinds of "creative" assignments will be performative (as, indeed, all essays and classroom presentations are at some level), academic essays rely on conventional marshalling of arguments and evidence and so are open to the kinds of traditional faults and fallacies that have been specified by logicians. Readers will hope to find in an academic essay that the arguments follow logically one after another, rather than jumping about from one point to another only tangentially related point. You should be able to control the logical sequencing of arguments partly through building paragraphs from topic sentence through to their conclusion, with a bridge to the next paragraph. Another control comes from a clear and articulate style, which will allow arguments to come forward in a clear and unambiguous way. But, in addition, there are informal and formal requirements to be met with respect to the logic of arguments. For instance, it is not logical to assert at the end of an essay a position that has not been introduced and demonstrated earlier in the paper. Nor can the dismissal of a particular position as rubbish be substituted for analysis and demonstration of *why* that position is rubbish. Similarly, when evidence does not support a thesis, when you argue beside the point, when you look at only some of the evidence, or when you distort the evidence, the logic is weak, often faulty, and there is a poor match between the position that is in the process of being developed and the marshalling of evidence.

Ideas must always be set out in a coherent fashion, usually proceeding from the strongest point to the weakest, or the reverse, which is a more difficult procedure. Generalizations will be supported or qualified by relevant evidence. For an argument to be convincing, the relationship between generalizations or assertions and supporting evidence must be considered carefully. Students have the most trouble at exactly this point: they either cannot qualify a generalization in the face of contradictory evidence and ignore the exception, or they suppress that evidence and continue to assert a generalization. Evidence will be reliable and pertinent if you take into account any contradictory evidence (for instance, by considering both sides of a question or by examining a text carefully for contrary evidence) or if you can modify your generalization (perhaps by claiming that it applies in most cases or in these specific cases, but not in others). Your argument will be much less convincing if it is apparent that you are playing up to a supposed reader's predispositions or views (toadying), basing your argument on bias or prejudice, or oversimplifying a complex topic.

TWO FUNDAMENTAL METHODS OF ARGUING A POSITION

To be convincing as well as valid, an argument must follow logical principles. However, many arguments convince readers and listeners without being particularly logical, or even by committing one or more well-known logical faults. Often it is because of the faults that the argument convinces unthinking people. Politicians are particularly expert in evading questions, appealing to popular opinion, or equivocating. Student essays often try to employ similar tactics. But critical thinking depends on using arguments that are both convincing and valid. To develop a reasoned position in a classroom presentation, essay, or examination is a considerable achievement.

Critical thinking makes use primarily of *informal logic*. That is, it applies the principles of logical concepts to the analysis of bodies of knowledge, of the materials studied in a course, and of specific readings in literature, history, sociology, or political science and to the writing of assignments. Students have to draw on a number of resources, including collected data, examples for readings, definitions of key concepts, counter-evidence, and prior studies of the same topic in books and periodicals. Then they have to assemble that material in some coherent order, not just to describe a situation, but to make an argument, to adopt and defend a reasoned position. Informal logic, then, is a kind of practical reasoning about the world. Since the 1970s, it has been the subject of much scholarly interest, as thinkers have tried to apply the conventional, older concepts of logic and to derive new ones from a wealth of material and language patterns available in the mass media, including newspapers, magazines, television, and music. Such studies have concentrated on the ways that logical connections are broken in arguments that appear in the media (chiefly through fallacies or errors in logic in informal reasoning), on the ways that rhetoric is used to persuade an audience of the validity of the argument, and on the ways that communication is established.

At the same time, informal logic depends on solid reasoning and to some extent on formal logic, the rules that have to do with the logical forms of arguments when they are stripped to their essential elements and are put into a coherent pattern according to conventional rules. Often, this formal logic is called *symbolic logic* because it uses symbolic abbreviations instead of "real" arguments to construct paradigms of arguments. In what follows, we set out the major kinds of arguments and show how you can recognize them. We indicate the basic patterns that these arguments employ and list a number of faults or fallacies that they are prone to. We also pay some brief attention to formal logic so that you can see some of its implications, though we leave detailed treatment of it to courses or books on symbolic logic.

Arguments depend on statements, assertions, or declarations that are connected to reach a conclusion. A declaration expresses what logicians call a *proposition*, a concept that is distinct from the sentence that expresses it. So the declarative statement "Mag loves Viv" expresses the same proposition as "Viv is loved by Mag." People use language in all sorts of ways—to express emotion, to give commands, to ask questions, to describe experiences—but propositions are different in that they make an assertion that is either true or false. Truth claims enter at the beginning of an argument, often unstated, when you make an assertion that you are about to defend in your argument. You may make a proposition, for instance, to the effect that the fundamental cause of the French Revolution was economic, or that all of Hardy's poems are pessimistic, or that the moon is made of Swiss cheese. Each of these statements can be defended or denied, but if it is asserted, a truth claim is being made about it at the beginning of your argument. Your audience might disagree, but they will have to withhold their judgment about the validity of the truth claim until you finish your argument. You might decide to proceed with your argument according to one of two traditional means, each of which depends on fitting your propositions together coherently: the *inductive method*, whereby you amass evidence to substantiate your claim, or the *deductive method*, whereby you begin with a broad premise and show how your theory can be defended in a sequence of logical moves.

From ancient times it was recognized that these two fundamental ways of developing an argument, often linked together in practice, are based on different kinds of reasoning processes. In the opening sentences of his treatise *Posterior Analytics* (*c.* 350 B.C.E.), the Greek philosopher Aristotle sets out the basic distinctions between induction and deduction, which continue to play an important part in logic:

> All instruction given or received by way of argument proceeds from pre-existent knowledge. This becomes evident upon a survey of all the species of such instruction. The mathematical sciences and all other speculative disciplines are acquired in this way, and so are the two forms of dialectical reasoning, syllogistic [or deductive] and inductive; for each of these latter make use of old knowledge to impart new, the syllogism assuming an audience that accepts its premises, induction exhibiting the universal as implicit in the clearly known particular (9).

In this treatise, Aristotle discusses in detail the means of making arguments, and in the *Prior Analytics* he sets out the methods for determining the validity of deductive arguments. In both cases he is concerned with showing how these means of argument lead to better comprehension or "instruction" and to new understandings.

To illustrate this point about different kinds of arguments, we provide an imaginary dialogue that might have occurred near a cave about a million years ago:

> Thog: "I've noticed that every time I throw a stone up in the air it comes down. And so if I shoot an arrow in the air now it must come down too."

> Nootun: "That's because of the law that everything that goes up comes down. If you shoot the arrow up, it comes down."

Thog is using inductive reasoning, arguing from his experience and previous examples to reach a general conclusion. Nootun, on the other hand, is using deductive reasoning, arguing from the general law (the law of gravity) and then moving to the specific. Thog is making a prediction about what will probably happen, on the basis of his observation, while Nootun is asserting what is certain. Or, to take a different example:

> Thog: "I've noticed that every time there is a drought we get rain. And so now, in this drought, we will get rain."

> Nootun: "That's because the rainmaker does his dance and says his prayers. So now, in this drought, we will get rain."

In this instance, the argument of Thog is again inductive, but unlike the first example, it is not based on an observation that all people would accept. In many droughts there is no rain. And if Thog has a science teacher, he might have to explain that that is why we have deserts. Nevertheless, Thog is still making an inductive argument, but it is a flawed one because it is based on too few examples and does not consider the contrary evidence. Nootun is using deductive reasoning again, stating what to him is a principle or axiomatic truth (when the rainmaker does his ritual, it rains) and a necessary conclusion, but his logic is also not very solid, because the rain may not be the necessary effect of the ritual. Thog and Nootun are stating their arguments pretty well, but more could be said about them. And both of them are making important arguments; neither way is inherently better or worse than the other. Each starts from a different basis and reaches a different kind of conclusion.

Inductive Reasoning

Inductive reasoning, as in Thog's arguments, begins with observation, experience, evidence, or facts. Then it compares all of these data, and after showing what the facts have in common, their similarities, or how they progress from one to another, draws conclusions. This is the process of induction.

The inductive method draws conclusions out of the facts or evidence that have been presented on the basis of some point of comparison or similarity. This drawing-out process is called *implication*. That is, the implications of the evidence are elicited to provide the basis for a conclusion. Induction, then, moves from the implications of particular details to a general principle or conclusion. The conclusion is then tested against the evidence, and new evidence starts the process off again.

The inductive method does not lead to any claims for absolute proof, but, rather, if the propositions are true, only to what is highly probable. For the method to be absolutely or conclusively valid, *all* of the examples would have to be considered, a practical impossibility. Normally, however, only a number of examples are chosen, and from them a generalization is made that is probable and usually convincing. But if a contrary example can be found, then the concluding generalization has to be modified. Hence, the inductive method can lead to conclusions that are probable, and the grounds on which that assertion can be made are either strong (or *cogent*) or weak.

Plausible inductive reasoning should be distinguished from stating a position and using one example to back it up as evidence, such as if you say, "The schools are in terrible shape. I know that because my brother is fourteen and cannot spell yet." In this instance, you are trying to prove your point by using only your brother's poor spelling to validate the weak claim that your position can be maintained. The schools might indeed be bad, and doubtless your brother is a poor speller, but the reasons might have nothing to do with the school. You might be drawing a false relation of cause and effect, or your sample might be far too small. You would presumably have to draw on a much wider and more varied sample. This kind of weak inductive reasoning, however, is a common fault among television talk show hosts and politicians, who frequently generalize from one instance to a principle, misrelate cause and effect, use examples to elaborate a point rather than argue a position, or draw false analogies. Instead of using induction to advance practical argument, they get lost trying to assemble evidence.

Strong inductive reasoning seeks to move from an accumulation of evidence to a probable conclusion. This method is often used in criminal procedures by the police and by lawyers in gathering the evidence to make a case (along with deduction in linking the parts of their arguments together). It is also the basis of the scientific method, in which the experimenter states a hypothesis, then proceeds through the experiment to examine all of the data to come up with a conclusion based on the evidence; one contrary piece of evidence means that the conclusion has to be modified. The scientific method then uses deduction to state the principle, to apply it to other specifics, and to draw a valid conclusion about it. In this way, the scientific method uses both inductive and deductive reasoning.

There are three major forms of inductive argument:

Inductive Argument by Means of Hypothesis and Evidence

This argument is presented as a hypothesis, followed by evidence to support it, leading to a general conclusion. In fact, however, the evidence is often gathered before the hypothesis is stated, or according to some working hypothesis that might have to be refined on the basis of further evidence. The scientific experiment is one example of the argument made on the basis of hypothesis and evidence. A series of experiments and observations leads to the formulation of a hypothesis that accounts for the evidence. That generalization is then claimed to be the conclusion of the experiment. This hypothesis and evidence method is also used extensively (often with other forms of argument) in law cases, and it involves making a claim or stating a thesis that you are going to test by means of facts, statistics, examples, evidence, or the opinions of experts. The lawyer builds the case on the basis of induction. Similarly, in detective fiction, the sleuth sifts through the evidence to find elements that can be compared and that point inevitably to the criminal: Sherlock Holmes in Conan Doyle's fiction is a master of inductive reasoning; Inspector Clouseau in the *Pink Panther* series is a failure in induction because he misses the points of comparison in the evidence, just as he fails in common sense, as when he asks the hotel clerk, "Does your dog bite?" When the clerk responds "No," he is still bitten. The clerk then explains: "It is not my dog."

University students commonly use the hypothesis (or thesis) and evidence form of induction in the academic essay. Most students use inductive reasoning in essays by making a thesis statement in the opening paragraph, supporting it with a series of examples (historical data, readings of specific passages in a text, comments on specific concepts, and so on) more or less associated with the topic, and reaching a conclusion in which the thesis is reaffirmed in somewhat different wording than in the opening paragraph. In fact, however, many of these essays use examples to illustrate or elaborate, or even to describe the claim made in the thesis, rather than to make an argument that actually defends the thesis. Such an argument in an essay is a weak form of inductive reasoning. It cites a series of instances as examples, rather than as evidence, and concludes with some generalizing comment on the basis of the examples. That comment is then turned into a thesis statement and is placed at the beginning of the essay. A thesis is not a self-evident truth or axiom, but a qualified conjecture or position that you are going to test or demonstrate: that is, you will have to argue for it. Evidence here is not merely a listing of examples, or a one-dimensional application of facts to prove a limited case over and over. Usually, your own first-hand experience falls into the field of opinion and is discounted or even dismissed as weak or unreliable evidence. The strength of your argument using this method depends largely on three factors: first, the formulation of your thesis; second, the way in which you organize your evidence into categories related to your thesis; and, third, how the evidence in each of the categories is put together to support the categories.

In more rigorously argued essays, the examples cited are in fact evidence, and they are arranged in some justifiable order, moving from stronger to weaker or the reverse in order to make a point. Hence, the thesis is well supported, and the paper takes the form of a more coherent inductive argument, much like that of the scientific experiment. The examples follow one another in a linked chain and rely on one another in important ways. The comparison of the evidence involves carefully assessing the points of similarity, noting which points are important and which are less so. Therefore, the similarities in the evidence, and the linking of them together, point with increasing probability to the claims of your thesis. To test your argument, you need to ask yourself why that order of your points appears as it does. If you cannot explain why the points follow in that order, each tied to the previous point, then you are not arguing logically, and might be setting out examples without apparent connections.

A more minor form of induction, that of proving a point by means of an example, is also frequently used by students, often with good effect. When a claim is being made about the interpretation of a particular passage in a text, and then some evidence is provided to support that interpretation, the proof is exemplified and validated, at least for this one instance. A marker can legitimately ask in the margin whether there is any contrary evidence.

When the evidence does not support the claims of the thesis the conclusion is unconvincing and implausible. That is, it fails to convince a reader. Reasons for failures in inductive arguments concerning thesis and evidence can include the following:

- The thesis is not clearly formulated.
- The thesis is not sufficiently qualified on the basis of your evidence.
- An opinion is mistaken for a fact or for an unsubstantiated position.

- An error concerning fact is represented as a truth.
- A position that has been discredited is represented as true.
- The evidence is based on errors of fact or interpretation or is drawn from an unreliable source (such as a disproved scientific position). The evidence must be presented in your argument without distorting or twisting it to make it fit your case, a trick much loved by politicians.
- The evidence is not substantial enough to warrant a generalization. A poll conducted using only two people is invalid. Two hundred people would be better, but many thousands would make a much better case. Proving a case from a work of fiction means that one example can support a focused or limited argument, but more evidence might be needed to make a more general case. On the other hand, it is possible to give too many examples as evidence to support a claim that has already been proven.
- The evidence is unrepresentative. To be valid, the evidence must be fair, balanced, and representative of the case you are arguing. If you conduct a poll among people who are ignorant of the subject, you cannot make any claim for its validity, unless your argument is related to something about the ignorance of people concerning this subject.
- The evidence is irrelevant to your hypothesis. If you argue that in a survey in your class of one hundred students' study habits, the half who listened to music while they studied did significantly worse than those who did not, your evidence is not necessarily relevant. Many other factors might have been involved: the need to work, the number of courses taken, students' ability, other claims on their time, familiarity with the subject matter, and so on. The evidence of listening to music is not relevant to performance unless both halves of the class are equivalent in other respects except for their music-listening habits.
- Sweeping claims are made for your evidence in either your thesis or conclusion. This mistake often occurs when students make universal claims about their evidence, using such words as *all, always, certainly, everywhere,* and *never.* Instead, a more qualified position, allowing for exceptions or special conditions, is more reasonable, as in arguments using such words as *a few, many, may, often, perhaps, possibly, probably,* and *usually.*

Inductive Argument on the Basis of Cause and Effect

The second common kind of inductive reasoning is used to show causal relationships among events, so that a specific cause can be claimed to have a particular effect, or the reverse. This kind of argument draws a connection between one assertion and another by saying that the cause A produces the effect B: for example, if enough heat is applied to water, it boils. It is assumed that there is regularity and uniformity in the physical universe and that on the basis of many observations this cause (heat) has this effect (water boils). For the water to boil, the heat is both a necessary and a sufficient condition or cause.

When we move away from physical phenomena (and even in them there may be variations that depend on other conditions being present in either the cause or the effect) to consider the causes and effects in historical events, in interpersonal relationships, in psychological experiments, or in works of fiction, the notion of a single and unambiguous cause for a single effect becomes much more difficult, if not impossible, to determine, and may be irrelevant. In such cases, the induction depends on even more careful observation of examples or instances, and on the very careful comparison of points of likeness. Drawing out the implications of cause-and-effect arguments, however, can be very difficult. Sometimes, the causes are remote, complicated, and complex; sometimes, they are immediate, direct, and singular. For instance, the cause of a person's ill health may be some bad fish, or it could be a complicated set of heart and lung problems. Trying to determine the effects of specific causes can produce a variety of alternatives. For instance, much medical practice consists of determining the proper causes for effects (symptoms) and prescribing appropriate remedies. In the field of psychoanalysis, Freud's study of hysteria in the case of *Dora* is based on exactly this issue: Dora's somatic symptoms of a cough, loss of voice, and a limp were not, in his analysis, the result of a physical malfunction (though they were actual physical symptoms); instead, he argued, they were caused by psychic disorders resulting from events earlier in her life that she had suppressed into her unconscious and that were outwardly manifested in the changed conditions of her body. Freud's method is that of induction, to trace the effects to their remote causes in her earlier life.

John Stuart Mill, a nineteenth-century English philosopher (1806–1873), sets out in *A System of Logic* (1843) five methods of testing whether the relationship between cause and effect is probable. The following tests or *canons*, as Mill called them, are explained with detailed examples by Copi and Cohen (486–510) and their examples have been adapted and simplified here:

1. *Method of agreement.* If two or more cases have only one circumstance in common, that circumstance is likely the cause (or effect) of the phenomenon. Suppose that four people come to the campus clinic with a rash that is diagnosed as measles, and a routine check indicates that they are all friends of Marsha (who also had the measles earlier), but have no other friends in common. The point of agreement indicates that Marsha is the probable cause of their infection.

2. *Method of difference.* If in one case something happens, and in another it does not, and both cases have everything in common except one circumstance (which occurs in the first case and not in the second), the circumstance in which the cases differ is the effect (or the cause) of the phenomenon. Two people who are roommates come to the clinic, and the first has an upset stomach while the other has not. A routine check indicates that they had each eaten the same things all day, except that the first had eaten Thai fish (without optional peanut sauce), the second turkey stew (with optional cranberries). Assuming that there are no other reasons, the fish is the probably the cause of the upset stomach.

3. *Method of agreement and difference together.* When the methods of agreement and difference are combined, there is a greatly increased probability of a justifiable relationship between cause and effect. Suppose that six students come to the clinic in pairs. In each pair one has a stomach upset, and the other has something different. All had the same meals, except that all with upset stomachs had eaten fish (no sauce); those who ate stew did not have upset stomachs. The strong probability is that the fish caused the upset stomachs.

4. *Method of residues.* When all effects but one are accounted for by all plausible causes but one, the residual effect is caused by the residual cause. A student arrives at the clinic with an allergy attack affecting breathing, a rash, and an upset stomach. An enquiry indicates that she was a friend of Marsha and had eaten fish. That accounts for two of the symptoms, but the third, upon enquiry, is explained by the fact that she added sauce to the fish. Two of the complex effects are explained by two of the probable causes. Whatever residual effect remains (the allergic reaction) must result from the remaining cause (the peanut sauce).

5. *Method of concomitant variation.* Whatever circumstance varies in any way whenever another circumstance varies in a particular way is either an effect or a cause of that circumstance. If the variable circumstances show increasing probabilities of the particular cause, there is a proportional relationship between the effects and the cause. Five students come to the clinic. One ate no fish and had no upset; one ate a little fish (no sauce) from a friend's plate and reported a headache; one ate half of the fish (with sauce) and started to feel ill and so stopped; the fourth ate all of the fish (with sauce) and had to lie down to recover; the fifth ate her neighbour's fish as well as her own (no sauce) and was violently sick. Therefore, the cause of the illness is probably the fish.

In each of these cases it must be assumed that the students' conduct and diet are relevant to the supposed causes of their complaints. And in each case the examination showed up a likely, but not certain, cause. With only the effects and no plausible cause, Mill's methods cannot prove a causal connection, as Copi and Cohen demonstrate in their critique of Mill (510–25). Mill's methods, nevertheless, are essential in exposing false causes and in pointing to possible or even likely causes, which will then have to be tested by other hypotheses that take into account other factors. Mill's tests do not help much with very complex causes and effects or with causes that have to be rejected. Even in a situation like Freud's *Dora,* the causes of her hysteria (in sexual repressions) that Freud finds are rejected by his patient, who also rejects him and analysis. The question of whether Freud pointed to the real causes remains.

The probable relationship between a cause-and-effect induction collapses in the following cases:

- *Post hoc.* Merely because one event follows another, the first is claimed to cause the second, or there is no demonstrated relationship between the cause and the effect: for example, *Nettie went to Africa and therefore Celie fell in love with Shug; or, I took Tylenol and a day later my migraine went away.* Technically, this fallacy is called the "After this and therefore because of this" fault, often given in its Latin form: *post hoc ergo propter hoc.* Other versions include the claim that when two events occur together they are causally related (*cum hoc ergo propter hoc*). The reverse is that there is no case for the claimed cause (*non causa pro causa*), because the claim that one event caused another was based on insufficient evidence or there was, in fact, no causal relationship.

- *Wrong direction.* There is a wrong direction in the causality sequence or antecedent effect, or causality with a wrong direction; the effect occurs before the cause, as when the door slams before the wind blows. Either the cause and effect are in the wrong order, or there must be a cause other than the wind.

- *Oversimplification.* A complex cause or effect is too simplistically drawn. To assert that World War II had a single cause (for instance, the rise of the Hitler's Germany) or that the Stock Market Crash of 1929 had a single effect (the Great Depression), are oversimplifications.

Inductive Argument by Means of Analogy

When various points of evidence are gathered in an inductive argument, they have to be compared, and the aim of that comparison is to find some points of similarity so that a generalization or conclusion can be drawn. That process often involves drawing an *analogy* between one set of evidence and another. At its simplest level, an analogy suggests that one object and its characteristic or effect can be compared to another object and its characteristic. Such a ratio or equivalence is common in speech and might not be used in argument. For instance, a writer might draw an analogy between the dying of a human body and the last days of a political regime, and such an analogy is descriptive, but it is not part of an argument. A more developed analogy can be used to persuade an audience that some things that are similar in some respects are probably also similar in some other respect: apes and humans are alike in characteristics A, B, and C. It is probable that they are also alike in characteristic D. Or one may draw an analogy between a well-known instance and a less-understood one, using the familiar and accepted points concerning the first to make a probable explanation of the latter.

One of the most famous of these analogies is the argument for the existence of God, called the argument from design, used by William Paley in his *Natural Theology* (1802). Paley argues that if you were walking on the beach and found a watch and examined it, you would have to assume that because the watch has parts that move in a certain fixed, orderly, and complex way, the watch had a maker (the watchmaker). Further, the watch was not made randomly but with a function and a purpose (to tell time). Paley then draws an analogy to the universe. Like the watch, the universe moves in a certain fixed, orderly, and complex way and similarly must have a maker as well as a purpose. The analogy depends on two of the four "causes" of Aristotle, the formal cause (what gives a thing its formal design or shape) and the final cause (what a thing's purpose is). Hence, the analogy compares the complexity of design and purpose between the watch and the universe (and quietly assumes a cause-and-effect relationship between maker and product, and between existence and purpose). Analogy here is a vital part of Paley's argument based on induction in the rest of the book, where he draws upon example after example of complex designs in the external world, each of them an analogy to this fundamental one at the beginning of his discussion. The point about analogies that makes them work in an inductive argument is that the common characteristics must be drawn out and expanded, and, as with cause and effect arguments, their common characteristics must be relevant.

Some analogies can be complex and tricky to untangle. For instance, when the fairy tale writer George MacDonald says how difficult it is to define what a fairy tale is, he resists giving a definition and, instead, uses an argument based on analogy: "Were I ... begged to describe the 'fairytale,' or define what it is, I would make answer, that I should as soon think of describing the abstract human face, or stating what must go to constitute a human being" (313).

Here the analogy is between the fairy tale and the abstract human face, and the human being. Each is said to be impossible to define, describe, or state. This kind of analogical argument is seen most clearly if its parts are set out like a mathematical ratio, so that *A is to B as C is to D*, or in the conventional pattern:

$$\frac{A}{B} = \frac{C}{D}$$

In the terms of MacDonald's argument the ratio becomes as follows:

$$\frac{\text{impossibility of describing}}{\substack{\text{the human face} \\ \text{in the abstract}}} = \frac{\substack{\text{impossibility of} \\ \text{saying what constitutes}}}{\substack{\text{the essence of} \\ \text{a human being}}} = \frac{\text{impossibility of defining}}{\substack{\text{a good fairy tale} \\ \text{in general}}}$$

Hence, the impossibility of description is to the abstract human face, as the impossibility of saying what constitutes the human being is to the essence of a human being, as the impossibility of definition is to the fairy tale in general. MacDonald's argument implies, however, that the contrary is possible, and he provides the concluding step of the analogy, "Read *Undine*: that is a fairytale.... I think *Undine* the most beautiful":

$$\frac{\text{a writer or painter can describe}}{\text{a particular human face}} = \frac{\text{a writer or artist}}{\text{can say what constitutes}} = \frac{\text{a writer can define}}{\text{one good fairy tale:}}$$
$$\text{"read } Undine\text{"}$$

Analogies, like other kinds of inductive evidence, are strengthened when there is an increased number of points of similarity (the watch is like the universe in more ways than one: it moves in a fixed, orderly, and complex way) and diminished when there is an increased number of differences. An analogy is also strengthened when the comparison involves many instances, rather than just one or two. If MacDonald had used only one stage in his argument, it would have been much weaker. If the analogy can also be based on a variety of instances, then the analogy is that much stronger. When Paley moves from the watch to the complex design of the eye of the fly, he is introducing just that kind of variety. So, also, the details that are compared have to be relevant: it would not matter if the faces, human beings, or fairy stories were young or old, as age is irrelevant; however, the difficulty of defining the existence or appearance of faces, human beings, or fairy stories in the abstract is relevant.

Analogical arguments fail in the following cases:

- *False or faulty analogy.* An analogy is faulty when the two events or objects that are being compared are alike in a number of irrelevant respects, but differ in the one relevant respect on which the analogy must depend. Put another way, the false analogy claims that two situations, A and B, are alike in many ways, and because situation A has the property X, so must situation B. Oscar Wilde's witticisms frequently depend on false analogy, as in the following examples from Lady Bracknell in the first act of *The Importance of Being Earnest*: "Ignorance is like a delicate exotic fruit; touch it, and the bloom is gone"; "To be born, or at any rate, bred in a handbag, whether it had handles or not, seems to me to display a contempt for the ordinary decencies of family life that remind one of the worst excesses of the French Revolution. And I presume you know what that unfortunate movement led to?"

- *Extended analogy.* Inductive comparison using analogy fails when it is assumed that because two situations are referred to in the same context, often the context of a proposed general rule, they are analogies. For instance, in a discussion of instituting laws on censorship, it is a faulty extended analogy to claim that censoring adult sites on the Internet is analogous to censoring books in high school libraries.

Deductive Reasoning

When Nootun made his argument to Thog about the law that everything that goes up must come down, and about how the rituals of the rainmaker bring rain, he was stating an axiomatic truth as his first principle. You could silently agree with him, or you could argue with him about the truth or falsity of his assertions, but in both cases, he began with a principle.

Deductive reasoning begins with some kind of position that can be defended or argued, often an *axiom*, or a self-evident truth, such as Nootun's statement that what goes up must come down. This opening declaration is called the first, or major, premise. Deductive reasoning then adds a second, or minor premise, in order to draw out the implications (in this form of reasoning they are called *inferences*) of the argument to apply them to a specific situation or set of data: an arrow is something that goes up. That is, a deductive argument moves from the general principle to the detail. Then it draws a conclusion: the arrow must come down.

In your studies you will encounter many courses that require both inductive and deductive reasoning. Many science, social science, and humanities courses depend first on inductive reasoning, assembling various kinds of evidence, building up a body of data, collecting problems or specific instances, and then drawing a conclusion or general principle from them that has a high degree of probability. Then a deductive phase can begin, in which the conclusion of the inductive phase is tested by application to other cases. Some other courses tend to use the inductive method without drawing attention to this logical structure, or even evading drawing connected conclusions. Such a course might proceed by examining examples each week, such as different texts (say, works of fiction) or concepts, without fitting them from the outset into an argument based on some critical or theoretical principle, and without drawing connections between them. Often, it is only during the final examination that a student (rather than a teacher throughout the course) has to perform the difficult task of moving to inductive comparisons among two or more examples, often by answering a question that states some general principle that appears for the first time.

Courses that stress critical thinking follow a different pattern. In the general design and argument of the whole course, the deductive method tends to be stressed. Such a course typically has a thesis or principle argument (functioning like a major premise), which is being tested or examined throughout the year, and each part of the course extends the argument of that premise by inferring other lines of argument that flow from it. Within that overall deductive argument, the individual lectures, seminars, and assignments also tend to stress the deductive method. The lectures are cast as arguments based on principles that are set out at the beginning of the year and that are elaborated as the course proceeds, building on the details and adding to the definitions and concepts to make a coherent deductive argument. In each lecture a minor premise is set out and is linked to the main argument about the course materials or concepts to draw a conclusion. If you understand that the lecturers are using this method consciously, you will see that they are not just setting out examples or moving randomly from topic to topic.

In your own writing you will often use an inductive method during your research as you gather examples to see whether there is any method of classifying them that will lead to a general principle under which they can be grouped as an argument. It is this principle that you will then be able to reshape into a thesis statement, the general position on which to build your argument, which will then follow a deductive method. Your thesis statement will move not through instances to support it, but from one position you are taking to a second position, and perhaps a third and fourth, all linked together in a chain of deductions.

Truth and Validity, Soundness of Arguments, and Fictions

It is necessary to distinguish between a valid argument and its truth claims. Logicians say that a deductive argument is "valid" when it is put together according to the rules of logic, when each of its premises is properly stated and proceeds toward drawing a conclusion that is based on the preceding propositions. Deductive arguments also make truth claims, beginning with the first premise, which is often a statement of an axiomatic or generally accepted truth. This truth claim is one that you can agree with or not, but it cannot be disputed in terms of the validity of the argument until it is put in relation to the second premise and the conclusion. If the argument is also put together correctly, then it is both true and valid, as in the following argument, one used frequently in logic textbooks:

All humans are mortal. (*major premise—axiomatic truth claim*)

Socrates is a human. (*minor premise—self-evident truth claim*)

Therefore, Socrates is mortal. (*conclusion—conclusion as truth claim*)

In this argument, all of the premises are true, and the argument is valid. However, it is possible to have a valid argument with false propositions:

All whales have four legs. (*major premise—false claim*)

All four legged creatures have tails. (*minor premise—false claim*)

Therefore, all whales have tails. (*conclusion—conclusion is true statement*)

In this argument, the first and second premises are false, though the conclusion is true. The argument is put together correctly, however, and so it is valid. If its premises were also true, it would be both true and valid.

A conditional argument depends on a stated conditional "if" or "when" concept:

When it snows the streets get slippery. (*major premise—axiomatic truth claim*)

It is snowing. (*minor premise—truth claim [observation]*)

The streets are getting slippery. (*conclusion—conclusion as truth claim*)

However, arguments that begin with a false statement, whether or not it can be considered metaphoric, might be valid in their terms and arrangement, but untrue:

All humans are baboons.	When it snows, balls of fire drop everywhere.
Socrates is a human.	It is snowing.
Socrates is a baboon.	Balls of fire are dropping everywhere.

It is also possible to have all of the premises and the conclusion true, but the argument invalid:

If this squeegee kid owned all of the money in the IMF, he would be wealthy.

This squeegee kid does not own all of the money in the IMF.

This squeegee kid is not wealthy.

The premises and the conclusion to this argument are true, but the argument is invalid, because it does not draw a correct inference from the premises as they are stated. The premises would remain true even if the squeegee kid were to inherit a lot of money from a regular customer who died, but the conclusion then would become false. For instance, if the terms were changed, this point would be even clearer:

If Bill Gates owned all of the money in the IMF, he would be wealthy.

Bill Gates does not own all of the money in the IMF.

Therefore, Bill Gates is not wealthy.

Thus, there can be invalid arguments with true conclusions, and valid arguments with false conclusions. When an argument is both true and valid, it is spoken of as *sound*. When it is an invalid argument (even with a true conclusion), or has a false conclusion, it is referred to as *unsound*. Hence, the logic of a sound deductive argument allows a conclusion to be drawn as a certainty. On the other hand, inductive arguments, moving from examples toward conclusions, always posit a high degree of probability, but never certainty. For further explanations of this relationship between arguments and their validity, truth claims, and soundness, see Peter Suber's "Truth of Statements, Validity of Reasoning," (**www.earlham.edu/ ~peters/courses/log/tru-val.htm**).

Many of the texts we read in courses, especially literary texts, are based on a major premise that is untrue. But rather than being called a false truth claim, such texts are often described as *fictions*, as assertions that, though false in fact, can be accepted as potentially true or as true for the purposes of representation in a text. For instance, when Dickens begins *Great Expectations* by saying, "So, I called myself Pip, and came to be called Pip," he is beginning a fiction, an invented narrative that purports to tell the "true" story of a boy's growth to manhood. It represents the data of the story as true, but, in fact, it is false: such a person has never existed. Even texts loosely based on historical narratives take one aspect of that historical narrative and fictionalize it so that it is untrue in point of fact. When Dickens begins his account of the French Revolution (a "true" historical event) in *A Tale of Two Cities*, his opening paragraph sets out a series of oppositions: "It was the best of times; it was the worst of times...." The truth of either part of the statement can be debated. The argument that Dickens advances in the narrative draws out the inferences of that statement and applies them to the cases of two men, Charles Darnay and Sydney Carton, at first the best and worst of men. However, the story that Dickens tells of their love affairs and their involvement in international intrigue and French politics is an invented fiction and is not a true story.

More pertinent to deductive arguments are those texts (both print and visual, as in films) that take some element of the external world and distort it as one of the axioms for creating the fictional world, as in science fiction, fairy tales, much children's literature, and fantasy. Often, this major premise is not stated overtly, but rather is implied, especially in the journey or transition from the represented real world to a representation of an alternative world. What follows in the narrative, however, unravels this false premise according to a logic that is entirely valid in its own terms, that is, according to the alternative world. In the alternative world, then, the false premise is accepted as true. For instance, in Lewis Carroll's *Through the Looking-Glass* a major premise is that everything works backwards. Within the alternative world of Looking-glass Land, this premise (false in the real world) is both true and valid. The premise is implied in the moment of transition, when Alice steps through the mirror. There are, of course, many other major premises that are advanced—for instance, Looking-Glass Land is constructed as a chess game.

In fact, however, propositions deal with the smaller parts of arguments, with the formal coherence between one statement and the next logically dependent statement and on the conclusion that can be drawn from the related propositions. It is only when we look at the major concepts of an intellectual position, say in abnormal psychology, or the causes of the collapse of Napoleon's march on Russia, or the logic of Looking-Glass Land as an alternative world, that we can see how a false assumption or assertion in the major premise can be carried forward logically to set out a coherent argument, and how the validity of the argument as a whole depends on the logical connections of the parts of the deductive argument.

Rules for Syllogisms

Most courses do not have either the time or the need to examine in detail all of the arguments that go into making a reasoned position or a deductive argument. However, it is important to see exactly how that reasoning can be applied, especially in crucial turns in an argument. Hence, it is useful to consider in a brief form how propositions work.

A number of formal rules govern the way deductive arguments work, a matter which can become a complicated study in itself. The most common errors, or fallacies, in students' arguments are suppressing the first stage of the argument (not stating the premise), using an opinion instead of an axiomatic truth for the first or major premise, and using too few or too many terms in the syllogism. Each of these difficulties is dealt with in textbooks on logic, often in very technical language. A summary of the rules for syllogisms and the fallacies in formal logic is given below. The discussion is not intended to be exhaustive, but it describes the main points that can be examined in greater detail in the suggested readings and Web pages. Put simply, trying to find the formal logical steps in your thinking can help you formulate your arguments with much greater precision and effectiveness.

The logic used in deductive reasoning is concerned with the relationships among propositions, how they can be arranged as major and minor premises to make arguments with valid conclusions. When two or more premises are arranged together, they are intended to provide support for the conclusion. The term *inference* describes the relationship of moving logically from proposition to proposition so that the end of one premise leads into the next by inference. The validity of the argument depends on its logical integrity or coherence, not on its truth claims, as we demonstrated above. It is possible for the propositions to be true and the conclusion to be invalid (because the logic is invalid), and for the propositions to be false and the conclusion valid.

A deductive argument is composed of several declarative statements that verbalize the position or concept being argued. According to traditional formal logic, every deductive argument can be set out in a logical form made up of propositions or declarative statements leading to a conclusion, a form called a *syllogism* (Greek, *syn*, together; *log izesthai*, to reckon > *logos*, speech, word, reason). A syllogism is composed of three propositions that contain three simple terms. Each of the three terms occurs in two of the three propositions. The first two propositions are the major and minor premises, and the last, which follows from them, is the conclusion. The standard form of a syllogism follows a specific pattern:

All A is X.	All university students receive grades.	(*major premise*)
B is A.	I am a university student.	(*minor premise*)
Therefore, B is X.	Therefore, I receive grades.	(*conclusion*)

Both the major and the minor terms appear in the conclusion, and it is in the conclusion that you can locate the parts of the syllogism. The subject term of the conclusion of the syllogism (B, or "I") is the minor term of the syllogism as a whole. The major term of the syllogism (X, or "grades") is the predicate of the conclusion. The third term (A, or "university student"), one that does not appear in the conclusion but only in the two premises, is known as the middle term. The proposition that connects the major term and the middle term is the major premise, that connecting the minor term and the middle term is the minor premise.

Normally, every deductive argument can be reduced to its logical components, the premises of a syllogism. In fact, however, most arguments abbreviate a syllogism, stating only one of its premises and its conclusion, especially in complicated arguments. Such an abbreviated syllogism is called an *enthymeme* (Greek, *enthymema*, a consideration > *en*, in; *thymos*, the mind). Part of the syllogism is unstated as still "in the mind." In readings, lectures, and even conversations people customarily leave out part of the argument, stating only part of it and the conclusion that allows them to proceed to the next point: for example, *all physicians are university graduates, and so all members of the Canadian Medical Association must be university graduates.* Normally, you would accept such a statement as almost self-evident, but if you wish to test its validity, you have to supply the missing premise to the syllogism:

All physicians are university graduates.

[All members of the Canadian Medical Association are physicians.]

So all members of the Canadian Medical Association must be university graduates.

One of the most difficult tasks for a student in considering the formal validity of categorical syllogisms is finding the major and minor premises and stating them so that they make a syllogism that is faithful to the terms of the argument, and so that its validity or invalidity can be recognized. The key is to find the conclusion of the argument and to begin there. As stated above, the major and minor terms of the argument both appear in the conclusion: for example, *Socrates is mortal.* The word *Socrates* is the subject of the conclusion, and therefore it is the minor term. *Mortal* is the predicate, and therefore it is the major term. The remaining term, found elsewhere in the sentence just before the conclusion, is the middle term, in this case, *human.* Hence the syllogism is:

All humans are mortal.

Socrates is a human.

Therefore, Socrates is mortal.

However, when the argumentation is more complex, the terms of the conclusion might be much harder to discover. For instance, in Chapter 8 of *Alice's Adventures in Wonderland* there is a dispute about the Queen of Hearts' order to cut off the Cheshire Cat's head, because the cat had dematerialized so that only its head was visible:

> The moment Alice appeared, she was appealed to by all three to settle the question and they repeated their arguments to her, though, as they all spoke at once, she found it very hard to make out exactly what they said.
>
> The executioner's argument was, that you couldn't cut off a head unless there was a body to cut it off from: that he never had to do such a thing before, and he wasn't going to begin at *his* time of life.
>
> The King's argument was, that anything that had a head could be beheaded, and that you weren't to talk nonsense.

TIPS: Adding Implicit Premises

1. Read the argument carefully to understand it and identify the explicit premises or conclusions.

2. Break it down into its major and minor premises with its conclusion.

3. Find the conclusion and determine what the major or minor premises might be if either is missing.

4. If there is no conclusion, reconstruct the conclusion from the available premises.

5. Rework the given conclusion to have it fit the stated premises more closely.

The Queen's argument was that, if something wasn't done about it in less than no time, she'd have everybody executed all round.

Aside from many other problems of logic in this passage (Carroll made substantial demands on his child readers, and he also published books on logic), the issue is what the Cheshire Cat's head can be cut off *from*. The executioner, the King, and the Queen all omit parts of their arguments, and so are stating their syllogisms as enthymemes. When they are expanded with their missing premises, all can be shown to be invalid.

When a deductive argument is made up of a series or chain of syllogisms, it is called a *sorites* (sōrī′tēz from the Greek, *soros*, a heap). In a sorites, the conclusion of the first syllogism becomes the first premise of the second, and so on, until the conclusion of the last syllogism is reached and is tied to the first premise. Some complex and complicated arguments are set forth in this manner, sometimes without the full stages in each of the syllogisms stated. Philosophers often use this method of constructing a deductive argument, as Socrates does in Plato's *Republic* when explaining the meanings of justice to his listeners. Another example might be the crazy ethics of the Duchess in Chapter 9 of *Alice in Wonderland*:

> She had quite forgotten the Duchess by this time, and was a little startled when she heard her voice close to her ear. "You're thinking about something, my dear, and that makes you forget to talk. I can't tell you just now what the moral of that is, but I shall remember it in a bit."
>
> "Perhaps it hasn't one," Alice ventured to remark.
>
> "Tut, tut, child!" said the Duchess. "Everything's got a moral, if only you can find it." And she squeezed herself up closer to Alice's side as she spoke.
>
> Alice did not much like keeping so close to her: first, because the Duchess was *very* ugly; and secondly, because she was exactly the right height to rest her chin upon Alice's shoulder, and it was an uncomfortably sharp chin. However, she did not like to be rude, so she bore it as well as she could.
>
> "The game's going on rather better now," she said, by way of keeping up the conversation a little.
>
> "'Tis so," said the Duchess: "and the moral of that is—'Oh, 'tis love, 'tis love, that makes the world go round!'"
>
> "Somebody said," Alice whispered, "that it's done by everybody minding their own business!"
>
> "Ah, well! It means much the same thing," said the Duchess, digging her sharp little chin into Alice's shoulder as she added, "and the moral of *that* is—'Take care of the sense, and the sounds will take care of themselves.'"
>
> "How fond she is of finding morals in things!" Alice thought to herself.

Although the chain of argument is frequently broken in this passage and over the next page of the novel, there is some effort to form such a linked set of arguments when the Duchess repeatedly explains "the moral of that" to Alice.

Rules for Standard-Form Syllogisms with Associated Fallacies

The standard form of the syllogism (sometimes called the *categorical syllogism*) contains three terms used in same sense throughout:

All A are X.	All children are creatures that need food.
B is A.	I am a child.
Therefore, B is X.	I am a creature that needs food.

Rules for Standard-Form or Categorical Syllogisms	*Associated Fallacies*

1. The syllogism must contain only three terms.

    All animals are mammals.
    Dogs are animals.
    Therefore, dogs are mammals.

2. All of the terms must be used in the same sense throughout, as in the example for rule 1.

1. Fallacy of four terms (*quaternio terminorum*):

    All dogs are mammals.
    All cats are animals.
    Therefore, all dogs are animals.

2. Fallacy of the ambiguous middle, or fallacy of equivocation (implies fourth term):

    Power tends to corrupt. [Lord Acton]
    Knowledge is power. [Francis Bacon]
    Therefore knowledge tends to corrupt.

    This example equivocates because the middle term, *power,* means different things, "political control over others" in the major premise and "mental ability or authority to control ideas" in the minor premise. If *power* is used in one sense throughout, one premise is false (Copi and Cohen 262).

3. The middle term must be distributed in at least one premise. *Distributed* means that the information about the middle term must apply to all members of the class. Hence, in the example for rule 1, what is said about animals is said about all members of that class.

3. Fallacy of the undistributed middle:

    All dogs are animals.
    All cats are animals.
    Therefore, all cats are dogs.

    The middle term, *animals,* is not distributed; nothing is claimed about the whole class of animals.

4. If either term is distributed in the conclusion, then it must be distributed in the premises, as in the example from rule 1.

4a. Fallacy of the illicit major (term)—the major term is undistributed in the major premise but distributed in the conclusion:

    All dogs are animals.
    No cats are dogs.
    Therefore, no cats are animals.

    The conclusion makes an assertion about *all* animals, saying that all of them are excluded from the class of cats. Hence, the major term in the conclusion, *animals,* is distributed. But the major premise makes no assertion about all animals, only that dogs are included in the class. Hence, the conclusion is invalid, since it illicitly goes beyond what the premises assert (Copi and Cohen, 263–64).

4b. Fallacy of the illicit minor (term)—the minor term is undistributed in the minor premise but distributed in the conclusion:

All terriers are animals.
All terriers are pets.
Therefore, all pets are animals.

The conclusion makes an assertion about all pets, but the minor premise makes no assertion about all pets (*pets* is undistributed), so the conclusion illicitly goes beyond what the premises warrant.

5. If one of the premises is negative, the conclusion must be negative.

All dogs are animals.
Some animals are not dangerous.
Therefore, some dogs are not dangerous.

5. Fallacy of drawing an affirmative conclusion from a negative premise:

All dogs are animals.
Some animals are not dangerous.
Therefore, some dogs are dangerous.

While this conclusion might be true, it is not valid.

6. Only one of the premises in a standard-form syllogism can be negative, as in the example in rule 5.

6. Fallacy of the exclusive premises (when a syllogism has two negative premises):

No Torontonians are Americans.
No Americans are Canadians.
Therefore, no Torontonians are Canadians.

7. If there is a particular conclusion (usually using the word *some*), one of the premises must be particular. Another way of stating this rule is that no valid syllogism with two universal premises can have a particular conclusion.

All dogs are animals.
Some animals are dangerous.
Therefore, some dogs are dangerous.

7. Existential fallacy:

All dogs are animals.
All animals are dangerous.
Therefore, some dogs are dangerous.

The minor premise is false.

All pets are domestic animals.
No unicorns are domestic animals.
Therefore some unicorns are not pets.

The conclusion asserts that unicorns exist, a false proposition (Copi and Cohen 266).

8. Each premise must be true or axiomatic, as in the example in rule 1.

8. Fallacy of invalid or impeachable premise—it is false, ambiguous, or of limited application:

All students like hamburgers.
Ahmed is a student.
Therefore, Ahmed likes hamburgers.

He might not. The first premise is of limited application.

Conditional Syllogisms with Associated Fallacies

A conditional statement in a syllogism is an "if/then" statement, with the "if" part the antecedent, and the "then" part the conditional.

The valid form of the conditional syllogism (*modus ponens*, way of affirming):

If A then B.	If it is raining, then the streets are wet.
A.	It is raining.
Then, B.	Therefore, the streets are wet.

Invalid forms of the conditional syllogism:

1. Affirming the consequent:

If A then B.	If it is raining, then the streets are wet.
B.	The streets are wet.
Then, A.	Therefore, it is raining. (No: the street washer might have gone by.)

2. Denying the antecedent:

If A then B.	If a bottle is marked "poison" it will kill me.
Not A.	This bottle is not marked "poison."
Then, not B.	Therefore, it will not kill me.

3. The way of denying *(modus tollens)*:

If A then B.	If it is raining the streets are wet.
Not B.	The streets are not wet.
Then, Not A.	Therefore, it is not raining.

Fallacies in Informal Arguments

A *fallacy* is a form of reasoning that should not be persuasive, though it often is. It depends on mistakes in logic, whether formal in propositions, or informal in thought or language forms. There are many more common mistakes in reasoning or argument than those we have listed above after the various forms of argument. Many are technical faults in the ordering of propositions (formal fallacies in formal logic), while others are usually called *informal fallacies* because they do not depend on the strict *form* or formal structure of the syllogism. Some informal fallacies have special names, usually their Latin names. The following list divides other common informal fallacies (in addition to those noted above) into two kinds, those that are based on an appeal to emotion and those that are based on mistakes in logical connection. This list is by no means complete, but if you are interested, there is an extensive compilation by Stephen Downes on the Internet, with many apt and current Canadian examples and with many links to other similar Web sites (**www.datanation.com/fallacies**).

Fallacies Based on the Appeal to Emotion or Audience Reactions

These fallacies distract the reader or audience by appealing to emotions or other psychological factors.

- The **argument or attack against the person** (Latin, *argumentum ad hominem*) is the most common of all of the appeals on the basis of emotion rather than logical arguments.

It is usually an attempt to win an argument by attacking the personal characteristics of an adversary, often in a derisive or abusive way. Characteristically, instead of attacking the logic of the arguments presented, the arguer committing this fallacy attacks the person making the argument—criticizing character (as in discrediting honesty or sexual activity or orientation), labelling, or name calling. Sometimes, this particular kind of argument against the person is called the *genetic fallacy,* since it attacks the source of an argument rather than the argument itself. Or the attack on the person may make the point that a particular position on one subject should be adopted by the adversary merely because of the adversary's special circumstance: for example, *Clinton's position on social reform is wrong for the country because he has admitted to cheating on his wife; Professor Smith's lectures are incoherent because he is dishevelled and dresses poorly.* Other forms of the attack on the person include guilt by association. This form is often used in political attack, perhaps the most famous being McCarthyism in the United States in the 1950s, when Senator Joseph McCarthy accused a number of civil servants, actors, and writers of being communists because of their friendships.

- A variant of this argument is the **"you too" fallacy** (Latin, *tu quoque*), when the action is deemed acceptable because the other party has also committed it, as when it is argued that a professor cannot deal harshly with a plagiarism case because he too had been convicted for the same offence, or, more generally, when it is argued "You've told a lie" and the response is "You are a liar too." A more minor version, creating misgivings, is to dismiss the arguer and the source of the argument by dredging up old, even unsubstantiated, charges against the arguer, as in alleging old rumours of prostitution charges against a rape victim.

- Another form is **to ridicule, mock, or laugh at the person** who is making the argument, rather than deal with argument made.

- The **appeal to force** (Latin, *argumentum ad baculum*), meaning to physical force, violence, or threats to cause someone to accept a conclusion, is often a last resort when an argument is slipping away and rage takes over. When all other arguments have failed, you make your point by punching your opponent. Governments bring in the army. The appeal is based on the notion that "might makes right" and is appealed to by the political lobbyist who reminds a politician of how many voters are annoyed with a particular position.

- The **appeal to the people**, the audience, a majority or popularity (Latin, *argumentum ad populum*) is the attempt to win over the readers or audience by claiming a position is true because it is widely held, rather than appealing to facts and established positions or making logical connections. This appeal to the people, the crowd, or the gallery also often involves the appeal to pity or an attack on the person. Shakespeare's Marc Antony uses this kind of fallacious argument in the funeral oration over Julius Caesar's body (combined with irony). This fallacy is much beloved of television commercial writers and evangelists.

- A variant of this fallacy is the **argument from numbers** (Latin, *argumentum ad numerum*), or the bandwagon effect, which states that because many people hold a position, it must be correct: *Because six million Canadians smoke, it must be good for you.*

- The **appeal to false authority** (Latin, *argumentum ad verecundiam*) arises when the authority appealed to is being adduced for evidence outside his or her field of expertise, just because he or she is an expert somewhere. Advertisers use this fallacy as a stock-in-trade: *Drink Pepsi because the Spice Girls say it represents girl power.* A variation of this fallacy is the appeal to anonymous authority: *A well-known government spokesperson says...,* or *Many scientists have claimed that eating broccoli prolongs life.*

- The **appeal to pity** (Latin, *argumentum ad misericordiam*) is an argument based on emotional sympathy. The many TV appeals to support children in the developing world exploit this fallacy: *The hunger of children in the third world means that we should always leave our plates clean (or adopt a child, or support a particular charity).* In courts of law, the argument on the basis of pity is often made to provide an extenuating circumstance for a breach of law: *I am poor and hungry, and that is why I stole the tarts.*

- The **appeal to consequences** or the **appeal to intimidation** is used when the audience is warned of unacceptable consequences to follow unless the argument is accepted: *Unless the City Council allows panhandling and the squeegee kids, tourists will be accosted and every tourist attraction will be picketed.*

- The **appeal to the holy cow** uses any concept, person, thing, or event that, in any given cultural context, is good and is immune to criticism, such as the American flag to a group of World War II legion members, or the Queen to members of the Canadian Monarchists League.

- Variants of this fallacy include the **appeal to tradition** (Latin, *argumentum ad antiquitatem*), which means arguing that because something has always been done this way, it is the best way (a favourite of city councils and local politicians who don't want to rethink a matter), or that older is better. A variant is the **appeal to modernity** (Latin, *argumentum ad novitatem*), that the newest is the best, the claim of most software vendors wanting you to upgrade to the most recent version, despite the possibility that the bugs have not been worked out.

Fallacies of Mistaken Logical Connection

Logical arguments connect assertions and propositions together in ways that move from evidence to principles, or from premises to conclusions. When the evidence is faulty in inductive reasoning, or the premises are false or poorly constructed or ordered in deductive reasoning, many faults in logical connection can occur. A number of these faults are used consciously by speakers and writers to skip over some embarrassing evidence, to raise a false argument to distract the audience, or to persuade the audience by some rhetorical (but illogical) trick. For instance, when a politician is asked a direct question about some unpopular social policy and responds by saying, "I have this to say about that" and then speaks of something altogether different, perhaps something very popular, this rhetorical ploy (changing the subject) is also an error in logic (dodging the issue), even though it might be an astute tactic. This fault is also called not answering the question, not facing the problem, or answering a question that was not asked—and this fault, like those that follow, exhibits weak or faulty links between evidence and proof.

- The **hasty conclusion or generalization** consists of jumping to a conclusion before you have proved it or to a generalization on the basis of too small or partial a sampling: *Fifty English fans rioted at the World Cup games in France, and therefore the English are a violent and lawless people.*

- A variant is the **sweeping generalization** (the fallacy of accident), in which a general rule is applied to a particular situation in which it does not fit, or when an exception should be made or when the context appropriate to the rule is ignored: *The law says you must drive past this school at 40 kph, so even though you are rushing your wife, who is in labour, to the hospital, you should not have driven faster than 40 kph.* Another variant is the inappropriate generalization (the fallacy of converse accident, the reverse of the fallacy of accident), in which the exception to the general rule is applied to cases where the generalization should apply: *Because Michelle, who was in the hospital, got an extension on her essay, all members of the class should have extensions.*

- **Fallacy of belaboured repetition** (Latin, *argumentum ad nauseam*) applies when an assertion is repeated rather than proved; the arguer believes that the more times a position is stated, the more likely it is to be true: *I've told you before and I tell you again that he is a habitual liar. He lies all the time. He is always telling lies. He lies, he lies, he lies.*

- **Fallacy of composition** applies to an argument in which what is true of the parts is argued also to be true of the whole: *Each of the parts of a machine is light; therefore, the whole machine is light.*

- **Fallacy of division** applies to the reverse of the fallacy of composition by stating that what is true of the whole is also true of the parts: *Yale University is excellent; Jane Bloggs is a student at Yale; therefore, Jane Bloggs is excellent.*

- The **appeal to ignorance** (Latin, *argumentum ad ignorantiam*) argues that a position is true simply because it has never been proved false, or the reverse: *There must be people on Mars because no one has ever proved there are not people on Mars;* or, *There must be ghosts, because they have not been disproved.*

- **Fallacy of many questions** (Latin, *plurium interrogationum*) occurs when two or more questions are made into one, as in the question "Have you stopped beating your dog?", in which answering either yes or no admits to the beating. The fallacy is sometimes called the complex question; it is a frequent device in Sophocles' *Oedipus the King*. This fallacy reduces the complex question into a simple either/or.

- **Begging the question** (Latin, *petitio principii*) uses as a premise the same proposition as is used in the conclusion. Usually, this circular argument begins with an assumption that you (and perhaps everyone) might think is true, and, after some arguments, you conclude that it is true. Often, the basic premise (or first argument) is hidden, is not stated, and so cannot easily be challenged: *Shakespeare is a greater writer than Agatha Christie because people of good taste prefer Shakespeare. And people of good taste are defined by reading Shakespeare.*

- **Assuming or asserting a position without demonstrating** it occurs when a statement asserts a case without evidence, a frequent problem in students' essays: *It is obvious that Alice hates all of the characters at the Mad Hatter's Tea Party.* Politicians frequently use this fallacy to their advantage in hiding behind "government policy" or concealed economics: *Tuition fees must rise because there is no money for universities and colleges* (the statement that there is no money is an assertion that is not demonstrated or that can be challenged). Readers will often mark such a statement as a defective argument that is not demonstrated with the letters Q. E. D. (Latin, *quod erat demonstrandum,* what must be shown—and is lacking).

- **Self-contradiction** occurs when two contradictory premises are joined together to make a claim: *Only after he kills himself in a car accident will he realize that he should not drink and drive.*

- The **false analogy** draws a comparison between two items on the basis of a supposedly common characteristic when, in fact, the items differ on precisely the point or context of the comparison. False analogies compare things that do not fit the case you are arguing: *Universities are like shopping malls. In shopping malls customers can enter any store and buy what they want and leave with it, and so it is with students at universities.* The analogy here could be unpacked usefully, and by pointing out differences between universities and shopping malls many cogent critical arguments could be developed. Although students do have choices and pay for services at universities, paying for a course does not mean passing it. There are many requirements and contractual rules that apply at a university; therefore, the argument draws a false analogy.

- The **vicious circle** (Latin, *circulus in demonstrando*) occurs when an argument proceeds to a self-contradictory conclusion, as in the famous paradox of Epimenides the Cretan: "All Cretans are liars." If he includes himself in the statement, then the statement is a lie, and therefore some Cretans are not liars and Epimenides may be speaking the truth. And yet he cannot be speaking the truth if he is included in his own statement that all Cretans are liars. Some logicians place this fallacy among the formal fallacies related to standard syllogisms.

- The **irrelevant conclusion** (Latin, *ignoratio elenchi,* ignoring the point) sets out to prove one thing and ends up proving another or may draw a conclusion that is irrelevant or beside the point of the argument: *Closing hospitals is necessary financially to keep the health care system running. Saved money will be able to be spent elsewhere in the system. Therefore, health care will be improved.* This argument begins with the goal of keeping the system running by saving money, and ends with asserting that health care will be improved; there is no necessary connection between closing hospitals and improving health care. On the face of it this argument also appears to be contradictory.

- The **red herring** throws the argument off track or diverts the audience by introducing irrelevant issues or questions: *Why should we worry about the raising of tuition fees when Pakistan and India are developing nuclear bombs?*

- The **domino fallacy** alleges that if one item in an argument can be dislodged, the whole structure of the argument will collapse: *In this course on feminist literature, this novel is not about women. Therefore, the whole argument of the course is invalid.* But it is usually the case that the parts of many arguments will stand independently; the fall of one is not necessarily tied to the fall of all. Sometimes, this fallacy is known as the "house of cards."

- The **"slippery slope"** maintains that if one exception is made, any number will follow from it, with dire consequences: *If I let one student bring coffee to class, and another a doughnut, soon they will bring in entire lunches and will be serving four course meals;* or, *If I let Suzie bring her gerbil to school, all the children will be able to bring their pets. Patrick will bring his turtle, Jemima her dog, and soon we will be run over with horses, and possibly elephants.*

- The **"straw man"** involves setting up a false opponent merely to advance your own position, or strengthening your own position by attacking an unrepresentative or weak oppositional argument. Usually two methods are used to employ this fallacy: first, making an appeal to the general audience, and second misrepresenting someone's position to set up your own: *Freud showed that his patients in Vienna suppressed their sexual feelings and experiences, and that is exactly why, as I shall show, civilization since him has been in great difficulty.* Freud's theory about suppressed sexuality is the straw man, an excuse for the arguer to advance his own theory about present-day civilization. This argument also shows the *post hoc* fallacy. In another example, the arguer uses a politician's comment as a straw man for an attack on an entire political agenda: *When the Premier cut milk money for pregnant women on welfare, his comment that they only spend it on beer exposed everything about his agenda.*

A number of excellent Web sites deal with logic, especially traditional formal logic and fallacies. The Longview Community College site is especially helpful in identifying fallacies, reconstructing arguments to show their parts, and understanding the arguments of complicated discussions (**www.kcmetro.cc.mo.us/longview/CTAC/corenotes.htm**). As well, the introductory logic page from the San Jose State University Critical Thinking page includes many do-it-yourself exercises for beginners in logic (**www.sjsu.edu/depts/itl/graphics/main.html**). See the Weblinks at the end of this chapter for more helpful sites.

USING QUOTATIONS IN BUILDING YOUR ARGUMENTS

Appropriate quotations from the novel, poem, play, scholarly book or article, or other document on which you are writing can greatly increase the intensity and persuasiveness of your writing. Such quotations can illustrate your point briefly and pointedly, can lead a reader through your ideas by means of example, and can allow easy comparison of texts, phrasing, images, words, and ideas. But they also have to fit with your argument and provide the kind of evidence that you need. You can support your own essay with quotations from recognized authorities to provide another scholarly opinion, or you could use a critic or scholar to highlight a particular approach or to create a point of departure for your own argument. As a general rule, quotations are used for the purposes of analysis or to demonstrate stylistic features of a particular writer or, perhaps, of a particular genre. They should not be used to support matters of acknowledged fact, nor merely to confirm what you have just paraphrased or summarized. Wherever you are using another writer's direct words, you need to use quotation marks and give the source for your quotation (see Chapter 12). We raise here a number of considerations regarding the use of quotations in constructing your argument.

Using Quotations to Support Arguments

Quotations can give powerful support to your argument. You should use a quotation if it makes the point you wish to emphasize in a clear and brief passage. However, nothing is accomplished if the quotation supports your argument, through a long, tortuous, and many-faceted passage. If the quotation is not brief and clear, you should summarize it in your own words and give a specific reference for the idea.

Using Quotations for Purposes of Disagreement

You may also use quotations effectively to provide counter-opinions, which you can then disagree with or qualify. Usually, more advanced students feel happier using this method, especially when they have done a good deal of work on a topic and consider that they have a fresh angle to pursue. An intemperate or unreasoned attack on a critic might seem to a sensitive reader like adolescent iconoclasm. Beware of the fallacy of the straw man in using this approach.

Using Quotations for Illustration

Complex arguments, difficult philosophical positions, and abstract reasoning often demand illustration, and sometimes a succinct quotation saves much lengthy and tedious explanation. Illustration, especially in essays on literary topics, is one of the primary ways of bringing in supporting evidence for your position. A quotation can summarize a character's qualities of mind, can give a vivid description, and can allude to figures of speech or qualities of language.

Explaining Your Use of Quotations

Because an apposite quotation can bring in a dynamic illustration, many inexperienced writers think that an illustrative quotation can replace argument. But good writers use quotations to illustrate their own arguments or to summarize them. You should use quotations to support (or counter) a position that you must argue on your own. Quotations need to be introduced with a phrase or an explanation to show how they relate to your argument as evidence or as proof, and they need to be commented on afterwards to draw out their implications, or to make a point. That is, the purpose of a quotation by itself is not self-evident, nor can your reader infer easily how you see it as applying to your argument or conclusion. You need to specify how and why you are using it and what you conclude from it.

FURTHER READINGS

Bergmann, Merrie, James Moor, and Jack Nelson. *The Logic Book*. 2nd ed. New York: McGraw-Hill, 1990.

Copi, Irving M., and Cohen, Carl. *Introduction to Logic*. 9th ed. New York: Macmillan, 1994.

Govier, Trudy. *A Practical Study of Argument*. Belmont, CA: Wadsworth, 1992.

Groarke, Leo, Christopher Tindale, and Linda Fisher. *Good Reasoning Matters!* Toronto: Oxford UP, 1997.

Hansen, Hans V., and Roberts C. Pinto, eds. *Fallacies: Classical and Contemporary Readings*. University Park, PA: Penn State UP, 1995.

Jason, Gary. *Introduction to Logic*. Boston: Jones and Bartlett, 1994.

Johnson, Ralph J. *The Rise of Informal Logic*. Newport, NJ: Vale Press, 1996.

Kelly, David. *The Art of Reasoning*. New York: W.W. Norton, 1988.

Ruggiero, Vincent Ryan. *Becoming a Critical Thinker*. Rapid City, SD: Houghton Mifflin, 1992.

Toulmin, Stephen. *The Uses of Argument*. Cambridge: Cambridge UP, 1964.

Weston, Anthony. *A Rulebook for Arguments*. London: Hackett, 1987.

WEBLINKS

- The Fallacy Zoo
  www.primenet.com/~byoder/fallazoo.htm

  Provides a substantial list, definitions, and examples.

- The Introductory Logic Page from San Jose State University
  www.sjsu.edu/depts/itl/graphics/main.html

- Longview Community College
  www.kcmetro.cc.mo.us/longview/CTAC/corenotes.htm

  A discussion of logic related to critical thinking across the curriculum. This site is especially helpful in identifying fallacies, reconstructing arguments to show their parts, and understanding the arguments of complicated discussions.

- Logic Resources and Definitions
  people.delphi.com/gkemerling/lg/index.htm

- Peter Suber's Logic Page from Earlham College
  www.earlham.edu/~peters/courses/log/loghome.htm

- Stephen Downes' Logic Resources
  datanation.com/fallacies/cgi-bin/portal/show_list.cgi?category=Logic_Resources

  Especially strong on fallacies.

RESEARCHING
PRINT SOURCES

C h a p t e r

THE RESEARCH STAGE

In Chapter 6, we discussed the ways to assess the scope and limits of an assignment topic and to position yourself in relation to what the assignment is asking you to do. We discussed the prewriting stage, when you consider your audience or reader and determine the purpose and subject of your paper. The next step is to plan your research and writing time and decide how much time you need for revision, final typing, and other preparation of the final form of the essay. A schedule that accurately and realistically outlines your time is often a great help.

In reading an assignment critically you will likely have become aware of the areas of your topic that need further research. For instance, in one of the assignment examples given in Chapter 6, on Thomas Hardy's despair or optimism, a survey of the critics of Hardy and a knowledge of the scope of his writings is fundamental. Your research will involve some library work for this topic and careful note taking, which entails indicating all direct quotations in quotation marks and noting the sources to avoid later accusations of unscholarly methods. You will also be evaluating the kinds of materials that you locate. The research stage will involve, as well, the careful reading of Hardy's novels and poems to select those examples from which you will finally develop your position. When you have gathered your notes, you will be able to determine how much more research is necessary.

You will also have to decide whether there are any central or difficult terms or concepts that have to be defined and where those definitions best fit into the paper. In general, essays that begin with dictionary definitions are as interesting as cold spaghetti. Nevertheless, some clarification early in the paper of terms, points of reference, and the general scope of the topic is very helpful to a reader. Dictionary definitions might be especially useful if you are presenting a historical topic, and dictionaries provide historically dated references. For a technical term you should consult a specialized dictionary. Otherwise, definitions are probably most useful to your reader when they are derived from the actual words of the writer you are dealing with, from contexts in the works, periods, or subjects you are writing on, or from the context in which the terms or concepts are used within a specific course.

RESEARCH METHODS AND LIBRARY SKILLS

The fundamental problem in researching a topic is finding a match between the specifics of what you are looking for and the general categories by which information is organized in your library. Indeed, the idea that knowledge can be classified is itself puzzling to many people.

Libraries organize knowledge according to institutional norms, which depend on modes of knowledge derived from the enlightenment tradition, as well as from the humanistic views of human nature and social activities that have dominated Western thought since the Renaissance. Those traditions tended to stress the works of major writers and thinkers, which were regarded as classics, and hence these writings came to be regarded as primary texts and the writings about them as secondary texts. This distinction was incorporated into library classifications systems, so that in the humanities and social sciences these works are privileged over secondary works of a critical, historical, and often technical or scientific nature. Much work in contemporary critical theory has challenged the ideological assumptions underlying this distinction. However, you should be aware that the systems of classification do have consistency—for instance, much of the classification system in the humanities is organized around concepts of nation, century, and individual author.

Critical thinking about where this information comes from and how it is organized should alert you to the fact that these systems of knowledge are deeply attached to the value systems and political affiliations of universities, libraries, and the Web. Such systems of organizing knowledge are not divine or written in stone; instead, they are chosen by a library or university for specific reasons of utility and conformity to the systems in other institutions. Awareness of at least some of these implications makes you a more questioning and perceptive user of the library and its facilities. Searching for information about your topic involves you immediately in these value systems and in the way they are put together.

The organization of any information retrieval system such as the library or the Web is set out according to topics, which are broken down into complex subsets. Knowledge of these topics and their subsets enables access to the specifics of your topic. The more knowledge you have about how information is organized and classified in the library and on the Web, the better you will be able to conduct a search. In the following section on research, we introduce you to a number of fundamental ways that knowledge is classified and suggest some practical strategies for accessing this information.

BOOK CLASSIFICATION SYSTEMS

All university and public libraries classify their books according to subject, then break down the subject within each broad general category. Two main systems are used, the Library of Congress (LC) classification system (devised by Charles Cutter and used in the reorganization of the national library of the United States when it moved into its present location in 1897)

TIPS: Using the Library

1. Your university's library is probably prepared to welcome you at the beginning of term with all kinds of orientation and instructional programs to acquaint you with its resources.

2. Many of these programs are offered regularly throughout the year. You should certainly take advantage of them early in your university career to get the most out of your research.

3. The library offers general tours, instruction on the card or online catalogues, workshops on the use of the CD-ROMs, and so on.

and the Dewey decimal system (first formulated by Melvil Dewey for the Amherst College Library in 1873 and later refined and expanded for the New York State Library and elsewhere). Most universities and colleges use the Library of Congress system, while most public libraries use the Dewey decimal system.

Outline of the Library of Congress Classification System (Twenty Major Categories in boldface)

A–AZ	**General Works**
B–BX	**Philosophy, Psychology, Religion**
C–CT	**General History**
D	**World History**
DA–DX	History by Country
E	**America, United States** (General History)
F	United States (Local History), Canada, Latin America
G–GV	**Geography, Anthropology, Sports**
H–HX	**Social Sciences, Economics, Business, Sociology**
J–JX	**Political Science,** Constitutional History, International Relations
K	**Law**
L–LT	**Education**
M–MT	**Music**
N-NX	**Fine Arts**
P	**Language and Literature**
PA	Philology and Linguistics, Classical Languages and Literatures
PB-PM	Other Languages and Literatures
PN	General and Comparative Literary History
PQ	Romance Literatures
PR	British Literature
PS	American and Canadian Literature
PT	Germanic Literature

Q	**Science**
QA	Mathematics
QB	Astronomy
QC	Physics
QD	Chemistry
QE	Geology
QH	Natural History
QK	Botany
QL	Zoology
QM	Human Anatomy
QP	Physiology
QR	Bacteriology
R	**Medical Sciences, Psychiatry**
S	**Agriculture**
T	**Technology**
U	**Military Science**
V	**Naval Science**
Z	**Bibliography and Library Science**

Outline of the Dewey Decimal System (Ten Major Categories)

000	General Works
100	Philosophy and Psychology
200	Religion
300	Social Sciences
400	Language
500	Natural Sciences and Mathematics
600	Technology and Applied Sciences
700	Fine Arts
800	Literature
900	Geography and History

At the reference desk in your library there will be a bound copy of the *Library of Congress Subject Headings (LCSH),* in which each of these subjects is broken down into its components, so that you can search the headings efficiently to find your topic. Information about the Dewey decimal system can be found at a useful Web site, CyberDewey (**ivory.lm.com/~mundie/CyberDewey/CyberDewey.html**).

GENERAL REFERENCE MATERIALS

All university libraries publish guides and offer tours to introduce students to the libraries' different departments and collections. Most libraries have several departments, such as reference (with librarians on duty to help with finding materials and to consult about library resources), periodicals (where current periodicals, serials, and newspapers are housed), a media library (with sound, film, and video resources), and perhaps specialized libraries, such as a map library, a law or science library, and a rare books library. The circulation department houses the catalogues (either in print form as card catalogues or in electronic form through computer access) and the checkout desks where books are borrowed. The reference section also has handouts and guides available to make your searches for materials easier. If your library catalogue is online, it likely has student aids to help you search the catalogue, as well as the special reference materials available on the Web. All of the information below applies to both print and electronic texts. Many of the works cited are available in both forms; some, in only one or the other. Your reference librarians can provide further information.

The general reference area of your library contains a kind of summary of the total library: here are located those books that are deemed essential reference sources in all of the subjects that the library contains; these books are not allowed to circulate, but they are available for all to consult. Becoming familiar with the kinds of resources located in your library's reference area is an essential step to becoming a good researcher. Specific kinds of books are located here:

- *Abstracts* are summaries of larger books or periodicals. Many disciplines summarize the research in their fields in abstracts or digests. For instance, *Historical Abstracts* indexes abstracts of articles of almost 2000 journals relating to all areas of the world except Canada and the United States. For these two countries you have to use *America: History and Life.* Major journals in the humanities and social sciences are covered in both. They are indexed by subject and author.

- *Almanacs* are registers of the days, weeks, and months of the year, sometimes with much other information a specific topic. See:

  The Almanac of Canadian Politics. 2nd ed. Ed. Munroe Eagles. Toronto: Oxford UP, 1995.

- *Atlases* are bound volumes of maps or charts or, sometimes, illustrations of a specific subject, such as an atlas of human physiology. See:

  The Atlas of African Affairs. 2nd ed. Ed. Ieuan L. Griffiths. New York: Routledge, 1994.

- *Bibliographies* are lists of books about a topic. Many writers and topics have bibliographies compiled about them. General bibliographies are guides to those bibliographies, such as:

  Bibliographic Index. New York: Wilson, 1938 to the present.

  Guide to Reference Books. Ed. W.P. Sheehy. Chicago: American Library Association, 1986.

  Harney, James L. *Literary Research Guide.* New York: Modern Language Association, 1989. A comprehensive guide useful in many fields other than literature.

- *Biographies and biographical indexes* provide information about people living and dead. Such books include the various national biographies and the *International Who's Who* (London: Europa, 1935) to the present, as well as various *Who Was Who* volumes. Many countries also have compiled indexes of their famous people, such as:

  Dictionary of American Biography. 11 vols. and supplements. Ed. Allen Johnson and Dumas Malone. New York: Scribner's, 1964.

  Dictionary of Canadian Biography. 11 vols. and supplements. Ed. George W. Brown, David M. Hayne, and Francess G. Halpenny. Toronto: U of Toronto P, 1966–.

Dictionary of National Biography. 22 vols. and supplements. Ed. Leslie Stephen and Sidney Lee. London: Oxford UP, 1967–68. British biography.

- *Dictionaries* contain information about words, and sometimes also subjects, in various languages, arranged alphabetically. Comprehensive dictionaries of the English language include:

The Oxford English Dictionary. 2nd ed. 20 vols. and supplements. Oxford: Oxford UP, 1989.

A Dictionary of American English on Historical Principles. 4 vols. Ed. William A. Craigie and James Hulbert. Chicago: U of Chicago P, 1960.

Webster's Third New International Dictionary Unabridged. Springfield, MA.: Merriam, 1986.

Canadian Oxford Dictionary. Ed. Katherine Barber. Toronto: Oxford UP, 1998.

There are many dictionaries of other languages, of course, as well as specialized dictionaries, such as:

A Dictionary of Slang and Unconventional English. Ed. Eric Partridge. London: Routledge and Kegan Paul, 1984.

Brewer's Dictionary of Phrase and Fable. 15th ed. Ed. Ebenezer Cobham Brewer. New York: HarperCollins, 1995.

Familiar Quotations. 15th ed. Ed. John Bartlett. Boston: Little, Brown, 1980.

- *Encyclopedias* are large compendia of information about specific topics or national cultures, for example:

Encyclopedia Americana. New York: Grolier, 1993.

Encyclopaedia Britannica. Chicago: Encyclopaedia Britannica, 1992.

The Canadian Encyclopedia. 4 vols. Toronto: McClelland and Stewart, 1996. CD-ROM edition: *1999 Canadian Encyclopedia World Edition.* Toronto: McClelland and Stewart, 1998.

- *Handbooks* provide specialized information or technical instruction. Almost every subject has one or more handbooks or guides, which are invaluable in critical reading for their definitions of terms, statistics and chronologies, and outlines of procedures or methods. Such data can fill in the blanks that inevitably come up in your reading. Some examples are:

Handbook of American Women's History. Ed. Angela Howard Zophy. New York: Garland, 1990.

A Handbook to Literature. 7th ed. Ed. William Harmon and C. Hugh Holman. Upper Saddle River, NJ: Prentice-Hall, 1996.

Eerdmans' Handbook to the Bible. Ed. David Alexander and Pat Alexander. Grand Rapids, MI: Eerdmans, 1983.

- *Indexes* point to where information can be found on a specific topic. For instance, the *Social Science Index (SSI)* indexes materials from some 350 journals related to anthropology, economics, environmental science, geography, law and criminology, public administration, political science, psychology, and sociology. The *Humanities Index* does the same for humanities disciplines.

- *Reviews* are books, collections, or articles that comment on or review other books, films, music, novels, or research. Reviews are useful both to summarizing the content of a text as well as to situating its scholarly, critical, or popular reception. Many indexes to these reviews may be consulted, including:

  Book Review Digest. New York: Wilson, 1905 to the present.

  Book Review Index. Detroit: Gale, 1965 to the present.

- *Serials* are regularly published periodicals and scholarly journals that contain research reports or summaries of recent research in a specific field, often in the form of a year-end review. For example, the journal *Victorian Studies* publishes annually a large survey of scholarship in the field.

SEARCHING THE LIBRARY CATALOGUES

Your first line of approach in researching any topic is to consult the library catalogues. Immediately you have a choice of one of five methods. Some online catalogues let you use a mouse to navigate by clicking on choices; others require you to type an abbreviation (such as *a* for author, *t* for title) to move through the search types.

Author Search

Authors include people, companies, organizations, government agencies, universities, societies, and so on. Type in the author's last name followed by the first name or initials. If you know only the last name, type it and you can search through all of the authors with that name to find your author, or if you get too many entries, limit your search by using the keyword search (see below). If your book has more than one author, all are listed in the catalogue.

Examples
> walker alice
> microsoft corporation

If you want books about an author, search by subject using the author's name.
Example
> hardy thomas

Title Search

Titles may be of books, journals, films, government documents, music, or computer databases.

Examples
> [The] Mayor of Casterbridge, Alice's Adventures in Wonderland
> University of Toronto Quarterly
> Apocalypse Now

Ignore *a, an,* or *the* in any language if it is the first word of the title. Include *a, an,* or *the* within the title. If you have a long title, enter just the first few words. If you have information about an article, search by the title of the journal or other source, not by the title of the article.

Subject Search

The organization of subject headings for a library search depends on the kind of classification system your library uses, either Library of Congress or Dewey decimal. The system is important because it determines the specific way that you define your subject in either the card catalogue or the online catalogue. Hence, when you search for a topic you need to be aware of the kind of logic used in the classification system. If you search for a proper name, such as Lewis Carroll, Melanie Klein, or J.M. Barrie, giving the family name first, you should have little trouble and will immediately find a sequence of categories that list, in order, works by your author, followed by letters, biographies, criticism, and detailed studies according to a wide variety of other subfields. Scroll down (or move through the subject card catalogue) until you find the category you want, and then search for individual titles that are appropriate.

If necessary, consult the *Library of Congress Subject Headings* index or a librarian for more sophisticated subject searches. Some subject searches may give related terms (with the words *see also*) or refer you to the correct subject term used in the catalogue. If you are having difficulty with a subject search, try using a keyword search.

Keyword Search

Keyword searches look for the word or phrase you type anywhere in a bibliographic record. That is, the words you search must be somewhere in the bibliographic entry, in the author's name, a word in the title, a subject as designated in the *Library of Congress Subject Headings* (specified in the long form of the bibliographic entry), the publisher's name, or the date. If you know one of the words in the title that you are searching for, you can enter that word in the keyword search category, and if that word actually occurs in the title it will be located. Or you can enter a phrase (such as French Revolution or war movies) or combine two areas of interest, such as an author's name and a subject term. Keyword searches usually display the most recent information first.

When searching by keyword, certain conventions are followed according to a system known as Boolean logic (based on connectives between keywords using words or mathematical symbols):

1. Use ? as a wildcard to search for variations in word endings:
    *   politic? [return] finds politics, political, politician, etc.
    *   litera? [return] finds literal, literate, literary, literacy, literature, literatures.

    You can also use $ to indicate a truncated word: govern$ finds governs, governing, governor, government, governmental, and so on. Avoid using ? or $ with very short words, as this will produce long lists of words, most of them irrelevant to your search.

2. Use ? with a number to search for a specific number of additional letters:
    *   litera?2 [return] finds literate, literary, literacy, but not literal or literature.

3. Use AND, OR, or NOT to combine keyword search terms:
    *   AND finds records with both (or all) of the terms (Shakespeare AND women).
    *   OR finds records with either (or any) of the terms (copyright OR photocopying).
    *   NOT finds records with the first term but not the second (Santa NOT Claus will find such instances as Santa Barbara, Santa Clara, Santa Scala, and so on).

TIPS: Searching the Library Catalogue

1. If you are looking for a title with *good* in it and you search good? you will get hundreds of entries; you need to be more specific. For instance, if you are looking for the novel *The Good Soldier Schweik* but cannot remember the last name or how it is spelled or the author, you can search under keywords for "good adj soldier," which will quickly produce *The Good Soldier Svejk* by Jaroslav Hasek.

2. If you do not know which system of searching your library uses for keywords, you can consult the Help button on the online catalogue, or in the library the reference or catalogue librarians.

3. If your search results in NO ENTRIES FOUND, you can check for spelling errors, try a keyword search, or make your search more general.

4. Use adj. to specify that keywords must be next to each other (asian adj. american). An alternative is to put the term in single quotation marks, such as 'gulf war.'

5. Use parentheses to express relationships among keywords:
   - (jazz OR ragtime) AND 'New Orleans' will search for either of the first two terms only in relation to the city of New Orleans.

   Some libraries also set up their keyword searches so that you can narrow the field, limiting the items found to those within a range of publication years or to works published in a certain language. Then, the items found can be arranged by date or by year of publication.

Call Number Search

A call number is the shelf mark that indicates a book's location in the library. Searching by call number (perhaps available from class handouts, library information forms, or your own records or earlier searches) will lead you to a specific location in the catalogue. You can then look as far as you wish on either side of that call number by keying or scrolling forward or backward to see other books on the same or similar topics. For instance, if you want to look up Thomas F. Kuhn's *The Structure of Scientific Revolutions* (1962), you will find that it is located in two different places in the Library of Congress catalogue and possibly also in your university library. First, it is catalogued by call number as part of the series in which it was first published:

Q   This letter is the Library of Congress letter designation for Science in general.

121 The number designates the subcategory of general encyclopedias and indexes of science.

I5   The letter *I* designates the first letter of the title of the publication or series in which the volume was published: *International Encyclopedia of Unified Science: Foundations of the Unity of Science*, vol. 2, no. 2.

The book is also listed as a separate publication by Kuhn and is catalogued along with other books in the field of scientific revolutions:

Q   This letter is the LC designation for Science in general.

175 The number designated as the subfield of scientific revolutions.

K95 Within this subfield, the books are arranged alphabetically by author. Sometimes the date is also added.

If your search results in a list, you can obtain more detailed information about your request by highlighting or entering the number of the item for one of the titles, authors, or other search results. Help screens are available at each stage of your search. You may start a new search from any screen. Additional commands appear near the top or bottom of each screen or are available as buttons or as highlighted hypertext links.

SAMPLE CATALOGUE SEARCHES

For more difficult topics, such as computers and writing, where would you begin? Since computers and writing is one of the topics of this book, we undertook a search for recent work in the area. The general topic of computers or writing appears to be too large and undefined. So, how can it be narrowed? Here it is useful to consult the Help buttons on the library catalogue main page or subject page to see how you might search for this topic.

For instance, if you do a subject search for "computers" (without the quotation marks) you will get a large number of entries that it will take you a long time to sift through. One of the headings near the top will be "see related headings for Computers" or some such advice to direct you to the cataloguing entries used in arranging this particular online library catalogue. Accessing that entry provides a number of useful lines to pursue. One is "Computer literacy," but that turns out to be related to a user's knowledge of and ability to use computers, not to the connection between computers and English language literacy and writing proficiency. The advice at the end of such a list to search also under headings beginning with the word "computers" eventually might lead you to "Computers and literacy," a far more promising heading, and there you will find a number of titles that you can scan for their relevance, many of which likely were written in the last decade, all of them dealing with how literacy can be addressed by computers, but not offering advice on how to improve your writing through the use of computers. If, by any chance, nothing shows up there, you might continue by searching the "related headings for Computers and literacy," which will eventually lead you into a search for the more general heading of "Literacy," and perhaps further off topic.

Your second recourse when this approach fails is to start with the term "writing." If your library uses this classification you may find the category "Writing computer-assisted instruction" and a reference to the periodical *Computers and Composition,* published since 1983 by Michigan Technological University. If your library subscribes, you can consult this journal for reviews of recent books in this field or other relevant articles. If your university does not subscribe, you can see if it is held by a library near you or is accessible online. Looking at the full bibliographical entry will show you that there is another LC subject classification specified for the book, "English Language—composition and exercises—Periodicals," which suggests that "English Language" might be another subject field to search.

As you read through the subject classification headings, you will soon be aware that the term *writing* has a number of very different meanings, including writing style and rhetoric (which is the central topic we are looking for), writing in various genres (poetry, science fiction, and children's literature, for example), and writing as the physical act of forming meaningful letters on a page or through some other medium (such as penmanship or the study of petroglyphs), along with the history of various kinds of writing or scripts from cuneiform to hieroglyphics. But ultimately, the subject search online was time consuming and failed to yield many significant materials, except for the periodical *Computers and Composition*.

A second approach is to use the keyword search. If you enter the phrase "computers AND writing" (the Boolean indicator that any items are to include both terms somewhere in the bibliographical entry), you will immediately find a number of items, some of which are almost certainly directly related to your topic. Some will relate to using computers to teach writing in the classroom, while others will relate to the actual practice of using the computer to improve your writing. Among these sources you might find *Writing, Teaching, and Researching History in the Electronic Age: Historians and Computers*, edited by Dennis A. Trinkle (1998). The LC subject headings for this book include "History—computer-assisted instruction," which suggests another place to look in the subject search. You might also find *Transitions: Teaching Writing in Computer-Supported and Traditional Classrooms* by Mike Palmquist et al. (1998), with seven LC subject headings, including "English Language—Rhetoric—Study and teaching—Technological innovations." Further examination of the LC subject heading "English Language—Rhetoric—Technological innovations" will lead to many other books on computers and writing style, including handbooks and guides and scholarly discussions of the impact of computers on writing in and for the classroom. You will then find that the books are located in the library stacks in a range beginning with the letters PE and then the numbers 1401 through to 1404, and you can search through the shelves for other appropriate books.

This subject heading is not one that might have popped quickly into your head, but the method for searching for it was quite logical and systematic, and it is a method that can be followed for most topics. Here, the keyword search proved most fruitful and yielded a lot of information fairly quickly. You can use this method efficiently if you have learned some of the Boolean short-cuts to make your keyword search more precise. The subject search, however, was time consuming and did not yield many items quickly. A combination of the two methods, using a keyword search to find relevant books and then searching the biblio-graphical entry for the appropriate LC subject headings, which you then examine in a sub-ject search, will yield a good number of items. Of course, if you are physically present in the library when you are conducting your online search, you can consult the *LCSH* yourself, or you can ask a reference librarian for suggestions and help. Similar procedures are used for the Dewey decimal system.

A more difficult kind of search is one in a relatively new field of enquiry that combines older subject headings in innovative ways, or one that relates specific texts to these categories in ways that challenge the assumptions built into the classification system. For instance, Peter Pan from J.M. Barrie's *Peter and Wendy* (1911) is traditionally seen as an eternal boy in a children's text, one who is always at play and who is often associated with the many spin-offs, from stage plays and musicals to Walt Disney's version of 1953. Recent work has begun to question the accepted view of the novel's innocence and has seen the story as re-flecting the imperial politics of the late British Empire. In particular, the story has been read as promoting the education of Edwardian children in the "white man's burden" ideol-ogy of the empire, which rationalized the right to conquest and colonize by purporting that it was the white man's responsibility. So, while you might legitimately expect to find a lot of material on Peter Pan and children's fiction, how might you begin to look for the more dif-ficult topic that relates it to education and empire?

One way, of course, would be to look up books under the subject heading of the author of *Peter and Wendy*, J.M. Barrie. There, you will find a list of subfields: a number of books will be on Barrie himself, mostly biographies and appreciations, followed by an alphabetized list of headings for adaptations, bibliography, biography, characters, criticism and interpretation, dramatic works, and so on. A check of the entry on "Criticism and Interpretation" will likely produce Bruce K. Hanson's *The Peter Pan Chronicles: The Nearly 100 Year History of the "Boy Who Wouldn't Grow Up"* (1993), an account of the versions, publication history, and reception of the novel and its variants. While this book will contain some material that is appropriate for you, the book by Jacqueline Rose, *The Case of Peter Pan, or, The Impossibility of Children's Fiction* (1984), deals critically with the general acceptance of Peter Pan as a children's classic. It is highly pertinent to your topic:

PR   subject classification letters [here for British Literature]

4074   subject subcategory classification numbers [Victorian and Edwardian number sequence where J.M. Barrie is located]

P32 R6   title and/or author numbers [*P* for Barrie's titles beginning with *P,* as *Peter and Wendy* or *Peter Pan,* with *R* as the author identification letter (Rose)]

1984   date of publication

The rest of the subject search, and even the LC subject headings in the main bibliographical entry for Rose's book, for instance for "Children's stories, English—History and criticism," do not carry you much further.

Since you are not looking for traditionalist interpretations, but rather for critical discussions of the British Empire and imperial education in relation to children's fiction, the next route to follow is to search for the keywords for the topic you are going to examine and into which you want to integrate your discussion of *Peter and Wendy.* It will be important for you to have some knowledge of the current discussions about the role of education in training citizens of empire. Here, the first keywords you might try would be "education AND empire," but such a search will turn up a lot of extraneous materials, from the Roman and Byzantine empires through to mission education policy in colonial Canada. One relevant book, however, is John Willinsky's *Learning to Divide the World: Education at Empire's End* (1998). The shelf mark, LC 1090 W53 1998, will lead you to other materials on education in Great Britain and the British colonies in a shelf check. Willinsky's book is a useful find for researching your topic, but the search really does have to be narrowed.

For one thing, you are not really looking so much for the notion of empire, though that word might appear in the titles or subject classifications of works that might be appropriate. Another word you might try is "imperialism," and since you are looking for materials that are also classified as literature, that would be a combination to try. In fact, a search for "imperialism AND literature" turns up a wealth of materials, including the following:

Bivona, David. *British Imperial Literature, 1870–1940: Writing and the Administration of Empire.* Cambridge: Cambridge UP, 1998.

———. *Desire and Contradiction: Imperial Visions and Domestic Debates in Victorian Literature.* Manchester: Manchester UP, 1990.

Brantlinger, Patrick. *Rule of Darkness: British Literature and Imperialism, 1830–1914.* Ithaca, NY: Cornell UP, 1988.

Bristow, Joseph. *Empire Boys: Adventures in a Man's World.* London: Unwin Hyman, 1991.

David, Dierdre. *Rule Britannia: Women, Empire and Victorian Writing.* Ithaca, NY: Cornell UP, 1995.

Dawson, Graham. *Soldier Heroes: British Adventure, Empire, and the Imagining of Masculinities.* London: Routledge, 1994.

MacDonald, Robert H. *The Language of Empire: Myths and Metaphors of Popular Imperialism, 1880–1918.* Manchester: Manchester UP, 1994.

Myrsiades, Kostas, and Jerry McGuire. Eds. *Order and Partialities: Theory, Pedagogy and the "Postcolonial."* Albany: State U of New York P, 1995.

Said, Edward. *Culture and Imperialism.* New York: Knopf/Random House, 1993.

At least one book, Laura E. Donaldson's *Decolonizing Feminisms: Race, Gender, and Empire Building,* deals with some of the same themes that Barrie deals with, the use of race and gender in defining the role of imperial colonizers, and, in fact, one of her chapters deals explicitly with *Peter and Wendy*: "The Problem of Discourse in a Marxist Never-Never Land: Of 'Piccaninnies' and Peter Pan."

One more route would be to check the subject heading for "Education—Great Britain—Colonies—History," where you will locate several books by J.A. Mangan that deal directly with the topic of imperial education:

Mangan, J.A. Ed. *Benefits Bestowed? Education and British Imperialism.* Manchester: Manchester UP, 1988.

———. *The Games Ethic and Imperialism: Aspects of the Diffusion of an Ideal.* London: Viking, 1986.

———.Ed. *The Imperial Curriculum: Racial Images and Education in British Colonial Experience.* London: Routledge, 1993.

TIPS: Finding More Information on Your Topics

Once you have found at least one book on your topic, preferably published recently, there are various ways of using it to locate other information:

1. Looking at other books that are near it on the shelf might yield other books on the same or similar topics.

2. There are three places in the book to find other information:

   ■ The first is in the bibliography or works cited list at the back of the book. Here, you are depending on the reliability of the author and the publisher for the integrity of the scholarly sources.

   ■ A second place is the preface, where often an author will give a brief summary of the recent scholarship on the topic.

   ■ Finally, the back of the title page includes details of the book's publication history but also yields various kinds of information, usually about the author (possibly birth and death dates, allowing you to look further into this period of history), and, most importantly, Library of Congress subject headings (enabling you to look that up in a subject search for other works classified there).

Finally, each of these books can be checked on the shelves for other books you or the cataloguers might have missed in the process, and each of the books you find can spur you on to other subject searches, based on either the bibliographical record in the online catalogue or on the verso of the title page, in the book's publication data in the print copy.

Perhaps a better way is to do a Boolean search that links two words in a string, in the form "empire+education" or "empire AND education" (omitting the quotation marks, of course, in the keyword search).

Another angle would be to look up the most general topics on the British Empire and imperialism, looking, especially, for studies written at about the time of the publication of J.M. Barrie's *Peter and Wendy*, in 1911. One of the first books to be located would be J.A. Hobson's *Imperialism: A Study* (1902). The catalogue entry gives other information about the Library of Congress subject headings that are used for this book, "Imperialism," "Great Britain—Colonies," and "Imperial Federation," so any of those headings could be searched for other titles. Perhaps the most efficient route would be to use the keyword method and search for "Peter+Pan AND Children."

Having found book titles and call numbers of books that are in your library, you are well on your way. You can now go to the stacks and follow the call numbers (or book classification numbers) to find the range where books on your topic are shelved. The shelf search involves looking for books adjacent to those you have already found in your catalogue search that are related to your topic.

To be a good researcher takes persistence and flexibility. If you don't find what you are looking for, that doesn't mean that there is no information available. You probably should adjust the categories you are using to search for that information and make adjustments until you find avenues to lead you where you want to go.

SEARCHING FOR RESEARCH MATERIALS IN NEWSPAPERS, PERIODICALS, AND JOURNALS

If you wish to find articles in newspapers, periodicals, or scholarly journals, you must use either the print copies of indexes or abstracts that list the contents of a large number of periodicals in your subject area or one of the specialized CD-ROM indexes that present this information in computerized format (some will be available for use only in the library, others might be available online from your home). Some of the standard indexes are:

- *Art Index*
- *Book Review Digest* (especially helpful for popular periodicals)
- *Canadian Periodical Index*
- *General Science Index*
- *Historical Abstracts* (scholarly monographs and journals)
- *Humanities Index* (scholarly monographs and journals)
- *International Political Science Abstracts*
- *MLA* [Modern Language Association] *International Bibliography* (scholarly monographs and journals)
- *Newspaper Index* (indexes major articles from the *Chicago Tribune, Los Angeles Times, New Orleans Times-Picayune,* and *Washington Post*)

- *New York Times Index* (lists all major articles in the NYT from 1913 to the present)
- *Psychological Abstracts* (scholarly works)
- *Reader's Guide to Periodical Literature* (for popular circulation periodicals)
- *Social Sciences Index* (scholarly works)
- *Sociological Abstracts* (scholarly works)
- *The Times Index* (indexes major articles in *The London Times*)

There are also sites on the Web that compile some of these indexes into computer-readable format, such as InfoTrac, which indexes 500 journals and has links to many others. You can begin this search through the University of Connecticut site (**www.lib.uconn.edu/gateway/infotrac.htm**).

Your reference librarian can help you find the index most appropriate to your topic. The following steps are usually necessary:

1. Define your topic.
2. Choose the index most appropriate to your topic and general subject area.
3. Find the subject headings. Often indexes and abstracts are arranged alphabetically by subject, and the headings may be located in a separate section to help the user. On electronic indexes you can use keyword searches.
4. Find the citation. Under each subject heading there is a list of citations, whether of authors and titles, journal entries, or numbered entries to look up elsewhere. You may have to search through the entire list of citations to find material that is pertinent to your search. The complete citation will consist of the following:

   - the author's name
   - the title of the article
   - the title of the journal in which the article appeared, with its volume number, date, and page numbers

5. Identify the journal title. Many indexes use abbreviations for journal titles to save space. There is a list of abbreviations in the front of the index or in a separate guide.
6. Search for the journal in the library catalogue, using the full title of the journal.
7. Using the call numbers, locate the journal in the stacks and find the issue that you need. Newspapers are probably stored on microform.

HINTS AND FURTHER REFINEMENTS

You may want to go into greater detail on a topic than the catalogue, shelf, book, and periodical searches yielded. Your next move is to consult the resources of other libraries. Many larger university libraries have one or two catalogues of the world's greatest libraries, perhaps the National Union Catalogue published by the Library of Congress (and covering 2500 major libraries) or the British Library Catalogue (sometimes shelved according to its old title, the British Museum Catalogue, referring to where it was located until the recent move to its own building in London). The Library of Congress Union Catalogue is available online at **lcweb.loc.gov/z3950/**. The catalogue of the British Library is also available online during specific hours and for limited search, mostly of books published after 1975: **minos.bl.uk/index.html**.

> ## TIP: Recording Sources
>
> Whatever method you use, record the bibliographical details when you record the quotations or information to avoid having to look for it again later or taking the more risky route of using the material without adequate citation of sources.

These catalogues almost exclusively are author catalogues, except for the titles of periodicals that are included in the general author alphabetical sequence and newspapers (in the BL catalogue, periodicals and newspapers are listed in a separate set of volumes and are classified according to place of publication). Looking up this catalogue can often give you the first date at which a particular work was published, since both of these national libraries are "copyright" libraries, requiring that everything that is published in the United States or in Great Britain be deposited free in the national library. The National Library of Canada is online at **www.nlc-bnc.ca/ehome.htm**.

The Canadian Library Index, located at **www.lights.com/canlib/**, provides links to all Canadian University libraries. Here, you might find that a library near you has the book that you want; however, your university's interlibrary loan department can locate and borrow books for you from other libraries throughout North America.

RECORDING YOUR SOURCES

When undertaking library research, it is important always to record the bibliographic data for your sources. Some people use index cards, recording the bibliographic information on one side (call number, author, title of book or article, [journal, issue, date], publisher, place of publication, date, and pages), and on the other side a summary of the article, a description of the book, or a quotation or other piece of information. Others prefer to use single sheets of paper for each source or document. Of course, some books may require you to use more than one sheet to record information, arguments, or summaries with quotations. If you are making your notes from the Web, it is easy to record the bibliographic information in the format that you will eventually use in your essay the first time that you access the site. You then can save the record (using the block and copy method) and all related records in the same file or folder. For information about how to record your sources, see Chapter 12.

FURTHER READINGS

Ballenger, Bruce P. *The Curious Researcher: A Guide to Writing Research Papers.* Boston: Allyn and Bacon, 1994.

Robertson, Hugh. *The Research Essay: A Guide to Papers, Essays, Projects.* Ottawa: Piperhill Projects, 1998.

WEBLINKS

- Auburn University Social Sciences Resources
  www.lib.auburn.edu/socsci/docs/netindex.html

- College of William and Mary Humanities Links
  warthog.cc.wm.edu/CAS/ASP/links.html

- Resources Useful for Researchers in the Social Sciences
  www.carleton.ca/~cmckie/research2.html

- Tusculum College Links
  www.tusculum.edu/college/links.html#libraries

- University of Toronto Library and Research Resources page
  www.library.utoronto.ca/resources/textonly.html

- Voice of the Shuttle: General Humanities Resources Page
  vos.ucsb.edu/index/html

  A site from the University of California at Santa Barbara, with many links to print and other sources.

- York Library Catalogue
  www.library.yorku.ca/

RESEARCHING ELECTRONIC SOURCES

NEW RESOURCES AND NEW METHODS

The widespread use of computers has not in itself revolutionized research. But libraries have been quick to adopt the new electronic technologies, and now most university libraries have a card catalogue for only small portions of their collections, perhaps for the older materials that have not yet been entered into electronic form or special collections, such as rare books. It is more usual, however, that the card catalogue has been replaced, first by a computer index to the library collection and, more recently, by a computer index that also provides other electronic resources:

- access to other libraries in the province or state through the Internet
- access to CD-ROM databases that are held in the library or other libraries
- access to all of the other libraries throughout the world through the Internet
- access to thousands of Internet research sites for books, collections, and other research materials

This availability of Internet and Web resources at your university library greatly expands the possibilities for systematic research, but it also complicates that research. Many university reference librarians have been thoroughly trained in the older book technologies and can greatly assist you in using the reference collections and other materials in your library. Some librarians will also be experts in the new computer technologies. These resources have necessarily involved new methods for research, which we address in this chapter.

RESEARCHING ON THE WEB

If you decide to use the Web for an early stage of your research for an essay, you first need to determine exactly which aspects of the topic can be best hunted for there, which are best looked for in the library in print or electronic sources, and which are best researched in your textbooks and other assigned readings. Whatever method you decide to follow for your research, you will have to spend some time reading what you have found—at least as much time as it took you to find it.

The Internet is an excellent resource for all kinds of current information and contemporary topics, such as computers and technology, recent developments in the natural sciences, current news, information from the governments of the world, information about products and business, including the possibility of buying almost anything online, and popular culture (music, films, other kinds of entertainment, travel, hobbies, food, and so on). But even with so-called current information, you will often find that Web sites have not been updated (you should examine the date at the end of the page, or note the date specified on the Web search engine).

Other fields, including many that are taught at universities, are still developing. In the humanities (English and other languages, literature, history, philosophy, religion, and the fine arts) and social sciences (anthropology, education, geography, political science, psychology, social science, and sociology), many new Web sites are being added daily. Many courses have Web sites, and there are now sophisticated search engines and indexes for thousands of pages in each of these general fields and particular disciplines. However, historical or contextual information about many topics in these fields is still more limited than current information.

Hence, it is more important than ever that you are aware of the purposes and functions of the various Web search engines. It is also crucial that you continue to focus on your topic and set limits on the amount of time that you spend searching. If nothing shows up within your time limit, you should reformulate your search or change search engines. You might also try searching at a different time of day if you find that the Web is slow because of excess traffic during peak hours. For other information on Internet library research, Net tools, evaluation, Web Browsers, and Netscape see: **www.lib.berkeley.edu/TeachingLib/Guides/Internet/FindInfo.html**.

TIPS: Researching on the Web

1. Be open to a number of different approaches to your topic.
2. If one term does not give any useful results quickly, move to another term, or try a different search engine.
3. Resist the temptation to follow up every lead, however trivial.
4. Distinguish between researching and surfing. To do research on the Net means to work on some of your academic projects. To surf is to spend time on the Net for entertainment purposes.
5. Keep a sharp eye on your topic, and refocus your research every few minutes to use your time on the Web to the best advantage.
6. If you find a useful site that you want to explore in greater detail, bookmark it and return to it later when you have accomplished the main purpose of your search.

COMPUTER DATABASES AND OTHER INFORMATION ON THE INTERNET

Most Web pages on the Internet are indexed, either by the title of the page, the address, a keyword, or the subject matter. This information is gathered by researchers who group these pages into categories, and also by mechanical searchers that gather and sort the data electronically. The resulting indexes are the databases to which the Web browsers have access. Of course, the database is never complete, since thousands of new pages are added every day, just as thousands of other pages disappear through lack of servicing, loss of the Internet provider, or inactivity. What kinds of information are on the Web that might be of use to you in your research, and how might you find it?

A number of strategies are particularly helpful to you when working on your essay, both in the prewriting and the drafting stage. These methods include accessing the university library and its online facilities over the Internet, accessing online research and reference tools, and accessing large collections of standard texts in what is in effect a "virtual library."

Internet Access to Libraries

Your University Library

The libraries of most public and university libraries are now accessible over the Internet. Gone—or at least going—are the card catalogues with "hard" information typed on each card. Instead of going to the library, queuing for a terminal, and then starting your search, you can search for materials from your home computer before you go to the library to get the book. You can also check whether the book is in the library or on loan, what other books are available on similar topics, and so on.

To access your university's library, you need a computer with a modem, an Internet server, and the access numbers and codes for the university system. In most institutions, the university provides or sells a package of software that makes online connection easy. Some institutions offer or require students to maintain a student account for online access. The advantage of having such an account is that you will then have access to some materials that are reserved for university users rather than the general public.

Most public institutions, including universities, allow the general public to access its catalogues. You do this by going to your university's main Web page via Netscape Navigator or Microsoft Explorer and then locating the library tab or icon, which will then give you a variety of choices, including searching the online catalogue. You can add this address to your bookmarks. Electronic searches of the catalogue enable you to hunt for an author, title, subject, and shelf number. Once you have found a book you are interested in, you can find others on the same topic by looking up the shelf number and scrolling forward and backward from that number. Or, you can use the Library of Congress subject classification codes or words that are used as descriptors in your book's information pages. Using those words, you can search the subject catalogue for other books on the same topic.

Catalogue information can be very useful in compiling a working bibliography. You might begin your library research on a topic by gathering one or two pages of bibliographical entries together and then checking the shelves of books in the library. Rather than transcribing all of that information manually with the potential for errors, you can save it to your word processor where you can compile and edit it later, send it to your e-mail address, or print it. You may block and save a single item, items from one screen, or even larger lists. Or you may compile many items to make a single list (see page 212 for instructions on downloading information from the Internet).

Other Libraries

You might wish to have information about a book that your university library does not own, or you might wish to see whether another university library nearby or a public library has materials you can use. You can access their information by going to your own library and clicking on "Other Libraries" or a similar link on the library home page. That will give you access to libraries in your area, in the country, and on other continents. One of the largest sources for bibliographical information is the Library of Congress, in Washington, which you can access in this way. Once you have gained access you continue your search in the usual way. You can also make a request to borrow those materials from another library (sometimes for a small fee) through the interlibrary loan office of your library. You should allow plenty of time for the materials to arrive before your research is due. There are many good collections of library links and catalogues on the Web, such as LibCat (**www.metronet.lib.mn.us/lc/lc1.html**) and webCats (**www.lights.com/webcats**).

CD-ROMs and Online Journals

Universities maintain subscriptions to a variety of CD-ROMs, specialized CDs that contain vast amounts of research information, which are available to users in the libraries. For instance, the many volumes of the *Oxford English Dictionary* are available on CD-ROM. So are the indexes of scholarly work completed in specialized fields over the many years, for instance, those compiled by the American Psychological Association and the Modern Language Association. Similar CD-ROMs are available in the sciences, social sciences and humanities, business, education, law, and religion. Some universities also make these resources available to the general public, but most require a user to log in to the library through a university-maintained server that is accessible only to members of that university community. In this way, the universities can provide the best service to their own members and also maintain the copyright and user restrictions placed on the CD-ROMs by the sellers. Any of this material, once accessed, can be saved to your word processor, sent to your e-mail address, or printed. You should check with your library for an information sheet on access to these materials.

As with CD-ROMs, universities may make available a number of journals online, both those that they publish and those that they purchase. Furthermore, a number of journals are now available only online. Restrictions about access to these journals may apply, as with CD-ROMs. It is also worth checking some sites that archive runs of journals, such as the University of California at San Diego Library (**gort.ucsd.edu/ejourn/jdir.html**) and the University of Florida Virtual Library (**www.clas.ufl.edu/users/gthursby/socsci/**).

If you find a journal index that is useful to you, you can make a note of the reference information and look it up in the hard copy in your library. Or, you can look further to see whether the article has been stored electronically and you can access it. If so, you can read the article online (although access time through your server might cost you money), download it to read later, or block and copy the text you want to use directly into your word processor (see page 212 on how to download from the Internet). You should always keep a careful record of the source. Alternatively, you can print the article or a blocked section of it using the print function on Netscape Navigator or Microsoft Explorer.

ONLINE REFERENCE TOOLS AND BOOKS

Dictionaries (English and other languages), style guides, handbooks of quotations, shorter encyclopedias, and so on, are also available online. Some might be available from your university's Web page. You can use, as well, the vast resources provided by Bucknell University at "A Web of Online Dictionaries," which offers over 500 dictionaries in 140 different languages and links to specialized dictionaries in popular and technical fields (**www.facstaff.bucknell.edu/ rbeard/diction.html**). Another site with the *Merriam Webster Dictionary* and the *Oxford English Dictionary* is Purdue University (**www.lib.purdue.edu/reference/dict.html**).

You can also use one of the numerous online reference shelves:

- Columbia University Bartleby Library: **www.bartleby.com/**
- Internet Public Library Reference Center: **www.ipl.org/ref/CenterNG.html**
- Research-It!: **www.itools.com/research-it/research-it.html**
- The Virtual Reference Desk: **www.refdesk.com**

The *Encyclopaedia Britannica* has now set up a free-access Web site (**www.britannica. com**).

Newspapers and other sources of daily information are also widely available, usually by entering the newspaper's name followed by .com. A long international list of newspapers generally available on the Internet is given at *The Reference Desk* (**www.refdesk.com/ paper.html**). Many newspapers have online sites:

- *The Globe and Mail*: **www.theglobeandmail.com**
- *The Toronto Star*: **www.thestar.com**
- *The Times* (London): **www.the-times.co.uk**
- *The New York Times*: **www.nytimes.com**
- *The Washington Post*: **www.washingtonpost.com**

Information about particular countries can be found on the site maintained by that country:

- Canada: **canada.gc.ca/main_e.html**
- United States of America (US Information Agency): **www.usa.gov/usa/usa.htm**
- Great Britain (Central Office of Information): **www.coi.gov.uk/coi/**
  and the BritIndex: **www.britindex.co.uk/government.html**

A wide range of links is collected about many countries at the Web site for Planet Earth (**www.tidusa.com/PEHP2000/Planet_Earth/info.html**).

Other specialized information is available also in the *Country Studies,* originally commissioned by the CIA (**lcweb2.loc.gov/frd/cs/cshome.html**). Virtually every country in the world is covered, with information that the CIA thought its agents should know when visiting, dealing with, or writing about such countries. Awareness of the political purposes originally involved in gathering this information should warn users to exercise appropriate judgment and methods of evaluation.

You might want to refer to a standard reference book that you do not have at home. You can, of course, look for it in the print books in your library, but another possibility is searching for it as an electronic text (called e-texts). There are several repositories of online books on the Web. The University of Michigan has been putting many books online (**www.ipl.org/**). Another collection is Project Gutenberg (**promo.net/pg**), named after the founder of the printing press. Many volunteers enter texts by scanning and typing them into electronic format. All of their books are available in ASCII format (that is, with no or very little formatting), to give easy access to all users. Other repositories include Great Books of Western Civilization (Mercer University) (**www.geocities.com/Athens/Atlantis/4360/**) and Alex: A Catalogue of Electronic Texts on the Internet (**www.lib.ncsu.edu/staff/morgan/alex/alex-index.html**).

If you wish to buy an inexpensive CD-ROM that contains many of these titles, you might try the widely available CD-ROMs produced by Walnut Creek Software or the collection *World Literary Heritage* produced by Sofbit, Inc.

One of the advantages of online books is that you can search for information in them. You can download the book, convert and format it for your word processor, and search for the relevant information using your word processor's find or search utility. Once you are finished with the book, you can archive it onto a floppy (perhaps using a compression tool, such as WinZip or PKZIP, to make it fit on a floppy) or delete it. For WinZip (shareware), see their Web site at **www.winzip.com/ibrowser.htm**. For PKZIP (shareware) see **www.pkware.com**. Shareware indicates that you pay for the product if you like and use it. Some universities have an onsite licence to distribute these products.

WEB BROWSERS AND SEARCH ENGINES

Web Browsers

Web browsers are search tools that are funded by banner and headline advertising fees. There are more than five hundred of these search engines. Your Web browser can also be used as a searcher, and so we discuss those first. Web browsers give you access to three basic kinds of engines: subject or category directories, keyword indexes, and metasearch engines. Usually, your university will have some of these engines already listed as hotlinks (you click on the name for access) on the university's Internet access page. Otherwise, you enter the URL of a particular search engine (see the addresses below) in your browser's location toolbar and click Enter. If you find the search engine useful, you can bookmark it and save it in a bookmark folder of search engines.

Subject Guides or Directories

Subject guides categorize Web sites according to content subject area. That is, the directory's staff assigns a site to a specific topic category, based on the Web page's content: computers, education, entertainment (books, movies, music), news, sports, and so on. You can narrow your search using the subject guides and options to access advanced features. This search will often lead you to good sources quickly, though there are fewer resources available in the database than in those of general search engines. Subject directories include the following:

- Andersonian Library in Glasgow for academic subjects: **bubl.ac.uk/link**
- The Argus Clearinghouse: **www.clearinghouse.net/searching/find.html**
- Galaxy: **www.einet.net**
- Inter-links: **www.nova.edu/Inter-links**

- Librarians' Index to the Internet: **lii.org**
- Magellan: **www.mckinley.com**
- NetGuide: **www.netguide.com**
- Yahoo!: **www.yahoo.com**

Keyword Search Engines

Search engines that use keyword searches are connected to vast Internet databases of millions of references through "spiders," or robots that circulate throughout the Web and collect information from millions of sites. Normally, these spiders read and index several hundred words on the Web page, as well as any keywords that the author of the page has built into the page. They then alphabetize the results and add them to a master list, giving greater stress to keywords in headings and to greater frequency of keywords in the body of the text (HotBot, for instance, indexes 110 million Web pages). Such browsers as Excite and HotBot usually allow you to search by keyword, a complete phrase, or a personal name and allow various inclusions (e.g., dates, countries) or exclusions (based on linking your terms with "operators," such as AND, NOT, OR, and so on).

The information keyword search engines return can be just the URL or Web address, the heading information, or a short abstract (the most useful). If you already know more or less what you want, such general search engines can be very helpful. On the other hand, if you are not focused, you will waste a great deal of time wading through several hundred irrelevant sites that are evaluated mechanically only according to your search criteria. Keyword search engines include the following:

- AltaVista: **www.altavista.digital.com**
- Excite: **www.excite.com**

TIPS: Using Search Engines

1. Use the advanced search options if available.
2. Search for several words rather than just one.
3. Select the "complete phrase" or "any of the words" options.
4. Narrow your search by date, country, or kind of site (for instance, .com for commercial, .edu for educational).
5. When you search for a complete phrase, include it in quotation marks.
6. Use + or – signs to indicate what must or must not be included in your results. The plus sign indicates that the following word must be present in the document you find, and a minus sign means that the following word must not be present.
7. Use limiters. All of the keyword search engines listed, except for InfoSeek, accept the limiters for a search used in Boolean logic. That is, the words AND, OR, and AND NOT may be used to include or exclude specific items in your search. The words must be typed in capital letters.
8. Read the search engine's help files for useful tips and hints.

- HotBot: **www.hotbot.lycos.com**
- InfoSeek: **www.infoseek.go.com**
- LookSmart: **www.looksmart.com**
- Lycos: **www.lycos.com**
- Northern Light: **www.northernlight.com**

Metasearch Engines

These engines use the term you provide to combine information from a number of other search engines. Because they combine the resources of different engines, they have to suppress the specialized search functions of those engines to achieve a common denominator, thereby bypassing some of the refined capabilities that you might wish to use. Some (such as MetaCrawler) collate the results; others (such as Dogpile) do not.

Metasearch engines include the following:

- Dogpile: **www.dogpile.com**
- Google: **www.google.com**
- MetaCrawler: **www.metacrawler.com**
- OneSeek: **www.oneseek.com**
- SavvySearch: **www.savvysearch.com**

Further information is provided by each of the Web sites for the browsers themselves or in the Internet article from *Information Technology* by Kathleen Webster and Kathryn Paul, "Beyond Surfing: Tools and Techniques for Searching the Web" (**magi.com/~mmelick/it96jan.htm**).

Using each search engine's optional or advanced features will help you to refine your search significantly. For further information about search engines in general, you can consult the following:

- Media Metrix: **www.mediametrix.com**
- Search Engine Watch: **www.searchenginewatch.com**
- University of California resources at Berkeley Library:

TIPS: Using Metasearch Engines

1. Use the appropriate search engine.
2. Start with a broad category search engine, such as Yahoo!, especially if you are uncertain about what you might find. If you are looking for information on current entertainment but do not have a category in mind, such an engine works best.
3. If you are clear about what you want, say the most recent Steven Spielberg film, enter either his name or the name of the film into a more specific topical index, such as All Movie Guide (**allmovie.com**), CineMedia (**www.afionline.org/CINEMEDIA**) or Movie World (**www.movieworld.com**).

Internet resources: **www.lib.berkeley.edu/TeachingLib/Guides/Internet**

Metasearch engines: **www.lib.berkeley.edu/TeachingLib/Guides/Internet/MetaSearch. html**

There are many more search engines. You can see a full and developing list at the "All-in-One Search Page" link on the Yahoo! site (**www.yahoo.com**). The "Searching the Web" link at the Yahoo! site compares the features of many engines and offers further information on conducting an effective search.

Strategies for an Effective Search on the Internet

As with traditional methods for research in print copies, you have to focus precisely on your topic for effective searches in electronic media. You should determine whether it is best to search your library catalogues or other electronic resources before going to the library to consult print copies. If you decide to use an online search of the Internet, you need to consider carefully how your topic can be defined or analyzed to make best use of the various search engines and their features. It is recommended that you use the search engines in the following order:

1. First, use metasearch engines to examine all of the databases at once.

2. In the second round, use the search tool with the most information for your topic, such as Infoseek, AltaVista Advanced Search, or Northern Light.

3. In the third round, look for bibliographies or other indexes concerning your topic by consulting Yahoo! using the limiters "topic" + indices. These limiters will restrict the search to those indexes that list information on your topic. Other places to look include the following:

   • Librarians' Index to the Internet: **www.lii.org**
   • WWW Virtual Library: **conbio.rice.edu/vl/database/**
   • UCB Internet Resources: **lib.berkeley.edu/Collections/acadtarg.html**
   • Purdue University's Internet Gateway: **www.lib.purdue.edu/vlibrary/inet_resources/**

4. In the fourth round, use one of the keyword search engines, such as Hotbot or Excite, modifying the search appropriately, and using Boolean logic forms ("topic" with limiters AND, OR, NOT).

Avoid general searches of databases without narrowing your topic. For further advice on search strategies, see the University of California site at Berkeley (**www.lib.berkeley.edu/ TeachingLib/Guides/Internet/**).

EVALUATING WHAT YOU READ: CRITICAL THINKING AND THE INTERNET

Many hours can be spent surfing the Web, for entertainment, for games, and for information. But is it a good research tool? The answer is that it can be useful, but you need to evaluate both the kind of information that you need and also the information that you find.

The Web can give you lots of information about popular culture, contemporary events, recent news items, and trivia, as well as access to libraries around the world, some reference books, many journals, and official data from almost every nation. But some of this information is hard to find unless you are an experienced Web researcher, and you might be better off,

TIPS: Conducting an Effective Internet Search

1. Use the advanced features capabilities of your search engine to help narrow your search.

2. Use an appropriate term for your search.

3. Make your term sufficiently general and sufficiently focused. If you search for "revolution," you will get far too much information. If you narrow your search to "French Revolution," you will be far more successful.

4. When searching print or electronic indexes for articles on a particular topic, gather about twice as many as you think you will need, since your library might not own all of the articles that you select.

5. Save time, lost references, and needless returns to Web sites or the library by noting down or printing all of the detail you will eventually need for your references and bibliography when you find your materials.

6. Ask your instructors and the reference librarians for help.

and much more efficient, in looking up a reference book. So it is important for you to judge first whether the Web is the appropriate source for the information you need.

If you do decide to use the Web, you should be aware that while many browsers or search engines (such as Yahoo! or Excite), and many servers (such as Geocities and AOL) monitor and sometimes limit what they carry, the Web itself is open to all who want to set up a page. There is no vetting of it by the Web for factual accuracy, grammatical correctness, freedom from bias or prejudice, and the like, although the makers of the Web page may be careful about these matters. Each site, then, needs to be assessed for its validity, and your guide here should be enquiring scepticism.

Most Web pages state the author or owner of the page. In the case of a company Web site, that company is the source for the information. But for other kinds of information sites, the sources may be less authoritative. There are numerous Web sites for movies and other forms of popular culture, but how can they be evaluated, since they are mostly maintained by fans? There are also numerous sites for the Holocaust. What authority does each have? What gives them their special knowledge and reliability? The site maintained by the Simon Wiesenthal Center (**www.wiesenthal.com/resource/gloss.htm**) has a distinguished history and impeccable credentials; so too do the sites maintained by the United States National Holocaust Memorial Museum (**www.ushmm.org/education/history.html**) and the Yad Vashem site in Israel (**truth.nizkor.org/hweb/orgs/israeli/yadvashem/**). But what about the Holocaust denial sites? Such an "authority" might be useful if you were doing work on the Holocaust deniers or on revisionist movements in recent history, but you could not rely on such a location for unbiased information. You would have to assess the site in the light of evaluation criteria available on such sites as those maintained by the Nizkor Project (**www.nizkor.org**).

Many Web pages are maintained by national and international organizations of great repute. The New York Psychoanalytical Society, for instance, maintains an important Web site on Sigmund Freud (**plaza.interport.net/nypsan/freudarc.html**), as does the Jung Institute on Carl Jung (**www.cgjung.com**). On the other hand, many high school classes,

BOX 9.1	**What to Do When You Have Problems**

Too few results:

1. When your search turns up no locations, first check your spelling.
2. Be less specific in your search terms.
3. Try some variations on the terms you are using.
4. Try another search engine.

Too many results:

1. Use more specific terms.
2. Link the words that narrow the topic even more, using Boolean logic terms (AND, OR, NOT).

Error messages:

1. *Error 404: Page/File not found.* The most common reason for this frequent error is that the URL is no longer functional. It may have changed, or the server may no longer carry this site. In any case, check the URL address again, paying particular attention to the upper and lower case characters, to the special signs such as _ or - or ~. Failing all else, move up one level in the address by omitting the last level after the slash (/) and try again.
2. *No answer* or the message that the server is not answering or might be down. Wait a few minutes, or perhaps a few hours.
3. *Page has moved.* If you are lucky you may be directed to the new address. If not, try moving higher in the address hierarchy by omitting what follows the last slash. Or, try searching for the topic or location again on another search engine.
4. *Permission denied.* Sometimes sites have restricted access during certain times of the day. Other sites are restricted to a specific membership.

interest groups, and individuals maintain Web pages and post information on their projects that can be useful or trivial, well or poorly researched, current or out-of-date. Many pages at least list a Web master or even the author, who may be contacted, often by e-mail, so you have a way of following up on the information. You can also find clues about the authority of a site from its Web address or URL, where the *domain name* might include a suffix that identifies it as a particular kind of site: .com (commercial site), .edu (educational site), .gov (government site), .net (network site), .org (nonprofit organization). A two-letter code often gives the country of origin: ca (Canada).

It is also wise to consider the accountability of a Web site. Knowledge presented in a scholarly format strives to be accountable by recording its sources, contextualizing its argument in relation to other scholarship, considering opposing views, and using language that is conventional and appropriate for the particular discourse. You can evaluate Web sites according to these criteria and judge the reliability and soundness of the information that a page presents. The key question underlying these criteria is whether or not the site is accountable—that is, whether or not it positions its information appropriately. For instance, there are several sites on the Web dedicated to white supremacy. Racist terms used as descriptives for groups of people clearly mark these sites as biased and as virtually useless as sources of information for any academic topic, except for a study of hate groups themselves.

Thousands of people put up Web pages on their favourite topics. Many Web browsers do not classify these pages with regard to their accountability. Therefore, the onus is on you as a user to make an informed assessment of their value. You should look for the kinds of attention given to references, sources, and links, look for the name of a person who is responsible for the page (often with an e-mail address), and resist being captivated just by attractive graphics. Many personal Web pages contain mistakes in spelling on the main page, and often the links are faulty and lead nowhere; however, some personal Web pages are maintained carefully by people who have a well-informed interest in a topic, and their information can be very helpful.

DOWNLOADING INFORMATION AT HOME FROM THE INTERNET

Having found information on the Internet that you wish to use in your research, how can you convert it from images and text on your screen to research notes in your assignment file or to essential data in your paper? One of the first steps you can take to preserve your research references is to bookmark your page. You can then use other procedures for saving text or graphics to your hard drive or for printing your present document.

Bookmarks

When you find a site that you want to make reference to or that you wish to return to later, you can bookmark it and file it among your own bookmarks by following these procedures:

1. Enter the site.
2. Double click on the Bookmark option in Netscape (or the Favorites option in Explorer) on the menu bar and choose Add Bookmark to record it. The title of the bookmarked site is then saved in your bookmark document, along with its URL. The bookmark remains as part of the list of recently added bookmarks until you press Edit Bookmarks in the drop-down menu and move your bookmark to an appropriate folder.

To edit bookmarks, you can follow these procedures:

1. Click on Edit Bookmarks in the drop-down menu attached to the Bookmark option on the menu bar (or Organize Favorites option in Explorer).
2. On the bookmark screen, choose Edit on the menu bar.
3. You now have several options, including adding a new folder for your new bookmarks. Having done so, highlight the file name you want to work with by single clicking it, and use your mouse to move the bookmark to an appropriate folder.
4. Create a list of addresses and sources that you consider important for your topic, or that you wish to reexamine later or preserve, by opening or closing folders with their contents (by pressing the + or - before each folder), editing by adding or removing files, and moving or deleting folders.

If you find Internet addresses when using a computer in the computer lab or library, you can either save them to a floppy disk or e-mail them to your address to file them later on your home computer.

Text

Text on the Internet is encoded in html format (hypertext markup language), which must be converted to be read by your word processor. So your first choice is to save the file you have found as an html file, which you can convert later. To save the file, you click on the file tab in the toolbar of Navigator or Explorer, and choose Save As. You have the choice of designating where you want the file saved and can change the name of the file to fit with your research needs. After you have logged off the Internet you can recall the file (Navigator or Explorer will run, but not online, to give you access to the file) and then proceed with the next step. You should be aware that some versions of Navigator and Explorer will not save graphics in this process automatically, or if they do the files may be very large. Perhaps a more useful method is to block the entire document, or the part of it that you need, and save it to your word processor. In detail, you should follow these procedures:

1. Log on to your server and Web program (Navigator or Explorer), and find the site from which you wish to download. Minimize this screen by clicking on the upper-right minimize arrow.

2. Start your word processor with a new document that you can name (such as "research" or some other title appropriate to your topic).

3. Click on the name of the Internet page you were consulting in the lower toolbar that indicates active programs or pages.

4. In the Internet page, use your mouse to block the text you wish to save (hold down the left button of the mouse and move it through the text to highlight it).

5. Click on the Edit tab in the toolbar, and choose Copy to save the highlighted text to your notebook.

6. Click on the name of your new document in your word processor in the lower toolbar to make it available full-screen.

7. Click on Edit → Paste to retrieve the document from your notebook and to format it for your word processor. At this time add a reference to the document you have copied: the author, title, URL, pages, and date you accessed the information. Your document will then have to be reformatted with new line endings, spacing, and the rest (see page 215 on decoding downloaded files).

8. Return to the Internet page to block, copy, and paste another part of your document or a new document. Any of these documents can be added to the same file or folder in your word processor, or you can begin another new file.

Some texts are encoded in yet another format, PDF, which can be read only by Adobe Acrobat Reader. This reader can be downloaded free from any number of sites, but especially from the home site (**www.adobe.com/products/acrobat/readstep.html**). This program is often bundled with software that comes with your computer. Once downloaded and installed (by following the advice given at the download site), this reader will be invoked to read Adobe files automatically; then they can then be saved in whatever format you wish.

TIP: Using Your Mouse

Even faster than blocking a whole document is the efficient use of your mouse. Clicking on the right button when in an html document automatically gives you a variety of choices for copying, saving, or printing the document. A little experimenting with these procedures will greatly improve your speed, efficiency, and accuracy in downloading research materials.

Graphics

Sometimes you want to save graphics (illustrations, maps, charts, headings, or banners) for use in your research or essay. Most Internet graphics are encoded in gif or jpeg format, indicating the kinds of capture and compression used in transferring an image into electronic bytes. To save a graphic image, you should follow these steps:

1. Locate your cursor on the image.
2. Using the right click on the mouse, click on Save As.
3. Save the image to the file that you designate on your hard drive. Normally that would be one of your research files for this assignment. Note that it will be saved in the same format that it was in when on the Web page.
4. For a your saved image to be used in an essay or other document, your word processor must be able to read the file or convert it to its own format. When that is not possible, you may have to use a third-party editing program to convert the graphic to a format your word processor can read. The newest versions of the major word processors are very good at reformatting graphic images. Consult your word processor manual to see which graphics files it can read.

Various graphics viewing and editing programs have the function of calling up your saved graphic, and saving it again in your word processor's format (possibly after you have manipulated its colour, detail, and so on). Some viewing and editing programs include the following:

- Adobe PhotoShop: **www.adobe.com/prodindex/photoshop/main.html**
- CorelDraw: **www.corel.com/products/graphicsandpublishing/draw8/index.htm**
- KeyView Pro: **www.keyview.com**
- LView Pro: **lview.com**
- PaintShop Pro: **www.jasc.com**

Printing from the Internet

Sometimes you may want to save the text or graphics material you have found by printing it, so you will have a hard copy of the information on the Web page. To incorporate any of this material into your own writing, you will have to retype it; on the other hand, the document is not taking up space on your hard drive or floppies. To print a document:

1. Click on the Print icon in the browser's toolbar.
2. Follow the instructions for your printer in the dialogue boxes that follow.

The speed of printing depends on the speed of your computer, the amount of RAM (memory) you have, and the amount of memory in your printer. If you are using a dot matrix printer, the process will take some time, and the graphics, if printed at all, will lack definition. On the other hand, if you are using a colour, bubble, or laser printer, the results should be excellent. Of course, the document will print according to the formatting instructions that you have chosen as the defaults in setting up the options for your Mac or PC, including your printer and Windows or another operating system. If the graphics do not print and you are certain that your printer has that capability, you should check your configuration to be certain that the box to print graphics as visuals rather than as text is chosen.

An alternative to using your printer to print Web pages vertically on one side of the sheet is using one of the add-on utilities that prints information from the Web in a special format that you specify. For instance, the utility "Click-Book" from Blue Squirrel software (**www.bluesquirrel.com/clickbook/**) allows you to print a Web document in a booklet format automatically. It reduces a full Web-sized screen page to half of an 81/2 by 11 inch page (printed in landscape or horizontally), and prints on both sides of the page, formatting them so that they read from front to back when stapled together. It also includes all of the graphics, prints the address of the page and the name of the site, and dates and numbers the pages. The same program can be used in printing from your word processor. You can download a free trial copy to see whether it suits your needs. Its advantages are that it works behind the scene and can be invoked on demand, it prints all of the necessary information that you need for referencing, and it saves space, paper, and hard-disk space while providing you with a hard copy.

DOWNLOADING INFORMATION IN THE LIBRARY

In the library you can download information in the same way as at home. You can send materials that you locate on the library catalogue to your e-mail address and print or save to a floppy information from the CD-ROMs. The library staff or the information bulletins the library posts can provide further information.

DECODING AND UNSCRAMBLING FILES YOU DOWNLOAD

Before you can use files in your essays, you need to be certain that you have the reference recorded accurately, in case you have to return for further information. If you refer to this document in your paper, you also must note it in your works cited list according to the proper form for citing electronic sources. Furthermore, many files that you download have to be reformatted with hard returns, margins, spacing, and so on. Unless you already have a macro (an encoded command sequence that you initiate through a macro shortcut with only one or two keys) to reformat such files, you will have to reformat the file manually. You should check the manual with your word processor to see whether yours has such a macro. Usually, manual reformatting involves using the search-and-replace function to convert all single hard returns into spaces (thereby correcting line endings to conform to your line length), five spaces into left tabs, and remaining double spaces into single spaces. Fancier macros will convert double hyphens to the longer en-dashes, triple hyphens into em-dashes, and plain quotation marks into "smart," or typographical, quotation marks (shaped like 6s and 9s).

Your word processor will convert files from other word processors, or if you have difficulty, you can save them by accessing your word processor's *Save As* feature and choosing the *Save as ASCII* or as generic word processor format. That means that most of the formatting codes are removed, and the text alone is preserved in a format that can be read by another word processor readily. Of course, the formatting codes (italics, underlining, and sometimes paragraph indentations) have to be reinserted. Most recent programs, however, convert files automatically from one word processor to another.

ORGANIZING YOUR READING NOTES ON YOUR WORD PROCESSOR

You can efficiently gather selected notes from your lecture notes and readings in preparation for writing class exercises, assignments, or research essays. Using a word processor will greatly assist you in making the best use of your time and resources.

Making reading or research notes on the computer is an easy task, especially if you are logical about how you organize your files. You may wish to open up a directory or folder for each course and within that place several subfolders, perhaps one for reading notes on your course texts, one for each assignment, and one for notes on lectures, seminars, and summaries for exams. Entering such research notes into your computer makes assembling them later for your essay much easier, and it also eliminates one more step in which errors in transcribing quotations can creep in. In the assignment folder, several methods are possible for keeping your materials easily accessible.

1. *Organizing your research materials by source.* You may organize your materials according to the books or articles you read in preparation for your assignment. As you read each item you can mark what you want to note afterwards, or you can make notes as you are reading. Frequently, the latter procedure results in making many more notes than you either need or can use, since you have not yet narrowed your topic to allow you to select strategically for your needs. It is important to read your materials critically and to record the pages where you want to make summaries or enter quotations. In either case, it is crucial to reference your work carefully.

2. *Organizing research thematically.* If you have already decided on your approach and the general topics under which your paper will be organized, it makes sense to set up your file according to the themes, issues, or problems that you will be discussing. Hence, the materials will already be assembled topically in preparation for your final paper.

3. *Grouping research materials.* A third method is to complete method one first, and then to move through each of the subfolders noting which material is to be grouped together. Then, you assemble the thematic file. As you can see, this method involved a cumbersome additional step. To make this step easier, some students print out the results of the first method, then annotate it, and use that to select for the preparation of the first draft, avoiding the thematic file completely. Again, it is important to emphasize that you should note carefully the references to all quoted or paraphrased passages that will be incorporated into your working and final drafts.

FURTHER READINGS

Burkle-Young, Francis A., and Saundra Rose Maley. *The Research Guide for the Digital Age: A New Handbook to Research and Writing for the Serious Student.* Lanham, MD: University Press of America, 1997.

Calishain, Tara. *Official Netscape Guide to Internet Research.* New York: Netscape Press, 1996.

Crump, Eric, and Nick Carbone. *Writing Online: A Student's Guide to the Internet and World Wide Web.* New York: Houghton Mifflin, 1998.

Harnack, Andrew, and Eugene Kleppinger. *Online! A Reference Guide to Using Internet Sources.* New York: St. Martin's Press, 1997.

Thiroux, Emily. *The Critical Edge: Thinking and Researching in a Virtual Society.* Upper Saddle River, NJ: Prentice-Hall, 1999.

WEBLINKS

- Beginners Central
  northernwebs.com/bc

- Beyond Surfing: Tools and Techniques for Searching the Web
  www.virtualref.com/_libdocs/12.htm

- College Connections Web Resource Directory
  www.rohan.sdsu.edu/dept/vsa/collegelinks/Welcome.htm

- Criteria for Evaluation of Internet Information Resources
  www.vuw.ac.nz/~agsmith/evaln/index.htm

- Evaluating Internet Resources
  staff.lib.utexas.edu/~beth/Class/evaluating.html

- Evaluating What You Have Found
  www.lib.uwaterloo.ca/howto/howto28.pdf

- Evaluation of Internet Sources
  www.vuw.ac.nz/~agsmith/evaln/evaln.htm

- Guide to Web Sites
  www.tusculum.edu/college/links.html#infotrac

- Internet Searching Strategies
  www.mgu.bg/pages/strategies.html

- Reference Sources on the Net
  ublib.buffalo.edu/libraries/e-resources/selected.html

- Searching the World Wide Web
  www.lib.berkeley.edu/TeachingLib/Guides/Internet/Strategies/html

- Thinking Critically about World Wide Web Resources
  www.library.ucla.edu/libraries/college/instruct/web/critical.htm

THE PLANNING STAGE

C h a p t e r **10**

We all face deadlines and wish that we had all the time in the world to complete our research, preparation, and revision before we hand in that important final copy. You know ahead of time the deadlines for your assignments and can usually make reasonable projections about the demands on your time. It is at the beginning of the writing stage, when they have gathered the appropriate research materials and must formulate them into a coherent argument, that many students face the greatest difficulty.

Many students have difficulty writing essays that satisfy their own intellectual standards and that meet the demands of the instructor. Students are puzzled by what seem like different requirements from department to department for what is often called standard written English, and they appear to receive contradictory instructions for almost everything involved in writing an essay: instructors require different formats for essay presentation; they propose different approaches to the materials to be researched for the essay; and they outline different expectations for analysis of texts or problems in the essay topic. It is true that expectations of essay styles will vary between a course in introductory economics and one in introductory English. But it is equally true that for either course, an essay that is written in standard English, that is well researched and cogently argued, and that is presented in an acceptable format will likely meet the demands of both student and instructor alike. Nevertheless, a student must be aware of the particular demands of individual instructors and of varying disciplinary norms in the presentation of research. Students also need to recognize that they are engaged in a struggle to control their own language, that they are both the producers and the products of their own language, and that in the classroom many different positions are competing for attention.

Students often feel victimized by these struggles, especially when they must hand in by Monday, for example, four pages on this novel or that topic in Canadian history. They ask themselves, "What can I possibly say? What can I possibly say that is new? What can I possibly say that hasn't already been said before—and better? What can I say to this teacher that he or she won't laugh or sneer at?" Or, the questions might move to a more practical level: "What should I assume about my reader? How do I begin? How will I be evaluated?" We all have been students in just this predicament. *Foundations* aims to help writers by giving voice to their critical language, weight to their words, and power to their position.

FROM THE READINGS AND RESEARCH DATA TO THE ORGANIZATION OF THE ESSAY

After you have completed your research, you are ready to begin organizing your materials into the shape of an essay. When you were making your notes, gathering references and quotations, and accumulating your research data, you were also making specific connections and links, which you now need to articulate directly. You should consider a number of subtopics for your paper and begin to group ideas, research materials, and quotations together, noting further possibilities for extension or any gaps. For each of the topics, you might try a topic sentence that summarizes, at least in a temporary way, your position.

Another method involves laying out your materials either physically, by grouping your research notes on a desk or on the floor, or by putting them under headings on your computer. Then, you are faced with the problem of moving from what you have found to what you will try to prove, from the raw materials to an argument. That move does not happen magically, randomly, or automatically. You need to think about how the parts of your materials are related, how they can be linked, what kinds of arguments they can support, what kinds of order they can be put into, and what the most effective presentation might be to meet the goals of your assignment.

Most essay topics demand analysis of events, ideas, or texts. Accordingly, mere narration, description, or enumeration of data will be insufficient. If you summarize a writer's ideas or arguments, it is important to do so briefly and clearly. Long summaries, extensive retelling of narrative, and elaborate enumeration of facts do not contribute to analysis. You need to remember that your instructors have also read the books; you have to gauge the audience that you are writing for. You are expected to understand the material, to be able to derive the key concepts of the course from your reading and research, and to relate them to the assigned topic. Doing so requires logical argument, analysis, and synthesis, a bringing together of ideas in an integrated way, often with a fresh approach. An outline will greatly help you with your organization, but a lot depends on how you set up your arguments to make your research and thinking work for you in your writing. The aim is to make your arguments communicate and to avoid impeding your ideas.

There are various ways of setting out arguments, a number of which are discussed in the following sections.

METHODS OF ORGANIZATION

Process or Predetermined Order

Ordering by process means moving through your material according to an order that is implicit in the material itself. Some topics, such as the description of a historical event, lend themselves to chronological order; some, such as scientific experiments, to cause-and-effect order; and some, such as the description of the action of a play or novel, to the order of events given in the work.

While it is effective and usually necessary to follow a process argument for certain stages of your argument, in isolating ideas for particular emphasis, it is important to avoid being dominated by the supposed "natural order," which might give your work an appearance of merely imitating or describing the concepts and patterns of the work, ideas, or event that you are writing on.

Parallelism, Comparison, and Contrast

A common problem beginning writers have in using comparison and contrast is discussing each work separately, detailing the particular ideas in each of the works without making meaningful connections. Such essays, in which work A is linked to work B with very little comparison or contrast, concluding with a summary paragraph, can have the shape of a string of sausages.

An effective method of lending unity and coherence to a paragraph or a whole paper consists of developing a thesis or topic sentence through parallelism, comparison, or contrast. Such an organization of ideas allows you to explain your idea by revealing similarities and differences with other examples. Furthermore, it demonstrates a broad reading background and shows that you are in control of the material that your course covers. An essay on Shakespeare's plays could draw parallels with his other works or with related ideas, characters, or events. Similarly, contrasts can highlight the effect that you wish to stress. In comparing, contrasting, or drawing parallels between works, you may use one of several methods for developing ideas in a paragraph, or, indeed, in a whole essay:

1. One method is to discuss work A first, and then work B, with cross-references to work A, and then to bring in work C to compare with works A and B. This is a ping-pong method, which may be cumbersome, and yet because it moves logically through each of the works, it appeals to the beginning writer. You need to be careful when using this method to stress the idea that you are explicating: it is your idea that should control your essay, not the logic of a whole work.

2. It is much better to discuss each of works A, B, and C by themselves briefly, and then to focus for most of the essay on the particular grounds or ideas that you are comparing or contrasting. The same principle of organization is applicable to disciplines other than literature; for instance, in the sample question on Canadian history in Chapter 6, you could discuss immigration, urbanization, and industrialization by themselves briefly and then write a series of comparisons and contrasts on their effects in the assigned historical period.

3. The best method is to choose key themes or ideas on which to base your comparison and to set each of them in some context ("Three of the central ideas in Shakespeare's tragedies are the role of nature, the freedom of the protagonist to act, and the theme of order. Each of these...."). Then, you can move to compare each work with respect to these key concepts. This technique gives far greater scope for integration of arguments, emphasis, synthesis, and coherence.

Classification and Analysis

Classification groups things according to similarities or differences; analysis takes them apart into their elements and examines their relationships. In almost every essay some classification will have to be undertaken to identify and set together similar ideas and arguments, to subordinate minor to major arguments, and to examine these classifications in a logical order. According to this method, the subject matter is divided into appropriate categories, both positive and negative. Consideration is given to which units may be related to larger divisions, which separated into smaller parts. When this method of organization is used a third stage of argument is usually needed, synthesis, in which the parts, analysis, and classification are brought together into a fresh insight to support your thesis.

Illustration and Example

Almost every essay requires some illustration, example, or citation from a text to support your argument, and so this method is used in each of the models of organization. By using illustrations and examples you develop the thesis from point to point, at each stage supplying some clarification. The method is useful for dealing with subjects that are made clearer with examples. For instance, when writing about freedom of speech and publication, examples of specific cases of the limitations of censorship would be particularly telling.

Illustrations are most effective when commented upon. You cannot expect that the connection an example or illustration has with the topic will be absolutely clear; examples need your comment to make their place in your argument clear. Examples that are counter to your position are often particularly illuminating because they give your argument something to push against.

The danger of this method is that it may degenerate into points and examples that are merely strung together. You can maintain your reader's interest by moving from minor to major points in an ascending order. A further danger of this method is that it may give example after example of a point that has already been made conclusively and that needs no further argument. This elaboration of examples will try your reader's patience, as you will appear to be either restating the obvious or merely filling space to meet the length requirements of an assignment.

THESIS STATEMENT

Having decided how you are going to organize your materials, you have already been thinking about how your topic can be turned into an argument. A thesis statement puts that argument in a single, assertive sentence. It formulates the position that your essay will try to prove. It usually gives the supporting reasons for your position, outlines your method, or briefly indicates the plan and main divisions of your argument. Put another way, the thesis statement answers your research question or formulates the controlling idea of your paper. A thesis statement gives directions to your reader about what and how you will argue. There are four marks of a good thesis statement:

1. It can be stated in one sentence.
2. It is restricted and focused.

3. It is unified—it has only one main idea.

4. It is precise, unambiguous, and clear.

A thesis statement is often the last sentence of the first paragraph.

The final thesis statement develops from a working thesis as the essay is written and is incorporated into the introduction after the essay is largely completed. As a student, you are writing as a professional; modern academic essay practice usually welcomes the first person in a thesis statement and opening declarations: "I shall argue that…, and my analysis will make use of the categories of…." Such formal directness is much preferable to the weakly anonymous and concealed agency of "One sees…," "This essay suggests…," or "We shall examine…." But you should check with your instructor if in doubt about using the first-person pronoun *I*. In phrasing your thesis statement, it is best to avoid weak assertions that begin "It is evident that…," "It is obvious that…," or "It will be made clear that…." Such phrasing in a thesis statement suggests that your whole argument is unnecessary: if it is already evident, obvious, or clear, why are you arguing it? Such weak claims to self-evident truths are just filler, and the real point that follows, perhaps still a self-evident truth that should be questioned or qualified, is what needs to be reexamined before you continue.

Once you have stated the general topic, you need to formulate a thesis about the topic. A thesis statement is not a hypothesis. A hypothesis is a supposition or conjecture, which serves as a starting point for further investigation: it responds to questions that you begin to formulate about the topic and that you will revise during your research and reading for the essay. The hypothesis will change and become more carefully framed, taking into account more aspects of the text or problem being considered. A thesis, on the other hand, is a proposition that is stated and that is to be argued and defended. It is the end product of the creation of various hypotheses and represents the argument that the essay will make.

A thesis statement needs to shape your specific topic to enable you to discuss the subject you have chosen to write on. If your statement is too general, it needs sharper focus and definition, perhaps by subdivision into relevant parts. Perhaps the assignment itself is broad, and it may be your responsibility to narrow it appropriately and to demonstrate your focus in your thesis statement (but you should see whether the instructor will allow the assignment to be more sharply focused). The more particular your thesis statement and the more focused your topic, the easier it will be to organize and write your essay.

OUTLINE OR ESSAY PLAN

After you have thought about your topic, completed your research, decided on a method of organizing your essay, and developed a working thesis statement, it is time to draw up an outline of what you propose to cover in your paper. It is often necessary to make outlines in your head, as in writing essay questions on examinations. But in preparing formal essays, a careful and thoughtful writer will usually draw up a formal outline, which is usually not meant to be submitted. The following guidelines will help you in creating an outline:

1. An outline should begin with a statement of the thesis or controlling idea in the opening paragraph.

2. Each major point should support your thesis. One way of checking your organization is to look at the topic sentences of each of the major divisions of your paper and ensure that they form a comprehensible argument. There will likely be three or four of these major divisions.

3. Each major division then should be subdivided into its parts, which are organized according to some coherent plan.

4. For a longer essay, even these subdivisions might be further divided into major and minor arguments or subcategories. However subdivided the outline becomes, there should be a category in the outline for each of the paragraphs.

5. From the topic outline, you can move to construct a sentence for each of the subdivisions; these sentences form the topic sentences. Often, you will complete this step in the actual writing of the paper, but if an essay proves difficult to organize, it could well form a independent step and would ensure a thoughtful and careful construction.

FURTHER READINGS

Paltridge, Brian. *Genre, Frames, and Writing in Research Settings*. Philadelphia: J. Benjamins, 1997.

Roth, Audrey J. *The Research Paper: Process, Form, and Content*. 8th ed. Belmont, CA: Wadsworth, 1999.

Steven, Laurence, Douglas H. Parker, and Jack Lewis. *From Reading to Writing: A Reader/Rhetoric and Handbook*. Scarborough, ON: Prentice Hall, 1989.

Veit, Richard. *Research: The Student's Guide to Writing Research Papers*. Boston: Allyn and Bacon, 1998.

WEBLINKS

- The Hyper Text Books
  papyr.com/hypertextbooks/index.htm
  Provides a full course on writing on the computer.

- Writing with Computers
  papyr.com/hypertextbooks/engl_103/compwrit.htm

THE WRITING STAGE

WRITING THE ESSAY

At this point many writers are well prepared to begin writing the first draft. Usually, that will involve starting not at the beginning, but rather with the first big argument for which you have collected most of your material. You will want to have that section in reasonable shape before you move to your supporting arguments. At each stage you should check what you write against three things: your preliminary thesis statement, your outline, and the assigned essay topic. As you proceed you should add your examples from your reading and research stage and pull other materials together, deciding what will have to be cut in the interests of space and time and what should be expanded in the interests of clarity and completeness. When you are fairly content with the shape of your main arguments, you can start to assemble them into a more final form. At this stage you will work on the paragraphs, begin to plan an introduction, add the first and concluding paragraphs, and perhaps print a rough draft to look over.

Some students, however, upon completing the research in good time, having made good notes and read all of the materials, are intimidated by the blankness of the first page, and, fearing having to fill twelve pages with their own thoughts, would rather have their teeth drilled. They are faced with writer's block.

Overcoming Writer's Block

None of the advice in the world will help if you are unable to put that difficult first mark on the page or start that essay file on the computer. Many writers, from the most experienced to the beginner, suffer anxiety about writing and find elaborate ways to put off the encounter with the blank page. All writers agree that practising the craft of writing helps to remove the anxiety. Writing letters, taking notes, jotting something down for a future essay, making a note of an idea on the computer in a miscellaneous file—all of these activities will keep you thinking about writing and, more importantly, keep you practising it. A number of tricks are known to be effective:

Writing against the Clock

Timing yourself is one trick. By this method you have a friend time you for five minutes while you write on your topic—you begin writing when the clock starts and then stop after five minutes. You are to begin on your topic, but if you cannot maintain ideas about it, you must write anything that comes into your head. It might well be that all you write has to be discarded; indeed, it very likely will have to be, but the purpose of the exercise is to begin the process of writing. This device can be used at any time to overcome writer's block, and you can write on any topic at all (sometimes called *free-writing*), or even on none, by merely setting out your frustrations in language that only you need read.

Talking Through

To talk through a topic also involves another person, preferably one who has some knowledge of your topic. As you talk about the topic, your friend takes notes of what you are saying and perhaps prompts with the occasional question or asks if you have thought of this or that argument. You might discuss the best means of organizing the paper, and you could even move toward an outline. Some teachers discourage involving other people in generating ideas or in overcoming writer's block because they are afraid that such collaboration will undermine the originality of your ideas. If you are in doubt, you should check with your instructor. If you do use this method, you need to make sure that what you produce is your own work. An alternative is to record your talk-through on a tape recorder, which will allow you to go back and reconstruct what is useful from the exercise.

Brainstorming

Brainstorming consists of setting out in as short a time as possible all of your ideas on a topic, however remote they may appear from your first thoughts about the topic. There is often little concern given in a brainstorming session to specific order—the point is just to get the ideas down. Then, you can organize them into a coherent shape, sequence, order, or outline. Several people can contribute to a brainstorming session, with one or more people recording all of the ideas. Again, you will have to find out whether your instructor recommends using such a process for your assignment.

Consulting with Your Teacher

Discussing your essay with your instructor can be important in getting started. You might wish to test an idea or an approach, or you might wish to get some feedback from your instructor about your choice of topic. Perhaps some aspects of it remain unclear to you, and you would like some further explanation. Meeting with your instructor will help you to refine your topic and will often serve as a stimulus to writing, especially if you record what happened at the meeting or even keep some notes of the main topics covered during the meeting.

Writing the First Draft on the Computer

Having completed all of your preliminary work at the prewriting stage, including organizing your notes, and developed your outline and thesis statement, at least in a preliminary way, you are ready to start setting out your paragraphs, beginning with those you have been working on in connection with your central argument. It should be stressed that you need not begin writing your draft from the beginning of the paper.

Writing your first draft of an essay on the computer will make it a lot easier for you to organize your materials, move them around, correct and add to text, and form your notes into paragraphs. You have great flexibility in jotting down your ideas, gathering them, and moving, changing, or deleting them, all the while editing what you write. Revision on a word processor avoids the seemingly endless typing and retyping that using a typewriter requires. Instead, as you revise by making corrections on the screen, you are learning the important skill of refining your writing, as well as saving time and paper.

Editing Tips

You can easily move words, lines, paragraphs, or large sections of your document with the word processor's "block and move" facility, using either a key or a mouse (left click and hold to block, move to the new location, and release). With this function you can incorporate your quotations, examples, illustrations, and data from other files gathered during your research and work on your paragraphs and thesis statement.

You will sometimes find that the corrections you have made are not as useful as the earlier version you had written, and you might wish to return to that stage. Most word processors have an Undo function that takes you back step by step through your most recent corrections, sometimes for a number of stages so that you can return to earlier versions.

On the other hand, if you are reasonably content with a longer section of your paper, you can save that (perhaps as a file "draft A" or "argument 1") before you go onto the next phase. If at this stage you wish to try a different direction, you can save that as "draft B." Eventually, you might decide that draft A was much better, so you can return to that version by calling up your saved document, which is a more efficient method for longer passages of writing than using the Undo function. At this stage, you might wish to combine the two drafts, using draft A as your base argument, but incorporating elements from draft B.

Split Screens

For this stage of editing, word processors offer another useful facility, the split screen. In recent programs, especially on the Mac and all versions of Windows on the PC, you can have two (and often more) files or windows open on your monitor at the same time, say the folders draft A and draft B. Using draft A as your basic document, you can move whatever sections from draft B you want into draft A with ease, and you can edit them there to make them fit into your argument. It may be necessary to reduce the size of the font to make more of the text fit onto the screen. Most word processing programs let you split the screen either vertically or horizontally, as you choose. In older word processing programs, such as

WordPerfect 5.1, you may have to use document one and document two (selected from the Screen option, CTRL-F3).

Search and Replace

The computer's Search and Search and Replace functions are very useful in helping you organize your paper in the early stages and correct it carefully in the later stages of the first draft. The Search or Find option allows you to move through your document to find the occurrences of a character, word, or phrase. This facility allows you to find other places in your essay where you have used the same idea or phrase; you might wish to link these two discussions with a comment. Or, if you have discovered a spelling mistake or other usage fault (see the list of commonly misused words on page 234), you can check for similar slips in the rest of your essay by using the Search and Replace function. You have the option of re-placing all occurrences automatically, or you can make a decision about each occurrence.

BUILDING PARAGRAPHS AND ARGUMENT

You have already been making notes about some paragraphs, following the outline of your essay. You have drafted your thesis statement in a preliminary way and have probably already written up some of your research notes in paragraphs. You are now assembling this mate-rial, writing the linking paragraphs, working on the coherence and persuasiveness of your ar-gument, and building the bridges between the phases of your thought and between your paragraphs.

A paragraph denotes a substantial division of thought. The movement from paragraph to paragraph through an essay should indicate the stages in the development of your argu-ment. Paragraphs build your argument in stages: short, choppy paragraphs often indicate fragmentary argument and lack of synthesis, and very long ones often indicate problems in defining the stages of your argument.

The Topic Sentence

Each paragraph should develop one main idea or topic. That topic is usually, though not always, announced in the topic sentence that opens the paragraph. At times, however, it is effective to have a paragraph build to a topic sentence at the end. Each sentence in a para-graph should contribute to the logical development of that topic sentence—adding infor-mation or examples, bringing out implications, advancing pro and con arguments, and so on (see page 229). If extraneous ideas are introduced that go well beyond the bounds suggested by the topic sentence, the reader will quickly become lost, as will your point.

The topic sentence unifies the argument of each paragraph. Assembled together, topic sen-tences should provide an outline of the essay's argument.

The Infant and the Overgrown Paragraph

Many inexperienced writers have difficulty in controlling larger passages of prose and fear that the topic sentence in a paragraph will be an inadequate umbrella for all of the follow-ing sentences. Out of anxiety, then, they break up their writing into "infant paragraphs," ones not fully grown, consisting of one or two sentences followed by another short paragraph, and then another. Such paragraphs usually need connecting, and so do the ideas. They need to be nourished with interrelated ideas and linked with guide words that inform the reader about the direction of the thought. On the other hand, fear of formulating a new topic sentence leads some writers to construct long paragraphs covering several topics and pages. To create paragraphs of a reasonable length, you should read over such long paragraphs and break them where a new topic begins.

Bridges or Links between Paragraphs

The reader should be able to follow the writer from paragraph to paragraph, and to accomplish that goal, a reader needs "bridges," or links, between paragraphs. Bridges help your reader follow the transitions in your argument. Certain signposts help, such as conjunctions and conjunctive adverbs, which indicate where your thought is turning a corner: *accordingly, after, although, because, before, consequently, conversely, finally, first, for example, furthermore, hence, however, instead, on the other hand, moreover, nevertheless, nonetheless, however, therefore, while.* Summary phrases indicate these changes in direction clearly. Transition phrases that include short summaries also help, such as "I have already shown that...," or "I have argued that...." Then, the next paragraph might begin "A second consideration is...." However, you should avoid clichés such as "Firstly I should like to...," "As mentioned earlier...," or "In conclusion...." Such phrases slow your argument down by unnecessary repetition and irritate your reader by stating the obvious. Another way of working on the bridges is to use some gathering phrase that summarizes the argument or thought from the previous paragraph, for example, "This devastation from the bubonic plague...."

Paragraph Unity

Paragraph unity depends on the effectiveness of your analysis and argument, on your grammar and style, and on the connection of ideas to the paragraph's topic sentence. In each paragraph you should stress main ideas and subordinate minor ones. Each part of a paragraph should relate to its central idea. A reader may stop at any point in a unified paragraph and see how the current sentence bears on the main topic. But the unity depends on more than the relationship of ideas to the main idea of the topic sentence. Unity is sustained through the logical development of ideas, so that a reader can follow what is being said. There are various ways of achieving that unity:

1. Unity of ideas is achieved by making sure that the paragraph is controlled by the topic sentence.

2. A key word is repeated from sentence to sentence, or suitable synonyms are used to keep the idea before the reader's eye: "A major factor in the decline of population was the arrival of the <u>bubonic plague</u> in Western Europe. The coming of the '<u>Black Death</u>' caused massive social dislocation. This <u>natural epidemic</u> was often interpreted in religious terms as a <u>judgment by God</u>. It was also interpreted as <u>the beginning of the end of the world</u>." The underlined passages are partly synonymous and parallel, and they are summarized in the second-to-last sentence by "this natural epidemic."

3. Unambiguous pronouns refer back to key ideas (in the last example, "it" in the last sentence refers back to "natural epidemic" usefully and reinforces the notion in the reader's mind).

4. Demonstrative pronouns are followed with some "gathering" word or phrase that focuses the ideas: for example, *this catastrophe; that disaster; these events; those developments.* The unreferential "this" or "that" phrase ("This shows that ..." or "This is ..."), which has no specific antecedent but usually refers to an idea earlier in the paragraph, is to be avoided. The vague "this" phrase leaves a reader to summarize the thought contained in the previous sentences without a useful gathering or summary noun, and without any clear certainty about the writer's precise meaning.

5. Conjunctive adverbs are used within a unified paragraph to connect thoughts and draw distinctions: *however, moreover, also, nevertheless, therefore, thus, subsequently, indeed, then, accordingly.* When they begin a sentence, they are usually followed by a comma.

6. The ideas in a paragraph are arranged in some kind of systematic order, perhaps based on chronology (describing the sequence of events: first came this, then that, then that), on logic (stating major to minor premises or cause and effect), or on space (describing a house, for example, in some order).

Paragraph Development

Paragraphs should move out from the topic sentence by way of illustration, contrast, or data. There are a number of conventional ways of developing a paragraph, many of which will occur to you when you are working through your research materials in the prewriting stage and when you are preparing your outline:

Using Definition, Explanation, and Illustration

1. Terms may be defined, or a topic may be divided into its parts. However, you should not use general dictionaries to reduce complex terms to simplistic definitions. They might be useful when arguing for their inadequacies, but they are not helpful in beginning an essay. You should define technical terms of a course (such as *fantasy, romance, horror, obsession,* or *monster*) through course readings or lectures, specialized subject dictionaries, or the *OED.* You should provide a definition only if it is integrated into your argument—in other words, you need not feel obligated to define what is common currency in your course unless you are pushing that definition in ways that you will develop in your argument.

2. An explanation may demonstrate how a phenomenon operates.

3. Examples or illustrations may explicate parts of your argument.

4. Persons, places, things, events, or ideas may be explained or described.

5. An anecdote or quotation may expand or qualify the topic.

Providing Evidence

1. Causes or reasons for discussing the subject may be explored.

2. Evidence or data may be cited to support the argument. Information may be in the form of statistics, facts, details, or precedents.

3. An authority may be quoted or paraphrased as testimony in support of the argument, with proper attribution of sources. An authority may also be quoted for purposes of disagreement; however, in the logic of evidence, such a statement must prove the contrary of your argument (pro and con arguments).

4. Something related to the topic may be compared and contrasted, or various degrees, conditions, or stages in the topic may be indicated.

5. Effects or consequences may be pointed out.

6. The relevance of evidence to your argument is demonstrated. No evidence is self-explanatory or naturally a part of an argument.

Providing Analysis

1. Analysis moves from definitions and descriptions to using the evidence to build a case, formulate an argument, assess the importance of the parts of a text or problem, and prepare a critique.

2. To do so, an analysis identifies and explains the relationships among parts of a text or problem, assessing the significance of the parts and their place in the whole. An analysis usually requires an argument about *what* is being said and *how* it is being said—how the argument or narrative in the text is put together or how a problem has been formulated, and how that construction contributes to the meaning of the whole. Sometimes, attention is given to how the reader is involved in creating an interpretation.

3. The analysis prepares for an evaluation, a summation of the strengths and weaknesses of the arguments about the problem or the text, a comment on the validity of those arguments, and a critique of its intellectual position.

These means of development of a paragraph are derived from the five ancient methods of inventing (or discovering) arguments in Greek and Roman rhetoric. The method could, and still can, be applied to any subject. You can also review a list of common topics as headings for suitable arguments and as a stimulus to new ideas. The five traditional categories of the discovery of arguments in classical rhetoric are as follows:

1. *definition*: defining by kind, or dividing an idea or thing into its constituent parts

2. *comparison*: showing similarity, difference, or degree

3. *relationship* (*causation*): showing cause and effect, antecedence and consequence, or contraries and contradictions

4. *circumstance*: considering the possible and the impossible, fact and future fact, differences or degree, or difference of size

5. *testimony* (*evidence*): citing authority, testimonial, statistics, law, maxims, precedents, or examples

Major and Minor Ideas

Arguments in paragraphs often move most easily from the general to particular details (the deductive method) or from theory to practice. They may also move from an assertion of a main point to a demonstration or analysis of it, and then to an explanation or evidence. Mere assertion does not constitute argument, nor does summary of either your material or someone else's ideas. Inductive reasoning, which entails moving from particular examples to a general theory, is a more difficult method of arguing.

In any case, you should place main ideas in main or independent clauses, and more minor ideas in subordinate clauses. Furthermore, you should place the main ideas in positions of emphasis in the paragraph, such as in the topic sentence: "The central reason for the widespread investment uncertainty is the weakness of the Asian economic markets, but other reasons also have an impact: the weakness of the Canadian dollar, soft domestic consumer demand, and wide-scale unemployment." In the paragraph following this topic sentence, each of the three reasons would be discussed in order.

Introductory and Concluding Paragraphs

The opening and concluding paragraphs state your thesis before and after proof. They shape the whole essay and so require a good deal of work in the planning stages. The actual writing of the introductory paragraph, however, might be the last thing you do in your rough draft.

The first paragraph should catch your reader's attention. There are various methods of doing so, such as opening with a controversial opinion or quotation, a counterposition (which can be argued against), a question (which can be answered), or a summary of your position or the issue in a balanced phrase or sentence. The topic and the thesis should appear prominently. For most papers, an introductory paragraph of five or six sentences is usually adequate, moving from the general toward the more specific statement of the thesis (sometimes in the last sentence) and offering a bridge to the main body of the paper. A note of caution, however, is needed here: beginning writers often misuse the funnel method, moving from a generalization to the thesis statement by beginning their introductory paragraph with sweeping generalizations that are only remotely related to or are banal formulations of their topic ("The Holocaust is an unforgettable event in the history of Europe"). Alternatively, they might begin badly by stating the well-known facts of a historical period ("World War I lasted from 1914 to 1918") or of an author's life or work. An opening generalization should always be governed by the specific focus of your topic. Many writers are tempted to go for some peripheral general context of the topic, rather than for a relevant point. For instance, if your topic were how Germany's emergence as a world power from its colonization of Africa in the 1880s contributed to World War I, it would probably be inappropriate to begin with the general effects of World War I or with banal assertions about how terrible that war, or any war, was, and how it changed the course of history. Such assertions may be incontestable, but they do nothing to introduce your topic. Instead, if you could locate a detail in Germany's colonization of Africa that raised the issue of competition with England and France (two recognized world powers), that detail could serve as a general template for your argument. Alternatively, you could formulate a generalization about Germany's emerging nationalism at the beginning of the twentieth century and be well on your way. To test whether your opening statement introduces your focused topic, you can ask how closely it is related to the specifics of your topic. If it is an extension of the topic, it is too remote and needs narrowing or rethinking.

The concluding paragraph is the summation of your essay, where you state the final position for which your argument and examples are the proof. The conclusions you draw should not exceed the limits of what you have argued or your evidence; in other words, you should not introduce new arguments in your conclusion. In concluding an essay, you should also avoid simply restating your hypothesis in the same words or in a banal or trivializing way that leaves your reader with the impression that you have run out of gas. As in your opening paragraphs, your conclusion should be free of empty generalizations ("Therefore, Alice Walker is a great writer" or, "Hence, World War I was hated by all the nations who fought in it").

The concluding paragraph should gather your argument into its final focus, moving from the details of the essay to the larger idea of your thesis again. Or it may move from a restatement of the thesis to a consideration of its implications as brought out in your evidence.

This ending should be emphatic, not apologetic. You should not use the deadly phrases "In conclusion ..." or "In summary...," which hide real integration at the end. Sometimes, a summary of your argument, if it has been complex, will help the reader recall your main points. Or, you may wish to point toward the conclusion that your evidence supports. Even a pithy example, summarizing your thesis, would make your conclusion strike home. Another strategy for concluding may be to call attention to the limits of your argument as stated in your thesis—that is, to restate your thesis to draw attention to the propositions and factors that went into your argument and suggest how changing these facts might lead to different questions, arguments, and even conclusions.

Writing a convincing argument takes more than ordering your points and marshalling sufficient evidence—much also depends on using language effectively. In the following section, we list a number of considerations that you should be aware of at all stages of your writing.

REVISING: STYLE AND PERSUASION

Your argument can be very well organized and your paragraphs carefully laid out, but if your writing contains grammatical or punctuation mistakes, your essay needs to be corrected (see Chapter 5). If it breaks with conventional usage or has faults in idiom or phrasing, your reader will be put off and the strengths of your argument will be obscured. On the other hand, if you have developed your rhetorical skills, the stylistic strategies to persuade your reader, your argument will be clear. In this section we address seven common rhetorical problems.

Revision of the draft is an essential step in the critical writing process. Revision has a variety of purposes: to correct mistakes in spelling, grammar, and punctuation, to improve paragraph structure and coherence, and especially to refine lapses in argument and examples. A thesaurus will help you think of synonyms; a dictionary or a spell checker on the computer is usually more useful in checking proper spellings at the revision stage than at the writing stage, when you want to set out your ideas. In the revision stage, you should note how your argument develops from topic sentences of paragraphs. You can ask yourself questions as you are revising, such as "What do I mean here?" "Is this point clear?" "Is this argument supported by pertinent evidence?" "How do I know this fact?" Often the question "What is my point here?" will clarify your argument.

Avoiding Meaningless Abstractions

It is important to avoid generalizations that are irrelevant to your thesis, that are undocumented, or that are unsubstantiated. Abstract concepts are used to provide distance from what is often taken to be a singular and common sense meaning of something. As such, they enable us to examine that phenomenon, whether it is a literary text, sociological data, or a historical problem, in new and different ways that open conventional interpretations to question. Such questioning depends on both the adequacy of the abstract argument and the relevancy of the examples.

An essay carries much more conviction when it is expressed in concrete language, using appropriate and telling details and illustrations. When using abstract language, you need to be careful that your concepts are actually communicating ideas and arguments that are relevant to your topic. A tendency in beginning writers is to use abstractions that are empty: "The militaristic hostilities of the United States instituted a process of tremendous deprivation, disorientation, and dislocation that traumatized the citizens of Iraq." This notion could be better expressed without the meaningless abstractions: "In engaging in carpet bombing, the United States caused tremendous suffering for the common people of Iraq."

Modifiers, whether adjectives or adverbs, should have a purpose in qualifying what they modify. Stringing together empty qualifiers, such as *excellent, meaningful, interesting, beautifully, widely,* and especially *hopefully,* makes your prose and argument vapid. As well, you should avoid circumlocutions (beating around the bush, or refusing to come to the point), unless you wish to achieve a special effect. You should also beware of slang, buzzwords (*interfaces, parameters*), colloquialisms (*I eyeballed him*), and technical jargon, such as the now current computer jargon (*boot up these ideas; get online with that plan*). Such language may be appropriate to particular audiences, but generally, for academic writing, it should be avoided.

Using Active Verbs in Assertive Sentences

Verbs in the active voice usually convey greater precision and power than passive ones. Assertions are more effective than weak, negative evasions. How feeble it is to say, "The memory of that wedding will not soon be forgotten." How much stronger to say, "We shall long cherish the memory of that wedding." To avoid introducing a personal perspective, opinion, or argument, many writers for newspapers, journals, and magazines use passive constructions. (Indeed, journalists and their editors would rewrite this sentence to read "Passive constructions are used by many writers"). Sometimes, passive constructions use the past participle ending in *-ed*: "This use of language is required by many teachers and editors" instead of "many teachers and editors require this use of language." Turning passive constructions into active ones almost automatically enlivens your prose and makes it more immediate by stressing the doer of the action rather than what is done.

You should also try to avoid the almost omnipresent copula verb. Instead of writing "Another set of circumstances is when the spots on the moon were seen by Galileo as bumps," you should write, "The world-view changed when Galileo looked at the spots on the moon and called them 'bumps.'" You should also avoid like the Black Death tiresome phrases, such as: "It is seen," "there is," "there are," or "an example is when." These unreferenced uses of the copula verb conceal the agent of the action.

Introducing Variety into Your Style

Variety in diction, phrasing, sentence structure, and paragraphs will improve your writing. Some of your ideas and sentences should be balanced; some sentences should be simple, some compound or complex. Sentences should begin and end differently, unless you are seeking a particular effect through repetition.

Using Descriptive Adjectives and Adverbs

Appropriate and precise adjectives and adverbs will qualify your position and enable you to convey far more subtle shifts in meaning. Vague and general descriptors will reduce your argument to meaningless platitudes. You should avoid the intensifier *very,* which rarely communicates the enthusiasm that you might feel, and above all, abominate *very interesting,* a bankrupt description. Modifiers should fall close to the words they modify. Other vague intensifiers include both the adjective and adverb forms of *apparent* (*apparently*): *clear, evident, obvious,* and other words that assert that something is self-evident. Such assertions of the self-evident indicate problems in your argument. (See the more detailed discussion of the thesis statement in Chapter 10.)

Using Precise Connectives

You need to be certain about the precise shades of meanings that you wish to convey by your use of conjunctions and conjunctive adverbs. Consider, for instance, the differences in meaning that can be accomplished by using a variety of them between the two clauses of a sentence such as: "Jane's mother was dying; _____ the doctor saved her."

although	because	before	nevertheless	nonetheless
however	therefore	moreover	indeed	while
though	hence	accordingly	meanwhile	consequently

Inserting the different conjunctive adverbs in the blank space shifts the meaning of the sentence. Some of the subordinating conjunctions have to be used at the beginning of the first phrase, as in "Although Jane's mother was dying, the doctor saved her."

Expressing Parallel Ideas in Parallel Grammatical Forms

Readers follow your ideas according to the patterns in your thought and your language, and they expect that when you set up a parallel it will be followed through in the thought and expression: "He likes reading and writing"; not, "He likes reading and to write" (linking two different kinds of verb forms, a participle and an infinitive). Verb forms should be parallel, of the same kind: "She was told to report to the teacher and to take her books with her" (parallel verbals). "Dogs are noted for their friendliness and for their loyalty" (parallel prepositional phrases). "The Bishop stated that he loved Bach, tolerated modern art, and hated contemporary architecture" (parallel clauses).

Avoiding Inconsistencies in Point of View

You should avoid shifts in point of view from first to third person: "I shall argue that…. One can demonstrate from this text that…." Also, you should ensure that moods or tenses of verbs do not shift. Historical events are usually put in the past tense: "Wellington defeated Napoleon at Waterloo." When writing about literary texts or other documents, it is better to use the present tense: "Hamlet kills Polonius before Ophelia goes mad." "Celie, in *The Color Purple,* writes to Nettie, 'I am so happy. I got love.'" "Aristotle discusses tragedy; Frye applies his terms to world literature." Other tenses need to be used logically for events before or after the main action: "Othello finally knows Desdemona has been faithful."

AVOIDING COMMONLY MISUSED WORDS AND PHRASES

To say what you mean, you require an adequate vocabulary. Building your vocabulary means regularly using a good dictionary when reading to discover the meanings of any unfamiliar words. Beyond that, saying what you mean involves having a sense of good usage and of the customary connotation of words (denotation involves the dictionary meaning; connotation involves the customary and contextual resonance of a word). Students often misuse a number of common words and phrases, such as the following:

A.D.: This abbreviation (Latin, *anno Domini*, in the year of our Lord) is placed conventionally before a date: A.D. 1492. B.C. (before Christ) is placed after the year number. The current convention is to use terms that are nonsectarian: B.C.E. (before the common era) and C.E. (common era).

all right: Two words, not *alright.*

almost: An adverb, meaning "nearly all."

among, between: Use *among* for more than two, *between* for two.

and with a verb: *Try and see* for *try to see* is a vulgarism.

anybody: Means "any person"; *any body* means "any corpse."

apt: Means "suitable, fitting". *Liable* means "exposed to danger, penalty"; *likely* means "probable":

He is apt to lose his temper. ✘ Jim's reply was apt. ✔

He is liable to lose his temper. ✘ The driver is liable for the damages. ✔

He is likely to lose his temper. ✔

beside/besides: *Beside* means "by the side of"; *besides* means "moreover."

centres around: Vague in meaning and image. *To centre* means "to place precisely"; hence, *centres on* is acceptable, but *to centre around* suggests both precision and diffusion simultaneously. This principle also applies to *focuses around.*

continually: "At regular intervals"; *continuously*: "without interruption".

data, phenomena: These nouns are plural and take plural verbs (from the singular forms in Latin, *datum,* and Greek, *phenomenon*).

different from: Not *different than* or *different to.*

due to: Implies a debt. Do not use it for *because of* ("by reason of") or *owing to* ("on account of"); *due to* is a predicate adjective and should be closely related to the noun or pronoun it modifies. Because it is not an adverb, it is *not* used by most stylists instead of *because of* or *on account of* to introduce a verb.

Due to bad weather, the match was cancelled. ✘

Because of bad weather, the match was cancelled. ✔

The cancelling of the match was due to bad weather. ✔

In particular, avoid the combination of *due to* with *lack,* which makes a sentence even more illogical:

Due to lack of study, she failed. ✘

e.g.: Means "for example" (Latin, *exempli gratia*). Students often confuse *e.g.* with *i.e.* (see below). For both abbreviations, write them out in English in a formal assignment. The abbreviations are acceptable (if used within the appropriate context) in summaries, lists, and notes.

farther: Is comparative of *far; further* means "moreover, or greater in degree."

fewer: Used for number; *less* is used for quantity or degree.

finalize and other *-ize* nouns made from verbs: These are usually a lazy evasion of precision. *Finalize* (complete), *utilize* (use), *minimize* (reduce), *publicize* (make public), *familiarize* (make familiar)—these words are the darlings of administrators and memo writers.

first: Preferable to the older *firstly* (*secondly,* etc.).

fix: Means "to make secure or fast," *not* "to repair."

hopefully: An adverb meaning "in a hopeful manner, with hope." In the phrase "Hopefully it won't rain," we mean "I hope it won't rain." Avoid "Hopefully it..." constructions.

however: This word is not a coordinating conjunction and cannot be used to join two sentences with a comma. It is a conjunctive adverb that indicates a new direction in thought: "Alice is an innocent; however, her real-world experiences enable her to be shrewd and questioning in strange situations."

i.e.: Means "that is" (Latin, *id est*), not "for example" (see *e.g.*). These abbreviations are rarely used in formal writing, but they may be used in summaries or notes.

if: Means "on condition that, on the supposition that"; *whether* implies doubt.

in depth: This cliché should be replaced with *detailed* or *profound.*

interesting: This word conveys only empty praise.

in the case of: This expression is wordy and unnecessary. Sir Arthur Quiller-Couch used to say that in the case of John Jenkins, deceased, the case was his coffin. *Case* technically refers to a case in law or police investigation and should not be used as a catch-all.

it: Should not be used as an unreferential pronoun: "It shows that...."

lend, loan: Either is a verb, but *lend* is preferable, and *loan* is more commonly used as a noun.

no one, none: Both words are singular.

participles: Words such as *being, falling,* or *jumping* can function as verbal nouns or gerunds. When preceded by a pronoun or noun, they govern the possessive case: "His being sick," "The hero's falling from power," "They insisted on my staying."

quite: Means "completely," not "rather." So "Judy is quite sick" means that she is at death's door, if not dead already. The expressions *quite a few* and *quite often* are, accordingly, silly expressions.

shall, will: The simple future tense of the verb *to be* is *I shall, you will, s/he will, we shall, you will, they will.* When you say "I will" you are using the subjunctive of intention, that is, you are not using the future tense but are making an oath or a vow: a realist can say "I shall die," but a suicide says "I will die." In formal usage, these distinctions are disappearing.

this: A demonstrative pronoun often used without any antecedent or "gathering" word to collect into a summary the complex of ideas that have gone before ("This shows ..."). This loose reference word refers back to a previous sentence or group of sentences. It can become highly effective when followed by a catchword that gathers the argument. However, *this* without an antecedent lacks any specific reference. You can make the reference particular and effective by pairing it with a catchword that gathers the argument together: "This material [or principle, difference, evidence, position] shows...." *Which, it,* and *that,* like *this,* are often wrongly used with no antecedent: "She gave us the essay topics, which scared everyone." "His first essay was better than his second; it was more coherent." (Which one was?) "That is a false assumption."

thus: Often followed by a present participle ("thus enabling ..."), this word is exceedingly vague, especially when the participle dangles, or is unconnected to a pertinent noun. Usually, a writer using this weak construction is suggesting some logical cause and effect, but the phrasing should be more precise. *Thus* means "in this way" or "consequently." *Therefore* is often used wrongly or weakly in similar fashion.

unique: Means "one of a kind" and so cannot be compared, as in "more unique."

USING QUOTATIONS EFFECTIVELY

In Chapter 7, we discussed how quotations can be used to support arguments, to serve as a point of disagreement in launching an argument, and to provide an illustration. We also pointed out that a quotation by itself is not an argument, but rather needs to be embedded in an argument. In this section, we consider how quotations can be fit into your paragraphs and your writing style.

Quoting Accurately

Direct quotations reproduce the words of another writer or speaker accurately. If you are using someone else's words, quoting from a character in a novel, from a critical article or document, from a book review, or whatever, you *must* use quotation marks (or single space and indent) and give the source for your information. Failing to do so involves you in serious problems concerning the illegal use of other people's words and can lead to charges of plagiarism (see Chapter 12). You can use various methods to summarize or otherwise change a writer's comments to adapt them to your style:

1. A *paraphrase* reproduces the content of the original in different words. A paraphrase retains all of the central ideas in the order of the original; however, those ideas and examples are all put into the (usually) simpler language of the writer.

2. A *précis,* or a summary, condenses the original while retaining the sense; it may omit substantial illustrations or examples, quotations, or subordinate arguments. A précis expresses only the main points.

When using either of these methods, you should acknowledge the source in a reference.

Avoiding Quotations at the Ends of Paragraphs

It is tempting to end a paragraph with a quotation from some authority on your topic, a quotation that sounds strong and unassailable. However, then you move on to the next paragraph, leaving the authority dangling in mid-air. It is much better to comment on the quotation you have used, showing how it makes your point or provides some useful qualification. You may also wish to note what is not said in the quotation.

Introducing Quotations

It is helpful to introduce quotations with an identifying phrase to show how they are being used in your argument as illustration or evidence. Their place in your paragraph and argument is not self-evident, so your reader needs to know why and how you are using a quotation. Quotations need introductions, usually including the author's name, to prepare the reader for your evidence and source. Just as quotations should not be left dangling at the ends of paragraphs, nor in the middle of them, they also need a word or two of introduction, telling the reader whom you are quoting: "As Freud observed, 'Hysteria is a fantasy carried to the level of sickness'" (direct quotation). "'Hysteria,' as Freud observed, 'is a fantasy carried to the level of sickness'" (direct quotation, source embedded). Or, you might wish to make the most of your own sentence: "Commenting on hysteria, Freud called it a 'fantasy' approaching a 'sickness'" (direct quotation of two words; the rest is paraphrase). You might wish to turn the ideas into indirect quotation and some paraphrase: "Freud said that hysterical persons were suffering from some fantasy that was so serious that it had become a genuine sickness" (the two words could be in quotation marks, but the direct quotation sense is not so clear, and quotation marks would tend to mean that the words are being used in a special sense). In every case, it is necessary to give the sources for your quotations. A quotation should almost always be followed by some interpretative comment of your own to explain its significance to your argument.

Using Short Quotations

There is no absolute rule about what makes a quotation short or long, and different sources specify different numbers of lines. Usually, quotations shorter than five lines should be integrated in your own prose, introduced with a colon or a comma, and enclosed in double quotation marks. A critic writes: "In the preface to *Jane Eyre,* Charlotte Brontë says that appearances should not be mistaken for truth" (4). If the lines are poetry, it is customary to set out more than two lines as block quotations. Shorter quotations of poetry indicate line endings by a slash with a space on either side: "In *Hamlet* Polonius offers his conventional advice to Laertes by first giving his blessing: 'There—my blessing with thee, / And these few precepts in thy memory' (1.3.57–58)."

Inserting Long Quotations

Long quotations of more than five lines of prose are usually separated from your own text. They are usually introduced by a colon, are indented ten spaces, and are typed double spaced. Many seminar leaders, however, prefer longer quotations of prose or verse in single-spaced and indented form in course essays. The indented longer quotation always appears *without* quotation marks, unless the passage quoted begins with quotations marks, in which case they are reproduced exactly as in the original. The quotation ends with the source reference in parentheses, after the final punctuation mark.

Inserting Explanations

A word or phrase of explanation added to a quotation should be enclosed in brackets. When you omit material from a quotation, you need to use three spaced dots for the omission (called an *ellipsis*), followed by any necessary terminal punctuation.

Including References for Quotations

Modern practice includes references in the text and makes them as clear and short as possible (see Chapter 12). Hence, unambiguous references to a document, poem, play, or novel repeatedly quoted in the course of a paper should be given directly after the quotation. References are made to line numbers in standard editions, to page numbers if a common text is used by the reader and the writer, or to chapter, act, scene, and line (for plays):

Milton tried to "justify the ways of God to men" (*Paradise Lost* 1.26).

This reference would be used in an essay where Milton is cited only occasionally; if the whole essay were on *Paradise Lost* the book and line references would be sufficient by themselves.

Hamlet said, "What a piece of work is a man!" (2.2.316).

Setting Quotations within Quotations

Single quotation marks are used for the internal quotation:

The actor said, "Hamlet's answer, 'Nothing,' is nonsense."

Periods and commas are usually put within the closing quotation marks; colons and semicolons are put outside them. Other punctuation is placed according to sense.

USING THE SPELL CHECKER, THESAURUS, AND GRAMMAR CHECKER

At this stage your computer will likely provide three services that are crucial to you as a writer. Each is found in the Tools tab in the menu bar.

The Spell Checker

After completing your first draft, you should run the whole text through the spell checker. However, you will still have to proofread the final copy (not with a spell checker) to catch any words that are spelled correctly but that are misused or any technical or special words that the spell checker misread. Recent word processing programs automatically highlight words that are either misspelled or unknown to it (such as proper names).

The Thesaurus

A thesaurus is a list of words that serve as alternatives (synonyms or close meanings) and opposites (antonyms) to a selected word. The Thesaurus function enables you to vary the words you use in your writing. With the cursor on a word, you can click on Tools and then choose Thesaurus. In a window, you will be given a choice of words to use as replacements for the word where your cursor is located. Clicking or highlighting a word from the list inserts it in your text. You might find it useful to check in a desktop dictionary the meanings of the words you are using for replacements.

The Grammar Checker

This tool is now sophisticated and helpful, but it has to be used on spell-checked text. To use it you open the file you wish to check and save it so that you have an up-to-date version in case you do not like the results the grammar checker produces. You can either select the entire document (by positioning the cursor at the beginning) or block a section to check. You then start the grammar checker in Tools. You have the option of modifying or customizing the checking style. By responding to the prompts on the screen, you work your way through your document. You will be offered corrections and suggestions and a printout of the results, or you may be shown a diagnostic analysis of your writing. If you are happy with the results, you can save them in a new document (choose File and Save As ...) and then can compare them with what you previously had saved. With each proposed change, you need to think carefully about what the grammar checker offers: Is it making the right assumptions about your audience and style, as well as your argument and its expression? Is it offering to change what you mean as well as how you are saying it? Do you understand why the changes are being proposed? Are the changes being proposed in any quotations? If so, you will not want to have these changed. Sometimes, the grammar checker finds mistakes where there are no problems, so you have to be alert to the proposed changes that are made.

SELF-EVALUATING YOUR ESSAY

To give you an idea of the criteria a grader might use to evaluate your essay, we include here a sample essay evaluation. We recommend that you go through the categories carefully and adopt them for self-evaluation of your work.

ESSAY ASSESSMENT

Organization and Argument

1. Thesis Statement: Is it on topic, clear, brief? Is the statement of claim made with or without reasons? Is the thesis statement well located?

2. Structure of Argument

    Main Points of Argument: Are central positions/issues set out? Subordinate Arguments: Do they support, extend, qualify the main argument?

    Logic: Is there a logical sequence to the argument based on the sequencing of arguments from major to minor, from claim to evidence, or from topic through a middle argument to a conclusion? Is the argument inductive (drawing conclusions from evidence) or deductive (moving from general principles to particular applications)? Are both sides of the question discussed? Is the argument based on information or assertion?

    Stages and Functions of the Argument: Are they marked in the text with either formal divisions (e.g., sections, sentences, paragraphs) or by indications in the wording (such as *to illustrate, consequently, in contrast, another example*)? Are these stages identified by their subjects or functions (e.g., definition, exemplification, qualification, restriction, illustration)? Is the overall structure coherent? Are nonfunctional repetition, redundancy, irrelevancy avoided?

3. Analysis

    Is analysis provided of key words, terms, evidence, and ideas?

    Is contextual analysis used, rather than dictionary definitions? If the dictionary is used, how is its "authority" incorporated, questioned, or located historically?

    Is the analysis of the primary text/document/monument comprehensive or selective? On what basis? What about secondary text(s), reference books? Do your illustrations and examples elaborate the analysis?

Are quotations used? Are they provided for evidence or illustration? How are they introduced or discussed?

Is the analysis at an appropriate level of complexity or level of abstraction? Is it supported with concrete evidence?

4. Factual Accuracy and Plausibility: Are data, statistics, dates, and points of fact accurate? Are points of interpretation plausible? Are sources of ideas, quotations, illustrations acknowledged?

Sentences, Paragraphs, and Language Strategies

1. Introductory Paragraph: Are opening ideas functional and well presented? Is there a "hook" to catch the reader's attention? Is the thesis stated?

2. Sentences: Is standard English used (e.g., correct subject–verb agreement, pronoun form, use of the apostrophe)? Is syntax correct (meaningful arrangement of words, phrases, sentences)? Is sentence structure varied and appropriate to essay's purposes?

3. Paragraph Unity: Is there a topic sentence? Are paragraphs developed? Are they internally organized? Are bridges and links provided between paragraphs?

4. Diction: Are words carefully chosen for contribution to meaning and argument? Is the level of diction consistent, and does it fit the essay's rhetorical demands and argument and level of formality? Are active verbs and descriptive adjectives used?

5. Conventions of standard English: Is spelling accurate? Is punctuation useful? Is the format for quotations correct? Are the method of citation and format and content of footnotes or endnotes and bibliography consistent? Is the essay format correct?

FURTHER READINGS

Floyd, Richard. *Success in the Social Sciences*. Toronto: Harcourt Brace, 1995.

Lester, James D. *Writing Research Papers: A Complete Guide*. New York: Longman, 1999.

Reeves, Phoebe. *What's the Big Idea? Writing through Reading and Thinking*. Upper Saddle River, NJ: Prentice-Hall, 1999.

Reinking, James A., Andrew W. Hart, and Robert von der Osten. *Strategies for Successful Writing: A Rhetoric, Research Guide, Reader, and Handbook*. Upper Saddle River, NJ: Prentice-Hall, 1999.

Richardson, Peter. *Style: A Pragmatic Approach*. Boston: Allyn and Bacon, 1998.

Troyka, Lynn Quitman, and Cy Strom. *Simon and Schuster Handbook for Writers*. 2nd ed. Scarborough, ON: Prentice Hall, 1999.

WEBLINKS

- Resources for Writers
  owl.english.purdue.edu/
  Numerous essay writing and research pages from the Purdue University Online Writing site.

- Resources for Writers and Writing Instructors
  andromeda.rutgers.edu/~jlynch/Writing/links.html

REFERENCES AND DOCUMENTATION: ACKNOWLEDGING YOUR SOURCES

When your teachers read your essays or other assignments, they want to know which sources you used and how you used them. A reader might want to follow up on a particular idea or might want to know how it is related to other kinds of thought. Adding references to your paper, or documenting your sources, ensures that your reader has a good basis on which to judge your scholarly abilities, protecting you from charges of plagiarism or other breaches of academic honesty.

In the sections below, we consider first the problem of plagiarism, then different kinds of references that you can use in your writing, and then the different styles used by humanities and social sciences disciplines. We also include up-to-date information on documenting electronic sources. The final section illustrates the stages in making various kinds of bibliographies or lists of works cited.

PLAGIARISM AND PROFESSIONALISM

Plagiarism is presenting work as your own that originates from some other source, which you have not acknowledged. It is an offence against academic honesty and is a breach of professionalism. As in any profession, there is a code of ethics for students, which demands that when using someone else's words or ideas you must acknowledge them. Sometimes, students fall into plagiarism through carelessness, by neglecting to make clear when taking notes from books or articles where the quoted material ends and where their commentary on that material begins; hence, it is important to make careful notes that distinguish between others' words and your own. Sometimes, students are caught in a last minute rush, and the temptation to steal someone else's argument, or even a whole paper, is too great. In this case the act of plagiarism is deliberate and if detected, as it often is, can result in dire consequences. Plagiarism is a serious academic offence and may result in a range of penalties, from a warning to failure in an assignment, failure in a course, being reported to the dean, annotation of transcripts, suspension from the university, and, in some cases, criminal proceedings.

Plagiarism can include entire papers, paragraphs, sentences, phrases, ideas, lab results, statistics, and graphics. The sources can include books and articles, encyclopedias, the Internet, or your friend's work. Sometimes, students use an essay service, paying large amounts for even a short paper. Universities have sophisticated means of detecting and prosecuting such offenders. Police recently investigated the use of essay services by students across Ontario. Ryerson, Toronto, and York Universities, among others, charged their offenders. Many were convicted and sentenced to failures in courses, failures for the year, suspensions, and, in the most serious cases, expulsion from universities in Canada for up to twenty-five years. Advanced methods of detecting plagiarism from Internet sources are now available for university instructors. The risk involved for students who use such services is extremely high.

Often, students are unclear about what constitutes plagiarism. Suppose you were writing an essay on James Whale's 1931 film adaptation (starring Boris Karloff) of Mary Shelley's novel, *Frankenstein*. In the course of your study, you have read a number of books and articles on the film, including Wheeler Dixon's article "The Films of *Frankenstein*" (1990), in which he talks of the film's complicated history of converting the novel to a different medium and its dramatic box-office and cinematic impact.

The full reference in a works cited (or references) list, which we discuss below, is as follows:

MLA Style

Dixon, Wheeler Winston. "The Films of *Frankenstein*." *Approaches to Teaching Shelley's* Frankenstein. Ed. Stephen C. Behrendt. New York: MLA, 1990. 166–79.

APA Style

Dixon, W. W. (1990). The films of *Frankenstein*. In S. C. Behrendt (Ed.), *Approaches to teaching Shelley's* Frankenstein (pp. 166–179). New York: MLA.

Dixon refers to the fact that the power of the film's images stopped other directors from taking a more searching look at Mary Shelley's novel. It would be perfectly acceptable for you to comment in your essay that the film caused a sensation at theatres across North America when it was first shown. Virtually all commentaries discuss this fact, and, indeed, it is almost common knowledge. However, if you say that Whale's film inhibited the development of other films that addressed the novel directly, you must give credit to Dixon's argument in one of the following ways:

Whale's version of *Frankenstein* was so powerful in its images and impact, however, that it inhibited new examination of Mary Shelley's novel for over twenty-five years (Dixon 169).

or,

Whale's *Frankenstein,* as Dixon argues, arrested fresh thought about the novel for over twenty-five years (169).

If you acknowledge Dixon like this, you are following good documentation practice; if you do not give credit to Dixon, you are using his ideas and argument as your own and are committing plagiarism.

In fact, this is the passage from Dixon:

> With this 1931 film Whale created a series of iconic conventions that rapidly became clichés in the decade and a half that followed and that, until the advent of the 1957 and 1976 productions, severely limited any serious approach to the novel's actual concerns (169).

If you refer to Dixon in either of the forms above, you are correct. However, if you paraphrase his words you are in serious trouble:

Example 1

In his 1931 film Whale created a series of iconic conventions that rapidly became common in the fifteen years that followed and that, until the productions of 1957 and 1976, limited any different approaches to Shelley's novel.

This close paraphrase is a plagiarism, even if you acknowledge the source in general. In fact whole phrases are lifted from the original, and the sentence structure of the original is copied. Only the opening and closing phrases are changed, along with "cliché" and "decade and a half." To avoid a charge of plagiarism, the passages that are quoted from the original should be in quotation marks, and the source should be acknowledged.

Example 2

As Dixon indicates, "Whale created a series of iconic conventions that rapidly became clichés" after 1931 and that, until the advent of the film of 1957, limited serious approaches to the novel (Dixon 169).

The writer of Example 2 does better than that of Example 1, since at least the source is acknowledged, and the first long phrase is in quotation marks. But the conclusion still borrows language that is often identical with the original, even though words are omitted, and the main idea of the passage is claimed as the author's own or is fudged—at any rate, it is not attributed to Dixon. Example 2 also is a plagiarism and is corrected in the same way as in Example 1.

Example 3

From 1931 to 1957 new approaches to Mary Shelley's novel were blocked in large measure because of the force and originality of the screen images that James Whale introduced into *Frankenstein*.

Although Example 3 is a clear paraphrase, changing the order of the ideas and the phrases in the sentence, and does not import any actual phrases from the original, it still constitutes plagiarism since Dixon's original point (concerning the way that Whale's film blocked rethinking) is not acknowledged. This example would be acceptable with a general reference (Dixon 169), since it avoids the problems of Example 1.

Example 4

Few film versions of Mary Shelley's *Frankenstein* have followed the novel closely. Instead, many have remained under the domination of James Whale's version of 1931. Indeed, as Dixon argues, Whale was so successful in creating "a series of iconic conventions that rapidly became clichés in the decade and a half that followed" that his version "until the advent of the 1957 and 1976 productions, severely limited any serious approach to the novel's actual concerns" (169). We could go even further, claiming that Whale's images continue to dominate not only the film versions of *Frankenstein* but are also clichés in popular culture.

There is no plagiarism in this example. General knowledge is used for the first and second sentences. But the exact reason for blocking new approaches, which is Dixon's main argument, is fully acknowledged by quotation marks and a reference.

These examples demonstrate different uses of sources and ways of acknowledging them. Different cultures have varying views about the authority of the text and the teacher, and so opportunities should be available to discuss these concepts and ways to avoid plagiarism as defined at your institution. If you are uncertain about the concept of plagiarism or are worried about a particular instance in a paper you are working on, you should seek advice from your teachers and perhaps the librarians. Another good source for information about plagiarism is the Internet, where a number of sites discuss the problem in detail and give elaborate examples. We provide addresses for several of these sites in the Weblinks at the end of this chapter.

The best way to avoid accusations of plagiarism is to use appropriate and accepted scholarly methods of study, research, and the presentation of that research in your submitted work. In particular, you need to document all references to the work of others, not only to avoid charges of plagiarism, but also to indicate the scholarly basis of your arguments and to lead others to the resources you have relied on.

DOCUMENTATION STYLES: ACKNOWLEDGING YOUR SOURCES

You must acknowledge all sources for your ideas and documents by giving a reference, either in the text or in a footnote or an endnote. Such references should indicate your sources in a clear, logical, and consistent form. At the end of Chapter 8 we pointed out that making careful notes while conducting your research will save you a great deal of time later, since you avoid the problem of having to go back to find sources that you did not annotate sufficiently the first time. In this chapter we discuss different kinds of methods for acknowledging your sources, using in-text citation, footnotes, and endnotes. Procedures vary from subject areas, and so we outline here the different formats or styles for acknowledging your sources as used by different academic disciplines. The system for providing that information is called *documentation style.* Your course instructor will tell you which documentation style is preferred for the course, and you should check to see what kinds of variations are acceptable. Once you decide on a particular style, you should use it consistently throughout an essay.

In general, the humanities disciplines (English, history, philosophy, and so on) use the style that has been developed by the Modern Languages Association of America (MLA style). It focuses on the author-page system in making references in the text.

In the social sciences (political science, psychology, sociology, and so on) scholars usually use the documentation style developed by the American Psychological Association (APA style), called the author-date system.

For scientific citation (in biology, chemistry, engineering, mathematics, medicine, and physics), the standard is set by the Council of Biology Editors in *Scientific Style and Format: The CBE Manual for Authors, Editors, and Publishers.* CBE style follows a number system. Reference is made in parentheses in the text to a numbered work and the page, and in the works cited the list is numbered and the works appear in the order of their first citation in the text, not in alphabetical order.

Some teachers (and many university presses) use a more specialized documentation style developed at the University of Chicago, summarized in their published manual, the *Chicago Manual of Style*.

As we discussed in Chapter 11, you usually will be integrating quotations into your own writing. We also discussed the methods of formatting quotations (using double quotation marks for direct speech, indenting quotations longer than four lines without quotation marks, and so on). Only rarely do students have to compile lists of quotations, though it is true that some essays that have been poorly written or analyzed look like compilations of quotations strung together with very little connective argument. If your assignment relies on one book, perhaps one of the books used in the course, and you are not expected to do outside reading or research for that book, most of the references likely will be placed immediately after your quotations or other summaries of the book's ideas and arguments. You will be able to insert these references as briefly and carefully as possible, according to the documentation style that is recommended in the course. If, however, your assignment involves more complicated research, either in the library or through electronic sources or the Internet, you will have to use more complicated methods of referencing your sources.

You will often have the choice of incorporating your references in the body of your essay (with a list of works cited at the end) or of adding references in footnotes or endnotes (see the discussion of formatting footnotes and endnotes below). In the following sections, we illustrate the various ways of making your references clear.

HUMANITIES FORMAT: MLA STYLE

In humanities subjects, academic essays generally follow the MLA style (before the adoption of this format in 1984, the footnote and endnote style was used for all references). The current method is easy and efficient for both writers and readers. MLA style documents sources in two ways: first, references to sources within the text of the essay are given in short citations (in-text citations), and second, a list of works cited is included at the end of the essay. MLA style uses the author-page method of citation. That is, the author's last name and the page number(s) from which the quotation is taken appear in the text, and a complete reference to the source appears in the works cited list.

In-Text Citations

Within the body of your essay you include references to each source you are using in parentheses right after your quotation, paraphrase, or summary. These in-text citations allow a

TIPS: Documenting Your Sources

1. Current practice favours incorporating most references to sources within your essay, adding notes (whether footnotes or endnotes) only for additional information that goes beyond citing a source.

2. Some course instructors still prefer that all citations of sources be included in endnotes or footnotes.

3. Check with your instructor to determine what is acceptable.

reader to refer to your works cited list for further information. Usually, an author's last name is used in an in-text citation to identify a source, together with the exact page numbers from which the cited material is taken. The author's name may be mentioned either in your sentence or in parentheses at the end of your sentence (or quotation); the page number is always given in parentheses, not in the text of your sentence. For the references in the text of your essay, after a quotation or use of an author's ideas, you include the author's last name and page number(s) with no comma or page abbreviation (Frye 354) or (Frye 354–56). The final period follows the citation reference. For instance, you might be working on an essay on the social and literary background to dystopias, including Margaret Atwood's dystopian novel *The Handmaid's Tale*, about a patriarchal republic called Gilead, where women are controlled as breeders. You may quote from the novel by summarizing, commenting in general, or citing the author:

Summary

Confined to her room for the most part, Offred memorizes all of the parts of her new world in the Commander's house, as a prisoner knows the parts of his cell. At the same time, she rejoices in the fact that at least she is alive (Atwood 7–10).

Commentary

While her language is descriptive, it also is evaluative, betraying the fact that Offred remains rebellious or is tempted to find ways to question the absolute authority that she is placed under. For instance, her own thoughts indicate that she is questioning the motives and words of the others in the household and their submission to authority (Atwood 12–13).

Citation

Illustrating Offred's need for human contact, Atwoood writes: "I would help Rita make the bread, sinking my hands into that soft resistant warmth which is so much like flesh. I hunger to touch something, other than cloth or wood. I hunger to commit the act of touch" (12–13).

Citation of a longer quotation

Offred links word to word, thing to thing, noting every detail and enumerating them, as each stands metonymically for something else, something more important, in the world she has left behind:

> I take the tokens from Rita's outstretched hand. They have pictures on them, of the things they can be exchanged for: twelve eggs, a piece of cheese, a brown thing that's supposed to be a steak. I place them in the zippered pocket in my sleeve, where I keep my pass. (Atwood 13)

In the first two instances, the name of the author is given in parentheses right after the passage you wish to document. Since this is the first reference that you are making to the novel, you need to identify the author. If you were writing only about Atwood and were citing only this text, and it was clear from the context that you were referring to the novel, you would not need to include the author's name. In the third example, the author's name is omitted because it is given in the introductory comment. In the final example, the period falls after the quotation, not after the parenthetical reference. In every case, there is no punctuation between the author's name and the page references, and the page numbers are given with no abbreviation, such as *p.* or *pp.*

In places where you may use an italic font on the computer (for instance, in book titles), MLA style still recommends that you underline to avoid the misreading of fonts.

However, underlining in texts on the Web and often in printed sources now usually indicates a hypertext URL, an active link to the Internet, rather than italics. You should check with your instructor about his or her preferences concerning underlining or italics. We assume that most students now use a computer in writing essays, and so have access to italic fonts. Hence, we have adapted MLA style here to give all of our citations with italic fonts where MLA would use underlining.

While this method of in-text citation for a single author and a single work is easy and efficient, it becomes more complex with other kinds of materials, but in every case the MLA style specifies how to format your references. The examples given below relate to Margaret Atwood and women's writing:

In-Text Citations from Print Media

MLA Style

One author
- Follow the format outlined above.

Examples of In-Text Citations

"I hunger to commit the act of touch" (Atwood 13).

Two or three authors
- Reproduce the order and spelling of authors' names as on the title page (or in the byline).

Critics [of Margaret Atwood] have addressed such themes as identity, Canadian nationalism, struggle for survival, sexual politics, and shamanism and concentrated on animal, mirror, camera, and other images in Atwood's work (Wilson, Friedman, and Hengen 2).

Recent US "patriotic" groups continue to use the names similar to those in Atwood. A recent *Toronto Star* article says that "they operate under such public-spirited names as the Guardians of American Liberties, the Constitutionalists, the Arizona Patriots, and the Association of the Sons of Liberty" (Wright and Meyer A11).

More than three authors
- Name all, or use the abbreviation et al. ("and others").

Women's development involves fostering independence of selfhood, the speaking voice, and the questioning and challenging mind (Belenky et al. 24).

More than one source by an author
- Include the title in a shortened form when you use more than one work by an author.

Again and again we find [Moodie] gazing at the sublime natural goings-on in the misty distance—sunsets, mountains, spectacular views—only to be brought up short by disagreeable things in her immediate foreground, such as bugs, swamps, tree roots and other immigrants (Atwood, *Survival* 51).

Two or more authors with the same last name
- Use the first initial and full last name for each author in the parentheses—usually, the full first name is used in your own sentence.

Old patriarchal psychologies of women that relate power to masochism have been radically challenged by Jean Baker Miller's claim that power is "the capacity to implement"(121), a claim that is negated in Offred's helplessness, historically established in one of Atwood's source books on puritanism (P. Miller 28–33).

Group or corporate author
- Use the group name as an author.

In *Our Bodies, Ourselves* the authors allude to current kinds of oppression that Atwood fictionalizes: "In the broadest sense, violence against women is any violation of a woman's personhood, mental or physical integrity, or freedom of movement through individual acts and societal oppression" (Boston Women's Health Collective 246).

Work cited by title
- Shorten the title in the parenthetical reference, using the first word as the one for alphabetizing in your list of works cited.

A brief but dated summary of Atwood's life and works is found in the entry in a standard Canadian reference book (*Oxford Companion* 28).

Multivolume work
- Include the relevant volume number in each citation, followed by a colon and space.

Nineteenth-century opinion held that "a woman's commitment to her own writing would destroy her femininity, threaten her marriage, and disrupt her household, and that literary women were often characterized by strong passions and notorious conduct" (Helsinger, Sheets, and Veeder 3: 6).

Novel, play, or poem
- Often, it is more useful to give chapter numbers, act/scene/line numbers, or stanza and line numbers; when you use a different text from the assigned one in a course, include chapter numbers after the page citations, separated by a comma.

The story of Orpheus and Eurydice to which Atwood refers on the last page of the novel is found in Ovid's *Metamorphoses* (10: 1–160) and the "vast darkness" perhaps echoes Horatio's phrase to Hamlet concerning the "dead vast and middle of the night" (1.2.199).

Work in an anthology or collection
- Use the author of the work in the in-text citation, and include information about the collection in your list of works cited.

In "Earth" the speaker is digging in the garden but is aware of the dead below the earth in a way that Serena Joy does not realize (Atwood 160–61).

Indirect source
- Use this format for quoted words in another source.

Christopher Lehmann-Haupt, an editor with the *New York Times,* says that only in the novel's final pages do we realize "how bleak and even terrifying" that world is (qtd. in Atwood, *Handmaid's Tale* 391).

In-Text Citations from Audiovisual Media

Audiovisual media include paintings, music, television, radio, and films. MLA style covers the various modes of citing such materials, including references in your writing to paintings (or sculpture or architecture), music, radio broadcasts, and films. In general, the artist, composer, writer, or producer/director is named, usually with the title of the work cited.

MLA Style	*Examples of In-Text Citations*
Work of art • Include the artist and list the title in italics.	... that landscape of greens and blues with a sky of stars (Van Gogh, *Starry Night*).
Musical composition • List the composer and include the title of the recording in italics or the title of the song in quotation marks.	*Apocalypse Now* begins with the music from a famous 1960s rock song (Morrison, "The End").
Television broadcast • List the title of the program in italics, the title of the episode in quotation marks, and the date.	One episode of the *X-Files* paid elaborate tribute to Mary Shelley's *Frankenstein* ("The Post-Modern Prometheus" 30 Nov. 1997).
Radio broadcast • List the title of the program in italics, the title of the segment in quotation marks, and the date.	The National Public Radio portrait of Alice Walker related the title of its program to the literary form of *The Color Purple* ("If God" 3 Mar. 1984).
Film • Include the producer and list the title in italics.	In setting much of his film in and around Boston, the director was true to the locale of Atwood's novel (Schlondorff, *The Handmaid's Tale*).

Many other forms of media exist and can be referred to in essays—including performances, personal letters, audio cassettes, and so on. In general, they follow the pattern set out above. Further details are given in the standard manuals listed in the further readings at the end of this chapter.

In-Text Citations from Electronic Media

Students are increasingly using a large and quickly evolving field of electronic sources that they access through computers and related technologies, much of it containing audio clips and visual images or graphics. According to the MLA Web site, such electronic media sources from the World Wide Web (Internet) include scholarly projects, reference databases, the texts of e-books (electronic books on the Net), articles in periodicals accessible electronically, and professional and personal sites. However, the MLA style has not kept up with the rapid changes in electronic media, especially on the Internet, in supplying methods for making clear in-text citations and relevant listings in works cited lists. For instance, the MLA page on the Internet (**www.mla.org**) specifies that Web addresses should be placed within pointed brackets (< >), a device used in instructing most e-mail programs to send to a specific address, and hence confusing to a reader. Accordingly, we have adapted the MLA style for electronic sources following Janice R. Walker and Todd Taylor in the *Columbia Guide to Online Style,* which has been endorsed by the Alliance for Computers and Writing, and by James D. Lester in *Citing Cyberspace.*

Electronic media change their references frequently, as new Web sites replace old ones. Many also become inactive. Hence, such references often do not have the durability or reliability of print or hard-copy media. Nevertheless, students must make acceptable references for any citations from such sources. In this evolving field, the following procedures are acceptable for in-text citations. Note that the Web address, or URL, may replace the author, title, and publication data. The date the Internet address was accessed (or the date on the Web page if it exists) is added after the Web address. Since Web pages are only one continuous page, regardless of length, a page reference is unnecessary, either in in-text citations or in lists of works cited.

Adapted MLA Style

Web sites
* Include the author's name, abbreviation, or alias if known, or the title or file name.

E-mail, listservs, and newsgroups
* Include the author's name, or alias, if known, with a short title or file address so a reader can identify it in the list of works cited.

Examples of In-Text Citations

At her Web site Margaret Atwood has made available a great deal of additional information about her novel, including detailed responses to questions. To one question about her heroine, she says: "I wanted an ordinary person, for the simple reason that most people subjected to these conditions are ordinary people" (Atwood, http://www.web.net/owtoad/q.html 17 Sept. 1998).

"Americacentrism and Eurocentrism mean that Canadian authors have never been chosen for the Nobel Prize in literature. It is disgraceful that Atwood has not been awarded a prize for literature given almost four decades of outstanding poetry and prose. Shame to the Nobel committee" (Charles, "Nobel Prize").

Works Cited List

The list of works cited follows the body of your essay and the page of endnotes (if any); it begins on a new page with the heading "Works Cited," and is numbered sequentially with the rest of your essay. The works cited list contains all of the materials to which you made reference in the body of your essay. It does not include the materials you consulted but did not use. Humanities essays that follow the MLA style list works cited entries in an alphabetized list by author (family name first). If there is no author, you alphabetize by the first main word in the title (omitting *A, An, The*). The author's name is placed at the left margin, and all subsequent lines for the same entry are indented five spaces or one-half inch (on a computer, you can use the hanging indent facility). Periods are used to separate the three main elements of the entry: the author, the title, and the place of publication with the date. For publishers' names, you can abbreviate *University Press* to UP or its equivalent: U of Chicago P. To simplify these entries, we have provided the citations for each of the examples of in-text citations given above.

Works Cited from Print Media

In the MLA style version of the works cited list a few conventions function to get all of the information down clearly. Each of the sections of the entry is set off by a period: the author's name, the title in italics, and the place and date of publication. The entries are arranged in alphabetical order. Everything else follows from this format.

In detail, that means that you give the author's name with the last name first (inverted order). If there is more than one author, only the first author's name is inverted, followed by a comma and the rest of the authors. If you cite more than one work by an author, you list each in alphabetical order by title, replacing the author's name with three hyphens and a period before each title after the first. If there is no author for a work, but only a title, you can use the title for your alphabetizing. All words in the title are capitalized, except prepositions, articles, and conjunctions. The first word in a title is always capitalized. Book titles, film titles, newspapers, and periodicals are all italicized. Articles in periodicals and chapter titles in a book are not italicized but, instead, are enclosed in double quotation marks. MLA style assumes that you are using a font with straight quotation marks instead of curly or typographical quotation marks like this (" "); however, most word processors now print typographical quotation marks automatically. We have assumed that you will use this feature of your word processor's program, and accordingly we have modified MLA and APA style in the examples that follow. The first line for each citation in your works cited list should begin at the margin; subsequent lines for the same entry are indented five spaces (one half inch, or one tab, or a hanging indent). Like the rest of your text, the list of works cited should be double spaced.

TIP: Remembering the Basic Format for MLA Works Cited List

In a works cited list use the following order:
    Jones, Henry. (author's name, inverted)
    The World According to Fido. (title in italics and caps)
    Boston: New World, 1997. (publication data)
Everything else is a refinement of this basic format.

MLA Style

One author
• Use the format outlined above.

Two or three authors
• Order and spell authors' names as on the title page; this applies to joint authorship or joint editorship.

• Note that MLA does not underline titles within titles. Many style books (the *Chicago Manual*, for instance) find this method confusing and put book titles within other titles in quotation marks.

More than three authors
• Name all or use the abbreviation et al. (Latin, *et alii,* and others)

More than one source by an author
• Include the full title in the list of works cited. Indicate a second work by the same author by three hyphens (on a long dash) and a period instead of the author's name; arrange titles alphabetically.

Two or more authors with the same last name
• Use the full name for each person, alphabetized according to their given names.

Group or corporate author
• Use the group name as an author.

Work cited by title (no author)
• Expand the shortened title from the parenthetical reference in the list of works cited.

Multivolume work
• Include the relevant volume number in each citation, followed by a colon and space.

Examples of Works Cited Entries

Atwood, Margaret. *The Handmaid's Tale.* Toronto: Seal-McClelland-Bantam, 1998.

Wilson, Sharon R., Thomas B. Friedman, and Shannon Hengen, eds. *Approaches to Teaching Atwood's* The Handmaid's Tale *and Other Works.* New York: MLA, 1996.

Alternative form:

Wilson, Sharon R., Thomas B. Friedman, and Shannon Hengen, eds. *Approaches to Teaching Atwood's "The Handmaid's Tale" and Other Works.* New York: MLA, 1996.

Belenky, Mary Field, et al. *Women's Ways of Knowing: The Development of Self, Voice, and Mind.* New York: Basic, 1986.

Atwood, Margaret. *Survival: A Thematic Guide to Canadian Literature.* Toronto: Anansi, 1972.

———. *Wilderness Tips.* Toronto: McClelland, 1991.

Miller, Jean Baker. *Toward a New Psychology of Women.* Harmondsworth: Penguin, 1976.

Miller, Perry. *Errand into the Wilderness.* Cambridge: Belknap-Harvard UP, 1956.

Boston Women's Health Collective. *Our Bodies, Ourselves.* New York: Simon, 1986.

Oxford Companion to Canadian Literature. Toronto: Oxford UP, 1983.

Helsinger, Elizabeth K., Robin Lauterbach Sheets, and William Veeder. *The Woman Question: Society and Literature in Britain and America, 1837–1883.* Vol. 3. Chicago: U of Chicago P, 1989.

Novel, play, poem
- Often, it is more useful to give chapter numbers, act/scene/line numbers, or stanza and line numbers; when you use a different text from the assigned one in a course, it is wise to include chapter numbers after the page citations, separated by a comma. Note that the first example gives the format for a translated work, and the second, for an edited work.

Ovid. *Metamorphoses*. Trans. Rolfe Humphries. Bloomington: Indiana UP, 1955.

Shakespeare, William. *Hamlet*. Ed. Barbara A. Mowat and Paul Werstine. New York: Washington Square-Pocket, 1992.

Work in an anthology or collection
- Use the author of the work in the in-text citation, and include information about the collection in your list of works cited, where you also list your author.

Atwood, Margaret. "Earth." *Poetry by Canadian Women*. Ed. Rosemary Sullivan. Toronto: Oxford UP, 1989. 160–61.

Editorial, letter to the editor, or review
- List the author if known, title if given, publication name, omitting *A* or *The* from the title, date, and pages.

Davidson, Cathy N. "A Feminist *1984*." Rev. of *The Handmaid's Tale* by Margaret Atwood. *Ms*. Feb. 1986: 24–26.

Signed article from daily newspaper
- Follow the format above, but add the name of the city of publication in brackets after the title, not underlined, if it is not part of the title.

Wright, Robin and Josh Meyer. "Righteous 'patriots' testing U.S. authority." *Toronto Star* 25 Apr. 1995: A11.

Article in a journal
—with continuous pagination
- Each issue continues the pagination from the previous issue. Cite the volume number only before the year, using arabic numerals throughout.

Godard, Barbara. "Telling it Over Again: Atwood's Art of Parody." *Canadian Poetry* 21 (1987): 1–30.

Article in a journal
—with separate pagination for each issue
- Each issue begins on page 1. Cite the volume number and the issue number, separated by a period.

Buss, Helen M. "Maternality and Narrative Strategies in the Novels of Margaret Atwood." *Atlantis* 15.1 (1989): 76–83.

Works Cited from Audiovisual Media

MLA Style

Examples of Works Cited Entries

Work of art
- List the artist, title in italics, museum or collection, and location.

Van Gogh, Vincent. *Starry Night*. Museum of Modern Art. New York.

Musical composition
- Include the composer, song title in quotation marks, album title in italics, medium, producer, and date; or, list the composer and musical form, without italics unless the work is titled.

Morrison, Jim. "The End." *The Doors*. LP. Elektra Records. 1967

Beethoven, Ludwig von. Symphony no. 5 in C minor, op. 67.

Beethoven, Ludwig von. *Moonlight Sonata*.

Television broadcast
- List the title of the program in quotation marks, series in italics, writer and director if known, and date of broadcast.

"The Post-Modern Prometheus." *The X-Files*. Writ. and Dir. Chris Carter. 30 Nov. 1997.

Radio broadcast
- Cite the title in quotation marks, series in italics, network, call letters and city of broadcast station, and date.

"If God." *Writers Today*. NPR. WGBH, Boston. 3 Mar. 1984.

Film
- Include the producer or director, title in italics, other information such as author of screenplay or actors, production company, date, and any subsequent release, as on videocassette.

Schlondorff, Volker. Dir. *The Handmaid's Tale*. Screenplay by Harold Pinter. Cinecom, 1989. Released on Videocassette by HBO, 1990.

Works Cited from Electronic Media

The general format for citations from electronic media consists of the following details, with punctuation and capitalization for each item. The lines listed separately here are combined in the citation list:

- Author's (Editor's, Compiler's) Last Name, First Name or Initials. [if known]
- "Title of Document Being Accessed." [title of article, Web page, or posting to a discussion list taken from subject line and put into quotation marks]
  - *Title of Complete Work* (*Project, Database, Personal Web Site*) [if known]
  - Version number or file number [if known]
  - Date of document or of last revision of Web site [if known, but often difficult to find]
  - Name of Institution or Organization Sponsoring the Web Site [if specified]

- Protocol and address [URL]
  - Access path [if specified]
  - Directories [if specified]
- Date of access [in parentheses]

The two essential items are the protocol and address, and the date of access. The protocol identifies the kind of electronic communication (such as CD-ROM, e-mail, ftp, gopher, http, or telnet), and the address is the URL. Some manuals specify that the URL is to be underlined. However, word processors such as recent and current versions of WordPerfect and Microsoft Word automatically underline and highlight Web sites or addresses as hypertext links that can be accessed on the Internet from within those word processing programs. The underlining (and highlighting in blue on the colour monitor) indicates that the address is "hot" and can be accessed on the Internet directly from the document. In a submitted essay, however, a reader would not have access to enter any site directly. Hence, there is no need to underline the URL as a hot address. The MLA style page on the Internet specifies that the URL should be enclosed in pointed brackets like an e-mail address. The preferred method of citing the URL without underlining or other notation is given here. It is a convention to give the URL all on one line; if it will not fit on one line, it can be broken after a slash in the address. The date of access is the date when you accessed the reference, and so it marks a time when the address was active and accessible. Most references also include an author's name and the title of the document or Web page. In other electronic media that do not accept italics, such as e-mail, the convention is to use an underline mark before and after text that would normally be underlined, _like this_.

Adapted MLA Style

Web Sites
- Include the author's name, abbreviation, or alias if known, and the title or file name, as in the in-text citation.

E-mail, listservs, and newsgroups
- List the author's name or alias, if known, with a short title or file address so a reader can identify it in the list of works cited.

Examples of Works Cited Entries

Atwood, Margaret.
   http://www.web.net/owtoad/q.html
   (17 Sept. 1998)

Charles. "The Nobel Prize Internet Archive."
   www.almaz.com/nobel/wwwboard/
   messages/705.html Posted by Charles
   on 07 Jan. 1998 at 14:04:37.

There is a large number of printed and electronic guides available for MLA style for printed materials. Many of these sources will be available at the reference desk of your library. In addition, most style handbooks have at least a summary chapter on how to make in-text references for the most common materials and how to create a list of works cited. The standard reference manuals, however, give detailed instruction on a wide variety of materials well beyond the possibilities of shorter handbooks. We list a number of these resources in the further readings at the end of this chapter.

SOCIAL SCIENCES FORMAT: APA STYLE

In the social sciences, the method of citation usually follows the standard format as set out by the American Psychological Association (APA) in the *Publication Manual of the American Psychological Association*. Like the MLA style, APA style uses in-text citation and a list of works cited (titled "References") at the end of an essay or article. The method of citation and reference, however, is somewhat different from MLA style. Citation is made in the text in parentheses to the last name of the author, the date of the publication, and a page reference (the author-date system). The list of references contains the author's name, alphabetized, followed by the date of publication, title, publisher, and place of publication.

In-Text Citations

In the social sciences disciplines, the same general principles for the need to acknowledge all sources apply. While the MLA style uses the author-page format, however, the APA prefers the author-date. If you refer to a source more than once in a paragraph, the APA style specifies that you refer to the author's name, the date, and the page for the first entry only, and then list only the name and page for subsequent references. APA style requires page numbers for all direct citations and recommends pages for paraphrases. To be safe, you should include page references for all derived materials, both those directly cited and ideas that are paraphrased. The abbreviations *p.* (page) and *pp.* (pages) are used. The examples provided here all relate to the question of how it is possible to change the priorities of the social structures of society, a topic that can draw on a wide range of materials in the social sciences.

In-Text Citations from Print Media

APA Style

One author
- Provide the reference after the quotation, outside the quotation marks and within parentheses: (Author, date, p. 143).

Two or more authors
- Give both names for two authors, all names for more than two for the first citation, and in subsequent citations, the first author's last name, with et al. Note that *and* is an ampersand (&) inside parentheses, but it is spelled out as *and* in text.

More than one source by an author

Examples of In-Text Citations

In assessing the potential for change in social policy affecting the most needy in society, a new look has to be taken at the concept of poverty that was defined at the beginning of the century as inadequate earning of the male members of a family, assuming that "every penny earned by every member of the family went into the family purse, and was judiciously expended upon necessaries" (Rowntree, 1902, p. 111).

The study of social change is problematic for sociologists because they rely on social order for their analyses, while change introduces the "unexpected and potentially explosive" (Crysdale & Beattie, 1977, p. 75).

or

Crysdale and Beattie argue ... (1977, p. 75).

- Distinguish sources by dates; several sources in the same year have letters added to the date: 1990a, 1990b.

Two or more authors with the same last name
- Use both initials for each author.

Group or corporate author
- Use the group name as an author.

Work cited by title
- Use the first words of the entry, usually the title.

Schudson's recent work on change and integration in national societies (1994), builds on his earlier work on newspapers as instruments of popular culture (1978, 1984).

The transformation of intercultural groups depends, among many other factors, on overcoming racial stereo-typing, or, rather, replacing racist stereotyping with "positive stereotypes that recognize but respect intergroup differences" (W. G. Stephan & C. W. Stephan, 1996, p. 124).

A government study determined that by 1980 integration was still severely limited in U.S. schools, since 69% of whites attended schools that were still less than 5 percent African-American (U.S. Commission on Civil Rights, 1987).

Shifts in "population, income, and church affiliation" have had little impact on the "cultural aspirations of most people" in Montreal ("Social Change," 1993, p. A4).

In-Text Citations from Electronic Media

The most recent print copy of the APA *Publication Manual* (1994) has information about references to electronic media that, like those in the MLA *Handbook,* are out of date. The director of the APA journals, Leslie Cameron, maintains a Web site that gives information on how to cite these sources according to the most recent thinking of the APA: **www.apa.org/journals/webref.html**. The APA also maintains a site that answers frequently asked questions (FAQs): **www.apa.org/journals/faq.html**.

The general procedure follows the conventions of HTML language and the Internet, in that pages are not referred to; however, if the site gives an author and/or date, that information is included. The URL is given in the list of references. APA style recommends that personal communications (such as e-mails) are to be referenced as in-text citations, but are not to be listed in the references. However, as with other matters on the Web, this field is in constant flux, and it now seems likely that e-mail and other electronic sources (such as chat lines) will become standardized for both in-text citation and notation in the list of references. Indeed, the current editions of print and electronic guides that amplify APA style do give details on just these matters. For instance, Janice R. Walker and Todd Taylor in the *Columbia Guide to Online Style* give detailed treatment of electronic sources, and James D. Lester in *Citing Cyberspace* does the same in his "Online Citation Guide": **longman.awl.com/englishpages/cyber.html**.

Adapted APA Style	*Examples of In-Text Citations*
Web sites • Use the author's name and date if known, and the title or URL.	A new "interdisciplinary theory for cultural change" has recently become available on the Web, and the author hopes that it will begin an online discussion of relevant issues (Fog, 1997).
Web-accessible journal • These journals are available through *WilsonWeb, Ovid,* and other databases. Cite in text as for any print publication; same for newspaper.	Foster's account shows that in Tennessee social change was impeded by the failure of legislatures and police regulators to stop both the drug trade and drug use (1996).
E-mail, listservs, and newsgroups • Use the author's name and date of posting.	The impact of new software in the field of cultural change and the role of Internet search engines in reducing student capacity for sustained concentration have been much discussed on the educational newsgroups, as Wertmuller has pointed out in an e-mail (May 14, 1998).

References List

The list of books referred to in an essay, article, chapter, or book is entitled "References" in APA style. The format generally follows the conventions set up in the in-text citations, based on the author-date method, arranged alphabetically. You add the page of references as the last page of your essay, numbered sequentially. The general format of the entries is the author's or editor's last name, followed by a comma and initials, the year of the publication in parentheses (or "No Date" if unavailable), the title of the source (no quotation marks for an article, but italics for a book or journal title), the publisher, and the pages if it is an article. APA style requires only the initials of the first and middle name of an author and capitalization of only the first word of a title (along with any proper nouns and the first word after a colon); titles of periodicals are capitalized. APA style specifies that titles of works be underlined, but as with MLA style, we use and recommend that you use italics on your computer. The names of university presses are spelled out. APA style also has the first word indented five spaces or one-half inch, and the second or following lines flush with the left margin. Other details are in the APA *Publication Manual.*

References from Print Media	*Examples of References Entries*
APA Style One author • Follow the format outlined above. • Only the first word of a title, and the first word after a colon are capitalized.	Rowntree, B. S. (1902). *Poverty.* London: Macmillan. or, Crane, D. (Ed.). (1994). *The sociology of culture: Emerging theoretical perspectives.* Oxford: Blackwell.

Two or more authors
- Reverse both names, and use an ampersand before the last name.

More than one source by an author
- Repeat the author's name for each publication, and put them in chronological order. For the article, note that there are no quotation marks around the title. The editor's name is in normal order, followed by Ed. in parentheses and the title. The pages of the article follow with abbreviation pp., and then the publisher.

Two or more authors with the same last name
- Use both initials for each author, and treat it as a book by two authors, above.

Group or corporate author
- Use the group name as an author.

Work cited by title
- Use the format for a newspaper article entry. If the article is in a journal, both the title and volume number are italicized.

Crysdale, S., & Beattie, C. (1977). *Sociology Canada: An introductory text.* Toronto: Butterworth.

Schudson, M. (1978). *Discovering the news: A social history of American newspapers.* New York: Basic Books.

Schudson, M. (1984). *Advertising, the uneasy persuasion.* New York: Basic Books.

Schudson, M. (1994). Culture and the integration of national societies. In D. Crane (Ed.), *The Sociology of culture: Emerging theoretical perspectives* (pp. 21–43). Oxford: Blackwell.

Stephan, W. G., & Stephan, C. W. (1996). *Intergroup relations.* Boulder: Westview Press.

U.S. Commission on Civil Rights. (1987). *The new evidence on school desegregation.* Washington, D.C.: U.S. Government Printing Office.

Social change in urban Quebec. (1993, May 23). *Montreal Gazette*, p. A4.

Decker, Jeffrey. L. (1993). The state of rap. *Social Text, 34,* 53–84.

References from Electronic Media

A reference should include the following (with capitalization and punctuation as shown):
Author's Last name, Initials. (date of publication or "No Date" if unavailable). Title of document. *Title of complete work.* [if applicable]. Protocol and address [complete URL] (date of access: month, day, year).

You should check with your instructor if you wish to vary any particular formatting instructions from APA style.

Adapted APA Style
Web sites
- Use the author's name and date if known, the title or URL, and date accessed.

Web-accessible journal
- These journals are available through *WilsonWeb, Ovid,* and other databases.

Examples of References Entries

Fog, A. (1997). *Cultural Selection.* http://www/datrix.co.za/docs/culture/cult.htm (October 10, 1999).

Foster, J. C. (1996). The rocky road to a "drug free Tennessee": A history of the early regulation of cocaine and the opiates,

Cite the author, date, title, and journal as for print; add the database producer, title, URL and date of access.

1897–1913. *Journal of Social History 29,* 547–564. From H. W. Wilson Humanities Abstracts http://wilsonweb3.hwwilson.com /cgi-bin/auto_login.cgi (July 24, 1997).

Web-accessible newspaper
- These are available through the newspaper's Web page.

Slater, E. (1999). Ex-wrestler sworn as governor. *The Record Online.* http://www. bergen.com/news/jesse05199901058.htm (January 5, 1999).

CD-ROM
- Indicate the author, title, medium, such as CD-ROM, and journal, as well as the source from which the information was retrieved.

Mulvihill, C. K. (1996). AIDS education for college students: Review and proposal for a research-based curriculum. [CD-ROM]. *AIDS Education and Prevention 8,* 11–30. Abstract from: SilverPlatter File: PsychLIT Item: 84-20138.

E-mail, listservs, and newsgroups
- Indicate the author, e-mail or other address, title of the communication, and, if possible, the source from which it is available and date of access.

Wertmuller, C. (cwertm@gosec.columbia.edu). Re: internet distractions... E-mail to Joe Blum (jblum@hotmail.com) (May14, 1998).

As with MLA style, APA style is continually being modified, especially with respect to electronic sources. Many resources are available for further information. Of course, the chief source continues to be the APA *Publication Manual.* The advice on electronic materials is revised at the APA Web site but does not remain current for long. Even more helpful are the many Web sites that offer guidance in using APA style (see the Weblinks at the end of this chapter).

FOOTNOTES AND ENDNOTES

Footnotes (at the bottom of the page) or endnotes (at the end of the essay, before the list of sources) are now used only for two quite limited purposes, although some faculty still prefer notes to the methods of in-text citation we discussed above (see further comments on this matter below).

Notes for Additional Information

Sometimes, you may wish to add a note (a footnote or an endnote) to amplify information in the text, or to provide other kinds of documentation (sometimes called a *content note*). Perhaps you are writing an essay on the French Revolution and are discussing the various factions that were in conflict later in the revolution, during the "Reign of Terror." You might, for instance, be discussing the opposing political theories of Robespierre and Marat and wish to provide some biographical information about each to your reader. You could introduce that biographical material into the body of your essay, but it might be seen by your reader either as filler or as digression. Perhaps it would be better to add brief biographical information on each revolutionary in a content note. Or, you might wish to comment in a little detail on the newspaper *L'ami du peuple*, which Marat published and in which he advanced his views of the revolution. A content note would let you do that without interrupting the flow of your argument.

To create a note, you insert a superscript number (that is, a number raised above the line) for the note at the point in your text where you want to draw the reader's attention to your information. Then you add the note and information, either as a footnote on the same page or as an endnote at the end of the essay, before the list of works cited. All current word processors have the capability of entering footnotes or endnotes automatically. For instance, in WordPerfect 8, you simply go to Insert and choose the Footnote/Endnote option; the correct number is added automatically in your text, and the footnote or endnote window appears, where you enter the information. In Word, the same procedure is followed. All word processors also allow you to format your footnotes and endnotes according to the requirements of the documentation style you are following in your essay.

A second use of content notes is to supply additional bibliographical information (called a *bibliographic note*). For instance, in your research on the Reign of Terror you might have come across a number of books and articles that you are not referring to directly in your essay or in your works cited list but that give an overview of the topic that a reader might find useful. In a footnote or endnote you can comment on these books and articles, indicating their range and importance. In fact, you are supplying a kind of annotated bibliography here to help the reader with additional information (see the discussion of annotated bibliographies on page 264).

For example, you might write the following with a content note to expand on Marat's medical condition without interrupting the argument you are making about his political position:

> Marat had lived a life of political intrigue, now in, now out of favour with the authorities and the populace of Paris. He had been put on trial himself and was acquitted, but he had been hounded into hiding in the Paris sewers, where it is alleged he contracted the skin disease that kept him confined periodically to cooling baths for the rest of his life.[1] When he was away from the meetings of the government (the Convention)....

Your note (following MLA style) might be as follows:

> [1] Simon Schama comments in detail on Marat's sickness: "Never particularly healthy, Marat had lately developed a crippling dermatological disorder which, on periodic eruption, would turn his skin into a roasting mess of scaly flakes and sores. The only relief for this arthritic psoriasis was to lie in a cool bath" (731).

If you were giving an annotated note on the Terror, it might look like the following:

> When the Terror had almost run its course, the Committee of Public Safety finally turned on Danton and had him executed, and then it was the turn of Robespierre, as the Terror took its most famous victim.[2]

> [2] In the extensive literature on the Terror, Marat, and Robespierre, the following sources are the most useful: Colin Lucas's *The Structure of the Terror* (London: Oxford Univ. Press, 1973) deals with the Terror in Paris and the provinces; R. R. Palmer's *Twelve Who Ruled: The Year of the Terror in the French Revolution* (Princeton: Princeton Univ. Press, 1989) sets out the leading figures and their activities. The reasons for and details of Marat's death are set out in Jean-Claude Bonnet's *La Mort de Marat* (Paris: Flammarion, 1986). The standard biography of Robespierre is J. M. Thompson's *Robespierre* (Oxford: Basil Blackwell, 1988), and the most

detailed account of his revolutionary activities is in David P. Jordan's *The Revolutionary Career of Maximilien Robespierre* (New York: Free Press, 1985).

DOCUMENTING REFERENCES IN FOOTNOTES AND ENDNOTES

Some instructors still require footnotes or endnotes rather than the current MLA or APA styles. If so, you should follow the following formatting procedures, checking them with your instructor if you are uncertain about them. Generally, faculty prefer endnotes to footnotes, and most students find endnotes easier to create. However, any word processor can create either automatically.

Your word processor can be programmed to modify the format you use for footnotes and endnotes. For instance, in WordPerfect 6–8, you can click on Insert and choose Footnote/Endnote and then Options. Then, you can select details in formatting, choice of fonts, and so on, in the text and in the note, along with styles of superscript, indenting, and so on.

If you are documenting by footnotes or endnotes, the usual convention in the humanities is to follow the "old" MLA format. The site at the University of Illinois at Urbana provides online help with this matter (**www.english.uiuc.edu/cws/wworkshop/oldmlamenu.htm**). The note should contain the information in the following format:

- the note number indented five spaces and in superscript, then a space
- the author's name in normal order, followed by a comma
- the title (in italic font, or, as in old MLA style, underlined)
- parentheses containing the place of publication, colon, the publisher, comma, and the date of publication
- the page number and a period at the end

Note that since 1984 MLA style has no period or comma between the title and the publication data, nor between that data and the page reference. The abbreviations *p.* or *pp.*, or *pg.* are not used. If the note continues to the next line, the second line begins at the margin. Footnotes or endnotes are single spaced internally, but double spaces separate each note.

In the text of your essay, the note is marked by a superscript number written slightly above the last word of your quotation and after all of the punctuation marks, like this.[1] The notes should be numbered consecutively with arabic numbers. The footnote (at the bottom of the page, added automatically by your word processor) or endnote (at the end of the essay) will read as follows:

[1] Northrop Frye, *Anatomy of Criticism: Four Essays* (Princeton: Princeton UP, 1957) 354.

Subsequent references to the same work, or to works by the same author, are kept as simple as possible:

[2] Frye 358. (a reference to the same work, different page)

MLA style does not use the abbreviations *ibid.* (the same) for a reference to the note or reference immediately preceding; *loc. cit.* (the location cited); or *op. cit.* (the work cited).

To refer to more than one book by an author, use an abbreviated title after the first full citation:

[3] Frye, *Great Code* 72–5.

For journal articles indent five spaces for the first line, and leave subsequent lines at the left margin. The author's name is given in normal order, followed by a comma. The title of the article is set in quotation marks, with a comma inside the last quotation mark; the title of the journal is set in italics or underlined, as is the volume number, and the date and page numbers are set as shown:

   4 Elaine Showalter, "Victorian Women and Insanity," *Victorian Studies 23* (1980): 157.

More complicated references also have conventional ways of setting them out: two authors (Jones and Black 91); more than one volume (Brown 2: 138); plays (*Macbeth* I. ii. 15); for other citation problems see the *MLA Handbook* or the *Chicago Manual*. Information about citation from the Writing Center at Purdue University is available from their Web site (**owl.english.purdue.edu/writers/by-topic.html**). The Web site **libweb.sonoma.edu/ instruction/guides/style/mlastyle.htm** provides a short guide on MLA style.

ANNOTATED BIBLIOGRAPHY

An annotated bibliography is a list of citations of books, articles, and other documents, including electronic sources. Each entry is followed by a brief description and evaluation of the citation. This annotation, or comment, informs a reader of the range and depth of the document referred to, and discusses its sources, validity, quality, and accuracy. The annotation is intended, therefore, to do two primary tasks:

- to describe the contents of the document, assessing its potential audience, level of difficulty, and range of coverage, and perhaps providing a quick overview of its contents
- to evaluate the relevance of the document and assess its accuracy and quality of argument

To create an annotated bibliography you will first have chosen (or will have been assigned) a specific topic. Perhaps an annotated bibliography is to be appended to one of your essays. You will have to decide what kind of coverage of the topic you wish to have in your bibliography. Do you want all of the books, articles, or Internet/electronic sources to be on one side of the argument? Do you wish to have a balance of pro and con positions? Should a variety of views on your topic be represented? Do you wish to have a balance between general and detailed treatments, scholarly and popular works? Whatever you decide, you need to gather about twice as many titles as you will finally use, and from those you make your informed selection.

You will have to examine and quickly review each of the texts to determine which are most appropriate. Then, you can create an entry for each citation, using the appropriate style, MLA or APA, or, if in science, CBE. You then add a short annotation that describes and evaluates the citation. Usually, each annotation is not more than four or five sentences or about 150 words. If you are preparing the annotated bibliography for an assignment, you should check with your instructor about whether it is acceptable to use fragments or point form in your annotations rather than complete sentences. If so, you can connect the fragments with semicolons.

You can add items to your annotated bibliography that might be useful to a reader, beyond those that you referred to in your list of works cited. You can also arrange the entries in categories ("Overviews of the Field," "Popular Treatments," and so on).

Your evaluation might consider the credentials of the author (institutional position, position in the field, past writings); the date of the work (republished, original date); the edition (first, revised); the publisher (how well known it is in the field); the reputation of the journal for an article and the range of the other articles in the issue; the audience (popular, educated, scholarly); the coverage in terms of providing new materials, updating old views or data, and dealing with primary materials (raw materials of the research process) or secondary materials (commentary on the primary materials); and how well reviewed the source has been. You might find reviews in the major book review indexes (*Book Review Digest, Book Review Index*).

After creating an annotated bibliography, you are well prepared to move into the writing of an essay. For some essays, an annotated bibliography is a valuable scholarly addition to the paper.

FURTHER READINGS

Amato, Carol J. *The World's Easiest Guide to Using the APA.* 2nd ed. Westminster, CA: Stargazer, 1999. Extracts available at www.stargazerpub.com/.

American Psychological Association (APA). *Publication Manual of the American Psychological Association.* 4th ed. Washington, DC: APA, 1994.

The Chicago Manual of Style. 14th ed. Chicago: U of Chicago P, 1993.

Gibaldi, Joseph, ed. *MLA Handbook for Writers of Research Papers.* 5th ed. New York: MLA, 1999. For senior high school and undergraduate university students.

Gibaldi, Joseph, ed. *MLA Style Manual and Guide to Scholarly Publishing.* 2nd ed. New York: MLA, 1998. For graduate students and scholars.

Li, Xia, and Nancy Crane. *Electronic Styles: A Handbook for Citing Electronic Information.* 2nd ed. Medford, NJ: Information Today, 1996. Includes both MLA and APA styles.

Walker, Janice R., and Todd Taylor. *The Columbia Guide to Online Style.* 1998. Columbia: Columbia UP, 1998.

WEBLINKS

Plagiarism

- Hamilton College
  www.hamilton.edu/academics/resource/wc/AvoidingPlagiarism.html

- University of Indiana
  www.indiana.edu/~wts/wts/plagiarism.html

- University of Minnesota
  condor.stcloud.msus.edu/~scogdill/339/paraphra.html
  This page deals with paraphrasing.

Documentation Style

- American Psychological Association: How to Cite Information from the Internet and the World Wide Web
  www.apa.org/journals/webref.html

- APA Style Guide
  www.stir.ac.uk/celt/study.htm

- Bibliographic Formats for Citing Electronic Information
  www.uvm.edu/~ncrane/estyles

- Bibliography Styles Handbook
  www.english.uiuc.edu/cws/wworkshop/bibliostyles.htm

- A Brief Citation Guide for Internet Sources in History and the Humanities
  www2.hnet.msu.edu/~africa/citation.html

- The Columbia Guide to Online Style
  www.columbia.edu/cu/cup/cgos/idx_basic.html

- James D. Lester. *Citing Cyberspace*
  longman.awl.com/englishpages/

- Guidelines for Writing in APA Style
  www.ldl.net/~bill/apatwo.htm

  Includes model pages for formatting an essay in APA style.

- MLA Style
  www.mla.org

- Online! Web page to accompany Andrew Harnack and Eugene Kleppinger. *Online!* New York: St. Martin's, 1997.
  www.bedfordstmartins.com/online/index.html

PREPARING THE FINAL COPY

Some students move immediately from the first draft to the final draft, revising the first draft on the computer and printing the final copy all in one exercise, perhaps even the night before the essay is due. Such horrors happen to all of us. But we urge one important and additional step, even in cases of emergency. If you do not treat the final draft as a separate stage of writing and put a proper amount of time into preparing that draft before submitting it, a great deal of hard work that went into the previous stages will be lost. In this chapter, we go through a logical order, from revision to proofing, and then to printing, which establishes a method for the final stage of writing your essay.

FROM THE FIRST DRAFT TO THE FINAL COPY

Format of the Final Copy

The final copy should be set out in a format acceptable to your reader. You should type or write on one side of the sheet only. A formal paper should be double spaced, on standard letter-size paper with ample margins: about one and one-half inches on the left and one inch on the other margins, or one inch on all sides, according to the *MLA Handbook,* the APA *Publication Manual,* and the *Chicago Manual of Style.* Length of assignments usually assumes "pica" pitch or twelve point for about 250 words to the page. A smaller font will be too difficult to read. As well, the trick of using a large font and wide margins in order to stretch a short essay to fit the minimum number of pages is immediately recognizable to a reader and gives a bad initial impression. You should check with your instructor whether the MLA style or APA style is the preferred model for setting out the format of your essay.

Title Page and Title

A separate title page is not usually required, but many students use them. If used, it should contain the essay title (without quotation marks, unless a quotation is included; book titles are set in italics), your name, the course and section number, and the date. If you give the title on the first page of the essay, the same information should be included. Spelling mistakes on the title page, such as in the instructor's name (which happens more often than you might think), set you off on the wrong foot.

   If you do not use a title page, you need to give the title on the first page of the essay. The title should be set two inches from the top of the sheet and should be double spaced if it runs to more than one line. Three spaces separate the title from the first line of text.

Paragraph Format

Usually, the first line of a paragraph is indented five spaces, except for the first paragraph, which is customarily not indented. In books that convention can be observed readily at the beginning of any chapter. Some writers also leave a larger space between paragraphs to mark them off, which is particularly useful in single-spaced typewritten documents. However, essays for class submission should always be double spaced.

Page Format

Pages are numbered throughout. The title page is unnumbered. The first page is numbered at the bottom. Margins should be one inch on all sides, unless you are instructed otherwise. Footnotes are at the bottom of each page; endnotes have a separate page, followed by the works cited page. Your name should be included on each page in case the pages become separated.

Proofreading

After writing or typing the final copy, you should go over it again to correct any typing or other errors. It is always useful to have a knowledgeable friend read the paper at this stage. You might have to retype a page or two, but the results will be worth it. Then, you can use your computer's spell checker on your final draft and use a good dictionary to check the meanings of unfamiliar, technical, or analytical words. Finally, you should read the draft you plan to hand in again to find any of the mistakes that the spell checker has not found, such as words that are spelled correctly but that are the wrong words. After the final revision and printing, you can make any necessary corrections on the final copy in ink if they are done neatly. However, you should retype or reprint major revisions on a page. It is important that you keep a copy of your paper and retain your rough notes and drafts.

Final Steps Before Submission

In moving from your working draft to preparing your final copy, you might consider the following steps:

1. When you have completed your working draft, save it both on your hard drive in the assignment file and on a floppy with a short essay title followed by the suffix .dft (draft). The floppy is for this assignment only, to be kept until the end of the year as insurance, showing the stages you reached in preparing your draft.

2. Print a copy of your working draft.

3. Relax. Then, with a pen or pencil read over your printed copy, as though you were a new reader looking at this piece of work for the first time, seeking to understand the argument and its transitions. This step in the revision process accomplishes two things. First, it makes you into a more objective editor than when you were writing on the computer, since going through your essay in the printed medium will help you to look at your writing in a fresh way. Second, it helps you to spot errors in punctuation, spelling, grammar, logic, and argument, as these mistakes are easier to see on the page than on the screen. It is particularly important to vet the work that the spell checker has done to ensure that no errors, such as words spelled correctly but misused, have crept in (such as *there* for *their*).

4. After you have gone through your final draft carefully, return to the computer, and make the changes you noted.

5. Then, pay attention to the formatting requirements, the references, and all of the finishing details that are necessary. All word processors assist with formatting type size, italics, boldface (which should be used sparingly and in places where you are certain it makes sense), or other variations, and with monitoring indents, tabs, and the like. Some word processors allow you to see the codes that are used to position such formatting. WordPerfect in all of its versions, for instance, allows a writer to use "reveal codes" to make these changes. Next, use the spell checker again. When you are through, save the copy to hard drive and to assignment floppy with a new suffix, .fnl (final), and print two copies, one to hand in and a second copy to keep in your course file.

6. Read through the essay once more for any last-minute mistakes, and correct them in ink. Many otherwise well argued papers are marred by slips and mistakes that are not caught in the final proofreading, an indication of a rushed or careless approach in the last stages of preparation.

SPECIAL CONSIDERATIONS FOR THE COMPUTER PRINTOUT

Formatting

Your word processor allows you to make systematic changes to a number of variables in preparing your final copy. Often, these variables will already be set up on your computer for your regular work. Many writers prefer to have them in place for the second or writing stage of assignment preparation. Formatting choices (accessible through the Layout or other relevant index tab or key) include the following:

1. *Page settings.* You should set the top and bottom margins at one inch and turn on the page numbering option to number your pages throughout.

2. *Page numbering.* The Layout → Page icon or tab gives a number of choices about page numbering. Normally, pages are numbered at the top right corner, except for the first page, which is numbered at the bottom centre. If a title page is used, it is not numbered. Page 1 is the first page of the essay. In any case, you need to be certain that your essay is numbered throughout, even if you have to enter the page numbers by hand after the final copy for submission is printed.

3. *Line settings.* You should set the left and right margins at one inch, justification at left justify, and tabs at the default setting of one-half inch.

4. *Spacing.* The essay should be double spaced throughout by changing the default setting of one space in the Layout → Line tab or key option. Long quotations may be indented one-half inch by using the Indent key and may be single spaced.

5. *Justification.* Justification refers to the way your line is filled out with spaces to give even edges on the left, right, or both margins. It is customary in essays and assignments to justify all text flush left, so that the left margin is even throughout and the right margin is ragged. Long quotations and quotations of poetry are indented so that each line of the quotation is also aligned with the indent.

Fonts

All word processors allow you to change fonts and font sizes. Most programs have a variety of the most common and popular fonts built in; other fonts can be bought or can be downloaded from the Internet if you wish further choice. Fonts have special names and belong to families that often have long histories, tied to the ancient civilizations of Jerusalem, Greece, and Rome, as well as to other forms of writing in central Europe, Russia, South Asia, and East Asia. In the Latin alphabet, used in English and other languages, our letter forms or shapes derive from the writing used in monuments, inscriptions, and manuscripts in ancient Rome and as modified during the European Renaissance with the development of literacy and printing. The "black letter" forms used by the monks in their handwritten manuscripts were used in the first printed books, but that style soon gave way to the forms we know and use today, the roman face (in which the letters stand upright on the line) and the italic face (in which the letters slant to the right, based on Italian court or chancery handwriting from the Renaissance). Fonts are also divided into those that have little feet on them (called serif) and those that do not (called sans serif).

Choice of Font

You should choose a highly legible and conventional font for your assignment and leave the fancy fonts to your birthday cards, or, perhaps, title page (if you have time). For the body of your essay, you may choose a font from among the following:

- *roman serif faces:* Baskerville, Caslon, Garamond, Goudy, Times Roman, or another standard roman font. Courier is a conventional roman serif typewriter-like font that is available on all word processors. All of these fonts also have italic versions, which are invoked automatically by your word processor when you use the italic font option.

- *roman sans serif faces:* Gill, Helvetica, Sans, Univers, or another standard roman sans serif face. Again, each has an italic version used automatically by your word processor.

Font Attributes

You should not use an italic font throughout your paper or set off quotations in italics (unless they are set in italics in the original). Italics should be reserved for specific purposes, such as book and movie titles. Words to be emphasized can be printed in italics or in boldface (printed darker). Some writers use boldface for subheadings in a long paper with subdivisions, but boldface or subheadings are usually not needed or useful in a shorter essay. Similarly, you should not use an unusual, decorative, or ornamental font throughout your essay to pretty it up; it is hard to read, and so fails to communicate your ideas effectively.

Font Size

Font size should not be smaller than eleven point (or ten characters per inch). Some fonts print smaller than others, so that, for instance, Garamond twelve point is about the same size as Times Roman eleven point. You should be aware that your assessor probably has a lot of essays to read and, thus, needs a font that is not too small. On the other hand, using a large font with large margins will not hide the fact that your essay is too short.

Graphics, Graphs, or Charts

Many other features are available to you in using the computer for your essays and other assignments. For instance, you can incorporate appropriate graphics into your writing to make a point, to add a pertinent illustration, or to provide an example. A graphic illustration, however, should contribute to the content and argument of your paper, and it should not be added merely to jazz up the page. It should also be accompanied by an explanation or comment. For instance, if you are writing on the art of the period of the French Revolution and want to discuss David's painting *The Death of Marat,* an illustration of the painting in your paper would be useful. You can do that in one of two ways. The older method is to photocopy an illustration and add the extra page to your printout, referring to it as "Figure 1" (and citing the source in your annotation and list of works cited). The newer method is to scan the image in (if you have access to a scanner) or download the image from the Internet.

Other possibilities include using graphics from the Web (such as illustrations from newspapers or magazines, especially for essays on popular culture or related themes), graphs or charts (for instance, showing population or land use, or other data in a schematic way), or summary tables of information. In each case, you will have to explain your illustration or other graphic and integrate it into your argument. Gussying up your paper with happy faces or graphics of Homer Simpson mooning the reader will not predispose that reader to take you seriously.

Printouts

Any printer attached to your computer, whether a dot matrix, ink or colour jet, bubble jet, or laser printer, can do a good job of printing your final copy. As with a typewriter, however, you need to be certain that you have an inked ribbon in your dot matrix printer or that your cartridges for other printers are sufficiently full. If you have changed your formatting drastically for your final paper, you should make certain that you have enough time to test your printer before you begin to print your final copy. Some printers do not take kindly to formatting changes; others readily adapt. If your printer has the capability of colour printing, you should use this feature sparingly or for strategic effect. You are not doing a layout for a glossy magazine, where headings should be in a fancy type with rainbow colours. On the other hand, some art reproductions, graphic charts, or tables benefit from appropriate use of colour.

Other Formats for Submitting Drafts and Essays

Drafts and Print Copies

Some instructors require you to submit working drafts, which they comment on before you submit the final paper. Others will read drafts if you are worried about your approach. Most are willing to discuss difficulties you are having in writing an essay. You should check with your instructor about whether you need to make an appointment for an office visit. As well, you should ask whether drafts can be submitted electronically, and if so, in what format. Courtesy requires that you do all that you can to submit your writing in a format that your instructor can read.

Floppy Disks

Some instructors now accept essays submitted on three-and-a-half-inch floppy disks. When submitting a paper on disk, you should keep a copy on a floppy. You probably will get back your paper with additions or corrections made on disk, and your instructor will also have made of a copy of the comments added during the marking process. Often, this procedure means that you get precise and detailed comment, but it might also be that you get a general comment at the end, without detailed correction throughout. You should check with your instructor concerning the preferred word processor and formatting you should use if papers may be submitted on floppies. Also, you need to find out how the instructor will mark them. Some instructors use boldface to add editorial comments, corrections, and suggestions for revision, which would be a problem if you had used a lot of boldface in your essay.

E-mail

Some instructors will accept drafts, and perhaps even the final essay, via e-mail. If you wish to use this procedure, you should check which format would be preferred. It is usually best to write a note to your instructor stating that you are enclosing the essay and then include the essay as an attachment. Most e-mail programs, such as Eudora, Pegasus, and Pine, as well as the e-mail functions on Netscape Navigator and Microsoft Explorer, allow attachments, though you must have the essay already prepared and formatted in a separate, designated file that you indicate when choosing the attachment option.

Network or Conferencing

Some courses use a special network arrangement or a program such as Powerpoint for the whole class, and students are invited to set up conferencing procedures to share ideas, writing samples, and even papers in process or final copies for peer evaluation. Sometimes, such courses allow students to submit final papers electronically over the network to the instructor alone; after it is marked it may or may not be shared with other students, according to the procedures of the course. Samples of such courses are abundant on the Internet, and if you are involved in such a course, you might be interested in consulting some of these sites (see **users.ccnet.com/~bmckinne/cheklist.htm**).

FURTHER READINGS

Rosa, Alfred, Paul Escholz, and John Roberts. *The Writer's Brief Handbook*. 2nd ed. Scarborough, ON: Allyn and Bacon, 1999.

Troyka, Lynn Quitman, and Cy Strom. *Simon and Schuster Quick Access: A Reference for Writers*. Toronto: Prentice Hall; Allyn and Bacon Canada, 2000.

Wilson, Wendy. *Print Out: Using the Computer to Write*. Toronto: Harcourt Brace, 1994.

WEBLINKS

Formatting

*   Bibliography Styles Handbook
    APA style: www.english.uiuc.edu/cws/wworkshop/apamenu.htm
    MLA style: www.english.uiuc.edu/cws/wworkshop/mlamenu.htm
    old MLA style: www.english.uiuc.edu/cws/wworkshop/oldmlamenu.htm

*   Psychology with Style: A Hypertext Writing Guide (APA)
    www.uwsp.edu/acad/psych/apa4b.htm

*   Psych Web Page
    www.psychwww.com/resource/apacrib.htm

    Provides a detailed list of APA formatting and style sheets.

Graphics

See the many art sites, such as the following:

*   ArtSource
    www.ilpi.com/artsource/artsourcehome.html

*   Internet ArtResources
    artsources.com/

*   World Wide Arts Resources
    wwar.com/

THE MARKED ASSIGNMENT AND WHAT TO DO ABOUT IT

Chapter

RECOGNIZING CORRECTION SYMBOLS

Many students get back papers with very few correction marks on them and wonder how their instructors want them to improve. The essay may contain appreciative and evaluative comments, but there may be few instructions about how to develop ideas, correct faults in expression or argument, or push the analysis further. Most instructors have many papers to mark and have limited time to make corrections. Some instructors mark in great detail, covering each page with corrections. Some markers give attention to one long paragraph, page, or section, marking it in detail. This kind of marking breaks down the whole argument into pieces and critiques the expression, grammar, and analysis. If you receive a paper marked in detail you are fortunate, because the instructor has taken your argument and analysis seriously.

It may be difficult for you to recognize what is important in all of the markings on the page. How can you determine what is most significant and to what you should give your attention before the next assignment? What, on the other hand, are the improvements or corrections in expression that might help you to put your case better? You need to be able to distinguish between corrections of major faults or serious flaws in grammar and more trivial corrections. Your instructor can help with this task, but you should be aware of some of the problems yourself.

First, you should correct serious faults in grammar. These faults include major problems with the comma (the comma splice, or the run-on sentence), with omitted or partial verbs or writing in clauses instead of complete sentences (the sentence fragment), and with faulty agreements between subject and verb. Faults like these will seriously inhibit a reader's comprehension of your argument, no matter how carefully you have tried to work it out. Second, on the level of argument, you should examine any circumstances the marker has noted where your evidence does not support your case or where there are serious problems in the continuity of your argument. A lack of continuity might involve poor essay organization (missing bridges from paragraph to paragraph or inadequate cause-and-effect sequences), or it might involve an inadequate thesis statement and supporting arguments. In either case, you should examine carefully the way that you have put your essay together.

Other common faults include missing the point of the assignment, failing to pursue the argument in enough detail, failing to support the argument with sufficient evidence, and neglecting to refer to detailed examples. Each of these gaps can be remedied in a rewrite, although you should have caught them in the earlier stages of essay preparation and writing. Using an essay-writing checklist would be helpful (see pages 240–241).

When you get your paper back, there may be many marks and abbreviations on the page that you do not understand. Some are quite mystifying. You need to be aware that many markers use the conventions developed by copy editors of manuscripts for publication. Hence, the Greek letter delta (δ) is often used to indicate that a letter, word, or phrase should be deleted. Or the number sign (#) is used to indicate that a space should be inserted where the mark is made, or where the slash-with-a-tail (the caret) is inserted into your text. The following chart lists the various marks that are generally used in the correction of essays, with the abbreviation and a comment on what the mark means. If there are other correction marks that you cannot read or understand on your marked essay, you should ask your instructor for clarification.

Correction Marks

abbrev	abbreviation
adj	adjective needed or wrong
adv	adverb required
agr	faulty subject–verb agreement
ambig	ambiguous
amp &	ampersand: write *and* out
apost	apostrophe
awk	awkward phrase
bridge	weak link between arguments or paragraphs
case	wrong case of pronoun, often *who* for *whom*
CB	comma blunder or comma splice
cf	Latin, *confer,* compare
clar	clarify unclear language or argument; needs rewriting
colloq	colloquial use
comp	comparative form of adj. is needed
concl	conclusion does not follow from argument
conj	wrong conjunction
contract	contraction (e.g., *they're, I'll*): spell out
coord	coordinate stces with coordinating conj. because ideas are related
CS	comma splice

d or δ	delete
dang part	dangling participle
det	details needed to substantiate argument here
dic	diction faulty: use dictionary or thesaurus
dict	consult dictionary
doc	documentation needed
e.g.	Latin, *exempli gratia*, for example; distinguish from *i.e.*
ellip or ...	ellipsis: three spaced periods to indicate omitted material, followed by terminal pc if at end of stce
frag	sentence fragment
gr	grammar faulty
1/2 stce.	half sentence
hy	hyphen
idiom	idiomatic usage required
i.e.	Latin, *id est*, that is; distinguish from *e.g.*
infin	infinitive needed or is split by other words
irrel	irrelevant material or argument
ital	indicate italics by underlining or print in italics
jar	jargon
lc	lower case needed
log	logic faulty
mod	modifier misplaced
nar	narrative being retold, not analyzed
non seq	Latin, *non sequitur*, it does not follow; a logical fault
no ¶	no paragraph
obs	obsolete or obscure
omit——	omit when line is drawn through words; do not use parentheses for omissions
p., pp.	page, pages
par ‖	parallelism weak
¶ para	paragraph problem or start new paragraph
parachuted quot	introduce stand-alone quotation with phrase and author's name
pass	passive verb construction; use active voice
pc	punctuation problem
pl	plural
poss	possessive problem
pron	pronoun problem or reference
QED	Latin, *quod erat demonstrandum*: what should be argued is only asserted

quest ?	reader questions validity of marked passage
quote(s)	quotation marks or use needs correction
red	redundant/unnecessary
ref	reference of pronoun or argument is unclear
rep	repetition
run on	run-on sentence: two sentences joined without punctuation
slang	lapse in appropriate language for audience
sp	spelling mistake
split infin	remove word that splits the infinitive
stce	sentence, sentence structure faulty
syllab	syllabification breaks faulty: check dictionary
tense	verb tenses not in agreement
tr or trans	transpose
ts	topic sentence absent
uc	upper case, capitals
v or vb	verb problems
vulg	vulgarism, inappropriate for formal essay
ww	wrong word
δ	delete (Greek letter delta)
← →	move in direction indicated
¶	paragraph
‖	parallelism
?	query, question the passage; meaning unclear
#	space needed where indicated
∩	reduce space to close up text
/ or ^	to locate correction

REWRITING YOUR MARKED PAPER

If you have spent some time thinking about and writing an assignment, chances are that you can consolidate your learning and understanding by carefully rewriting the assignment. Even if you were rushed and did not give an adequate amount of time to the work you handed in, you would profit from a rewrite. You might have been confused about some aspects of the argument or of the readings, you might have been uncertain about how to best arrange the points you wanted to stress, or you might have been imprecise in arguing your case or expressing it. You might have received a good grade but are not sure what exactly you did right. Whatever your grade, and however you performed, a revision will help you understand and improve your knowledge of this particular aspect of the course. In addition, you will have the sense that you have understood the assignment better and can now move on to the next stage of the course with a better grasp of its materials. Finally, you will be much better prepared for writing your next assignment. For all of these reasons, it is a good idea to rewrite at least some of your papers.

There is, of course, another very important reason for rewriting—to improve your grade on the assignment. Your instructor might announce in class whether he or she is willing to accept a rewritten paper. Some instructors never do, some always do, and still others set out specific regulations: you must hand in the rewritten essay within so long of the original due date of the assignment, you can choose one assignment per semester to rewrite, or the instructor will read a rewritten essay but will not change the grade, and so on. If your instructor has not clarified such conditions, you should check with him or her about the policy on rewriting and grade changes. Even if a grade change is not possible, you should ask whether it is possible for your instructor to read a rewritten paper. You can still benefit from such a rewriting exercise.

In almost every case an instructor will want you to resubmit the original marked assignment with your rewritten paper in order to be clear about how well you have profited from the rethinking stage and to see in detail how you have revised your work.

If you decide to rewrite your assignment, you should be very clear about the terms of the assignment, about what your instructor's markings on your paper mean, and about what your purpose is in revising. An office interview with your instructor can help to clarify these procedures and goals.

LEARNING FROM YOUR MARKER'S COMMENTS

When many instructors hand back assignments in class, they make detailed comments about how well the class understood and executed the assignment. Those comments can be of the greatest help in the process of rewriting. When papers are given back, you may be too embarrassed to even look at the grades or marks on your paper. You should try to get over this block, and read the corrections on the paper carefully. It is important that you ask about any corrections that are unclear and that you know before you leave the class the instructor's policy about rewrites.

Above all, when the assignment is taken up in class, you should mark down on your own paper or in your notebook the instructor's comments on the major faults or problems in understanding or writing the assignment. Often, those comments will be on points that directly concern you and your work, and they will indicate ways in which you might improve, either in a rewrite now or in preparation for a future assignment. Grade profiles for

---

TIPS: Rewriting

1. Ask your instructor if rewriting is allowed.
2. Be clear about whether or not the grade can be changed.
3. Find out if it is possible for the grade to be lowered if the revision is not sufficiently careful or thorough.
4. Make an appointment with your instructor to go over your paper in detail before you consider a rewrite.
5. Resubmit the original marked assignment with the rewrite.

the assignment will indicate where you stand in relation to the rest of the class and can help to guide you in revising an assignment.

Requesting an Office Interview

If there is any point on your paper that you are unclear about, or if the assignment went completely over your head, it is a good idea to make an appointment to see your instructor in his or her office. Above all, if you are unclear about rewriting, would like to rewrite, or have been asked by your instructor to rewrite, you should make an appointment to go over the paper in detail.

University instructors hold office hours, and you can take advantage of these special times set aside for consultation. Many students do not realize that office consultation is a regular and expected part of university instruction. You should think about the assignment before you come to the office and reread your paper and the assignment topic so that you are well prepared. You will want to have some questions in mind (you might want to write some of them down). By referring to them, you are showing to your instructor the seriousness of your intent and indicating that you have given the matter some thought beforehand. You should also bring your marked assignment and any books that are central to your essay, such as a particular novel, play, or historical document that you wrote your paper about. It might be that your instructor will want you to reconsider some aspect of this document that you dealt with in your paper. If your paper was a research paper for which you went to the library or did work on the Internet, you should bring your rough notes and any other materials that were helpful to you in your preparation. Often, a particular problem can be traced to some difficulty in taking notes, evaluating information, or constructing arguments at the planning stage.

You should also have some idea of how long you can spend in the interview. Some instructors are greatly pressed for office time and can afford only five or ten minutes for a first meeting; others are able to give up to half an hour for concentrated work like this. If you need more time, you should ask whether you can book another appointment soon, perhaps outside of regular office hours so that you can spend more time discussing your assignment.

When you are in the office, you need to state your reason for coming and then produce your marked assignment and ask the instructor to go over the first few pages so you will understand the instructor's intention in marking the assignment. Usually, an instructor will want to look over the marked assignment quickly to get a grasp of the mistakes that were pointed out. He or she will then begin the process of reevaluation and will make comments, ask questions about what you meant here or there, and explain any of the points in the marking scheme that are unclear to you. Your job at this point is to respond to and absorb what is being discussed. This office interview is an important part of your learning experience, and most instructors are efficient and helpful in leading you through the process. It is not intended to be a mini-examination, or a grilling about what you might have done on your paper. Instead, it is an opportunity for you to understand better what you have written and for the instructor to explain the terms and expectations concerning the assignment and your performance in meeting those expectations. At this stage you should be ready to make notes quickly and efficiently, perhaps on your paper, or, more usefully, in your notebook, so that you can refer to them later in detail. You will not be able to take down all that your instructor is saying, but you should make heading notes of the main points and write them up as soon as possible after the office interview.

Conceptual and Mechanical Problems

If your instructor has not gone over the conceptual problems in your paper, you should ask for advice about its major conceptual defects and understand them before you get down to details. You need to try to distinguish between the conceptual problems that you have in understanding the topic and the problems you might have in expressing those ideas. You should try to find out what the strong points of your argument are in the estimation of your instructor, and also what areas of your paper need improvement. Are there any exercises that he or she could recommend to help you in formulating these concepts better? Did you have problems in understanding the reading for this assignment? If so, you should ask whether you can go over that reading again, now, or look at a short passage with the instructor to see whether you are getting the right points out of what you are reading.

When you are clear about the major conceptual strengths and weaknesses of your paper, you may wish to look again at the mechanical problems in your writing and expression. Again, you should ask your instructor what he or she considers to be the major problems in your writing style. Are there problems with the organization of your argument, your thesis statement, topic sentences for paragraphs, or grammar and punctuation? Your instructor can suggest ways to work on those problems and may suggest exercises, perhaps on the Internet, that you could undertake to overcome these defects. Remember that you are at this interview to get help for rewriting your assignment and for improving your grades in this and the next assignments in this course. Before you leave the office, you need to be certain that you understand the kinds of writing faults that you make and how you can overcome them.

Problems in General Comprehension and Analysis of the Topic

You need to look more carefully and systematically at problems in general comprehension of your topic. If you have seriously misunderstood the assignment or the readings involved, you have to get to the bottom of *why* you misunderstood, so that you do not make the same mistake again. Had you missed the relevant lectures or seminars in which the work was discussed? Were your notes on these matters unclear or incomplete? If either of these problems fits your case, the answer is not hard to find: be certain to attend the classes around the time when assignments are due and take as complete and careful notes as you can. Often, a lecturer will comment in detail on the requirements for an assignment, will give special instruction in a seminar, or will answer specific questions that students ask about the assignment.

If the reasons for your misunderstanding really do result from failing to comprehend the course materials, you should use the office time to try to understand them. You should state exactly what it is that you do not understand. Or, if you do not know where to begin (which is often the case for many students), you should say so and ask how you should first move to understand the readings or the topic.

The next stage is to consider the defects in your analysis. Often, these defects will result from a failure to ask appropriate and searching questions of your materials in order to answer the problem in the assignment. You might try formulating a different set of questions to see what each set of questions prompts you toward in terms of an analysis. You might bring these questions to the office interview and ask your instructor what set of questions he or she thinks would yield the best results.

You also need to examine the stages in your argument. You should go back over Chapter 7 in this book, which deals with the organization of an argument, and see whether you have met those objectives. Your instructor might have marked on your assignment various places where your argument does not measure up, through lack of appropriate evidence, a weak balance of general points and detail, faults in logic, an inability to get beneath the surface of the materials, or an argument based on a too cursory or superficial reading of the materials. For any of these cases, you need to see what kinds of materials would be more appropriate and what kinds of arguments would best present them. When you come to the office appointment, it is a good idea to have some of these materials ready and to have thought about them beforehand.

Your aim should be the general improvement of the entire assignment. However, if time is short (either yours or your instructor's), you should try to leave the office with at least one page clear in your head, understanding the revisions that are recommended there, related both to conceptual argument and to mechanical expression in proper grammar and clear punctuation.

Having understood at least one page of the corrections and the marking scheme, you can then ask how you can extend that page throughout the whole assignment. Or, even better, you can state how you believe you can extend what you have learned throughout the paper. You should ask if there are any important dangers or pitfalls that you should watch for in your own argument or in the topic generally. Before you leave the interview, you should summarize in your own words what you understand about the main points that you will need to rewrite. You also need to be clear about the due date for resubmission and any other details.

SUBMITTING THE REWRITTEN ESSAY OR PREPARING FOR THE NEXT ESSAY

It is important to ask your instructor what you should submit with the rewritten assignment. Usually, you should hand in the marked copy of the assignment with your revision. But other materials might also be required, such as rough notes, outlines, or reading notes. You should keep all of these for each assignment, together with the marked and returned assignment, until the end of the year. They serve as protection for you in the case of appeals, difficulties in completing the year, faculty labour disputes, health problems, and many other possibilities. It is important that you submit the final rewrite on time (as agreed with your instructor), along with any other materials.

SUBMITTING DRAFTS OR OUTLINES FOR COMMENT

Many students ask whether an instructor will read outlines or drafts of essays. Many faculty will readily agree to do so, especially for students who have shown that they can profit from in-office advice. Usually, an instructor will suggest what forms of draft will be acceptable for reading and will indicate whether they will be marked or commented upon orally. You will, of course, be well aware of the deadlines for the finished assignment and should be prepared to hand in a draft or outline, if it is acceptable, well in advance of the due date. You should check with your instructor about an appropriate timetable. It is likely that you will be doing this work before the materials have been covered in class, so you might want an earlier office meeting to check your interpretation of the materials and topic for the assignment.

You should be prepared to suggest what kinds of drafts would be most helpful, from your viewpoint, to submit. Also, you need to be clear about whether you should submit these drafts or outlines, marked or not, with your final assignment, or whether they are for your own preparation only. If your instructor is willing to read a draft or outline, you should submit it double spaced and with questions included about places in the argument where you are uncertain about meaning or interpretation. You also should try to make the outline or draft as clear and complete as possible in order to get the most benefit from your instructor's reading. Finally, you should use the information gained from the marked draft or outline to improve the preparation of the final version of your assignment.

The rewrite stage, then, can greatly contribute to your comprehension of a particular stage of a course and will help you to move on to the next stage with understanding and confidence.

WEBLINKS

- Making the Grade
  www.waikato.ac.nz/humanities/history/mtg_main.html

  A site from the History Department of the University of Waikato.

- Student Conferences
  darkwing.uoregon.edu/~uocomp/confer.html

  A University of Oregon site.

PART SIX
EXAMINATIONS

PREPARING FOR AND WRITING EXAMS

Chapter

RECOGNIZING THE OPPORTUNITY TO PERFORM

Like death and taxes, examinations are inevitable. They come with the territory. All over the world the spring rituals of agony are played out in different ways. In India the largest halls are taken over for the dreaded procedures. In Japan students and parents alike scan the results of examinations to determine who will succeed, who will not. At Oxford a week of daily examinations in formal dress is the culmination of the B.A. degree, celebrated with friends immediately after the last examination by uncorking champagne bottles in the quadrangle. And in North America examination time brings the familiar sight of chairs lined up in the gymnasium before desks, where brain and memory are put to the test on the examination paper.

Bound up with tradition, and a characteristic of university teaching from the early middle ages, the examination is the culmination of a course, its climax, when a teacher sets out those questions that will push every student in a limited time to draw the course together, to make sense of it, and to show what he or she knows. Term examinations and in-class tests are good preparations for the final examination, but it is the final examination that carries most of the weight. Gone, in most instances, are the courses in which the grade depends entirely on this final exercise. Examinations now make up a part of a grade, often about a quarter to a third, and so are weighed along with all kinds of other assignments. This rearrangement, at least in North America, has very much reduced examination anxiety.

The threat of the examination hangs over a course from the moment the instructor hands out the syllabus and describes the tests and exams in the course. And the threat is the motive for that banal and all-too-common bleat of the anxious student, "Are we expected to know this for the exam?" as though the teacher were simply passing out optional information, just to hear him- or herself talk at random about whatever topic comes into his or her head, or as if the course were so full of data that no student could possibly be expected to digest it for an examination. In fact, most teachers are clear about what will be on examinations, and many go to great lengths to explain the format and kinds of questions beforehand, sometimes even giving samples or setting out limits on the kinds of things that students will be examined on.

An examination is an important exercise for you to perform and excel in (it *is* a performance, and as in other art forms, the rules, moves, and procedures can be learned and perfected). Here is an opportunity to pull up a borderline grade and to bring a body of learning into focus. After all, you have been studying this material for a term, or for a year, and have already invested a good deal of money, time, and intellectual effort in this course. Here is the occasion for you to bring it all off. It used to be claimed that examinations are an important life experience, forcing you to concentrate in a situation of tension your ability to recall, think through, analyze, and organize a body of material. And it is true that many people will undergo other tests later in life, perhaps not written summaries and analyses of intellectual content in a specific disciplinary field, but possibly tests to show their competence in a job and in a variety of life skills. Above all, however, the examination is an opportunity for pulling together all that you have been working on in a course over a long period of time, for learning it afresh and in an integrated way, and for demonstrating your control over that learning. In this chapter we examine various resources that you can draw on as you prepare for examinations, we consider problems you might face, and we work through different procedures for different kinds of examinations. Finally, we consider ways of reducing examination anxiety, and we provide a survival kit to use before, during, and after the examination.

ORGANIZING YOUR TIME, RESOURCES, AND METHODS

Examination skills depend not on doing far more work than other students, but on taking advantage of all of the learning opportunities that are offered in a course and bringing them into systematic focus during the weeks and days before the examination. Many studies have been devoted to knowledge retention rates. Generally, they demonstrate that without any systematic effort to keep your academic work up-to-date, without weekly and monthly reviews, you will have forgotten more than 80 percent of what you have read and heard in lectures over a four-month period. The effort required to pull that percentage up to an acceptable level in two or three days is enormous. But if you have consolidated your work regularly with reviews, you will have retained about 80 percent by the end of the year and will be in excellent shape to prepare for writing the examination (see Walter Pauk for the grim details about forgetting and retention rates and examination performance in *How to Study in College* 168–69).

Bringing your work into focus for the examination requires mobilizing several of your resources. First, you have to be crucially conscious of time. You will be under a lot of pressure to complete courses, assignments, and readings in the final weeks before a test or examination, and other sorts of details will interfere, such as moving and interviewing for summer or permanent jobs. So you need a schedule of your courses, with a note about which courses have term tests (with their dates), which have final examinations, and the weight attached to each exam. When the final weeks before the examinations approach, you are faced with a series of critical judgments:

- Decide which course is in the best shape, and which one is in the worst. Arrange your time to devote a proportion to each course. Block off the time in large sections, so that you have a morning, an afternoon, or an evening for a specific task that can be completed within that time.

- From your examination schedule calculate how best to divide your study time according to the timetable and your preparedness.

Second, you have to consider your resources.

- Assemble all of your resources for a particular course together. That would include your lecture notes, tutorial notes, essays and rough notes, other assignments, notes for class presentations (your own and others'), the books for your course, reading notes on course textbooks and other books, library research notes, and so on. Generally, some of this material will be in good shape, but some will have gaps. Make certain that you have a complete set of notes and go over them to make sure they are together and in order.

- Go over your lecture and seminar notes with highlighters or other markers. Note in the margins the terms in one colour if you have not already done so. You will have saved a lot of time if you had already prepared your lecture notes week by week in this way. Also, note any concepts that are developed in the lectures, and on separate sheets begin your summaries—of terms, of concepts, and so on.

- Gather your reading notes together, along with the annotations in the assigned books in your course. You should already have some summaries available. Some will be in the course kits, some will be in your lecture notes, and some you will have made during your reading and studying for that part of the course. If you are missing any of these summaries that are readily available, get them in order now.

- Be realistic in your assessment of what you can do. If you have not read or finished reading some of the books on the course (and who has not been there?), do not try to read them now. Instead, find the summaries to fill in the gaps.

Having mapped out your time and assembled your course materials, you are ready to develop a method for moving to the actual preparation for the examination:

- Begin to make your lists of key terms, concepts, arguments, examples, and other details. Put the summaries of course readings together and start to assess them on the basis of similarities and differences.

- Look closely at the last few lectures on the course for clues about the test or examination. Most instructors give detailed comment about what is expected and what kinds of questions might be on an exam.

- The last lecture or seminar is often a summary of the course, just as the opening lecture or section of the course is often a general introduction. Put these two kinds of materials together for a quick overview. Then, move to your own summaries and charts or study sheets.

MAKING SUMMARIES OF THE COURSE: FROM THE SYLLABUS TO THE EXAM

Understanding Course Patterns and Design

At this stage your greatest resource is your syllabus for the course and your course kit (if one is used). These documents set out the goals of the course, usually in a general way, and set out the lectures week by week, providing an overview of the year. Often, the syllabus will contain general materials or weekly assignments that greatly amplify the overall concept and intention of the course, its intellectual goals, and the kinds of skills that you are expected to have mastered.

From this understanding of the course concepts and goals, you can move in your preparation to try to formulate the conceptual framework of the course. What are the assumptions about knowledge, human nature, the discipline? What are the first principles of the course? How many are there? Can you state them? Is there one basic concept on which all of the rest of the course depends? (You need to beware here, lest you oversimplify what is a complex subject.) You should be able to formulate some of these principles and basic concepts to organize the course.

Now, you can look for the development of ideas. Throughout this book, we have stressed the linking of critical thinking to skills in organizing an argument. As the course comes to a close, you have to draw on those skills to see how the course was developed. You can do so by asking yourself a set of questions: Does this course depend on a series of more or less separate sections with little connection? On the other hand, is the course a progression of ideas, each building on the last? Do the same words recur in the syllabus from week to week as the lectures are outlined? If your instructors wrote outlines on the board for each lecture, was there similarity in the terminology and concepts used there? How are they arranged?

It is probable that there are large sections of the course that have subheadings. The divisions may be chronological: Canada before colonization; from exploration to colonization; toward Confederation; Confederation: the first years; rail and commerce and the unification of the country; from the turn of the century to World War I; the Great Depression; from World War II to the Cold War; contemporary issues in federalism. Or, the course may be organized around concepts that depend on sociological analysis: the colonial family; the extended family; break-up of First Nation families and cultures under the Native education acts; contemporary stresses on the family; the nuclear family as ideal; the single-parent family as reality. In a literature course, has the material been covered chronologically or thematically? Have the readings (or novels or plays) been grouped, and if so, how? Why?

When the course was being taught, were you asked to look for connections, to find patterns and design structures? If so, what are they? Were different kinds of information and different modes of analysis used for these different sections? By answering these questions, you are seeking now to "read" the materials on the course inductively to see the patterns and concepts and to derive the organizing principles from the details.

Distinguishing Essentials from Examples

In the section on taking notes in lectures and seminars (see Chapter 1), we discussed the differences between main points in the argument of a lecture and the examples used to illustrate it, and we pointed out that many students get bogged down in the detail of the examples rather than noting the kind of example or the page reference to be filled in later and concentrating on the main point. In studying for examinations, your purpose is different.

You already have a good outline of the course and have set out the major concepts in a coherent order. Now you have to fit the details into that same pattern. Your aim is to get one or two examples, perhaps more for important points, that illustrate the concepts you have identified. You might do this by making a chart that lists the concepts on one half of the page, from top to bottom. On the other side you can fill in several columns with appropriate examples, historical events, statistical data, experiments, and so on so, so that your page, when completed, will include several examples for each of the major concepts of the course. It would be wise to choose examples that fit the concept clearly and to make a note about which particular aspect of the concept the example illustrates. You should note any way in which the example does not fit, either next to each example or in a separate column. You should choose examples from different parts of the course (to exemplify your own coverage of the course materials). You might also pick out similarities from among the examples.

This exercise is an important one because it requires you to do an exercise in critical thinking with the course materials. You have already extracted the main principles, concepts, or terms of the course, and now you have to pull from the full range of the course the illustrations that will make sense of your reading of the course, not necessarily those given in the lecture. You are putting the course together for yourself. These pages of synthesis are good for review just before the examination.

Creating Blocks of Material, Details, and Comparisons

Some instructors will spend the last lecture or seminar summarizing the course. They might suggest ways in which you can make your own summaries. Some approaches, of course, work better for one kind of course than for another. In a literature course, for example, one method of preparing your summary is to go through the course from the beginning and note in the left-hand column week by week the titles of the readings. In the other columns on the page you can make your own summaries of the texts in various categories, covering either traditional or nontraditional materials (see the sample below).

Title and Date	Author	Major Characters	Minor Characters	Functions	Settings	Summary of Action	Questions or Examples
Jane Eyre (1847)	Charlotte Brontë	Jane Eyre	Mrs. Reed Miss Temple	Aunt Teacher	Gateshead Lowood	[to be filled in as appropriate]	[to be filled in as appropriate]
		Mr. Rochester	Adèle	Master, pupil	Thornfield		
		Bertha Mason		Mad in attic			
			Grace Poole	Servant			
		St. John Rivers		Teacher	Moor House		

The details about the characters, the actions, and the questions and examples will depend on what you have done with the novel in your course. But you might also want to have several kinds of study sheets about such a text, one dealing with the settings in more detail, including specifics about the locations, the kinds of families there, class and economic status, and dominant images and metaphors (such as the books at Gateshead, leading to those at the school at Lowood and the contrasting school at Moor House, and the chestnut tree at Thornfield). That is, the summary chart in which you list all of the details of one book after another might draw together the separate charts that you make for each book. If you considered other aspects of the text, you could also include them, such as patterns of sign systems and signification, elements of narratology (plotting, modes of narration, metafiction, focalizations), historical and political contexts (education in England; colonization, plantation ownership, and intermarriage in the West Indies; missionary activities, the dominant culture, and racism), or the roles of gender (governesses, inheritance laws, codes of master/servant, conventions of marriage).

You can make similar charts, though with different headings and categories, for readings in any course. Charts for historical or political readings would list the documents, date them, give something about their historical or social context, and then note the main points, the chief persons or issues that they address, and perhaps their immediate and longer-term impacts.

Assembling the charts is an important stage, because you are putting together the large blocks of materials and are setting out the details of the course coherently. But you have not yet moved to making the comparisons. That requires a further step. Once you have your charts together, you need to think more analytically about how the various course materials are linked together, how they can be compared and contrasted. You might find it helpful to jot down possible points of comparison or to draw arrows to make links.

WHAT TO DO ABOUT ...

What You Don't Understand

The time for dealing with concepts, readings, or lectures that you have not understood is well past once you are preparing for examinations. Most of those difficulties should have been solved much earlier in the year. However, even several days before the examination it is possible to patch a leaky intellectual boat, to get some help about matters that you do not follow. Your first source of information is your teacher. Some instructors have special office hours for discussing the exam in the final two or three weeks before the examination. During these office hours students are free to bring materials that they do not understand, as well as questions about readings or lectures. Some teachers are also available for consultation by appointment or by e-mail, but you should be careful not to abuse this opportunity nor to reveal that you have really been doing too little work earlier in the year. A second source of information is your fellow classmates. Some students study in groups, which often can be helpful in filling in gaps of knowledge, definitions, and so on. A third source is an encyclopedia or other reference book in your subject area. This route, however, is probably useful only in an emergency, since consulting such a book in the library will draw away valuable time from your preparation and might also be a source of distraction. Furthermore, it might not have the kind of focus that was so important in the course that you are gathering together.

What You Don't Know

There always will be some areas of a course that you know better than others. On the whole, it is wise to try to balance your studying to give attention to all parts of the course, weighted, of course, according to the time devoted to the various materials in the lectures and readings and to the instructions given by the teaching staff. However, there might well be some areas that you know almost nothing about. In the final preparation for an examination, you have to evaluate carefully whether you can safely avoid filling in that gap, whether you can do short-term first aid to patch it up partially, or whether you have to sacrifice time from other areas of the course that you know better to devote time to the area that you know nothing about.

If you know nothing about one or two of the course's major concepts, perhaps fundamental ideas upon which other ideas are built, it obviously would be wise to recognize that fact and remedy that defect. Otherwise, your lack of a solid foundation will betray you at every stage in your examination answers. It is often very difficult to conceal such a gap. On the other hand, if you simply have not covered one of the course topics, perhaps one among many, then your judgment about its importance in the course will be a determining factor. Of course, you are taking a serious risk. If one of the compulsory questions involves that material, you will be out of luck. You might gain some insurance, or perhaps some assistance about probabilities, by checking previous examinations. It used to be said that what you don't know won't hurt you, but that maxim does not help you go into an examination with a calm mind and the knowledge that you are well prepared. Studying throughout the year and drawing the materials together effectively at the end is the best procedure.

What You Haven't Read or Researched

Just as there will be some areas in which you lack proficiency, so too there will be some parts of the textbook, other readings on the course, or specific research areas that you have skimmed too superficially or have not read at all and now cannot recall the first thing about. The two or three days before the final examination are not a good time to remedy this defect. However, as with ideas or topics on the course that you do not know about, you have to judge the importance of the reading in the overall argument and intellectual framework of the course. Is this reading fundamental? If so, you should find some way to cover it—first by skimming, and then by reading the most important parts more carefully. You might also consider getting an aid to the reading. Some readings have summaries, student cribs, or other reading aids available. Using these tools here is an emergency measure. Study aids (laminated sheets, crib notes, reading guides, and the like) are sometimes recommended by instructors. While some of them are written by leading authorities in the field (some major Milton scholars have written crib notes to *Paradise Lost*, and they are used in some courses on Milton to supplement the other readings), some teachers frown on their use, so you should be aware of this potential problem. However, if you decide to simply ignore some of the major readings on the course, you are putting your examination at risk.

STUDYING ALONE, WITH A FRIEND, OR IN A STUDY GROUP

Some students find it best to study alone, while others want to work with a friend or in a small group. However you study, you need to follow your timetable and resist the temptation to be distracted by food, music, the TV, other people, or even the people with whom you are studying. Many students find that it is good to do some basic work alone first, and then to pool their resources with a friend or a group. Beginning with others means that you have little chance to pull your own work together independently. If you decide to study with a friend, you need to be aware that you should not engage in merely pooling ignorance. It is important to choose the friend with whom you decide to study carefully. Having studied a body of material, each of you can explain a concept, a text, or a chapter of the text to the other person, and the other person can then ask questions. You both can then check the materials for errors or deficiencies and assess performance. Then, the roles are reversed for the next body of material.

Studying in a group can also be a great help. However, you should set aside enough time to do your individual preparation, too, and you should not plan to study in a group right up to the last minute. A study group made up of people who are willing to work and who can share knowledge with you and use your abilities can give you great support. For your own peace of mind, it is good to find out that others are also worried about this exam, that they share at least some of your difficulties, and that they can help you over hurdles that you thought were impossibly high. At the same time, the approaches that other people use should stimulate you to a better performance level. Again, the process that a group uses to get through the material means that they will be relying on you for help (stimulating you not to let them down), so your own abilities will be appropriately challenged. Explaining both what you know and what you are shaky about helps you to consolidate your information and formulate your questions more sharply.

A study group also needs some ground rules to function effectively. Usually, one person acts as the convener, and all agree on a timetable for the studying and for the work the group wants to cover together.

STUDYING FOR DIFFERENT KINDS OF EXAMS

Multiple-Choice and Short-Answer Exams

So-called objective examinations often test for detail that a student either knows or does not know. Far more demanding are the more sophisticated objective examinations that require distinctions between close alternatives. For instance, the kinds of questions used on the SAT (Student Aptitude Test), LSAT (Law Student Aptitude Test), and GRE (Graduate Record Examination) are very sophisticated methods of evaluation, and people who look at educational trends look over carefully the results of these examinations. Indeed, many universities and private organizations sponsor short courses to train people to perform well in these examinations.

It is crucial that you read the exam instructions carefully. Often, multiple-choice exams are divided into sections, and sometimes different instructions, different numbers of required answers, and different weightings apply to each section. You also need to note whether there is a penalty for guessing. It might still be worth your while to guess if you are fairly certain that you are correct. You should plan your time in relation to the numbers of questions that you have to answer and the weight given to each, then proceed carefully and methodically, pausing from time to time to stretch, breathe deeply, and relax your muscles, before resuming with focused concentration.

Multiple-choice examinations or tests give a variety of alternatives for responding to a particular statement or question. Usually, one alternative will be definitely wrong, but several others will be close to correct. You are looking for the best match between the question and one of the alternatives. You first need to read the opening statement in the question and think about what the answer might be. Then, you can read all of the alternatives before you answer. You should note any qualifying words that determine correct answers. If the root statement is all-inclusive—"All members of category X ..." or "Members of category Y always ..."—then the choice you make must fit all of the instances included. On the other hand, if the root statement includes the words *some* or *often,* these relative words allow for a degree of interpretation, and you have to be even more careful.

Yes/no and true/false examinations depend on detailed information that enables you to identify the point being made in the governing statement and judge its truth or falsity. The danger with this kind of examination is lingering or ruminating over a question too long, so that eventually your doubts take over and you are unable to decide. If in a true/false examination you are absolutely stumped about which is the correct response, you should guess. You have a 50 percent chance of being correct, so you should not leave any question unanswered. Finally, you should note carefully when reading each statement the presence of any qualifying words (*all, most, some, few,* and so on) and all negative words, especially *not.*

Short-answer exams ask for particular information that you have to supply in a succinct, abbreviated form, often in point form. Such answers require you to know your material well and to be able to summarize it accurately and efficiently.

For each of these kinds of examinations, similar methods of study can be used.

- First, go to the examination record office or to the part of the library or other facility where old examinations are kept. Make photocopies of the most recent examinations, and look closely at the kinds of questions that are asked. Which parts of the course are stressed? Which concepts appear again and again?

- Build your vocabulary in the field of study on which you will be examined. Multiple-choice examinations often hinge on the meaning of a particular crucial word in a statement. If it is close to the materials involved in the question, it might fit the answer; if it is remote from that field, it is likely not the right answer. But your ability to distinguish between possible correct answers and wrong answers will depend in large measure on your familiarity with the course concepts and language and on your general vocabulary skills.

Problem-Solving Exams

Problem-solving examinations set out a problem and ask you to solve it, using formulas, theory, or mathematics. They are often used in mathematics and computer science examinations, in some areas of sociology and the social sciences, and in economics. More rarely, they are used in humanities courses where the problem might be more closely related to game theory or to the construction of an alternative reading of data based on some stated preconceptions or assumptions. In any case, you are expected to apply the knowledge that you have of techniques, theory, formulas, and practices to new conditions.

If the exam requires you to learn a lot of formulas, you should write them out at the beginning of the examination so they are clear to you and so you can refer to them. Then, you need to read the examination over carefully and select those problems that you think you have the best chance of answering correctly, within the allowances of the exam instructions. When you set to work on a particular question, you should mark or underline the operative words so you fully understand what is involved in the problem. Then, you can move toward a solution, asking appropriate questions as you proceed: How do I get there? Is this the first step? Are my assumptions correct? Is this formula or principle or theory the right one for the data? Sometimes, you will have to make mathematical calculations; if so, you should be careful to enter them accurately on your calculator (if allowed) and transcribe them accurately in the exam booklet. It is a good idea to check the numbers again before you move on. You should continue to work in a concentrated and methodical way, solving each step as you come to it. If you get stuck after a reasonable effort, you can move on and come back when you have time at the end. You should also try to make time for a review.

Essay Exams

In preparing for the essay examination, you will have gone over a number of the old examinations so that you know the kinds of questions that you will be expected to answer if the exam follows the same format. If you are uncertain about this point, you should ask your instructor. In preparing for the exam, besides all of the preparation we have noted above, you should decide on the major themes, issues, and categories of knowledge covered by the course, and make up thesis statements about each. Then, you should list a number of points—at least three, perhaps four—in the form of topic sentences for your leading paragraphs. You might create outlines of the kinds of questions that you have been asked on previous examinations, and then go over your notes from lectures and readings to see where they could be filled in.

It helps to do an outline on the examination itself or on the back of one of the pages (usually in a different book so that you can have the outline before you as you write and can add to it as you are answering the question). You should begin with a thesis statement and reformulate it if necessary once you have completed the outline. You will recall that a thesis should be a complete statement that summarizes what you intend to argue in the answer. It is not merely a statement of an opinion, but rather an attempt to state some reasoned position. It should give the main points that you will be developing in your answer. Some students take the terms of the exam question and turn it into a thesis statement, adding their own twist to it and including the three or four points that they will be arguing. However, merely restating the terms of the question in the same words does little for you in setting up an argument. You should avoid spending too much time on your outline. Once you have your main points set down, as well as any references to details, illustrations, or examples, you can begin to write. You should copy out the thesis statement and continue from there.

In reading the question, you should be aware that instructors use a variety of different directions. The most common instruction is to "compare and contrast"; you should note that whenever you are asked to compare two or more items, you are expected to give both the similarities *and* the differences and to discuss them. You are forced in such a question to make a more complex answer than in a question that simply asks you to provide information. You may have to use specific categories of knowledge in your comparison of these two novels, these two political parties, these two social phenomena. Or, you may have to use certain tools in your analysis, but the essential thing is that you must compare and contrast. It is not sufficient to choose three items, write an introductory paragraph saying that you will compare and contrast the three items in such and such categories, and then write three paragraphs, one about each item individually, without any comparison or contrast, followed by a conclusion. Such an answer fails to achieve its most central goal, that of making a comparison and drawing a contrast. You cannot ask the marker to step in and supply the comparison and contrast for you.

TIPS: Writing Essay Exams

1. Write a thesis statement.

2. Do an outline in another examination booklet so you will have it before you as you write.

3. Add key words about details or illustrations to the outline to remind you to include them as you write.

4. Include some details (in parentheses) as you write to show the marker that you know what you are writing about, such as names, dates, historical contexts alluded to briefly, technical terms, and brief quotations of a word or phrase.

5. Give one or two longer examples that you can develop in more detail, and give brief examples to illustrate other points. Again, use parentheses for quick examples to avoid being distracted and writing too much.

6. Make certain at the end that you have not moved too far away from your thesis, and also that your main points have covered what was asked for in the question.

Many other words are used in examination questions that require particular tactics for response, as in Box 15.1. For instance, the following questions ask you to do very different things:

1. Identify the major results of World War I and II as they affected Europe and North America.

2. Explain the major results of World War I and II as they affected Europe and North America.

3. Compare the major results of World War I and II as they affected Europe and North America.

4. Evaluate the major results of World War I and II as they affected Europe and North America.

5. Justify the major results of World War I and II as they affected Europe and North America.

In each case, the verb at the beginning of the sentence determines how you should organize your answer. The first question asks for a list of results or effects of the two wars in the form of information. This question demands that you state detail, and it is a hard one to fudge. The second asks you to explain or give reasons for the particular results that you already have enumerated: you have to answer the question, Why? The third question asks you to compare two sets of results, and, as always, a comparison asks that you point out both similarities and differences. The fourth question involves evaluation, judging the comparative results of the two world wars. This question is of a level of difficulty greater than the earlier three, because you already will have had to make a comparison, and then you are asked to assess the value or worth of the particular results. Finally, the fifth question asks you to make an argument defending or upholding the results that you have stated. Here, you have to advance your own view of how those results can be supported (or give the views of others and align yourself with or argue against those views). In this answer you have to know the materials well enough to position yourself with respect to the details and to defend your position.

BOX 15.1	Common Verbs in Essay Questions

- **Identify:** exemplify, enumerate, list, describe, define, state, summarize
- **Explain:** analyze, discuss, illustrate, interpret, outline, trace
- **Compare:** contrast, distinguish, relate
- **Evaluate:** appraise, criticize, review, weigh
- **Justify:** agree/disagree, debate, defend, prove

Note that each of these verbs has a different connotation. For instance, under *identify,* to *exemplify* means that you have to list specific instances or examples; to *describe* means that you have to specify the characteristics of something; and to *define* means that you have to explain the meanings of a particular term by isolating its qualities. Under *explain,* to *illustrate* means that you have to clarify an issue by means of particular illustrations or examples to illuminate what you are discussing, while to *trace* means you have to set out the development or history of a particular idea or happening. Of course, many of these terms overlap somewhat, but you should be aware of the nuances of the operative terms of each examination question.

Essay exams have three major dangers. First, there is the danger that the answer will not address the terms of the question, either by missing some important aspect of the question or by failing to go deeply enough into the material of the course to answer adequately. Second, the answer can be too general, lacking detail, examples, or evidence to back up what you are arguing. This fault is common not only among students who are ill prepared and who do not have the examples in mind at all, but also among students who are well prepared but who remain on the level of generalization, never coming to grips with detail. The third danger is that the detail will take over. This problem is the rarest, but it happens among students who have done all of the work but who find it difficult to rise above the detail to the terms of an argument. For these students, the outline with a thesis and major points is crucial to keep recalling them to the point that has to be argued. Even if you are a student who is following a good outline and who has a good balance of general argument and examples, you need to beware of becoming sidetracked by an example that takes over or that draws you into spending too much time. If you find that happening, you should just end and move on, leaving some space that you can return to during the exam review time to correct with a bridge to the next point.

Take-Home Exams

While the sit-down three-hour examination is in many ways a trial by fire, at least it is a limited period of agony. The take-home exam, however, sits there as an unformed and disturbing threat. The expectations might be less clear, and the time is much more open. Even a limited take-home, in which there are only two or three days to complete the work, means that those days are full of potential hazards. At the same time, take-home examinations are being used less frequently because of the possibility of cheating by using the Internet.

If you are assigned a take-home examination, you should pay particular attention to the instructions, both in the seminars or lectures before the examination is assigned and in the assignment itself. Are you being asked to use only the course materials, to extend the readings in certain ways, or to research in the library or elsewhere? Answers to these questions will determine in large measure how you prepare for and answer the examination. Above all, you will be aware that the kinds of answers you are expected to give are not flip, casual, or superficial. You are being given more time to consult your course materials and are expected to give thoughtful and reflective consideration to the course. You should use the time to prepare your answers carefully, balancing the ideas of the course and illustrating your points with appropriate and detailed examples. You can now afford the time (not available on an essay exam) to write a take-home exam that can be qualified, discriminating, and subtle. You can get help from the learning skills program at your university or read the information on preparing for tests and exams at various sites on the Internet, such as the York University site (**www/yorku.ca/cdc/lsp/ep/exam.htm**). The Web site at the University of Victoria also has brief and helpful information on taking multiple-choice, true/false, and essay exams, as well as general tips (**www.coun.uvic.ca/learn/exam.html**). Another site, at the University of Guelph, has brief tips and advice on a variety of exam-related questions (**www.uoguelph.ca/csrc/learning/ep-res-b.htm**).

CRAMMING TO GOOD EFFECT

Everyone who has studied the technique of cramming, including those researchers who have done it themselves, point out that the short-term acquisition of knowledge is a sure path to quick loss of retention. Materials acquired in cramming are not retained. If the course you are taking is a basic course in your discipline, or if it is one that you are expected to use as a foundation to build on later, cramming can get you through the exam, but you will not be able to draw on the course later because much of it will be gone.

That said, however, many students have to cram. But there is cramming and cramming. Working hard for the three days before the exam when you have kept your coursework up-to-date is not cramming. It is consolidation. You already have completed what we have discussed above, and you now can take that time to go over your rough notes, draw together your course summaries and charts, and work through the thesis statements, outlines, comparisons, and examples that will set you up for a solid examination. However, seeking to cover coursework in three days that for much of the year you had not consolidated, that you read sketchily in the first place, and that perhaps you only partially understood, *is* cramming. It might bring on a justifiable attack of anxiety. You might be able to impose upon a friend, even at this late date, to lend you the notes that he or she will be needing now, or to sit in on a study group without participating (for who would have you?) to hear what is going on and to get some clues.

You will be tempted to do some of the reading that you had neglected all year. At this stage, some of that reading might still be useful, but it is impossible in a short time to go over all of the material in any detail when you have not looked at it before. So, you need to adopt the shortcuts. Read, or at least skim, the introductions to each of the readings, and fit the introductions into your plan of study, which is now expanding. Add extra pages to it. If you are marshalling this material on the computer, leave spaces where you want to add new information. Do not rewrite it, but add. If you are working with pen and paper, use scissors to cut and paste to add new materials from your reading of the introductions. Your aim is to have an overview of the course, but not to know it all only superficially. It would be better to have an overview and to have more detailed knowledge about several major parts of the course. In that way, you can write about them with more confidence. Of course, you are taking a chance that those items will be on the examination, so all will depend on choosing the right areas carefully.

Keep a firm eye on the clock, and even though you have had bad study habits in the course throughout the year, redeem yourself now by working solidly and with concentration. Allow yourself short, limited breaks for a coffee, a stretch, or a quick jog (five minutes), but then get back to it.

Halfway through your time, turn away from your notes and look at old exams. You should see some questions that you can start working on. Do an outline for one or two of them, starting with a thesis statement that states what you intend to argue, and then presenting three or four major stages to your argument. Quickly flesh out the outline with an example (with similarities and differences) for each of your major stages. Then leave it and try another. For the third example, choose a question that you cannot answer, and formulate, however shakily, a proposed thesis topic and perhaps some stages, or at least one. Then go back to your syllabus to locate the place in the course where this material was covered, and consult your notes (it is to be hoped that you have some) and try to pull together some of the information that you need. If you draw a blank, look over the books on the course or the textbook to see what should be considered, and by skimming try to arrive at something. Even if you cannot complete a full outline for this question, get something down so that you are not left with that desperate feeling that your world is slipping away from you.

At the end of the day, before you go to sleep before the exam, plan to know something about several of the major concepts, themes, or divisions of the course. And the next morning, before the exam, go over these major concepts again, and have the examples in mind. After the exam, strengthen your resolve never to let yourself get into this situation again, and write yourself a letter to be opened at the beginning of the next term, as advice from the foolish to the wise.

WRITING EXAMS

Countdown to Zero

In the final day before writing the exam, it is a good idea to go over the syllabus again, to check the study sheets that you prepared, and to look over systematically the thesis statements, the major points you outlined, and the examples you listed. You might add further details. You should also check the readings again to make sure that you have the facts straight and memorize any of the final points that you want to be clear about. During the last day it is important to eat regular meals and to do some regular exercise. Finally, on the night before the exam, you can get together your equipment for writing the exam (see below), and have a good sleep, at least six hours. You have prepared well. Now is the time to put your preparation to good use.

Equipment

What aids are allowed, such as mechanical or electronic devices like calculators (with an extra set of batteries)? The class should have been informed before the examination whether textbooks, notes, dictionaries, or other reading aids are allowed. Some exams are "open book," but you should be aware that arriving with a book trolley full of sets of encyclopedias, an author's collected works, and so on, might not be smart. You need to think of the time it would take you to look materials up, read it, and then write a response, then calculate rationally what books you will need for an open book exam.

What other materials are allowed or needed? You should take a good watch, two or three pens and pencils, erasers, some white-out, tissues, drinks or snacks if they are allowed in the examination hall (bring coffee, juice, or some sugared drink to give you energy, and perhaps some chocolate), some scrap paper, hair elastics, and, above all, your photo-ID as issued by the university.

Location and Time

Every year students miss the first half-hour or more of an examination because they slept in, missed the bus, or went to the wrong location at the wrong time. Finding out about the time and place of the examination beforehand is your responsibility. The dates and times of exams are published by most universities, but you should make it a point to check those details in the last class. Sometimes the examination halls are in areas of the university that you might be unfamiliar with (gyms, assembly halls, cafeterias), so you need to know how you are getting there well in advance and plan to be better than on time—at least ten minutes early so that you can use the final few moments before the exam either to relax or to go over the details that you have been having the most trouble with. Arriving early to hear your friends boasting about what they know or going over details that are important to them but not to you will reduce your confidence, and you don't need that kind of help. You need to stick to yourself and compose yourself for the big race. When you enter the exam hall, you should choose a seat where you will not be distracted, either by the examiners (some of them like to chat during exams) or by other students. Then, you can arrange your desk, making sure the table does not rock, and collect your thoughts. You should listen carefully to any instructions or explanations that the invigilators give at the beginning of the exam. These comments might include explanations of typos on the exam or some other mistake that you should know about.

Reading the Exam Questions

Even before you read the examination questions, you might want to jot down some of the details of that pesky outline, or that trick for remembering those facts in order, or whatever terms you do not want to forget. Then you can set your mind at rest and get on with reading the exam paper.

We have already stated the basic requirements for any examination in the section above on different kinds of exams. It is important to read the instructions carefully. Then read them again. Then read each of the questions carefully, and read them again. On any given examination, some student misses marks unnecessarily though misreading of the instructions and questions. You should note especially any of the words we discussed above (*list, explain, analyze, compare,* and so on). As you go through the exam, you should mark the questions you can certainly answer, and those that are possible. Then, you can take at least four or five minutes to read the questions over, circle any words or questions that are confusing, and seek advice from an invigilator if you do not understand either the instructions or the questions. Usually, it is best to begin by answering questions that you are certain of, and a little later, raise your hand and ask the invigilator your questions when he or she approaches your desk.

TIPS: Reading Exam Questions

In reading the exam note:

1. the time allowed for the exam
2. the number of questions required for a complete exam
3. the weightings for each part of the exam, and even for each question
4. the key words in each question (underline these key words or use your highlighter to mark them)
5. any inclusions or exclusions (such as no works from the fall term may be used on the final exam).

Pacing Yourself

It is crucial that you plan your time and map out your strategy, allowing at least half an hour to reread parts of your exam and to fill in any blanks that you left. You should check again the weighting for each question and plan your answers so that you have enough time for each. Halfway through the exam, you will need to check the time to be sure that you are on track.

You should begin the exam with the questions that you can answer best, or with the ones that you want to get out of the way. You do that to build on your successes. But you should not be tempted to overkill on the answers that you are familiar with. It is better to answer what is asked, leave some blank space for later, and go to the next question.

With essay questions, you should take the time to write out some kind of outline, perhaps in a separate booklet. You should be sure to hand it in with your finished books, because you may not have time to finish completely, and the outline will be a help to you. Some examiners do not take into account any rough work. Even if that is so, the outlines will show that you have taken the answers seriously and might help an examiner to give you a more favourable or insightful reading. Other examiners say that rough work cannot count against you but only for you, and they will read it to your benefit. At any rate, rough work will help you to organize your answer better. The outline should follow the form that you prepared in studying for the exam—a thesis statement and three or four summary points with the examples noted but not sketched in detail.

Tactics for Good Answers

Examiners are looking for you to show off what you know, but your knowledge has to be directed to what the question is asking. You should continue to ask yourself at the end of each page whether you are still on topic. You are also being assessed for your knowledge of the course as a whole and its concepts. Are you including the course concepts in each of the answers? The key terms for the course? Are you including concrete examples (dates, authors, events, short quotations, references to documents, alternative theses)? You should answer short-answer exams by coming to the point quickly. If you are allowed to use point form, using verbs before your answers will kick-start your ideas. If you are required to write in paragraphs, you need not waste time by rephrasing the question, but rather should proceed directly to your answer. In essay exams, you can use the thesis-outline method and fill in the references to your examples.

After you have finished, you should still have a small amount of time left for review. That was part of your planning at the beginning of the exam, and now it is vital for you to go over your answers carefully and quickly, adding detail, examples, and comparisons and correcting mistakes as you proceed. Your aim in this review should be to improve your answers, not just to reread the answers. Finding the energy for this last effort is difficult but important.

Exam Anxiety and What to Do about It

Panic

Everyone feels panic. Sometimes it happens before you have started to draw the course together at the beginning of the pre-exam study period. You trigger anxiety by wondering over and over: How can I ever get this into focus? And you conclude that you are washed up and hung out to dry. Panic sets in. Or it happens the day before the exam, when you are done and are ready to go, when suddenly all of your self-doubts surface, and you cannot sleep. You should get up, do some exercise, have some cereal, call a friend for a *short* chat, and consider this:

- You have prepared as well as you could in the time and given your resources.
- You have a general grasp of the whole course, and you know some of it in detail.
- You already have a passing grade in the course, perhaps a pretty good grade, and this exam is weighted much less than your other coursework.
- You know enough to get some marks on the exam, and you will pass.
- Even if the exam counts for a lot of marks, you still know enough to pass.
- You have done the best that you could.

Then, you can get together the stuff you need for the exam—pens, your watch, the notes you will read in the morning—set your alarm, and go to bed and get a good sleep.

Panic during the exam can also be a problem. Now, you have to use your writing and not your studying to get through the anxiety. You should take some deep breaths and focus on some object in the classroom, not the clock. Then, you need to recall that you have done a good deal of work in this course, have attended many lectures, and have read the books, and assure yourself that you will do fine, take some more deep breaths, and start writing. If that fails, you might ask the invigilator for permission to go to the washroom, and wash your face and come back refreshed and resolved to begin.

Too Little or Too Much Food or Drink

You will be working hard for some time on the exam. Chances are that you have also been up early and have done some cramming. You have driven or walked to the exam, and now you need energy to get through the last hours. It is important to have eaten something (but not too much—no need for the three-egg-and-steak breakfast—you don't need to doze off during the exam) and to come with some snacks and juice or coffee. You might not want them, but you also might need them. You should avoid bringing food that is noisy to unwrap or consume.

Not Knowing the Answer

Many exams, especially essay questions, allow you to choose between alternatives. If the question is compulsory, and you don't immediately see how to answer it by any of the alternatives, you need to think about it some more. You should choose the most likely alternative and jot down any ideas you have that might be pertinent on the blank page opposite to the answer. Then, you can ask yourself questions and write two or three of the questions down: What is this question asking? Then narrow the focus: How might I answer it? What are the possibilities? What would work here? You should not leave the question until you have some ideas written down. Then, you can leave some blank space and move to the next question, reserving time to return to this question later in the exam. Often, ideas will occur to you that you can add to your questions and that you can fill out into an answer before the exam is finished.

Special Needs

If you need special consideration for exams because of a physical or learning difficulty, you should make the arrangements well beforehand. Most universities have a special office that deals with students who have these needs. Your professor will be only too happy to cooperate. You need to speak to your teacher well before the exam and explain that you are making arrangements to write the exam under the auspices of the student help office (or whatever it is called on your campus). You need to make certain that your instructor knows whether you need extra time or equipment, such as a computer. Like other students, you should come well prepared and with all of your special equipment, such as pens, notebooks, snacks, and a good watch.

IF YOU MISS THE EXAM

If for health reasons you missed an examination, you should first get a letter from your doctor stating when he or she saw you and any other appropriate details. You should take a copy of the letter to your course director, who might allow an informal makeup exam. If the exam is a formal end-of-year exam, then you have to take the letter to the student affairs office or to the registrar's office—to whomever looks after such appeals in your university. Universities have in place specific regulations that govern such cases, either by giving you deferred standing, which will allow you to write the exam later, or an aegrotat standing, which means your work is evaluated exclusive of the examination.

If you slept in, mistook the date or time, had a car breakdown, or suffered whatever natural disaster, you have to move quickly to plead for help from your instructors (sometimes they are sympathetic) or through a petition in your faculty–student offices. You might begin with your teacher, then with the chair of the department or director of undergraduate studies, and then with the various faculty officers. A formal petition may be required, and you might have to submit all of your coursework along with your petition, one more reason for keeping it all on hand at least until you receive the final grade in the mail.

AFTER THE EXAM

When the exam is handed back (especially mid-term exams or in-class tests) and is taken up in class, you should make notes on your exam or in your notebook about the instructor's comments. Often, they will be important clues about what she or he will want you to do on the final examination. Furthermore, these comments provide insight into the marking scheme and into the kinds of errors to avoid. If there are any markings on your paper, you need to make sure that you understand them; if you don't, you can go to your instructor for enlightenment. Were comments addressed to the way you developed your argument or to your grammar, punctuation, and expression? Those points are certainly important in this course, and you will need to improve in your exam-writing skills.

Later, you can go over your answers and rework them to see why your correct or high-scoring answers did well. You should look up your notes from lectures and readings and from your exam preparation sheets to see what information you have there about each question. How complete was your response? What were its strengths and weaknesses? If you missed out on a question altogether, you need to determine the reason. Was it because you simply had not covered (and so did not know) that material? Did that omission happen because you misunderstood what was important in the course? If so, you should think about why you were misinformed. Perhaps you misread the question, in which case you should be careful not to let that happen again. In your analysis of the exam questions, you need to ask yourself whether most of them related to the lectures, the readings, or other sources. Were you expected to make a synthesis of the course material or to answer and relate facts and concepts from the course content? Answers to these questions will help you to prepare for the next test or exam in the course.

On the matter of the content of the exam, did your answers in essay questions state what was asked for and what you intended to say? Try to read your answers with fresh eyes, as though you were looking at it as a marker. How would you assess this answer now? Does it have an argument using critical skills? Does it have a thesis and clear argument? Is there a good balance of general argument and detail? Are your examples and illustrations on topic and accurate?

More generally, you should ask yourself if you were well prepared for this exam, and if not, how your preparations could have worked better for you. Were you prepared for the length and difficulty of the exam? Had you gone over previous exams? Did you complete the exam with time to review your answers? Did you run out of time? If you misjudged the timing or weighting of the questions or did not pace yourself well, how could you correct that for the next exam?

During the exam, did you have any difficulties with discomfort, anxiety, or blank spots (blocking) when you just could not write? How serious were these problems, and did they interfere with your completing answers or the exam as a whole? If you did have these difficulties, you should certainly work on them before your next test, perhaps by seeking aid from your counselling office, or perhaps by arranging with your instructor to write some practice answers that he or she could mark.

If you gave the exam your best shot, you can go away happy. You have brought all of the year's activities into focus. All of the learning skills that you have acquired have come through a final evaluation process, and you are a wiser person. You have mastered a large and complicated body of intellectual material, and the skills you take away after writing this exam and finishing his course you can easily and profitably export to other courses. You are well on your way. Now is a good time to go to that party at the end of the year with your friends. You deserve it.

FURTHER READINGS

Jalongo, Mary Renck, Meghan Mahoney Tweist, and Gail J. Gerlach. *The College Learner: How to Survive and Thrive in an Academic Environment.* Englewood Cliffs, NJ: Merrill, 1996.

Longman, Debbie Guice, and Rhonda Holt Atkinson. *College Learning and Study Skills.* St. Paul, MN: West Publishing, 1993.

MacFarlane, Polly, and Sandra Hodson. *Studying Effectively and Efficiently: An Integrated System.* Toronto: Guidance Centre, Faculty of Education, U of Toronto, 1983.

Taylor, Catherine, Heather Avery, and B. Lucille Strath. *Making Your Mark: Learning to Do Well on Exams.* Toronto: Harcourt Brace, 1994.

Warren, Russell G. *Carpe Diem: A Student Guide to Active Learning.* Lanham, MD: University Press of America, 1996.

WEBLINKS

- Preparing for Tests and Exams, York University:
  www.yorku.ca/admin/cdc/lsp/

- Study Skills, University of Toronto
  snow.utoronto.ca/~ggay/study.skl.htm

- University of California at Berkeley
  www.-slc.uga.berkeley.edu/CalREN/TestsGeneral.html
  Provides brief and helpful information on taking multiple choice, true/false, and essay exams, as well as general tips.

- University of Guelph
  www.uoguelph.ca/csrc/learning/ep-res-b.htm
  Provides brief tips and advice on a variety of exam-related questions.

- Virginia Tech University
  www.ucc.vt.edu/stdysk/stdyhlp.html

Works Cited

BOOKS

Adams, Marilyn. *Beginning to Read: Thinking and Learning about Print.* Washington: Sponsored by the Office of Educational Research and Improvement of the U.S. Department of Education, 1990.

American Philosophical Association. *Critical Thinking: A Statement of Expert Consensus.* Millbrae, CA: California Academic Press, 1990.

Anderson, Richard, Elfreida Hiebert, Judy Scott, and Ian Wilkinson. *Becoming a Nation of Readers.* Washington: Sponsored by the National Academy of Education, National Institute of Education, and Center for the Study of Reading, 1985.

Aristotle. "Posterior Analytics." Trans. G.R.G. Mure. *Introduction to Aristotle.* By Richard McKeon. New York: Modern Library, 1947. 9–109.

Bettelheim, Bruno. *The Uses of Enchantment: The Meaning and Importance of Fairy Tales.* New York: Knopf, 1976.

Board of Education for the City of London. *A Parent's Guide to Whole Language.* London, ON: The Board, 1990.

Breland, Hunter M., Robert J. Jones, and Laura Jenkins. *The College Board Vocabulary Study.* New York: College Entrance Examination Board, 1994.

Brody, Jane E. "Procrastinate No More: You Can Help Yourself." *New York Times* 5 June 1996: C12.

Brownmiller, Susan. *Against Our Will: Men, Women and Rape.* New York: Bantam, 1976.

Carroll, Lewis. *The Annotated Alice.* Ed. Martin Gardner. London: Penguin, 1970.

Chamber's Twentieth Century Dictionary. Ed. Thomas Davidson. Edinburgh: W. & R. Chambers, 1901.

Copi, Irving M., and Carl Cohen. *Introduction to Logic.* 9th ed. New York: Macmillan, 1994.

Council of Biology Editors. *Scientific Style and Format: The CBE Manual for Authors, Editors, and Publishers.* 6th ed. New York: Cambridge UP, 1996.

Donaldson, Laura E. *Decolonizing Feminisms: Race, Gender, and Empire Building.* Chapel Hill: U of North Carolina P, 1992.

Flesch, Rudolf. *Why Johnny Still Can't Read: A New Look at the Scandal of Our Schools.* New York: Harper and Row, 1981.

Garner, James Finn. *Politically Correct Bedtime Stories.* New York: Macmillan, 1994.

Grimm, Jacob. *Household Stories from the Collection of the Brothers Grimm.* Trans. Lucy Crane. New York: McGraw-Hill, [1882] 1966.

Humm, Maggie. *Dictionary of Feminist Theory.* Columbus: Ohio State UP, 1995.

Lester, James D. *Citing Cyberspace.* New York: Addison Wesley, 1997.

Levy, Harold. "Madame Guilty in Sado-Sex Trial." *Toronto Star* 10 Oct. 1998: A6.

Lieberman, Marcia. "Someday My Prince Will Come." *College English* Dec. 1972: 383–95.

MacDonald, George. "The Fantastic Imagination." *A Dish of Orts.* 1893. London: Edwin Dalton, 1908. 313–22.

Metz, Christian. *Film Language: A Semiotics of the Cinema.* Trans. Michael Taylor. New York: Oxford UP, 1974.

National Council of Teachers of English. (NCTE). "Elementary School Practices." *Current Research on Language Learning.* Urbana, IL: NCTE, 1993.

Paley, William. *Natural Theology.* London, 1802.

Partridge, Eric. *Concise Usage and Abusage.* New York: Citadel, 1965.

Pauk, Walter. *How to Study in College.* Boston: Houghton Mifflin, 5th ed./1993.

Pei, Mario. *The Story of Language.* Rev. ed. New York: New American Library, 1966.

Ratnesar, Romesh. "The Homework Ate My Family." *Time* 25 Jan. 1999: 36–45.

Sapadin, Linda, and Jack Maguire. *It's About Time.* New York: Viking-Penguin, 1996.

Snow, Catherine, Susan Burns, Peg Griffin, et al. *Preventing Reading Difficulties in Young Children.* Washington: Sponsored by the Office of Special Education Programs, the Office of Educational Research, the National Institute on Child Health and Human Development, and the National Research Council of the National Academy of Science, 1998.

Traugott, Elizabeth Closs, and Mary Louise Pratt. *Linguistics for Students of Literature.* New York: Harcourt Brace, 1980.

Tuttle, Lisa. *Encyclopedia of Feminism.* Harlow: Longman, 1986.

Walker, Janice R., and Todd Taylor. *Columbia Guide to Online Style.* New York: Columbia UP, 1998.

Yarington, David. *Surviving in College.* Indianapolis: Bobbs-Merrill, 1977.

Zipes, Jack David. Trans. *Beauties, Beasts, and Enchantment: Classic French Fairy Tales.* New York: New American Library, 1989.

WEB SITES

Atwood, Margaret. "Margaret Atwood Speaks to the TCTE May Gathering—May 25/95." *The Margaret Atwood Information Web Site.* 7 Nov. 1997. www.web.net/owtoad/q.html

"Coaching Winners." *Critical Thinking Across the Curriculum Project, Longview Community College.* 5 May 1998. www.kcmetro.cc.mo.us/longview/ctac/winners/htm

"Concentration." *Dartmouth College.* 10 Sept. 1998. www.dartmouth.edu/admin/acskills/lsg/concentration.html

Cornell Method. www.dartmouth.edu/~acskills/lsg/cornell.html

Critical Reading. www.cmli.dist.maricopa.edu/critR/index.htm

Davis Dyslexia Association Home Page. www.dyslexia.com/quest.htm

"Elementary School Practices: NCTE Guidelines and Position Statements." *National Council of Teachers of English (NCTE) Home Page.* 19 Oct. 1998. www.ncte.org/positions/elem.htm

Paul, Richard. "Three Definitions of Critical Thinking." *Foundation for Critical Thinking Home Page.* www.criticalthinking.org

Special Education Legal Primer. micriconnect.com/journal/legal

Index